ARAB MiGs, Volu

Tom Cooper & David Nicolle, wi tin Smisek

# ARAB MiGs
## Volume 5

**October 1973 War: Part 1**

Tom Cooper & David Nicolle, with Holger Müller, Lon Nordeen & Martin Smisek

HARPIA
PUBLISHING+

Copyright © 2014 Harpia Publishing L.L.C. & Moran Publishing L.L.C. Joint Venture
2803 Sackett Street, Houston, TX 77098-1125, U.S.A.
arabmigs@harpia-publishing.com

All rights reserved.

No part of this publication may be copied, reproduced, stored electronically or transmitted in any manner or in any form whatsoever without the written permission of the publisher.

Consulting and inspiration by Kerstin Berger
Artworks and drawings by Tom Cooper, James Lawrence and Sander Peeters
Maps by James Lawrence
Editorial by Thomas Newdick
Layout by Norbert Novak, www.media-n.at, Vienna

Harpia Publishing, L.L.C. is a member of

Printed at Grasl Druck & Neue Medien, Austria

ISBN 978-0-9854554-4-6

## Contents

**Introduction** .................................................................................................... 7

**Acknowledgements** ........................................................................................ 9

**Abbreviations** ................................................................................................. 11

**Addenda/Errata:** Arab MiGs, Volumes 1 to 4 ................................................ 13

**Chapter 1:** No Peace, No War ......................................................................... 27

**Chapter 2:** Patience Before Purpose ............................................................... 55

**Chapter 3:** Seeking Revenge ........................................................................... 103

**Chapter 4:** A Long and Miserable Day .......................................................... 157

**Chapter 5:** Hold the Line ................................................................................. 181

**Appendix I:** Deliveries of MiG-21s to Arab Countries, 1961–1973 .............. 203

**Appendix II:** Deliveries of Aero L-29 Delfins to Iraq, 1968–1974 ............... 211

**Appendix III:** Logbooks of Egyptian Pilots ................................................... 215

**Appendix IV:** EAF squadron commanders, October 1973 ........................... 219

**Appendix V:** Artworks ..................................................................................... 223

**Bibliography** ................................................................................................... 241

**Index** ................................................................................................................ 247

# Introduction

Volume 5 of the *Arab MiGs* series has several objectives. The primary purpose is to continue providing an in-depth analysis of the Arab air forces that became involved in conflicts with Israel, with an emphasis on the operational history of Soviet-manufactured aircraft designs – foremost those of the Mikoyan i Gurevich and Sukhoi Design Bureaus. While the previous four volumes provided in-depth coverage of the period 1955 until late 1970, *Volume 5* covers the period between late 1970 and mid-October 1973.

The second objective is to shed light on air warfare during the first phase of the October 1973 Arab-Israeli War, and especially so upon its more obscure aspects. While – or perhaps because – nearly all literature in the English language is based on Israeli sources, many events from the October 1973 War remain unknown even after 40 years. Furthermore, and as surprising as it might sound, especially to many Western observers, much of the Israeli operations during this conflict remain well outside the Israeli academic world. The majority of works about the October 1973 War consist of memoirs intended to preserve war stories and eyewitness accounts of participating Israeli officers and soldiers. In turn, Israel appears to have covered up a number of major engagements in which the Arab forces did well. Equally, although some Israeli publications appear authoritative at first look, they contain a number of contradictions that do not stand up to closer cross-examination.

Wars are always two-sided affairs: no matter to what degree any side claims to be 'telling the truth', or party to knowledge, no one actor is capable of providing a complete picture or an understanding of historical 'truth' – even less so when emotionally involved. In order to gain a better picture of the events, we have to understand what both sides planned to do, and did. Therefore, another centrepiece of this study is an attempt to analyse and reconstruct the full flow of operations and their results, and the reasons for these.

This is not to say that under-reporting of the air warfare during the October 1973 War is limited to Israel. It is undeniable that the 'Arabs' have released even less information to the public – especially in regard to air warfare. The vast majority of Egyptian publications only pay tribute to the Egyptian Army's comprehensive preparations for this war and the crossing of the Suez Canal, in the period 6–8 October. Reference to the rest of the conflict – from 8–24 October, and especially to the Israeli counter-crossing and subsequent encircling of the Egyptian 3rd Army – is usually omitted from reporting in the public, as is obvious to all visitors to the October Panorama in Cairo, for example. Similarly, with the exception of two Egyptian Air Force (EAF) units – a small squadron deployed in Syria during the October 1973 War, and a squadron operating Dassault Breguet Mirage 5 fighters owned by Libya – not a single account has so far been released that provides the operational history of the EAF during the October 1973 on a blow-by-blow basis.

Although corresponding laws were relaxed by the responsible authorities nearly 30 years ago, the Egyptian military stubbornly refuses to publish any of its documentation regarding the October 1973 War. The Syrian government has not released a single authoritative account about the intentions, planning or conduct of operations concerning the Syrian Arab Air Force (SyAAF) during the October 1973 War. Indeed, there is not even one authoritative Syrian publication concerning the general conduct of military operations during that conflict. Given that the country became involved in an extremely bloody and highly destructive civil war in 2011, this is unlikely to change for years to come. In the case of the Algerian Air Force (QJJ) and the Iraqi Air Force (IrAF), the situation is slightly better. This is almost exclusively due to private initiatives, although the availability of primary sources remains somewhat limited. Regrettably, this is unlikely to change any time soon: although the so-called 'Arab Spring' resulted in the release of at least some official documentation, and some of this can be found in this book, this also occurred on the basis of a few private initiatives, randomly, and in haphazard fashion. Because of this, most of our efforts related to reconstructing the history of the Arab air forces involved and their activities remain limited to recording the 'battlefield memories' of Arab officers and pilots.

Considering this set of circumstances, the authors decided to include in *Volume 5* more comprehensive data about Israeli air operations during the October 1973 War than was the case in previous volumes. The aim is to provide a more accurate insight into the backgrounds of specific operations. Another reason for this approach was the attempt to provide a précis on the number of aircraft per type as available on either side at the onset of hostilities in October 1973, and a detailed reconstruction of confirmed losses. As previous volumes of this series have shown in great detail, nearly all publications that emerged since the start of the Arab-Israeli wars in 1948 have contained data that was far from what could be considered as 'definite'. Furthermore, most earlier publications never cross-examined information about the losses of Arab air forces losses provided by local sources and thus ended up grossly exaggerating these. Such works also downplayed the losses suffered by the Israel Defense Forces/Air Force (IDF/AF). Although various Israeli researchers frequently stress that all their publications – including those touching the topic of the October 1973 War – are based on official documentation, none of this has been seen in English language to date. On the contrary, this book is the first in the English language to include details from one such Israeli document related to the air war.

As authors of this book, we believe that we have provided the best assessment currently available. Our information does not claim to be 100 per cent complete, but it is nevertheless far more complete than anything that has previously been published. Therefore, we offer conclusions based upon our 'almost complete' information, with confidence in our own objectivity. Meanwhile, we are happy to admit what we do not know and to highlight gaps in our available information. Thus, we remain open to objective criticism and to other interpretations. We would not only welcome additional information but remain eager to hear alternative interpretations based upon other information that might be currently available. That, after all, was our purpose in writing this series of books, and will remain so until the final volume appears.

*Tom Cooper, David Nicolle, Holger Müller, Lon Nordeen & Martin Smisek,*
*June 2013*

# Acknowledgements

This book is the result of enthusiastic and intensive cooperation on the part of many individuals and several organisations. Many of the personal stories retold in this volume are intriguing and throw an especially interesting light on specific events. While in some cases we do not feel free to mention any names, and prefer to express our gratitude personally, we cannot emphasise sufficiently the fact that this work became possible only thanks to so many different persons providing precious help, often despite no uncertain risk to themselves and their families.

The list of those to whom we owe our gratitude is long, and as usual begins with the officers, pilots, non-commissioned officers and other ranks of various Arab air arms, particularly (in alphabetic order) those in Algeria, Egypt, Iraq, Jordan and Syria. They include the late AM Taher Zaki (EAF), the late AM Mustafa Shalabi el-Hinnawy (EAF), the late AM Alaa Barakat (EAF), Lt Gen Arif Abd ar-Razzaq (IrAF, ret.), AM Badr Domair (EAF, ret.), AVM Qadri Abd el-Hamid (EAF, ret.), the late AVM Mohammad Abdel-Moneim Zaki Okasha (EAF), AVM Nabil el-Shuwakri (EAF, ret.), AVM Mamdouh Taliba (EAF, ret.), Maj Gen Ahmed Abbas Faraj (EAF, ret.), Maj Gen Alwan Hassan al-Abossi (IrAF, ret.), Maj Gen Ayman (ADC, ret.), Maj Gen Zia el-Hefnawi (EAF, ret.), Maj Gen Mamdouh Heshmat (EAF, ret.), Maj Gen Reda el-Iraqi (EAF, ret.), Maj Gen Mohammed Abdel Wahhab al-Jabouri (IrAF, ret.), Maj Gen Hussein el-Kfass (EAF, ret.), Maj Gen Ahmed Kilany (EAF, ret.), Maj Gen Mustafa Nabil al-Masri (EAF, ret.), Maj Gen Samir Aziz Mikhail (EAF, ret.), Maj Gen Nassr Moussa (EAF, ret.), Maj Gen Mohammed Najji (IrAF, ret.), Maj Gen Salim Saffar (IrAF, ret.), Maj Gen Ihsan Shurdom (RJAF, ret.), Maj Gen Siad Shalash (EAF, ret.), Maj Gen Ahmed Yusuf el-Wakeel (EAF, ret.), Maj Gen Magdy el-Wakeel (EAF, ret.), Maj Gen Medhat Zaki (EAF, ret.), Brig Gen Ahmad Sadik (IrAF, ret.), Brig Gen Faysal Abdul Mohsen (IrAF, ret.), Air Cdre Farouk el-Ghazzawy (EAF, ret.), the late Air Cdre Mustafa Hafez (EAF), Air Cdre Fikry al-Gindy (EAF, ret.), Air Cdre Fuad Kamal (EAF, ret.), Air Cdre Gabr Ali Gabr (EAF, ret.), Air Cdre Abdel Moneim el-Tawil (EAF, ret.), Wg Cdr Kamal Zaki (EAF, ret.), Wg Cdr Talaat Luca (EAF, ret.), Wg Cdr Usama Sidqi (EAF, ret.), Lt Col K. M. Molodtsov (V-PVO, ret.) and others.

Special thanks are due to a number of other researchers for their kind help, comparable with near-authorship of this book. In particular, Group 73 in Egypt – including Dr Abduallah Emran, Nour Bardai and Ahmed Zayed. Their interviews, often with the same individuals originally interviewed by David Nicolle and Lon Nordeen some years ago, have provided numerous clarifications of various matters that were previously unclear. They were able to ask more detailed questions, arising from the greater amount of information that has become available in the meantime, with the end result of this team effort being a far more detailed picture.

We would like to express our special gratitude to Patricia Salti from the United Kingdom for sharing her recollections and original documentation concerning the Royal Jordanian Air Force, much of which is still waiting to be published. Our special thanks also go to Ali Tobchi from Iraq, for spending days and weeks patiently helping us reconstruct IrAF operations during the October War. They did so in cooperation with various retired officers, pilots and other ranks, who – sadly – do not feel free to be mentioned in public. Sander Peeters from the Netherlands went to great extent to compile various obscure data on specific Western weapons systems, and to help in any other possible fashion, and we owe him a lot for his help.

We would like to thank Mr Tarek el-Shennawy, Mr Ahmad Keraidy, Mr Ahmad Moukhalad, Mr Ahmad Turaiba, Mrs Leila, the late Mrs Khouda and the late Mrs Mona Tewfik, for their kind permission to use their family archives. Furthermore, we would like to thank Mohammad Hassan, Abdul Salam al-Maleki and Hayder Aziz in Iraq, who provided plenty of their own documentation, photographs, publications, as well as contacts to a number of former IrAF pilots and officers, and who helped with additional translations of original documents and publications; to Yasser al-Abed, R. S. and other friends in Syria for their selfless sharing of documentation concerning SyAAF officers, pilots and history in general; to Yawar Mazhar and Usman Shabbir in Pakistan, as well as Jagan Mohan in India, for kindly sharing the results of their research and helping with contacts relating to the Pakistan and Indian Air Forces, respectively; to Albert Grandolini in France for his immense patience and endlessly kind permission to use his extensive archive of photographs and various data; to Jean-Marie Langeron in France and Tomislav Mesaric in Croatia for their fantastic help with extensive and in-depth studies of the flying performances of various fighters discussed in this book; to Yoav Efrati, Zvi Kreissler and other friends in Israel for providing pointers and for help with background research on specific Israeli operations; to Vatche Mitilian from Lebanon; to Mark Lepko in the United States for selflessly providing the results of his relevant research, based on plenty of hard work over the years; to Sherif Sharmi, Franz Vajda, Jeroen Nijmeijer, Menno van der Wall, Frank Olynyk, Robert Szombati, Peter Weinert, Thomas Nachtrab, Alexander Hunger and Ferenc 'Franz' Vajda, for their kind permission to use some of their research, and to Hicham Honeini from Lebanon for his patience and kind help with the translations of various publications and documentation from Arabic.

Last but by no means least, we would like to thank a number of friends who have helped with additional information, commentary, translations or encouragement over a prolonged period of time, foremost Farzad Bishop, Ugo Crisponi, Christof Hahn, and Tom Long. All of them, as well as our families, have consistently supported our work with the greatest enthusiasm and patience, and our special thanks are due to each one of them.

## Abbreviations

| | |
|---|---|
| **AAA** | anti-aircraft artillery |
| **AAM** | air-to-air missile |
| **AB** | air base |
| **Air Cdre** | air commodore (military commissioned officer rank, equivalent to brigadier general) |
| **AM** | air marshal (military commissioned officer rank, equivalent to lieutenant general) |
| **An** | Antonov (the design bureau led by Oleg Antonov) |
| **APC** | armoured personnel carrier |
| **Brig Gen** | brigadier general (military commissioned officer rank) |
| **CAP** | combat air patrol |
| **Capt** | captain (military commissioned officer rank) |
| **CAS** | close air support |
| **CBU** | cluster bomb unit |
| **C-in-C** | commander-in-chief |
| **CO** | commanding officer |
| **Col** | colonel (military commissioned officer rank) |
| **EAF** | Egyptian Air Force (official designation from 1952 until 1958) |
| **ECM** | electronic countermeasures |
| **ELINT** | electronic intelligence |
| **EO** | electro-optical |
| **FFAC** | fast forward air controller |
| **Flt Lt** | flight lieutenant (military commissioned officer rank, equivalent to captain) |
| **FM** | field marshal (military commissioned officer rank) |
| **FTU** | Fighter Training Unit |
| **GCI** | ground-controlled intercept |
| **Gen** | general (military commissioned officer rank) |
| **GP** | general-purpose (bomb) |
| **IDF** | Israel Defense Forces |
| **IDF/AF** | Israel Defense Forces/Air Force |
| **IFF** | identification friend or foe |
| **IR** | infrared |
| **IrAF** | Iraqi Air Force (official designation since 1958) |
| **IIAF** | Imperial Iranian Air Force (official designation until 1979) |
| **Il** | Ilyushin (the design bureau led by Sergey Vladimirovich Ilyushin, also known as OKB-39) |
| **IP** | initial point (typically a visual reference on the ground used as an aid to begin attack run) |
| **IRBM** | intermediate-range ballistic missile |
| **KIA** | killed in action |
| **Lt** | lieutenant (military commissioned officer rank) |
| **Lt Col** | lieutenant colonel (military commissioned officer rank) |
| **1st Lt** | first lieutenant (military commissioned officer rank) |
| **Maj** | major (military commissioned officer rank) |

| | |
|---|---|
| **Maj Gen** | major general (military commissioned officer rank) |
| **MBT** | main battle tank |
| **MHz** | Megahertz, millions of cycles per second |
| **Mi** | Mil (the design bureau led by Mikhail Mil) |
| **MiG** | Mikoyan i Gurevich (the design bureau led by Artyom Ivanovich Mikoyan and Mikhail Iosifovich Gurevich, also known as OKB-155 or MMZ' 'Zenit') |
| **NWC** | National Water Carrier (Israel) |
| **OCU** | Operational Conversion Unit |
| **OTU** | Operational Training Unit |
| **PoW** | prisoner of war |
| **QJJ** | al-Quwwat al-Jawwiya al-Jaza'eriya (Algerian Air Force) |
| **QRA** | quick reaction alert |
| **R-3S** | Soviet air-to-air missile, based on US-made AIM-9B Sidewinder (ASCC codename AA-2 Atoll) |
| **RAF** | Royal Air Force (of the United Kingdom) |
| **RHAWS** | radar homing and warning system |
| **RIO** | radar intercept officer (see also WSO) |
| **RJAF** | Royal Jordanian Air Force |
| **RS-2US** | Soviet air-to-air missile (ASCC codename AA-1 Alkali) |
| **RWR** | radar warning receiver |
| **SAM** | surface-to-air missile |
| **Su** | Sukhoi (the design bureau led by Pavel Ossipowich Sukhoi, also known as OKB-51) |
| **SyAAF** | Syrian Arab Republic Air Force |
| **Tu** | Tupolev (the design bureau led by Andrei Nikolayevich Tupolev) |
| **UAR** | United Arab Republic (Union of Egypt, Syria and Yemen, 1958–1961) |
| **UARAF** | United Arab Republic Air Force, designation of Egyptian and Syrian air forces between 1958 and 1962, and of the Egyptian Air Force until 1969 |
| **UAV** | unmanned aerial vehicle |
| **USAF** | United States Air Force |
| **USN** | United States Navy (includes US Naval Aviation) |
| **V-PVO** | Voyska Protivo-Vozdushnoy Oborony, the Soviet Air Defence Forces |
| **Wg Cdr** | wing commander (military commissioned officer rank, equivalent to lieutenant colonel) |
| **WIA** | wounded in action |
| **Yak** | Yakovlev (the design bureau led by Alexander Sergeyevich Yakovlev, also known as OKB-115) |

# ADDENDA/ERRATA: ARAB MIGS, VOLUMES 1 TO 4

The authors would like to make the following amendments and corrections to *Arab MiGs, Volumes 1 to 4*.

## Volume 1, Chapter 4: Follow-Ups, pp91-93 & Volume 2, Chapter 4: Mixed Fortunes, pp139-140

Breaking the established tradition of opening every new volume in this series with a photograph of a British-made aircraft in service with an Arab air force, Volume 5 opens with a photograph provided by Samir Aziz Mikhail, veteran MiG-pilot from Egypt. It is showing him early during his career, while serving with No. 31 Squadron of the United Arab Republic Air Force (UARAF, as the Egyptian Air Force had been named from 1958 until 1972), in 1964. The unit in question was equipped with MiG-17PFs (radar-equipped variant), originally purchased by Syria immediately following the Suez War of 1956, and initially commanded by Sqn Ldr Munir al-Garudy. Following establishment of the United Arab Republic, on 1 February 1958, this unit was incorporated into the UARAF, and moved to Inchas air base, in Egypt. While in Egypt, it came under the command of Sqn Ldr Hafez al-Assad, future Commander-in-Chief (C-in-C) Syrian Arab Air Force (SyAAF), Minister of Defence and then President of Syria. Following the coup in Damascus that led to break up of the United Arab Union, on 28 September 1961, the MiG-17PFs were retained by Egypt. However, No. 31 Squadron soon moved to Abu Suweir, as recalled by Mikhail, who found it there in mid-1963:

'I graduated in 1963, with Generation 14, and was assigned to serve with a fighter wing based at Abu Suweir. This included a MiG-17PF unit commanded by Col Mohammed Naibh Messeri. I served with that squadron only shortly before joining the first group of youthful lieutenants that converted to MiG-21s.'

Samir Aziz Mikhail in front of a MiG-17PF of No. 31 Squadron, in summer or autumn 1963. (Samir Aziz Mikhail Collection)

(Albert Grandolini Collection)

## Volume 1, Chapter 4: Follow-Ups, pp99-102

Albert Grandolini kindly provided a photograph (see left) of one of four Hawker Fury F.Mk 11s (also known as 'Baghdad Fury') donated by Iraq to Morocco in 1961. Furthermore, he found another photograph of one of these aircraft (see above) on the blog maintained by Col Abbdesslam Bouziane (FARM, ret.), one of the first 12 Moroccan officers trained at the French Air Force (Armée de l'Air, AdA) Academy in Salon de Provence. Although of rather poor quality, these are nicely showing that the original camouflage pattern was retained, but Iraqi markings and serials removed and replaced by contemporary markings of the Aviation Royale Chérifienne (ARC), including a red star and serial numbers (2 on the photo to the left; a wingtip of the same aircraft can be seen on the right side of the photo above and is indicating that this was repeated in 'RAF-style' on bottom surfaces of either wing). Furthermore, the aircraft with serial number 2 appears to have received three white 'invasion stripes' added ot the wings of those Iraqi Furies loaned to Egypt during the latter part of the 1948-1949 Arab-Israeli War.

## Volume 1, Chapter 6: Yemen, pp139-141; Volume 2 Addenda/Errata, pp37-38; Volume 4, Addenda/Errata pp26-27

David Kohlen from Germany provided the following correction relating to the USAF F-100 unit based at Dahran, in Saudi Arabia, between early July 1963 and January 1964:

*'The F-100s that can be seen on p37 actually belonged to the 523rd Tactical Fighter Squadron (TFS), not the 23rd TFS, as stated in your book. The 23rd TFS was never part of the 27th Tactical Fighter Wing, but that of the (Bitburg, West Germany-based) 36th TFW. Instead, it was a detachment of the 523rd TFS, itself a part of the 27th TFW, that deployed to Dhahran, starting in early July 1963. The other squadron of that wing, the 481st TFS, also deployed a detachment to Saudi Arabia, in the period 14 November 1963 to 1 February 1964 (as per Special Order T-808, issued on 5 November 1963). However, it seems that there were never more than eight USAF F-100 fighters at Dhahran at any time, and even then two F-100Ds and one F-100F (two-seater) were actually based at Jeddah International instead.'*

## Volume 2, Chapter 1: Turbulent Times in Iraq, pp66–71

In *Volume 2* of this series and in sister publication *Iraqi Fighters: Camouflage and Markings, 1953–2003*, we have written about Iraqi acquisition of MiG-19S and MiG-19PM fighters, as recalled by Brig Gen Ahmad Sadik (IrAF, ret.). Accordingly, after purchasing examples of the MiG-19S, then C-in-C IrAF, Maj Gen Jalal Jawad al-Awqati, began drawing up plans for increasing the total number of that type to 50. The Soviets delivered all of the aircraft from this order, but the IrAF never put more than 16 of them into service. The remaining MiG-19s were left packed in their crates and stored inside a hangar at Wahda air base (the former RAF Shoibiyah).

Meanwhile, our further research into this topic has provided additional confirmation of Iraq ordering – and the USSR delivering – 36 MiG-19PMs, together with their primary weapons, RS-2US air-to-air missiles (ASCC codename AA-1 Alkali). This confirmation was provided by Iranian military historian and aviation journalist Babak Taghvaee. Namely, while working on his book *Iranian Tigers at War: Northrop F-5A/B, F-5E/F and Sub-Variants in Combat Service since 1966* (to be published in October 2014 by Helion & Company), Taghvaee worked through the archive of the Islamic Republic of Iran Army's Political Conscience Organisation. Among others, he found several tapes with recordings of meetings between the former heir of Iran, Shah Mohammed Reza Pahlavi, various Directors of the Iranian Organisation for Intelligence and National Security (SAVAK), and members of the US Military Advisory Assistance Group (MAAG) in Tehran, in 1960. On one of the tapes the contemporary director of the SAVAK could be heard expressing great concerns about deliveries of MiG-19PMs to Iraq at a time when then Imperial Iranian Air Force (IIAF) was still flying obsolete and worn-out North American F-86F Sabres and Republic F-84 Thunderjets:

*'Iraq ordered 14 MiG-19s in 1960. The first 14 machines delivered were the basic MiG-19S, armed with NR-30 cannon and capable of carrying 250kg [551lb] bombs or ORO-57K pods for unguided rockets. But the second batch of aircraft of this type ordered by Iraq belongs to the MiG-19PM variant. This is equipped with the PR-2U radar which provides compatibility with RS-2US air-to-air missiles. Iraq received 36 such MiG-19PMs, together with 100 RS-2US missiles.'*

Obviously, this raises several questions. If retired IrAF generals recall deliveries of such aircraft, and official Iranian military documentation confirms it, why did they never enter service and what happened to the no fewer than 36 MiG-19PMs after their arrival in Iraq?

As mentioned in *Volume 2*, Iraq was already experiencing significant problems with the technical realiability of their MiG-19S fleet. Because of the endemic involvement of the military in political affairs, the IrAF lacked crews for the only unit that operated the type, No. 9 Squadron. As a result, it was decided not to introduce the MiG-19PM to service. These were stored – in a disassembled condition – inside a hangar at Wahda. Because these MiGs were never assembled and test-flown, Iraq never formally accepted them and never paid for them. Correspondingly, these 36 MiG-19PMs remained in Soviet possession. The authors consider it most likely that all were returned to the USSR following two coup d'etats in Baghdad in 1963, as was the case for certain other Soviet-delivered equipment that did not enter service with the Iraqi military.

The reason why the IrAF never accepted these MiG-19s is further confirmed by another tape found by Taghvaee in the same Iranian archive. The document contains records of another meeting between the Shah, the director of the SAVAK, and members of the MAAG, held in 1961. On this occasion it is clear that Iranian intelligence has learned that Baghdad has received Moscow's permission to order 'at least a squadron worth' of brand new and more advanced MiG-21F-13 interceptors armed with R-3S missiles, and Tupolev Tu-16 bombers.[1]

Further confirmation of this fact was obtained in an entirely unexpected fashion. Namely, while deciding not to accept the MiG-19PMs, Iraq retained the stock of 100 RS-2US missiles delivered with them. An Iraqi engineer who formerly worked for Iraqi Armament Industries, and interviewed (on condition of anonymity) in the process of research for another publishing project, recalled what happened more than 20 years later:

*'In 1987, we converted a number of R-3S missiles that were out of shelf life into unguided air-to-ground rockets for our [Mil] Mi-8 and Mi-17 helicopters. The diameter of the R-3S is 127mm [5in], and so we removed their seeker heads and attached 130mm [5.1in] artillery shells instead. The resulting weapon was a big success that made our pilots very happy: in this fashion, they obtained unguided rockets with a considerable punch, which they were capable of firing at the Iranians from distances well outside the range of enemy air defences.*

*'Because of this success, the idea was born to try and do the same with the stock of RS-2US missiles – one of my colleagues called them 'pigs' because of their shape – left behind from the times of the attempted acquisition of MiG-19PMs, back in the early 1960s. I know that a project to convert them into unguided rockets was launched in early 1988, but don't know what happened with it: I left the company before the research and development process was completed.'*

## Volume 2, Chapter 2: Compromised Solutions, pp80–81

Concurrent with information regarding Iraqi orders for MiG-19PM interceptors, in the course of a recent interview with Group 73, Maj Gen Nabil Shuwakry (EAF, ret.) revealed the precise number of MiG-19S fighters ordered by Egypt from the Soviet Union in November 1959:

*'The Air Force bought 56 MiG-19s. They were delivered only starting in 1961, and became the first supersonic aircraft in service in Egypt. Because of technical problems we soon lost interest. Instead, the Air Force then opted to buy the MiG-21F-13, equipped with a radar and two air-to-air missiles.'*

## Volume 2, Chapter 3: Political Games, pp113–114 & pp118–121

A reader from Iraq, who prefers to remain anonymous, sent us the following additional information regarding the coup in Iraq, on 8 February 1963:

*'Capt Munthir al-Windawy was not alone during his attack on Rashid AB, on that morning. Flying a Hunter F.Mk 6 he destroyed one row of MiG-19s of No. 9 Squadron. But, a few minutes later a pair of MiG-17s from No. 7 Squadron attacked Rashid AB too, and they strafed and destroyed four MiG-21F-13s of No. 11 Squadron. I do not know the names of the pilots involved…'*

Addenda/Errata: Arab MiGs, Volumes 1 to 4

We intend to pursue this issue in our further research and would welcome any additional information.

## Volume 2, Chapter 4: Mixed Fortunes, pp142-144 & Volume 3, Chapter 2: Fighting the Lost Battle, pp99-103

A reader from Algeria who prefers to remain anonymous has kindly provided a number of scans of photographs published in Algerian newspapers in the early 1970s. While most are rather small and of insufficient quality for print, several depict Algerian Air Force (al-Quwwat al-Jawiyya al-Jaza'eriya, QJJ) MiG-17F and MiG-21F-13 interceptors, and Ilyushin Il-28 light bombers as seen shortly before the June 1967 War:

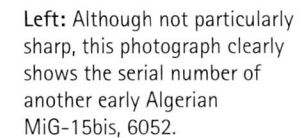

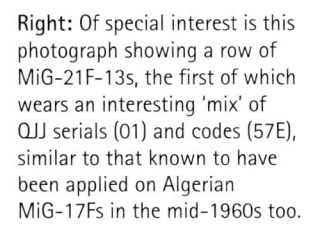

**Left:** Although not particularly sharp, this photograph clearly shows the serial number of another early Algerian MiG-15bis, 6052.

**Right:** Of special interest is this photograph showing a row of MiG-21F-13s, the first of which wears an interesting 'mix' of QJJ serials (01) and codes (57E), similar to that known to have been applied on Algerian MiG-17Fs in the mid-1960s too.

**Left:** Although photographed around the same time, the MiG-21F-13 with serial number 69 has received no code.

**Right:** Another view of the MiG-21F-13 with serial number/code 01/57E.

Detail view of the front part of an Il-28. While its serial number – 207 – applied below the cockpit appears to have been removed by the censor, that on the door of the front undercarriage bay was left in place, offering an interesting supplement to the photograph published on p144 of *Volume 2*.

## Volume 3, Chapter 7: Repercussions, p203

The emergence of the *Arab MiGs* series has prompted quite interesting reactions from a number of Israeli readers, researchers and enthusiasts. Many private individuals and even some state-owned companies have welcomed our publications and accepted them enthusiastically. Viewing our research and publishing efforts as 'anti-Israeli', others have replied with fierce critiques. Accusing the authors of (citate) *'hating Israel'*, Shlomo Aloni – considered the leading historian of the Israeli Defense Force/Air Force (IDF/AF) by many – has declared the content of *Volumes 1 and 2* as *'Arab stories from 1001 Nights'*. Surprisingly enough, he limited his specific critique to our description of one incident along the Israeli-Jordanian ceasefire lines, in 1966. At least as interesting is the fact that, contrary to his practice in reaction to certain previous of our publications, he did not forward any 'letters to the publisher', supposedly written by IDF/AF pilots in 'protest' against the 'lies' published in our books.

Much more interesting – and more useful – was a reaction from another historian, author and publisher about the IDF/AF, Ra'anan Weiss. While not failing to observe that, *'Arabs always lie, always'*, he kindly provided the following – official – IDF/AF document listing claims for Arab aircraft destroyed during the June 1967 War.

Scan of the Document AG-10-428, p44, 'Table 40: Total Loss of Enemy Aircraft'
(IDF via Ra'anan Weiss)

| | Lebanon | Iraq | Jordan | Syria | Egypt | Total | Type of aircraft | | |
|---|---|---|---|---|---|---|---|---|---|
| | ז | ו | ה | ד | ג | ב | | א | |
| 1 | 1 | 23 | 29 | 61 | 338 | 452 | Total | סה"כ | .1 |
| 2 | 1 | 20 | 21 | 56 | 232 | 330 | Total fighters | | .2 |
| 3 | - | 15 | - | 33 | 100 | 148 | MiG-21 | | .3 |
| 4 | - | - | - | - | 29 | 29 | MiG-19 | | .4 |
| 5 | - | - | - | 23 | 89 | 112 | MiG-15/17 | | .5 |
| 6 | - | - | - | - | 14 | 14 | Sukhoi | | .6 |
| 7 | 1 | 5 | 21 | - | - | 27 | Hunter | | .7 |
| 8 | - | 1 | - | 2 | 59 | 62 | Total of bombers | | .8 |
| 9 | - | 1 | - | - | 30 | 31 | Tu-16 | | .9 |
| 10 | - | - | - | 2 | 29 | 31 | Il-28 | | .10 |
| 11 | - | - | 2 | 3 | 11 | 16 | Helicopters | | .11 |
| 12 | - | - | 2 | 3 | 1 | 6 | Mil-4 or similar | | .12 |
| 13 | - | - | - | - | 10 | 10 | Mil-6 | | .13 |
| 14 | - | 2 | 6 | - | 32 | 40 | Transport | | .14 |
| 15 | - | 2 | 6 | - | 24 | 32 | Il-14/Dakota | | .15 |
| 16 | - | - | - | - | 8 | 8 | An-12 | | .16 |
| 17 | - | - | - | - | 4 | 4 | Unidentified | | .17 |

Essentially, this list citing 452 Arab aircraft as destroyed between 5 and 10 June 1967, is the same as that published in the English edition of the *Jerusalem Post*, on 11 June 1967, and in every other account of the June 1967 War until the appearance of *Arab MiGs Volume 3*. The only difference is that most other lists contain additional entries for aircraft shot down in 'air combats', usually listed in parenthesis.

In light of Israeli insistence that 'Arabs always lie', and in an attempt to offer an interesting comparison that enables our readers to gauge the reliability of sources from both sides of the Arab-Israeli conflict – including the famed 'Israeli intelligence', often cited as being the original source behind almost everything published about Arab air forces to date – we are re-posting the official list of UARAF losses for the June 1967 War, originally published in *Volume 3*, p203:

**Official list of UARAF aircraft and losses by type for the period 5-30 June 1967 (EFM, Document No. 44)**

| Type | Before 5 June 1967 | 10 June 1967 | Operational Losses | Deliveries from USSR | Deliveries from Algeria | Deliveries from East Germany | End of June 1967 |
|---|---|---|---|---|---|---|---|
| MiG-15 | 26 | 11 | 15 | - | - | - | 11[1] |
| MiG-17 | 70 | 26 | 44 | 93 | 21 | 30 | 166[2] |
| MiG-19 | 27 | 11 | 16 | - | - | - | 11[3] |
| MiG-21 | 100 | 22 | 78 | 65 | 20 | - | 98[4] |
| Su-7 | 34 | 1 | 25 | - | - | - | 41[5] |
| **Total fighters** | **257** | **71** | **178** | **158** | **41** | **30** | **327** |
| Il-28 | 34 | - | 34 | 10 | 12 | - | 30[6] |
| Tu-16 | 23 | - | 23 | - | - | - | - |
| **Total bombers** | **57** | **-** | **57** | **-** | **12** | **-** | **30** |
| Il-14 | 48 | 29 | 19 | - | - | - | 27 |
| An-12 | 22 | 15 | 2 | - | - | - | 15 |
| **Total transports** | **70** | **44** | **21** | **-** | **-** | **-** | **42** |
| Mi-1 | 6 | 6 | - | - | - | - | 6 |
| Mi-4 | 21 | 20 | 1 | - | - | - | 26[7] |
| Mi-6 | 12 | 2 | 10 | - | - | - | 2 |
| Mi-8 | - | - | - | 10 | - | - | 10 |
| **Total helicopters** | **39** | **28** | **11** | **10** | **-** | **-** | **44** |
| **Total losses 6 June – 4 August 1967** | | | **267** | | | | |

1   Seven of these aircraft were stored, while the other four were under repair.

2   No fewer than 52 MiG-17s were in storage as of early August 1967, of which 11 were MiG-17PF night-fighters and 26 MiG-17s (without afterburner).

3   Eight of these 11 aircraft were under repair.

4   This figure included 40 newly delivered MiG-21PFS – all of which had been previously brought up to a standard similar to the MiG-21PFM (including SPS flaps) and should therefore have been properly designated MiG-21PFS – as well as MiG-21FLs (considered 'all-weather fighters' by the UARAF), plus 19 'original' MiG-21PFMs (considered 'night-fighters' by the UARAF). Interestingly, the Egyptians tended to designate all of these variants as 'MiG-21FL'.

5   12 of these aircraft were in storage.

1   Ten of the aircraft still available as of late June were Il-28R reconnaissance-bombers. Note that eight additional Il-28s were stationed in Yemen.
2   16 out of 26 in service with the UARAF were assigned to the Egyptian Navy.

While it is generally acknowledged that exaggerations of enemy losses are frequent in air warfare – foremost due to the extremely high speed at which the encounter develops and the effects of combat stress – and therefore understandable, the conclusion is on hand that Israeli writers insist on 'their' data no matter what type of evidence to the contrary is provided. Correspondingly, it is not a little ironic that in more than 40 years since, none of the authors and researchers working on this topic has ever attempted to cross-examine such Israeli data with Egyptian or information from other Arab sources. For example, considering that Egypt neither had 148 MiG-21s, nor 112 MiG-17s or 30 Tu-16s at the start of the war, and that it wrote off 267 different aircraft within the period 6-30 June 1967, it is obvious that the UARAF could not have suffered as many as 338 losses in the period between 6 and 10 June 1967 alone.

## Volume 4, Addenda/Errata, pp27-28

Referring to the photo of Hunter F.Mk 6 coded XG236, Andy Marden sent us the following correction:

*'This was one of two aircraft from No. 66 Squadron Royal Air Force loaned to the Iraqis in 1957 to provide a reserve for a flypast over Baghdad. It was returned to the RAF and was lost while still in service with No. 66 Squadron, on 14 February 1958.'*

## Volume 4, Chapter 1: Defiance and Active Defence, p54

Several readers made us aware of a mistake regarding the date of the sinking of the Israeli Navy destroyer *Eilat* (hit by up to three P-15 Termit/SS-N-2 Styx anti-ship missiles fired from two Komar-class fast missile craft of the Egyptian Navy). We cited this as, 'the night of 11-12 July 1967', rather than 21 October 1967. A different incident on 11-12 July saw the destroyer, together with two Israeli torpedo boats, uncover two Egyptian torpedo boats off the Rumani coast. Both Egyptian vessels were sunk in the engagement that followed.

It was AM al-Ezz that took over as the C-in-C UARAF during the night of 11-12 June 1967 (he was replaced by AM Shalaby el-Hinnawy on 23 October 1967).

## Volume 4, Chapter 2: A Long and Bitter Battle, p68, p96, p110; Chapter 6: Friends Old and New, p192

A reader who prefers to remain anonymous provided the following corrections regarding specific SAM systems sold to Egypt by the USSR during the late 1960s.

*'Concerning the SA-2s and their lack of NRZ-1 IFF system, as cited on p68: actually, even the latest variants of the SA-3 did not have a separate IFF system, except*

*for the NRZ-12 and/or the NRZ-15 systems installed on the P-15 and P-18 radars, respectively. These were elements of the Kremny 2 system.*

*'The photograph on p96 shows a P-30 radar that had its upper antenna inclined in order to provide a height-finder. As such, this was the first Soviet radar to provide a 3D picture. The radar picture provided had a significant error built in: it showed the wrong altitude of the target, which was usually about 2,000m [6,562ft]. This was the reason why the Soviets abandoned this system and rapidly replaced it with the P-35 and P-37.*

*'On p110 you mention the P-37 with an integral D-band IFF system. The reason why the NRZ-20 IFF system was integrated on the P-37 was that it did not disturb the work of the main antenna: the NRZ-20 emits at a frequency of 668MHz, which is different to any of the frequencies at which this radar works. The same is the case with the P-19 and P-40. On the contrary, metric radars – like the P-12, P-14 and P-18 – needed a separate small antenna to send the IFF signal.*

*'On p192, you mention 'Brigadier General Mohammed Taher Bouzroub', as commander of the Algerian air defence brigade deployed in Libya. At that time Algeria was rulled by President Boumedienne, who had left the military with the rank of colonel. Because of this, it was completely out of the question for anybody else in the military to have a rank above him. Correspondingly, although bearing the responsibilities of a brigadier general, Bouzroub wore the rank of colonel. It was only once Col Chadli Benjedid became president that he decided to let officers acess the rank of general in order to distinguish between the military and civilian authorities.'*

## Volume 4, Chapter 2: A Long and Bitter Battle, pp78 & Chapter 4: Syria – Still Alone, pp177

As mentioned by Mohammed Okasha in *Volume 4*, the UARAF temporarily deployed one squadron of MiG-17s to Syria in 1969. The latest research by Group 73 historians has uncovered another Egyptian pilot who served a tour of duty with the unit in question and provided more details about this deployment. Hussein el-Kfass told us the following about his early career and his tour in Syria:

*'I am originally from Ismailia. My father was a foreman on the Suez Canal. I wanted to become a naval officer, but I loved flying and was fascinated by the pilots that would come to Ismailia, or whom I saw at Abu Suweir… I initially failed for health reasons and because I botched up my tests, but managed to enter the Air Academy during my second attempt, on 26 November 1966, with the generation 21… I experienced the June 1967 War while serving as a cadet during my first year at Bilbeis, where one of our instructors was an Indian, named Labora, who helped me become a pilot… In February 1968, 18 of us were sent to the Soviet Union for further training. Additional cadets joined during that course, so that we were 29 that qualified, with three of us – including Atif el-Sadat, half brother of then future President of Egypt – qualified on Su-7s, while the others were taught to fly MiG-17s…*

*'We returned to Egypt on 20 June 1969, and subsequently I got myself into trouble that not only landed me in prison, but FM Fawzy wanted to get me out of the Air Force. I was saved by AM Baghdadi and Maj Gen Mubarak and ordered to go to Beni Suweif, together with seven MiG-17 pilots. They then took us to Aswan, where I*

A youthful Hussein el-Kfass (kneeling in centre, front row) seen during training in the USSR, in 1968. (Hussein el-Kfass Collection)

*joined No. 89 Squadron of Air Brigade 206. Shortly after the Soviets deployed to that air base with their aircraft and thus we were first re-deployed to Daraw and then to Luxor. After finally starting our training on MiG-17s, we eventually got the order to prepare for deployment to Syria…*

*'I spent only a few months in Syria, but developed a strong relationship with a number of their pilots, who had a very high fighting spirit. For all of that time, the Syrians were engaged flying defensive sorties. The Israelis would suddenly appear from behind Jebel Sheikh, attack their targets on the ground or hit some Syrian aircraft, and then disappear. In October 1969, we were replaced by the unit led by Mohammed Okasha.*

*'When I got back to Egypt, in 1969 I was assigned to a MiG-17 squadron based at Qutamiyah AB. I did not like some of the training procedures there, had a strong disagreement with the squadron CO and thus got myself into troubles again… My commander wanted to send me to one of the units flying transports… Only an intervention by Maj Gen Abdel Moneim el-Shennawy prevented this, and thus I ended up at Abu Hammad AB, newly constructed outside Zaqaziq, joining No. 62 Squadron while this was commanded by Samir Farid.'*

## Volume 4, Chapter 2: A Long and Bitter Battle, p119 & p138

Ahmad Keraidy from Egypt, the son of late Il-28 and Tu-16 bomber pilot Mohammed Abdel Wahab el-Keraidy, kindly provided the following photograph and information confirming a report by Y. V. Nastenko, a former Soviet advisor in Egypt, according to whom the first victim of Soviet air defence units equipped with S-125 (ASCC codename SA-3 Goa) surface-to-air missiles was an Egyptian Il-28:

This photograph is showing UARAF Il-28 crews in Yemen, during a visit by Marshal el-Salal to Rawda AB, in 1963. On the far left is Flt Off Dorry Riyad Sakr. He died while flying an Il-28U that was shot down by Soviet SA-3s over Cairo West AB.
(Ahmad Keraidy collection)

An Il-28U conversion trainer as flown by Dorry Riyad Sakr when he was shot down by Soviet SA-3s. Currently it remains unclear whether this happened in December 1969, as reported by some Russian sources, or in March 1970. Only two Egyptian squadrons continued to operate this type in October 1973: the survivors were withdrawn from service during the first half of the 1980s.
(Albert Grandolini Collection)

## Volume 4, Chapter 3: Other Egyptian Wars, pp145-150

Commentary from Egyptian sources relating to foreign mercenaries flying for the Nigerian Air Force during the Biafran War prompted Ares Klootwyk, a South African that flew MiG-17s in Nigeria, to submit the following reply, provided via renowed military journalist Al J. Venter:

'I have no recollection of any taunting of Egyptian aircrews by mercenary pilots regarding the wars of 1956 and 1967. I also don't recall Egyptians ever flying [Aero] L-29s delivered from Czechoslovakia during my time in Nigeria. We were friendly with both their pilots and mechanics and got on well together. We actually had no option because they were responsible for keeping our planes airborne.

'During my time, and in my experience, none of our MiGs were equipped with rocket rails. I cannot recall Bond and Kuzupski being referred to as 'Whisky pilots' by name, and I never personally knew of them flying inebriated. I do vaguely recall Bond flying with a bottle in his navigation bag, but he always appeared to have completed his mission successfully.

'The first night operations by the MiGs started in November 1968, with Jimmy Webb and me bombing the Uli airstrip. We experienced very, very heavy anti-aircraft fire and so did not try our luck again at night bombing.

'Concerning the 22 May 1969 raid by [Malmö Flygindustri MFI-9B] Minicons: there were no more than two Il-28s at Port Harcourt at any time and none were destroyed by the Minicoins on that raid. Arriving from the hotel shortly after the Minicons had left, I only saw one MiG-17 on fire. No Canberras were ever deployed by Nigerians and during that raid there was no [de Havilland] Heron aircraft at Port Harcourt. At the time there was also no [Curtiss] C-46 there.

'The 19 November 1969 attack by a [North American] T-6 Harvard at Port Harcourt did not cause any damage to any aircraft on the field.

'The 29 November 1969 (not 19 November 1969, as stated in your report) confrontation with a pair of Minicons happened when I was scrambled from Port Harcourt in a MiG-17 to search for two Minicons that had attacked an oil installation. The order came to search for them at Uli airstrip and towards the north.

'When I came to Ozubulu, which was north of Uli, I saw what I thought were two vehicles coming towards me at high speed along a tarmaced road. As I got closer, I made them out to be a couple of small aircraft on the road. I didn't have time to cock my guns and fire as I was too close to them.

'When I did come around for the second time, one Minicon had exited the road on to a dirt track and disappeared under trees. The second Minicon had come to a stop, still on the surfaced road, and the pilot had disappeared into the bush.

'I didn't fire... but went around again and on the third pass I opened fire and the Minicon seemed to disintegrate (later on I learned that it was rebuilt and was flown again).

'As I could not see where the first Minicon had disappeared to, I went back to base, loaded up with two 100kg [221lb] bombs as stated in your report, returned to Ozubulu and dropped my bombs individually on positions where I suspected the aircraft might be. I subsequently learned that no damage was one.

'By the time of this episode, all the Egyptian MiG pilots were long gone.'

## Volume 4, Chapter 3: Syria – Still Alone, pp183-184

This recently rediscovered photograph was taken by Tom Cooper in August 2004, and shows the memorial to the late Col Fayez Mansour at the former Military Museum of Damascus (closed in 2010). Mansour was killed in an air combat with Israeli Mirages while flying a MiG-17F, on 12 May 1970. Noteworthy are Mansour's decorations and flags of various (sadly, unknown) SyAAF units.

(Tom Cooper)

1   These new aircraft were considered such a threat for Iran, that they eventually prompted the IIAF and the Shah of Iran to enter negotiations for acquisition of at least comparable, if not superior fighters and interceptors. This drive resulted in Iran purchasing Northrop F-5A/B Freedom Fighters and, later on, McDonnell Douglas F-4 Phantom IIs.

# Chapter 1

# NO PEACE, NO WAR

The story of the October 1973 War between the Arab nations and Israel is as complex as it is long, and hard to simplify. It was directly related to the outcome of the June 1967 War, when Israel seized the Sinai Peninsula as far as the Suez Canal from Egypt, Jerusalem and the West Bank from Jordan, and the Golan Heights from Syria. It was directly related to the protracted discussion at the United Nations Security Council, which resulted in the ambiguous Resolution 242 that in turn fit the US objective of supporting Israeli territorial acquisitions until the Arab states would be willing to negotiate peace on Israeli conditions.

The 1973 War was also directly related to the stunning Israeli victory of 1967 that created a sense of invulnerability in that country: primarily based on occupation of 'buffer zones' in the Sinai and the Golan, and a myth of the invincibility of the IDF that gradually developed. Finally, it was related to the stalemated peace efforts in the Middle East, caused by Israeli unresponsiveness to Egyptian overtures and negotiation attempts by UN envoy Gunnar Jaring and US Secretary of State William Rogers, and also the limited motivation to encourage negotiations on the part of successive administrations under US Presidents Lyndon B. Johnson and Richard B. Nixon.

There is little doubt that Johnson and Nixon defined the situation in Cold War terms and treated Israel as a Cold War ally that had to be armed, no matter how little Israel actually contributed to the struggle against the communist block. Nevertheless, the US wanted stability in the Middle East and would have preferred a general settlement, but because that was impossible they were prepared to accept the status quo and an avoidance of conflict. The reason was that they were 'busy elsewhere': as of 1973, US power was floundering in the morass of Southeast Asia, Washington was making strenuous efforts to prevent an epidemic of revolt in Latin America, and President Nixon then became involved in the Watergate Affair that eventually forced him to resign. Therefore, the US continued arming Israel in the belief that the very imbalance of power between Jews and Arabs would prevent a new conflict.

Egyptian President Gamal Abdel Nasser was without equal in the Arab World. He was the only Arab leader to attain world stature. His decision to accept the Rogers peace plan, in August 1970, which prompted the US to exercise enough pressure for Israel to follow in fashion, was of critical importance for Egypt: the Egyptian president knew that his country required a period of calm in order to complete the necessary political and military preparations for a counterattack in the Sinai. However, this approach, as well as requiring a compromise between King Hussein of Jordan and the Palestinian guerrillas in order to end the inter-Arab war that was raging in Jordan,

Two Mil Mi-8 helicopters of the UARAF seen while bearing the coffin of the late President Nasser, on 28 September 1970. At that time, most Egyptian Mi-8s were still painted overall olive green.
(Tom Cooper Collection)

required nerves of steel. Ultimately, this claimed Nasser's health: he died suddenly, on 27 September 1970.

Nasser was succeeded by Anwar el-Sadat. Like Nasser, Sadat was another of the so-called 'Free Army officers' who had overthrown Egyptian King Farouk in 1952. Compared to Nasser, Sadat seemed insignificant and desined for only a short time in office. Nevertheless, he quickly showed his mettle.

Having little faith in diplomacy, Sadat gave it a try during the first months of his leadership, but then concluded that such efforts were futile since the US would not pressure Israel into making any concessions. Sadat instead concluded that a military option would be necessary to secure another political intervention by the US, and to facilitate negotiations with Israel. However, Egypt lacked the weaponry considered necessary to exercise the military option, primarily because the Soviet Union – meanwhile involved in negotiations with the US in order to decrease Cold War tensions – was not interested in enabling 'the Arabs' to start a new war in the Middle East, as much as having doubts about Arab preparedness to wage such a war. Therefore, Sadat had to accept Israel's military dominance as well as the fact that the ever-increasing provision of US military and political aid to Israel ensured that this superiority exceeded the combined military power of all the Arab states bordering Israel.

Against this backdrop, between 1970 and 1973 the United Arab Republic Air Force (UARAF) – as the Egyptian Air Force had been named since 1958 – experienced a period during which the high pace of training and combat operations were slowed down, while the force received batches of new equipment sporadically sold by the USSR. At the same time, the UARAF made efforts to convert its pilots and ground personnel to these new aircraft while preparing them for a new war. Time and again, minor clashes with the Israel Defense Forces (IDF) did occur, but with both sides interested in maintaining the ceasefire from August 1970, none of these caused a major conflagration.

# Facing Reality

Early in his presidency, Sadat undertook a review of the existing military plans for a counteroffensive that would return the Sinai to Egyptian control. Dissatisfied by these, in February 1971 he abandoned all the three plans prepared by War Minister, FM Mohammed Fawzy (including 'Plan 200' and 'Granite', at least one of which was to be concluded by a liberation of the Gaza Strip), declaring them unrealistic because Egypt was facing an enemy that was supervisor in all regards. Sadat then proposed a new peace plan that envisaged a partial Israeli withdrawal and an opening of the Suez for navigation, as well as the return of Palestinian refugees to their homes. He took care to prevent Yasser Arafat from entering a new confrontation with King Hussein of Jordan, and then ensured the unity of Egypt, Syria and Libya before quashing a threatened coup by pro-Soviet elements in Cairo (and launching an anti-Soviet counter-coup in Khartoum, as described in Chapter 6 of *Volume 4*). Nevertheless, Israel turned down Sadat's offer, and in June 1971 the new Egyptian president made his final decision to launch a new war.[1]

On 1 March 1971, Sadat visited Moscow accompanied by Fawzy. Intent on ensuring Egyptian parity with Israel in terms of arms, he pushed for deliveries of offensive weapons including Tupolev Tu-22 supersonic bombers and advanced MiG-23 and MiG-25 interceptors. These were considered necessary to provide Egypt with the means to neutralise Israeli air power by attacking IDF/AF air bases while the Egyptian Army was on the offensive. Soviet Premier Leonid Brezhnev agreed to supply them, but – aware that delivery of such weapons would endanger the detente with the US – he conditioned deliveries on the Kremlin having the final say on their operational deployment. Although Egypt eventually agreed to such conditions, months passed and nothing arrived.[2]

Meanwhile, Sadat returned to Cairo only to find himself facing a coup plotted by a group of Nasserist officers and others with close ties to Soviet officials, led by his Vice President (and former Air Force officer), Ali Sabry, and Fawzy.[3] Sadat struck first: he dismissed Sabry and placed him under house arrest, on 2 May 1971. When Fawzy attempted to lead a squad of tanks to liberate Sabry, his column was overwhelmed by the Presidential Guard. More than 90 other officers were arrested and, together with Sabry and Fawzy, sentenced to years in prison. Among others, Sadat then appointed Maj Gen Sa'ad ad-Din el-Shazly in place of Fawzy as the new Chief of Staff Egyptian Army, on 16 May 1971, and ordered him to start planning and preparations for the liberation of the Sinai.

Having secured himself in power, Sadat signed a friendship treaty with Moscow on 27 May 1971, aiming to pacify Soviet suspicions over his purge of pro-Soviet officers. At the same time, he re-opened diplomatic channels to Washington. Alarmed at the pos-

Three Egyptian Su-17s (including serial number 7754 on the left side of the photograph) as seen during a post-October 1973 War parade in Cairo. Despite the poor quality of this scan, the aircraft can be clearly distinguished as Su-17s thanks to the following details: 'missing' fences on the wing gloves, conduits for wiring on top of the fuselage, 'big' rear fuselages, (necessary to house the original Lyulka AL-31 engine), and housings for Sirena-3 radar warning receivers (RWRs) above the rudder. (via Tom Long)

sibility of Egyptian-US reaproachment, Moscow this time reacted by providing some of the armament demanded by Cairo, including 16 Su-20s. The aircraft that arrived in Egypt actually belonged to the 0-series of Su-17s, as recalled by Ahmed Abbas Faraj, who was with the first group of Egyptian pilots to convert to this type:

*'I completed my training at the Air Force Academy in 1968... and was appointed – together with 12 other pilots – to the Helwan-based brigade equipped with Su-7s and commanded by Col Mohammed Abdel-Rahman. Later on we transferred to Jiancalis AB, where our training was supervised by Soviets. Our primary instructors were Egyptian, though, including Sa'ad Zaghloul and Salah Danish. After five months of rigorous training, often lasting from 0500 in the morning until 1700 in the afternoon, we received a short leave... then moved to Bilbeis AB, where I was assigned to No. 52 Squadron under the command of Kamal Zakaria, from whom I learned a lot about military flying. The other unit within our brigade was No. 53 Squadron under Lt Col Abdul Rahman Sidki, and there was a dedicated reconnaissance squadron from another brigade... It was there that I was selected to join a group of pilots that would convert to a new type we were about to get.*

*'Our test pilots flew the Su-17 variant in the USSR, in 1970, and their reports about it were not especially positive. However, they were told that we 'must' be satisfied with whatever aircraft the Soviets were ready to deliver. Furthermore, the new aircraft could carry more weapons and was more manoeuvrable than the short-ranged behemoth that was the Su-7BMK, and thus a decision was taken to order 16 Su-17s. The first of these were delivered to our squadron in May 1972, and we underwent a conversion course at Jiyanclis AB. The first CO of our squadron was Hazem al-Gharby.*

*'The first impression of the new Sukhoi was that it was very large, as large as a [McDonnell Douglas F-4] Phantom, and powered by a very large engine, too. Its introduction to service was marred by technical problems and during the first eight months of training I flew only 17 minutes. Once the problems were solved, we concentrated on training CAS for ground troops, but trained air combat versus one, two and more aircraft too – primarily against Bilbeis and Inchas. We reached a very*

Providing a comparison with the Su-17s, this is a post-October 1973 War photograph of four genuine Egyptian Su-20s. As can be seen, all were painted in a standardised camouflage pattern in beige and olive green (known as 'sand and spinach' in the West). Powered by Tumansky R-29 engines of smaller diameter, they have slimmer rear fuselages, additional fences on top of the wing gloves, no wiring conduits on the upper fuselage, and the Sirena-3 RWRs are positioned directly above the braking parachute housing. (via Group 73)

*high readiness rate within a few weeks. After our conversion, the squadron was redeployed to Cairo West, in order to keep us away from US reconnaissance aircraft that were regularly flying along the Egyptian coast of the Mediterranean. Indeed, some of our first operational missions saw us being scrambled to intercept such aircraft. We climbed to 14,000m [45,932ft] altitude, but the Americans escaped.'* [4]

Namely, production of the Su-20 was launched only in early 1973, and the Soviets could thus not deliver any such aircraft to Egypt the year earlier: what they had were Su-17s from the 0-series, which saw a short service with the Soviet Air Force (Voyenno-Vozdushnye Sily, VVS). Indeed, once the deliveries of Su-20s to export customers began, it seems that the first batch of these was sent to Syria instead, because Egypt is not known to have received any additional aircraft of this type – whether Su-17s or 'genuine' Su-20s – before sometimes during or immediately after the October 1973 War. Meanwhile, another group of EAF pilots converted to Su-17s, including Muhammad al-Ibrahim:

*'I underwent my flying training in the USSR, and flew MiG-17s and Su-7s in Egypt before converting to the Su-17 at Beni Sueif, in July 1973. The Su-17 was faster than the Su-7, carried 3,500kg [7,716lb] of weapons – half a ton more than the Su-7 – and was more powerful, more manoeuvrable, and had a better acceleration. The gunsight was better and it could carry two R-3S missles for self-defence.'* [5]

# Slowing Down

Throughout the period between August 1970 and spring 1971, the ceasefire between Egypt and Israel was largely respected. Therefore, the end of the 'War of Bloodletting' (a term introduced by Nasser, usually translated as 'War of Attrition' in the West) enabled Egypt to considerably improve its positions along the Suez Canal. Free from the necessity to maintain high readiness rates, the Air Defence Command (ADC), led by Maj Gen Mohammed Ali Fahmy, finally received the opportunity to reorganise and

Maj Gen Mohammed Ali Fahmy, commander of the Air Defence Command and mastermind of the Egyptian air defence doctrine for the October 1973 War. (via Tom Cooper)

assert itself along a 20km (12.4-mile) strip west of the Canal and thus protect the Army, which now began preparations for a major counterattack.

Simultaneously, the ADC raced to establish additional units and equip them with new equipment, including the first batches of S-125 Pechora (ASCC codename SA-3 Goa) surface-to-air missiles (SAMs) and ZSU-23-4 'Shilka' self-propelled (radar-controlled) anti-aircraft guns (SPAAGs). In this fashion, the ADC became strong enough to ring most of the 20 major UARAF air bases that became operational by late 1970, deploying both SAM sites and additional AAA units. The UARAF – which as of August 1970 had reached a total personnel strength of 18,500, including 700-750 pilots (of which 290 were qualified to fly fast jets, while 220 others were undergoing various stages of training) – could afford to somewhat relax its alert level.

The Air Force experienced a period of immense pressure upon all its ranks between 1967 and 1970, during which it was forced to maintain extremely high readiness rates and fight the IDF/AF while at the same time analyse recent experiences and draw necessary lessons, as well as train large numbers of new pilots and ground personnel. One of the instructors recalled by most of the Egyptian pilots that earned their wings during this period – and also by Faraj in the aforementioned citation – was Salah Danish. This former MiG-19 pilot was in the process of converting to Su-7s when the June 1967 War broke out. He was shot down and captured by Israeli forces during this conflict, but released in the course of a prisoner exchange in 1968. Danish returned to Egypt to find himself in an unpleasant situation, but subsequently emerged as one of the hardest-working instructors at the Air Force Academy:

*'For the first few months, I underwent a period of debriefings and security checks, and was kept isolated, but also fed with delicious food to recover my health. It was a very difficult period of time for me, because I was forbidden from meeting my wife and newborn daughter and could see them only from a window of the building in which I was held… After a lengthy period of recovery in Luxor I went*

MiG-21FL serial number 6128 seen while under repairs at one of the factories at Helwan, shortly after the October 1973 War. Even before that conflict, Egyptian maintenance facilities were overburdened by demand, and the EAF had to send dozens of its aircraft abroad for such work of its aircraft abroad for such work, including to the VEB Flugzeugwerft Dresden, in former East Germany. (David Nicolle Collection)

No Peace, No War

S-125 Pechora (ASCC codename SA-3 Goa) SAMs of the ADC, as seen after the October 1973 War. Notable is the original twin-rail 5P71 launcher for V-601P missiles: later variants introduced quadruple launchers. (Tom Cooper Collection)

*to [AM Shalaby] Hinnawy's office and requested to be posted to one of the combat units. I wanted to go back and fight the Israelis again. He told me he appreciated my wish but it would be more useful for me to serve as an instructor at the Air Force Academy. So I ended up doing refresher training on Yak-18s and conversion courses on L-29s and Su-7s, before starting my new job of training cadets at Bilbeis and Marsa Matruh… We worked feverishly and successfully graduated more than 400 new pilots by early 1972: nearly 70 per cent of those who fought in 1973 were my former students and I considered them my 'children'…*[6]

New Egyptian military commanders concluded that the high intensity of operations by the ADC and the UARAF had both positive and negative effects, as explained by Shazly:

'The Air Force was our weakest arm… in the air, our pilots still depended on their own skills and whatever they could coax from their machines; and in their many encounters since 1967 our men had frankly not matched the enemy's. Was the problem lack of skill or inferior aircraft? Our pilots were always blaming the machines; the Soviets blamed our pilots. I saw it as a combination of both… Our pilots needed intensive training; yet even relatively raw ones had to bear the burden of the War of Attrition. By 1970 pilot exhaustion had pushed training accidents to an alarming rate. We eased off the training pressure. But that merely meant training would take longer.'

Indeed, the intensity of operations reached such proportions during the War of Attrition that even the Egyptian defence sector proved unable to simultaneously develop new weapons and the necessary modifications for available equipment, and also satisfy the demands for technical support from the armed forces. This in turn was the reason why the UARAF – followed by the SyAAF – began the practice of sending large numbers of its MiG-15bis, MiG-15UTI, and MiG-17F aircraft for overhaul abroad, foremost to the LZR-2 works in Poland, during the period 1968–1973.[7]

Unsurprisingly, many of the preparations begun after the defeat of June 1967 remained to be completed. These included finding solutions to a number of problems including unrealistic training and planning, unworkable mobilisation plans, unemployable tactics, and equipment-related insufficiencies.[8] Indeed, the lack of equipment and very low stocks of spares and ammunition – primarily the result of slow deliveries from the USSR – also proved a hindrance, and led to the realisation that the Egyptian military had to increase its total manpower if it were to become able of launching a major attack into the Sinai, while simultaneously securing all important installations around the country from Israeli counterattacks.

As the intensity of training was slowly decreased, many units were rotated around newly constructed bases. Although heavily hardened, some of these proved not entirely suitable for combat operations – often for entirely unexpected reasons, as recalled by Medhat Zaki, then flying MiG-21F-13s with No. 26 Squadron:

*'In 1971, the newly constructed Wadi Qena AB was complete, so our unit moved there. That air base was in the middle of the desert and surrounded by mountains, far away from any urban centres. There was no radio, no TV, and we felt very isolated. Soon after moving in, our aircraft began developing technical issues. After a lot of searching, we found out that these problems were caused by mice that sneaked into the fuselage and bit through the electric wiring. The situation became so serious that eventually our unit had not a single aircraft fit to fly.'*

## Death of a Stratofreighter

During summer 1971 the conflict between Egypt and Israel entered a new phase, known as 'No Peace, No War'. Despite the ceasefire, the IDF/AF began launching reconnaissance sorties not only around, but also deep inside Egyptian airspace, attempting to track down and map positions of new SAM sites, as well as to monitor the construction of new UARAF air bases. Medhat Zaki recalled that one of the first such sorties was undertaken over the newly constructed Wadi Qena air base:

*'Before long, an Israeli reconnaissance plane flew over our new air base. Because of the problem with mice, to our great shame, we were unable to scramble and intercept. Eventually, this resulted in the decision for our unit to switch back to Inchas.'*

While the 20km (12.4-mile) strip along the Suez Canal generally remained quiet, time and again Israel would send its aircraft over this area as well. The UARAF responded in kind. Around 12.40 on 11 September 1971, a pair of Su-7BMKRs – a locally modified variant of the Su-7BMK fighter-bomber – was on a reconnaissance mission along the western side of the Suez Canal, when Israeli forces opened fire. One of the Sukhois was hit and crashed around a kilometre from the northern end of the Canal.[9]

Aiming to return the favour, Shazly ordered Fahmy to set up an ambush. During the following night, the 414th Air Defence Battalion (one SA-2 site) was clandestinely re-deployed closer to the Suez Canal, and ordered to wait for its opportunity. This came on 17 September 1971, when a lonesome Boeing KC-97G Stratotanker of the IDF/AF (registration 033/4X-FPR, serial number 52-2683) approached the Canal – precisely with the intention of searching for Egyptian SAM sites. The CO of the 414th Air Defence Battalion (established in September 1967), Ahabadin Ayman recalled later:

*'It was a Friday, and shortly after the noon prayer our early warning radars reported an aircraft approaching Port Said from the north, at slow speed and an altitude of 9,144m [30,000ft]. We went on alert, and soon saw this aircraft flying*

No Peace, No War

During the 'No War, No Peace' period, Egyptian MiG-21RFs and other reconnaissance aircraft continued to fly intelligence-gathering sorties along the Suez Canal, but – on the direct orders of Shazly – they remained outside Israeli-controlled airspace.
(Albert Grandolini Collection)

*parallel to the Canal. Our radars were on standby, but did not emit: if we activated our radar, the Israelis would know we were there and the plane would fly away. Instead, we tracked our target visually, patiently waiting for it to enter the engagement envelope. I climbed into the cabin of our Fan Song radar and I was surprised to see this slow reconnaissance aircraft coming this close to the Canal. It was clear that it could not avoid any missiles. At 15.11, we fired two SA-2s. One detonated next to the target, spraying it with shrapnel. There was a big ball of flame and the plane crashed. We saw one parachute.'*[10]

Out of the Israeli crew of eight, seven were killed. According to Israeli reports, the aircraft was shot down while under way 27km (16.8 miles) east of Ismailia; according to Shazly, its wreckage came to the ground less than 4km (2.5 miles) *'south of the Bitter Lakes'*.[11] Expecting Israel to respond with an attack on their SAM sites, the Egyptians prepared accordingly. Ayman continued:

*'We knew the Israelis were mad and would try to hit back. We also knew the US had recently delivered AGM-45 Shrike anti-radar missiles to Israel, which the Americans developed in response to their experiences from fighting SA-2s in Vietnam, and that the Shrike homed in on emissions from the Fan Song radar, used to direct the fire of the SA-2 site. What the Israelis did not know was that we had already studied American experiences and their new weapon. We expected the Israelis to make use of anti-radar missiles, and prepared appropriate countermeasures…'*

Starboard view of the same MiG-21RF from No. 22 Squadron. These two photographs show it following a post-October 1973 overhaul, while wearing an adapted variant of the Nile Valley camouflage pattern. For a comparison with its original Nile Valley camouflage pattern, see Appendix V.
(Albert Grandolini Collection)

35

Israeli soldiers inspecting the wreckage of KC-97G 033/4X-FPR shot down by SA-2s from the 414th Air Defence Battalion ADC – commanded by Ahabadin Ayman – on 17 September 1971, while flying east of the Suez Canal. (Albert Grandolini Collection)

The IDF/AF returned in force on the next day, deploying F-4E Phantom IIs equipped with AGM-45 Shrike anti-radar missiles (ARMs) to hit back in force. Ayman concluded:

'On Saturday, we suddenly detected several formations of Israeli aircraft heading in our direction. When they were still 10km [6.2 miles] away from the Suez Canal, they started firing Shrikes. We deployed our countermeasures and confused the Shrikes so much that all of them fell halfway short of their targets.'

Out of 12 AGM-45s fired by the Israelis, two caused some damage to one Egyptian and one Soviet SAM site, but all others missed. An unknown number of Shrikes failed to detonate and were captured intact by Egypt.[12]

This KC-97G survived long enough to end up on display in the IDF/AF Museum at Hatzerim. (Tom Cooper Collection)

No Peace, No War

## Reconnaissance Games

In a further reaction to Israeli provocations, and in great secrecy, the USSR drew aircraft and personnel from the 4th Centre of Combat Employment and Personnel Training of their Ministry of Aviation Industry, from the Scientific Research Institute of their Air Force at Lipetsk, and from the 47th Independent Guards Reconnaissance Aviation Regiment of the VVS, and deployed them to Cairo West air base, in March 1971, where these detachments were reorganised as the 63rd Independent Reconnaissance Aviation Squadron (63rd ORAE), and put under the command of Col Alexander S. Bezhevets.[13] The 63rd ORAE included pilots Nikolay Stogov, Vladimir Uvarov, Nikolay Borshov, Yuriy Marchenko, Viktor Gordienko, and Chudin. The aircraft operated by this unit was one of the most advanced in the USSR at that time: the Mach 2,83-capable MiG-25R (construction numbers 0501 and 0504, Bort numbers 40 and 41, respectively), and its variant with bombing capability, the MiG-25RB (construction numbers 0402 and 0601).[14] The secrecy surrounding the 63rd ORAE was so great that the part of Cairo West assigned to it was protected by Soviet soldiers and no admittance was granted to any Egyptians. For the duration of the deployment, the aircraft was codenamed 'M-500'.[15]

The 63rd ORAE was declared ready for operations about one month later, and its aircraft initially flew above the Nile Delta before turning west to make training runs over the unpopulated area south of the famous World War II battlefield of el-Alamein. All flights were undertaken in total radio silence and by pairs of aircraft, so that if one was lost for any reason, the other could better guide the rescue teams. The MiG-25 and its equipment were still under development at that time. For example, the Soviet technicians required several months of intensive work to fine-tune the engines and make them capable of propelling the aircraft to the maximum speed of Mach 2.83 – and then only for a maximum period of eight minutes. The aircraft required special fuel, desig-

One of four 'M-500s' deployed by the 63rd ORAE at Cairo West, beginning in March 1971. These aircraft usually wore only a bare minimum of national markings, including fin flashes and roundels on the upper and lower surfaces of the wing. The national markings on the front fuselage were usually burned off during operational sorties over the Sinai, turning into black circles.
(el-Djeich)

nated T-6, which was not available in Egypt, and had to be brought by Soviet tankers to Alexandria.

The Soviets wanted to make their operations as safe as possible. Correspondingly, all four aircraft were equipped with A-72, A-87 and A-10-10 cameras with focal lengths of 150, 650 and 1300mm, respectively, enabling photographs to be taken from altitudes up to 22,000m (72,172ft), which was above the maximum ceiling that could be reached by Israel's MIM-23 HAWK SAMs. Furthermore, they carefully coordinated all sorties with the HQ of the 135th Fighter Aviation Regiment (135th IAP) at Bani Suweif, and protected their MiG-25s with flights of Soviet-flown MiG-21s during each take-off and landing.

Once all the officers and engineers involved were satisfied with the function of the aircraft and their systems, permission was granted for operations close to the areas under Israeli control. On 10 October 1971 – by which time they were operating from specially constructed underground hardened aircraft shelters (HASes) – a pair of MiG-25s climbed to an altitude between 23,000 and 24,000m (75,459 and 78,740ft) over the Mediterranean, and then turned east. They approached the coast of northern Israel and then accelerated to Mach 2.5 while turning southwest and flying along almost the entire Israel-Sinai coastline, from Acre to the Suez Canal. Of course, this operation led to alerts on all IDF/AF air bases, but Israel lacked suitable means for the interception of such fast and high-flying aircraft.

Following additional studies of Israeli air defences, the decision was taken to fly the first mission over the Sinai. On 6 November 1971 two MiG-25Rs repeated the exercise from October, but instead of turning in the direction of Israel, they took a southeast course and thundered high over the Sinai, crossing the peninsula from the eastern end of Lake Bardavil to Ras al-Sudr, in the Gulf of Suez, within less than two minutes. From December 1971, two flights over the Sinai were undertaken every month, until the mission on 10 March 1972 – flown with help of giant underfuselage tanks containing 5,300 litres (1,166 Imp gal) of fuel – covered almost the entire length of the Sinai on a north-south axis.

In each of these cases, all Israeli attempts to intercept the two high-flying intruders failed: theoretically, the F-4Es of the IDF/AF could catch a MiG-25R and attempt to shoot it down with their AIM-7E Sparrow missiles. However, such operations required perfect vectoring by the GCI and faultless work by the aircraft's crew, with the aim of bringing the Phantom into a specific position below and ahead of the MiG-25, and from which it could bring the target to the edge of the Sparrow's engagement envelope within a very short period of time. Despite numerous scrambles, no IDF/AF crew ever managed to attain such a position – even though there was at least one case when Bezhevets felt forced to accelerate his aircraft up to a speed of Mach 2.83 while passing high above Refidim; this was against instructions since it was likely to cause damage to the engine. Egyptian and Soviet crews of different radar stations monitored failed Israeli interception attempts with great satisfaction, as recalled by Fuad Kamal:

*'We saw Phantoms being scrambled from bases in Israel, but especially so from Meliz [Refidim] and their new base in the southern Sinai [Ophir]. They were climbing at maximum speed, but never came even near. Sometimes they would manage to cross the flight paths of MiG-25s, but in reality were much lower than the MiGs. Israeli HAWK SAMs were equally helpless.'*

No Peace, No War

A map showing routes taken by Soviet MiG-25s during four flights over the Sinai Peninsula and along the Israeli coast in late 1971 and spring 1972. (Map by James Lawrence, based on *AW&ST*, 22 May 1972).

IDF/AF crews work on a Teledyne Ryan Model 124I photo-reconnaissance drone (note that the wing has been removed). This UAV operated according to a programmed flight regime after ground launch, but could also accept corrective radio commands. (UPI)

Throughout all of their overflights, the MiG-25s experienced only two minor technical breakdowns. One of these forced Bezhevets to make an emergency landing at Aswan, in the course of which one main tyre burst while the aircraft was approaching the end of runway. This caused the wing on the same side of the aircraft to touch the ground. However, because the aircraft was already rolling at a very low speed, damage was minimal, and the MiG was flown back to Cairo West after a short repair.

Unable to tackle the threat, the IDF/AF 'responded in kind' – by deploying Teledyne Ryan Aeronautical Model 124I remotely piloted vehicles (RPVs, nowadays colloquially known as 'unmanned aerial vehicles', UAVs) over Egypt. The Model 124Is were made in the US and were previously successfully deployed during the Vietnam War, in the period 1967–1971.[16] Delivered to Israel in July 1971, they entered service with the newly established No. 200 Squadron IDF/AF in September of the same year. These subsonic UAVs, equipped with reconnaissance cameras made by the CAI Division of Bourns Inc., were ground-launched from different sites in the Sinai, from where they undertook several high-altitude flights as deep as Cairo in May 1972. After being slowed down by a parachute, the 124Is were usually recovered by mid-air 'snatch' from a helicopter. Despite all the possible security precautions, at least two were shot down over Egypt during the first year of their operations.[17]

In comparison, the Soviet MiG-25s remained 'untouchable' for the Israelis. On 16 May 1972, the 63rd ORAE launched its most daring mission, sending two M-500s to photograph the entire length of Israeli positions along the eastern side of the Suez Canal and down the coast to Sharm el-Sheikh. The MiGs entered the airspace around 10.30 and Israel scrambled four F-4Es from Refidim and Ophir, but their GCI made an error. The Soviets zoomed high above the first of the Phantoms that approached, without its crew getting a chance to open fire. Around 10.35, another F-4E managed to approach and fire a single AIM-7E, but the missile motor burnt out before reaching its target. Indeed, this Sparrow then failed to detonate when reaching the end of its flight, and finally landed almost intact on the western side of the Canal. It was recovered by Egypt and Sadat decided to give it to the Soviets.[18]

After this failure, the IDF/AF launched a frenzied search for an air-to-air missile that could be launched from the F-4E and shoot down what the Israelis thought was a 'MiG-23'. Among others, this eventually resulted in the stillborn Project Distant Thunder (or Distant Reach), which saw an attempt to target the MiG-25's Doppler navigation radar using the AGM-78 Standard anti-radar missile.[19]

In the meantime, the IDF/AF returned to the practice of attempting to drag Egyptian MiG-21s into ambushes, and on 13 June 1972 was successful in doing exactly this. When the ADC scrambled two MiG-21s to intercept a reconnaissance sortie under way over the Nile Delta, the Israelis dragged them in front of two Phantoms and two Mirage IIICJs waiting low over the Mediterranean and shot down both the Egyptian fighters. Finally, Israel may have launched the rumour that it was about to acquire US-made MIM-14 Nike Hercules SAMs, which the Soviets knew were capable of intercepting their MiG-25s. Russian sources differ about the subsequent fate of the 63rd ORAE. According to one version, they subsequently ceased flying over the Sinai and only flew operations along the western side of the Suez Canal. According to the other, the 63rd ORAE closed its shop at Cairo West already in April 1972, after Moscow concluded that the unit had completed all the work there was to do in Egypt. While the crews returned to the USSR, the aircraft were stored inside their underground HASes at Cairo West.[20]

## Granite and Minarets

Far behind the scenes and in great secrecy, top Egyptian military commanders meanwhile began developing their plan for a counteroffensive into the Sinai. The task in question was primarily the job of Maj Gen Shazly. Using Fazwy's plans as a basis, and driven by his own and Sadat's ideas that Egypt did not have to win a war, but foremost needed a good start and initial success that could produce more favourable political conditions for a superpower intervention, his first ideas in this regard called for a limited attack, known as Operation 41 (later Granite Two). This envisaged an advance of up to 60-70km (37-43 miles) east of the Canal. Although considered unrealistic by Shazly, since it depended upon the availability of equipment and supplies Egypt did not possess, this plan was developed in full collaboration with Soviet advisors, such that these could form their own conclusions about the required quantities of armament, equipment and supplies. As expected, the Soviets accused the Egyptians of exaggerating their needs. As a result, when Sadat and his Minister of War, Mohammed Ahmed Sadek travelled to Moscow in October 1971, not all of their requests were met, even though they were promised deliveries of 100 additional MiG-21MFs and equipment for 10 2K12 Kvadrat (ASCC codename SA-6 Gainful) air defence brigades.

However, in total secrecy from the Soviets and in agreement with Sadat, Shazly meanwhile developed a plan based on the actual capability of the Egyptian armed forces, which became known as The High Minarets. Based on an Egyptian adaptation of Soviet doctrine, this plan envisaged a limited offensive thrust over the Suez Canal with a goal of a 5-10km (3.1-6.2 mile) penetration, followed by consolidation of bridgeheads and construction of comprehensive ground defences. The crossing operation would be undertaken on the widest possible front and would be spearheaded by infantry reinforced with light anti-tank weapons, and supported by deployment of heliborne commandos behind enemy lines. The plan was then to protect the bridgeheads from counterattacks by Israeli regular armoured units until enough armour and artillery could be brought to the Sinai to establish comprehensive ground defences. Commandos were expected to slow down the arrival of Israeli reinforcements and reserves, expected some 10-12 hours after the start of the war, and Israel's first major counterattack, expected some 15-24 hours after Egypt began its crossing. Through crossing the Canal and advancing on the widest possible front, Egypt hoped to make it impossible for the IDF to detect the direction of the main Egyptian effort or concentrate effectively for one of their typical flanking attacks. Finally, during all this time the Egyptian ground forces could operate within the effective cover of ADC's SAMs, which in turn meant that the Air Force – which Shazly assessed as *'hopelessly outclassed by the technologically superior IDF/AF'* – did not have to wrestle for air superiority. Instead, it would be the ADC that would bear the brunt of responsibility for air defence over the front lines, while the UARAF would instead concentrate on air defence further behind, and limit itself to flying local counterattacks under carefully controlled conditions.[21]

While The High Minarets was outright rejected by Sadik, as *'politically unprofitable'*, Shazly ramped up the related training of the Army and expansion of the ADC, while Sadat began searching for officers that would understand his concerted two-stage effort in which diplomacy played the dominating role, well ahead of that of the military.[22]

In April 1972, AM Ali Baghdadi, who insisted on keeping the UARAF out of unnecessary clashes with Israel, retired and was replaced by Maj Gen Hosni Mubarak. Five months later, Sadat prepared his final coup. On 24 October 1972, the Supreme Council of the Egyptian Armed Forces convened in his office in Giza, discussing the decision that Egypt should go to war with the weapons on hand. During the meeting, the president made a number of rulings, the main one being *'to have the military put some muscle into the matter'*. Sadik, who was not only in disagreement with Sadat's and Shazly's ideas on fighting a 'limited war', but who also proved unable to find solutions for Egypt military's deficiencies in general, was dismissed and replaced by Maj Gen Ahmed Ismail Ali (a former intelligence officer recalled from retirement). Maj Gen Mohammed Abdel Ghani el-Gamasy was appointed the new Chief-of-Operations Army (and therefore supreme commander of the units deployed along the Suez Canal), only four days later. Like Shazly before them, Ismail Ali and Gamasy understood the implications of Sadat's order, and accepted both the change in objective and the operational attack plan. Together with Shazly, they completed the work on The High Minarets in the first half of the January 1973.[23]

From that time onwards, there exist essentially two parallel Egyptian histories of the October 1973 War. One is usually represented by Sadat and his closest aides including Ismail Ali, Gamasy, and Mubarak, and is usually supported by Western observers. According to this version, it was this goup that developed – or at least understood and accepted – Sadat's (actually Shazly's) idea of a limited war, supposedly based on Ismail Ali's *'intuitive understanding of the abilities and limitations of the Egyptian solider'*.[24] Furthermore, these officers apparently insisted on emphasising professionalism and merit as the key to promotion, and encouraged plain speaking and self-criticism among the Egyptian military ranks. The version supported by Shazly, as well as a number of Egyptian and even Israeli researchers, appeared more recently. It links the appointment of new commanders less with their expertise, and much more with internal politics (i.e. securing Sadat's presidency), their ability to overcome fears and self-doubts, and above all a huge dose of sheer luck. Some of the arguments pro and contra either version can be seen in examples like that recalled by Abdel Aziz al-Marsa, meanwhile a seasoned MiG-17 pilot assigned to No. 62 Squadron UARAF, and related to an event that occurred a few months after the end of the War of Attrition:

*'After the end of the War of Attrition, our unit re-deployed to Gardeka, and we began training to fly combat operations by night. The tactics were to have an Il-28 bomber drop flares in a circle around the target, so that we could acquire it visually while approaching, and then hit with bombs and rockets. Eventually, we abandoned this idea for several reasons, including the lack of flares and other equipment. Still, this affair was not yet over. It was around this time that our unit received a visit by the then defence minister, FM Mohammed Fawzy and C-in-C UARAF, AM Ali Boghdadi, our brigade CO Col Samir Farid and his deputy, Lt Col Hassan Fahmy. During that visit, Fawzy asked us if we were ready for a war against Israel, or not. Our squadron CO frankly stated, 'No, we are not ready to fight by night'. Because of this, he was relieved of his command – even though it was certainly not his fault that our unit was not equipped to fight by night.'*

In comparison, according to Mohammed Okasha, a former MiG-17 and Mirage pilot and leading historian of the Egyptian Air Force, Mubarak's appointment in particular was related to sheer luck:

*'Mubarak was a good pilot, working tirelessly, and particularly excelling at administrative work and studies. He was trained on Supermarine Spitfires, Il-28s and Tu-16s, among others, educated in Soviet Union, and ran the Air Force Academy for no less than four terms. It was good for Egypt to have people like him, with efficiency and ability to plan and arrange everything. However, beyond that, Mubarak was not really good for anything else. There were many other, much better warriors, better planners, and much better commanders – foremost brigade and squadron commanders – like Barakat, Manawy, Saima (an ex-RJAF Hunter pilot who defected to Egypt in 1962), etc…*

*'Mubarak was simply lucky. Following the 1967 War, he was sent to Iraq, together with all our other Tu-16 crews. Our Air Force lost all of its bombers of this type in*

Serving as Deputy Chief of Staff EAF and Fighter Commander as of April 1972, AVM/Maj Gen Mahmoud Shaker Abd el-Moneim was originally expected to take over as C-in-C. Mubarak was picked instead of el-Moneim due to the latter's health problems.
(Nour Bardai Collection)

President Nasser (in suit) with AM Shalaby el-Hinnawy (next to Nasser) during a visit to the UARAF Academy, in October 1967. Days later, el-Hinnawy picked Mubarak as his Chief of Staff, indirectly re-launching the career of the latter officer that was to lead to Mubarak being appointed the C-in-C EAF, and – in 1981 – President of Egypt.
(Nour Bardai Collection)

Maj Gen el-Moneim seen during inspection of an unknown EAF fighter unit, in early 1972. In the minds of many Egyptian fighter pilots, he was the actual mastermind of the Egyptian Air Force as it went into the October 1973 War with Israel. (Nour Bardai Collection)

*the June 1967 War and thus these crews were sent to Iraq to continue their training on Iraqi Tupolevs. That way Mubarak evaded purges that followed immediately after that war. While in Iraq, many officers complained about Mubarak and his leadership and thus he was sent back to Egypt. By accident, he arrived in Cairo on the same day Nasser dismissed AM al-Ezz and 21 other top UARAF officers, and appointed AM el-Hinnawy in his place, on 23 October 1967. Appreciating his administrative skills, El-Hinnawy then picked Mubarak as Deputy Operations – the third position in the overall UARAF hierarchy. Due to differences between el-Hinnawy and FM Fawzy, el-Hinnawy was forced to leave, and thus Mubarak ended as Chief of Staff (the second position in the overall hierarchy), in June 1969 – and this opened the way for his subsequent appointment as the Commander-in-Chief Air Force.*[25]

Ultimately, a crucially important rift within the High Command of the Egyptian armed forces was to result at the height of the October 1973 War. This was apparently created by problems that emerged during cooperation between some of these aforementioned officers and Sadat, their mutual disagreements and mistrust, and above all by some of their command decisions during the conflict. In turn, the 'winners' of that struggle were to dictate how the history of the war was subsequently presented – especially to the Egyptian public, but also in the West.

## Tensions with the Soviets

Relations between the Egyptians and their Soviet advisors continued to deteriorate during the first half of 1972, until they degenerated to unacceptable levels. The reasons for this were a combination of boredom caused by the ceasefire, differences of a professional and ideological nature, but foremost the continuous delays in the arms deliveries promised by the Soviets and the fact that Moscow was doing little to help Egypt recover the Sinai.

Differences of an ideological nature were primarily caused by the Soviets understanding their presence in Egypt as serving the purpose of 'bringing the United Arab Republic into the socialist camp.'[26] While generally apolitical and only eager to fight Israel, Egyptian pilots had what appeared as 'pro-Western orientation' to the Soviets, and many were devout Muslims. Therefore, the Soviet advisors – most of whom tended to consider Arabs to be 'living in a feudal system' – attempted to 'convert' the Egyptians, which many Egyptians found unacceptable.

Similarly, while the Soviet advisors were expected to provide advanced military expertise at tactical level, many of the Egyptian pilots and officers rapidly concluded that their instructors not only lacked the required experience – despite including several aces from World War II – but were foremost 'preaching' obsolete and useless tactics that were causing losses to the Egyptians.[27] Nevertheless, the Soviets insisted on considering themselves 'superior' to the 'defeated Egyptians', as noted by Alaa Barakat:

*'I often quarrelled with our Soviet instructors. As for the reasons… For example, once I led a mission over the Sinai and wanted to split my flight into two pairs before we crossed the Canal, so that each pair would attack our target from a different direction. The Soviet advisor insisted on a direct, single-line approach by the entire formation. I asked for support for my standpoint from the HQ – but was told to follow the advisor's instruction. The result: two aircraft lost.*

*'The problem was simple: we flew the British tactical formation known as 'fluid four'. Our tactics was actually a sort of British-Egyptian system, which provided a greater tactical freedom and initiative to the pilots. If we found it suitable, the two pairs operated independently from each other. The Soviets insisted on their 'finger four', where only the number 1 had anything to say. We found that useless in combat against the Israelis.'*

Abdel Aziz al-Marsa confirmed this:

*'Single aircraft in our formation were under way 1,000m [3,281ft] from each other in line abreast, with a vertical separation of 150m [492ft]. Much to the distaste of our Soviet advisors, the number 2 in our formation did not fly in front or behind our formation leaders, nor were they limited to strictly following the leader's instructions.'*

Other Egyptian commanders found that the only solution was to ignore the Soviets, as concluded by Marsa:

*'The Russians were lacking combat experience and tactical knowledge, knowledge about modern air combat and weapons, and the understanding of our situation, and our brigade CO decided that nobody should listen to them. We left them on their own and instead concentrated on our training.'*

Finally, the Egyptians were furious that their pilots trained in the USSR received a much lower standard of training than expected, as recalled by Reda el-Iraqi, another pilot flying MiG-21F-13s with No. 26 Squadron:

*'Our pilots returning from Russia were only taught to take-off and to land. We had to train them in all other aspects of flying. At the time we were overburdened by the task of training hundreds of new pilots at home – the Soviets simply failed to help us.'*

Medhat Zaki, seen later during his career. Like most EAF officers, he considered the Soviet presence more of a nuisance than of any serious help.
(Medhat Zaki Collection)

Due to slow deliveries, the MiG-21MF only began entering service in numbers in 1971. Based on a serial number – 8228 – that is in the range originally applied to Soviet-flown aircraft in 1970, this example was operated by either No. 56 or No. 82 Squadron EAF and was probably purchased by Egypt during the Soviet withdrawal, two years later. (Tom Cooper collection)

In other cases, the Egyptians – and also officers of other Arab air forces advised by the Soviets – felt hampered by the Soviets as regards the conduct of their operations, as recalled by Medhat Zaki:

'After the end of the War of Attrition, five pilots from No. 26 Squadron were chosen to do a tour of duty in Syria. There we met several Pakistani pilots, trained in the US and with combat experience from the war with India. The Syrians and Pakistanis taught us the zero-speed manoeuvre. When we returned to Egypt, the Russians could not believe what we did with the MiG-21. They said, 'If you decrease your speed to less than 320km/h [199mph], you're going to crash'. Actually, this

An unsmiling Soviet Marshal Gretchko shakes hands with Egyptian pilots during a visit in 1969, together with Shalabi el-Hinnawy. Due to Moscow's preoccupation with countering the West within the framework of the Cold War, and Egypt's preoccupation with Israel, relations between Egypt and the USSR were very rarely cordial. (David Nicolle Collection)

*manoeuvre had a profound impact on our pilots, increasing their confidence to the maximum. In No. 26 Squadron we practiced it on MiG-21F-13s and became so good at flying it that nobody wanted to convert to newer models, like the MiG-21MF, although this was much more modern.'*

Of course, pilots that converted to the MiG-21MF rapidly adapted and then developed the manoeuvre for the new variant, as recalled by Dia el-Hefnawy

*'After the ceasefire of August 1970, our brigade was reinforced through the arrival of MiG-21MFs, which entered service with the newly established No. 27 Squadron, based at Abu Hammad. Among the pilots assigned to this unit were Ahmed Atef, Farid Harfush, Hussein Ismail and myself. The MF was heavier and manoeuvred differently to the F-13 I used to fly with No. 25 Squadron, and thus we flew plenty of air combat exercises against each other. The MF proved especially useful for slow-speed manoeuvring, taught to us by five Pakistani advisors in Syria, and thus we developed the zero-speed manoeuvre into an offensive movement – to slow down and move below the target while raising the nose and then fire at the opponent as this was passing by. This became possible due to the improved thrust of the MiG-21MF's engine. Of course, the Russians couldn't stop cautioning us not to try doing this...'*

It was the zero-speed manoeuvre that resulted in a first major crisis, in April 1971. This began when an Egyptian pilot named Safay el-Zanaty was reassigned from one of the Su-7 units to serve as section leader with No. 26 Squadron at Inchas. In the course of his conversion course, he clashed several times with Col Vyacheslav Petrov, a particularly arrogant Soviet advisor to the CO Air Brigade 102. After Zanaty repeatedly questioned the purpose of Petrov's advice, the Russian challenged him to a simulated air combat, as recalled by el-Iraqi:

*'There were several such incidents, and each of them ended with a reprimand for the Soviet instructor. Flying the new variant of the zero-speed manoeuvre, Zanaty easily outmanoeuvred Petrov and 'shot him down', twice. After landing, Petrov insisted on another dogfight session. During that exercise, Zanaty outmanoeuvred the Russian again, but Petrov continued insisting until he flew Zanaty into the ground. Our pilot was killed. Petrov was instantly removed from his position and sent back to the Soviet Union. The word was that he ended up in a gulag in Siberia.'*

Actually, Petrov did not end up in Siberia, but all such 'challenges' between Egyptians and Soviets were subsequently strictly prohibited, and the influence of the Soviet advisors on the operations of Air Brigade 102 decreased to zero.[28] True enough, the Soviets were not only to blame. Many EAF officers, and a number of leading Egyptian military commanders – foremost among them the Minister of War Gen Sadek – were fiercely anti-communist, and they repeatedly bullied the family members of Soviet advisors when these visited Egypt. The situation became even tenser once the Egyptians began suspecting the Soviets of treachery, according to Barakat:

*'There was strong evidence that somebody in the Soviet mission was passing sensitive operational information to the Israelis. Especially our Su-7s almost always encountered Israeli fighters waiting for them over their targets. On one occasion a mission was cancelled at the last moment, but still our radars tracked Israeli fighters climbing over the designated target - even though no Sukhois were approaching. Later on, one of the Soviet advisors defected to Israel while on his way back to the USSR, after a tour of duty in Egypt.'*

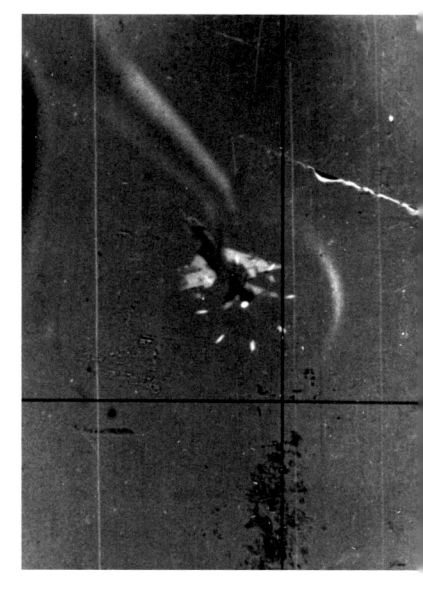

A gun-camera photo taken by Ali Wagedy during a training sortie between two units freshly re-equipped with MiG-21MFs. (David Nicolle Collection)

An Egyptian pilot with a recently overhauled MiG-21M (or MF), in 1971 or 1972. The pilot's face and the serial number of his aircraft were censored before the photo was handed over to David Nicolle and attempts to remove this chemically were only of limited success.
(David Nicolle Collection)

Ultimately, such suspicions may have been proven correct. In early September 1971, Egyptian counter-intelligence uncovered an American espionage ring centred upon Tanashi Randopolo, an Egyptian of Greek parentage, and a member of the US mission in Cairo. Randopolo provided an extensive confession, in which he stated that he had established contacts to Soviet pilots named Belekov and Yuri, who were based at Jiyanklis air base between May 1969 and March 1971. On several occasions the Soviets invited Randopolo for dinner at their private quarters at the base, during which he gathered much information. In this way, he obtained data about the SAM sites that protected Jiyanklis, the Soviet views on Egyptian capabilities, and other details. However, it remains unclear if Randopolo was capable of obtaining information about the planning of Egyptian operations sufficient to provide advance warnings for the IDF/AF. The Soviets insisted that their personnel did nothing wrong and that the Egyptians tolerated their insistence on not sending any of the relevant officers home. 'In the interest of Egyptian-Soviet friendship', Sadat decided not to take any action and all the officers in question were reassigned to units deployed in the desert.[29]

## Break with Moscow

The inevitable rift between Cairo and Moscow followed within months. In the meantime, Sadat certainly made some use of the Randopolo Affair during negotiations for the next major arms deal in Moscow, beginning on 21 September 1971. Unusually, this time the USSR agreed to deliver weapons and equipment worth USD195 million. This included 10 Tu-16 bombers with air-to-surface missiles, 100 MiG-21MFs (including 50 to be delivered by the end of the year, and a workshop for overhauling their engines), 20 MiG-23s (to be delivered in 1973), one air defence brigade equipped with new 2K12 Kvadrat SAM systems, various heavy armament and ammunition for the Army, and assistance in the construction in Egypt of several factories for the manufacture of other equipment and spares, including one that was to be capable of maintaining

No Peace, No War

MiG-17s, MiG-21s, Su-7s and P-15 radars. Known as the 'October Deal', this arrangement was to finally provide Egypt with the arms necessary to launch a war to 'recover the Sinai'.[30] As usual, the USSR was slow to deliver, and only a fraction of this order ever reached Egypt, most of it not before early 1972. Sadat's government, which had announced 1971 as 'the year of decision', was thus discredited in the public, after an entire year passed without anything happening.

Farid Hafrush compared the various MiG-21 variants – which meanwhile formed the backbone of the Egyptian Air Force – as follows:

*'The MiG-21F-13 was a fantastic aircraft in terms of manoeuvrability. It had a very poor weapons system, the ranging radar was obsolete and there were almost no other avionics. The gunsight was poor and there was only one cannon with 60 rounds – sufficient for five seconds of firing – and two missiles. Getting the R-3S to function in combat was very difficult, primarily because it could not be fired at an acceleration of more than 2.5g, while in dogfights we were all the time pulling more than that. One had to be careful with the sun, clouds and even reflections from the ground. It was a very poor missile.*

*'The MiG-21FL was more stabile than the MiG-21F-13 and much more powerful. Acceleration was better. Still, it had only a very poor radar, no cannon and almost no navigational aids – only compass and radio direction-finder. The MiG-21PFS and MiG-21PFM were practically the same, but with the addition of an automatic data-link to the GCI, which never functioned. These aircraft had a good autopilot,*

President Sadat shakes hands with pilots of No. 26 Squadron, including Medhat Zaki (centre, second from right). By 1973, this unit primarily consisted of older and more experienced pilots, who preferred to continue to fly the more agile but older MiG-21F-13s instead of the more modern but heavier MiG-21MFs. (Medhat Zaki Collection)

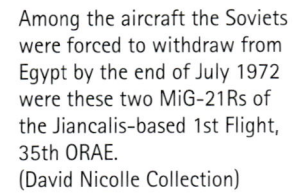

Among the aircraft the Soviets were forced to withdraw from Egypt by the end of July 1972 were these two MiG-21Rs of the Jiancalis-based 1st Flight, 35th ORAE.
(David Nicolle Collection)

*and were very manoeuvreable, especially in roll. But they were good for sports flying only: they had no cannon; only two R-3S missiles, which was the same as no armament at all.*

*'The MiG-21MF was a very good aircraft, stable and much more powerful than any of the earlier variants. It had four underwing hardpoints (two of these could take drop tanks, for a maximum total of three, instead of one as on earlier variants), and two levels of afterburner, but afterburner could only be used at high altitude. Except for the capability to carry four missiles, it had a 23mm internal cannon, with a useful load of ammo, but this was effective only at short ranges.'*

Concluding that even MiG-21MFs did not constitute a significantly improved defensive capability, Egypt launched a new effort to obtain more potent offensive arms from Moscow, in February 1972. This time the Soviets agreed to deliver not only the equipment promised in October 1971, but also 20 Tu-22s (of which the first two were to arrive in March 1972), 25 MiG-17s modified with ECM systems, and assistance in launching domestic production of the MiG-21MF by 1979. However, when Egypt – in an attempt to avoid the payment of salaries for Soviet personnel deployed in the country – also demanded the USSR begin withdrawing its air defence units, Moscow was dismayed. Concerned about what it saw as the 'increasing influence of anti-Soviet elements' within the Egyptian government, the USSR began demanding up-front payments for the Tu-22s in hard currency, effectively quadrupling their price.[31] Once again, negotiations were fruitless, although the Kremlin promised delivery of eight battalions of SA-3s, another SA-6 brigade and 16 additional Su-20s. Only small batches of this equipment began arriving in March 1972, and it did not include any of the much-needed additional fighter-bombers. Concluding that the Soviet presence in the country only impeded Egyptian interests, on 16 July 1972 Sadat informed Moscow that 970 Soviet advisors and around 7,000 other military personnel were to leave Egypt by the end of the month.[32]

International reactions to this decision varied. The USSR not only had to launch a massive air and sea bridge to evacuate its personnel and equipment, but was also left concerned that Sadat's 'expulsion' of its personnel would have considerable influence upon Moscow's foreign policy in the Middle East and Africa for decades to come. Reinforced in their opinion by fake reports purposely aired by Cairo in order to confuse its opponent, Israel was convinced that the Egyptian military would collapse without Soviet support. In fact, Sadat carefully timed his decision and brought it to bear only once his leading commanders had provided assurances that they could keep the IDF/AF at bay with the help of recently delivered SA-6s (provided Egypt launched a limited offensive that would advance no further than a few kilometres into the Sinai, as Shazly – supported by Fahmy – insisted). The ADC and EAF lost the services provided by the four Soviet-owned MiG-25s, a Soviet electronic reconnaissance and countermeasures squadron, as well as the ground-based stations equipped with SMALTA stand-off jammers, which were necessary for the support of operations against Israeli HAWK SAMs. However, the loss of these capabilities was not seen as significant by the responsible Egyptian officers. Nabil Shuwarky, meanwhile undergoing a staff course in the USSR and about to be put in command of Air Brigade 102, provided the following analysis:

*'It didn't matter that they provided us with weapons and some training. It was like after that Israeli ambush for Soviet pilots in June 1970: brigade commanders called each other to congratulate. We were all fed up of Soviet abuses and offense and there was a sense of celebration everywhere around the Air Force. Our morale soared when they left.'*[33]

Indeed, Ahmed Abbas Faraj recalled the reaction of the majority of UARAF pilots:

*'We were relieved when they were ordered to go. Only one of them remained with our brigade, and he was a technical officer that helped our technicians to maintain recently delivered Su-17s.'*

Reda el-Iraqi, who still flew MiG-21F-13s with No. 26 Squadron, explained:

*'President Sadat's decision to expel the Soviets from Egypt in 1972 was one of the most important decisions made by him: it started a period of serious preparations that led to the war, slightly over a year later… Because of evidence of Soviet espionage activites, after their departure we first changed everything in our squadrons: all codenames and radio-calls, even the distribution of tasks between different officers.'*

Despite Sadat's 'kick out' order, several groups of Soviet 'technical experts' remained in Egypt. Among them were members of the 9th Guards Reconnaissance Bomber Aviation Regiment, which delivered a batch of 10 Tu-16KSR-11 aircraft to Aswan in autumn 1971, where these entered service with the newly established No. 36 Squadron. The training of Egyptian crews for these bombers was primarily undertaken over the Mediterranean and the Western Desert, and included flights at altitudes as low as 50m (164ft) – which stunned more than a few Soviet instructors, who were not used to flying at altitudes below 100m (328ft). Together with the new bombers, Egypt also received around 100 KSR-2 and KSR-11 (ASCC codename AS-5 Kelt) air-to-surface missiles, a number of which were fired during training – in the course of which the crew of Maj Mohammed Abdel Wahab el-Keraidy scored highest.[34] One of the Egyptian Tu-16 pilots recalled:

*'After their delivery and review of their documentation, we discovered that these 10 Tu-16s were already based in Egypt in 1969 and early 1970. Back then, the Russians used to keep them in well-guarded hangars and we were not allowed to even approach them. The ADC reported to have tracked them flying reconnaissance sorties over the Mediterranean. Only once did the Russians ask us to let one of the Egyptian pilots fly as co-pilot on one such sortie. While flying over the US fleet, the bomber was intercepted by US fighters and then the crew asked our pilot to take off his oxygen mask and show his face through the window, so as to make it 'obvious' that the crew was Egyptian.'*[35]

Tu-16K-11-16 serial number 4407 as seen after October 1973 War, accompanied by four MiG-21PFS fighters. (Ahmad Keraidy Collection)

Serial number 4406, this Tu-16K-11-16 was one of 10 aircraft delivered to No. 36 Squadron EAF in autumn 1971. Notable is the nose-mounted antenna for the Ritsa radar-detection and target indication system (necessary for deployment of KSR-11 anti-radar missiles) and the underwing pylon for an air-to-surface missile. (Christ Knott Collection)

1. Sadat, *In Search of Identity*, pp178–195; Ovendale, *The Origins of the Arab-Israeli Wars*, pp189–192; Shazly, *The Crossing of the Suez*, pp17–20 and Carlowitz, *Egypt at War*, p8.
2. Shazly, *The Crossing of the Suez*, pp17-20 and Heykal, p115.
3. It seems that Fawzy's reason for opposing Sadat was his insistence on 'all out war of liberation to eradicate all traces of Israeli aggression', and Sadat's refusal to sign a decision to go to war no latter than the Spring of 1971, as originally envisaged by Nasser. According to Fawzy, it was not only so that everything was foreseen and planned for a new war with Israel by mid-1970, that it was him who re-established the Egyptian military, 'based on the Egyptian people's potential, the enemy's capability, and his estimate of the arrival of Soviet supplies and the army's ability to absorb them', that Egypt attained military superiority over Israel in July-August 1970, and that operational plans for liberation of The Sinai – including the general plan (Plan 200) and stages plan (Granite) were presented to Nasser shortly before his death. See Fawzy, *The Three Years War*, Chapter 3. His claims are rejected by nearly all historians in and outside Egypt, foremost Hamad.
4. Faraj, interview with Group 73, February 2012; this and all subsequent quotations from Faraj are based on transcriptions of the same interview.
5. Al-Ibrahim, interview, March 1999; this and all subsequent quotations from al-Ibrahim are based on transcriptions of the same interview.
6. Danish, interview with Group 73, 2010; this and all subsequent quotations from Danish are based on transcriptions of the same interview. For details on Danish's earlier career see *Volume 3*, pp60-62, 82-89, 94-97, 101, 107, 110, 111.

7. For specific details about large numbers of Egyptian and Syrian MiG-15bis', MiG-15UTI's and MiG-17Fs overhauled at the LZR-2, see Volume 1, pp194-203
8. For details on equipment-insufficiencies related to the Egyptian air force, see Volume 4, pp37-44
9. The downed pilot was reportedly killed in the crash of his aircraft.
10. Ayman, interview with Group 73, July 2010.
11. Shazly, *The Crossing of the Suez*, p82.
12. Dmitry Shevchuk, unpublished manuscript for article *The Soviet-Israeli Air War*, 2008. The reason for the failure of this Israeli operation lay in the seeker head of the Shrike: once this was tuned in to the frequency at which the targeted radar was operating and the missile was fired, the seeker head remained locked on to that frequency. If the targeted radar stopped emitting or changed its working frequency, the missile would lose the target and fall to the ground. Furthermore, the Shrike could become confused if its seeker head was 'saturated' by emissions from two (or more) different Fan Song radars.
13. Creation of the 63rd ORAE can be traced back to 27 May 1969, when the General Staff of the VVS issued a directive for creation of the 47th Independent Reconnaissance Aviation Regiment, equipped with 10 MiG-25Rs, 20 Yakovlev Yak-27Rs, 6 Yak-28U conversion trainers, and a single Antonov An-2 liaison aircraft. Selected pilots and ground crews were gathered in Gorky during November, while flight training on MiG-25s began in July 1970, at Shatalovo AB. Because only three MiG-25Rs became available by the end of that year, the unit had very little time to prepare for deployment to Egypt. See Steffan Büttner and Alexander Golz, 'Foxbat Finale' *Combat Aircraft*, March 2014.
14. Although colloquially described as 'Mach-3-capable', the MiG-25 could not reach such high speeds. Usual operational speed was between Mach 2.1 and Mach 2.3. The plane could accelerate up to Mach 2.83, but only in the case of emergency and at the risk of damaging engines. This is exactly what happened to one of Soviet MiG-25R during one of subsequent sorties over the Sinai.
15. Ibid; Shevchuk further detailed that the four MiG-25s were assembled inside hangars damaged by the Israelis during the June 1967 War, while used by workers from Gorky Factory to help Egyptians assemble newly-delivered MiG-21s. According to same source, the two MiG-25RBs arrived together with stock of FAB-500T bombs, which were covered in special coating protecting them from temperatures of up to 300°C, caused by friction during high-speed operations. However, no FAB-500Ts were ever deployed by MiG-25s of the 63rd ORAE.
16. The Model 124I was a derivative of the Model 147 Lightning Bug UAV and was specifically developed for Israel, where it was also known as the Mabat ('observation').
17. AW&ST, 22 May 1972 & Newdick, *Modern Israeli Airpower*, pp142. Notable is that according to Iraqi Military Intelligence, sometimes between 1971 and 1973 the IDF/AF should have modified at least one of its two recently acquired Lockheed EC-130H Hercules electronic warfare aircraft for airborne release of 124I UAVs; Sadik, interview, March 2006
18. Shazly, *The Crossing of the Suez*, p158.
19. Interview with former DIA analyst, provided on condition of anonymity, October 2001; according to same source, this was what prompted Israeli interest in obtaining then two newest US-made interceptors, the Grumman F-14A Tomcat and McDonnell Douglas F-15A Eagle, leading to the purchase of the later in the mid-1970s.
20. Büttner & Golz, *Combat Aircraft*, March 2014. According to the manuscript for the article 'The Unknown Heroes: Soviet Pilots in the Middle East, 1955–1974', provided to Group 73 by Russian researcher Mikhail Zhirokhov, the two MiG-25Rs of the 63rd ORAE were subsequently deployed to South Yemen, from where they flew additional sorties later in 1972. Some of these supposedly saw additional overflights of Israel and ended in landings in Egypt for refuelling, before the jets returned to South Yemen.
21. For discussion of influence of the Soviet warfare doctrine upon Egyptian planning for October 1973 War, see Asher, *Egyptian Strategy*, pp103.

22  Only indirectly indicating the importance of Saddat's and Shazly's approach as a breakthrough in Egyptian strategic thinking, even Hassain Heykal, Nasser's most faithful follower, admitted that, '...it took Egypt a long time to get used to the idea of a limited offensive that was aimed first and foremost at opening political prospects'; Heykal, *The Road to Ramadan*, p168.

23  Asher, *Egyptian Strategy*, pp81; Gamasi actually claims that there was only one offensive plan, the Badhr Plan, and that he was the chief architect, Gamasi, p212.

24  Description used by Pollack for Ismail Ali, in *Arabs at War*, p99; for comparison of differing standpoints between these groups, see Sadat's *In Search of Identity*, Gamasy's *The October War*, Badri et all's *The Ramadan War*, and Pollack's *Arabs at War*, in comparison to Shazly's *The Crossing of the Suez* or Blum's *The Eve of Destruction*, and various other works cited in endnotes and Bibliography. While most of these stress that it was Ismail Ali's skills and his 'intuitive understanding of the abilities and limitations of the Egptian soldiers' that proved crucial for successful planning and conduct of Egyptian operations early during the war, Shazly's memoirs, supported by numerous other sources cited in this book, clearly indicate that corresponding planning was well developed.

25  Okasha, interview to al-Masry al-Youm magazine, July 2011.

26  Asher, *Egyptian Strategy*, p67.

27  According to Asher, *Egyptian Strategy* (p69), the role of Soviet advisors in Egypt was officially defined as, '...to use their practical experience to elevate the combat proficiency in units and sub-units, and maintain the armed forces' levels of combat readiness. The Soviets will extend practical assistance to commanders and officers in the following areas: the preparation of troops and command centres, field training, operational planning, control and improvement of combat readiness, instruction of individual soldiers in secondary units.'

28  El-Iraqi's account of this incident was – indirectly – confirmed by the recollections of Victor Rozhkov, posted at http://www.hubara-rus.ru/egypt_period.html. Notably, when describing this incident to Rozhkov, Petrov described Zanaty as 'Squadron Commander', while the Egyptian was a section leader, but novice on MiG-21.

29  Asher, *Egyptian Strategy*, pp111 and 'Air Defence Forces: Remember Veterans', *Aviarus* volume 21, 2005.

30  Shazly, p113.

31  By Soviet standards, the salaries paid to Soviet personnel deployed in Egypt by the Egyptian government were quite handsome. Ivan Mishchenko, a radio-intelligence technical officer, recalled that he could save enough from his monthly wage of 90 Egyptian Pounds to buy himself a Moskvich 412 car. See Irina Temirova and Vladimir Shunevich, 'During the War in The Sinai, the Israelis exchanged Egyptian Prisoners for Watermelons', *Fakty i Komentarii* (in Russian), Kiev, 26 December 2000.

32  While the 'expulsion' of most of the Soviet advisors from Egypt in 1972 certainly became part of Sadat's 'feint', aimed to convince Israel that Egypt was not about to launch another war against Israel, various Arab publications – and foremost Sadat's memoirs – leave little doubt that the decision was primarily related to Moscow's failure to press Israel into concessions and Soviet refusal to supply Egypt with the arms required to launch a new war with Israel. The expulsion became a part of this feint rather by accident than by design, despite what various Israeli, Russian – and even some Western – accounts have claimed (for example, see Alvin Rosenfeld, *The Plot to Destroy Israel: The Road to Armaggedon* [New York, Putnam, 1977], pp112–113). Despite the points of view in Moscow, Tel Aviv, Washington or elsewhere, Cairo saw that a lack of Soviet diplomatic action and postponements of arms shipments were forcing the nearly bankrupt Egypt into a new war, one in which it would have to fight a technologically superior opponent while unable to operate freely because of the lack of necessary armament and equipment.

33  Shuwakry, interview with Group 73, October 2013

34  Mustafa Mohammed Hassan, interview, March 2010.

35  M. Z. (former UARAF/EAF Tu-16 pilot), interview provided on condition of anonymity, August 2001.

# PATIENCE BEFORE PURPOSE

Indirectly, the apparent break in relations between Cairo and Moscow had relatively positive effects upon the otherwise cool alliance between Damascus and Moscow – in the short term, at least. In the long term, it actually had a beneficial effect on relations between Cairo and Moscow, too. After Sadat had evicted most of the Soviet advisors, Moscow turned to Damascus with a request for help in improving relations with Egypt. Through Syrian mediation, the USSR struck another arms deal with Egypt, in October 1972, envisaging delivery of one squadron of MiG-23s and another squadron of Su-20s during the final quarter of 1973, and a brigade of 9K72 Elbrus system equipped with R-17 surface-to-surface missiles (ASCC codename SS-1c Scud-B) during summer 1973. It was in this way that Sadat – among others – finally secured deliveries of armament capable of hitting Israel. Therefore, Sadat's decision clearly had the effect Cairo was hoping for. However, and although Egypt accepted these attractive offers and the USSR eventually delivered this equipment, the reconstruction of the alliance between Cairo and Moscow was never successfully completed.[1]

Syrian involvement soon became of interest for Egypt as well, foremost because Sadat – in pursuit of his multi-prong policy of preparing for war, and in order to disperse the IDF by forcing it to fight a multi-front war at the same time – entered negotiations with Syrian President Hafez al-Assad regarding cooperation during the forthcoming conflict. Syria's position through the period 1970–1973 was different to that of Egypt. Assad's government was isolated on a diplomatic level because of the country's staunch anti-communist and anti-Israel position and its refusal to negotiate. Foremost, Syria was seriously lagging behind in terms of reorganisation and re-equipment of its military. Because of continuous Syrian support for militant Palestinian Arab irregulars – colloquially known as 'Fedayeen' – based on its own soil and also in southern Lebanon, the country found itself exposed to fierce Israeli attacks, too. Ironically, it was a corresponding agreement between Cairo and Damascus that resulted in a calming of the otherwise tense situation along the Israeli-Syrian ceasefire lines, in February 1973. This apparent 'break' in the continuous struggle between the Arabs and Israel was in turn exploited by the Egyptian and Syrian militaries to finalise their preparations for the coming war.

## Battle Days

Moscow's reaction to the expulsion of its advisers from Egypt was very swift. Because Damascus was fiercely critical of Sadat's failure to launch an attack on Israel, in 1971 and 1972, the Soviets saw an opportunity to exploit. Within only a few days, they signalled their interest in improved relations with Damascus, and so it happened that a number of their advisors were re-deployed to Syria. The Soviets arrived right in the middle of ongoing clashes, as recalled by Maj Gen Alexander G. Vagin, who arrived in Damascus in August 1972:

*'I came to Syria almost straight from Egypt and found the Syrians having higher combat readiness,* [and] *much stronger minded and better than the Egyptians as pilots. Ultimately, they proved to be the only Arab pilots capable of 'appeasing' the Israelis in air combat. They were true hooligans of the sky, and would not listen to the instructor. They flew ever slower and slower, below 300km/h* [186mph], *until their MiGs would slip into a tailspin. We told them, 'You can't do that', but they kept on going. It turned out they had found a 'secret weapon' against the Phantom. They would pull up, the Phantom would follow, then they would stall their aircraft, decelerate until slipping into the tailspin. The Phantom was heavier, so it was always the first to 'go down'. Then the MiGs would slip behind them and open fire. The Phantoms accelerated much faster and often avoided fire, but the Syrians were good at using their cannon.'*[2]

As of that time Israel and Syria were involved in a spate of clashes provoked by the attack by the Palestinian militant group Black September on the Israeli Olympic team during the 1972 Summer Olympics in Munich, West Germany, which ended with the death of 11 Israelis and one German police officer, on 6 September. Two days later, the IDF/AF bombed 10 PLO bases in Lebanon and Syria.

Feeling bolstered by increased Soviet support, but also in order to give his reorganised military some combat experience, President Assad felt he was in a strong enough position to authorise a limited war against Israel. This would allow his officers to test various concepts, gain experience and confidence, but also test Israeli detection capabilities and reaction times. Most of these operations were very limited, but were widely publicised by the Syrian media, which nicknamed them 'Battle Days'. Battle Days struck a responsive chord in many Arab countries, raising Syrian popularity and prestige, which had been at low ebb for years. Correspondingly, after Israel deployed its air arm to silence Syrian artillery, on 9 September the SyAAF was ordered to respond in fashion.

Around 14.00, eight Su-7BMKs armed with 250kg (551lb) OFAB-250 bombs sent to attack Israeli positions in the Qunaitra area encountered strong Israeli resistance. Two fighter-bombers from the leading flight were shot down by ground fire (Syria assessed them as shot down by HAWK SAMs, although Israel claimed both as hit by Mirages), and then the Mirages and Phantoms caught the two survivors. Following a pursuit low between the hills of the Golan Heights, one Su-7 was shot down. All three pilots were killed, and no fewer than 16 MiG-21s that waited for their return failed to intervene. 'Adad', a veteran Syrian Su-7BMK pilot commented:

*'Our pilots flying Su-7s were always short on fuel and because of this they were advised to avoid dogfights at any cost. We depended on flying low and at high speed to avoid enemy interceptors. Even flying evasion manoeuvres could be deadly because it necessitated activating the afterburner, which was likely to burn all the fuel within a few minutes. And we were flying so low, the chances of a successful ejection were nil. Whenever possible, we planned our missions so as to reach our target, attack and return beyond our front lines before enemy interceptors could catch*

*us. We had no radar warning receivers, no electronic countermeasures, no chaff and flare dispensers. We also had next to no navigational aids: we navigated with the help of a map, compass and watch until reaching our 'initial point'. Then we would engage the afterburner and pull up to climb while trying to visually acquire our target, roll out and enter a dive for the attack. If we did not find the target that was the end of the mission: we had no fuel to search for the enemy.*[3]

Another major battle day ended on 9 November 1972, when no fewer than 12 Phantoms dropped over 50 bombs on one of the first Syrian SA-2 sites to become operational, positioned near Sheikh Miskin. The site was completely obliterated and most of the crew killed, but Syria learned its lesson and subsequently began combining SAM sites within an overlapping network, like Egypt before them. When Syrian artillery reacted by shelling Israeli positions on the Golan, around 14.00 local time, Israeli jets returned to hit these positions as well, provoking a major air battle with SyAAF MiG-21s scrambled in response, as recalled by Vagin:

'*...We were sitting in the command post and listening to radio transmissions from an air combat between eight MiG-21s and eight Phantoms. We could listen to transmissions from both sides, and the Israeli and Syrian pilots sounded very much the same. We could hear them calling, 'Attack! ... Break! ... Someone is burning! ...' And we started counting. One shot down, the second... the fourth... All four of our own shot down? Then I heard the fifth... and then the sixth! We were amazed: six of our MiGs shot down? However, it turned out that 'ours'* [the Syrians] *had shot down four, and lost two...*'

The SyAAF subsequently claimed four Israeli aircraft shot down, in exchange for two losses; Israel denied having suffered any losses, and claimed two MiG-21s instead.

Following an attack by Palestinian Fedayeen on Israel, the IDF/AF returned to the skies over Syria on 21 November 1972, this time to bomb positions along the Purple Line. Syria hit back – starting around 14.00, as usual – with artillery, tanks and MiGs, and even deployed a large formation of aircraft to hit the National Water Carrier (NWC) system near Lake Tiberias, inside Israel. A pitched battle ensued, which was to last for eight hours, and during which Israel claimed six MiG-21s and 15 MBTs as shot down and destroyed, respectively. Syria officially confirmed only one MiG loss (the pilot reportedly ejected safely over friendly ground troops), but Vagin recalled yet more dramatic SyAAF losses, as well as the reason for these:

'*...The attack on the NWC was a mission planned to be launched in response to an Israeli raid. We had spent an entire day calculating everything and intended to have several groups of aircraft attacking from different directions, separated in speed and altitude, and along carefully selected routes, depending on terrain. However, Naji Jamil* [C-in-C SyAAF] *changed the plan at the last moment without consulting me. The result was that two of the attacking groups were intercepted and became involved in a big dogfight. The flights under way at low altitudes managed to escape, but those flying higher became involved in a dogfight. We lost nine out of 14 aircraft involved, and shot down only two Israelis.*'

While Moscow agreed to replace this huge loss, and delivered 16 MiG-21MFs to Syria before the end of the month, Soviet advisors once again put the blame for all their problems upon the Arab pilots.[4] Vagin argued in typical fashion:

'*The Syrians complained that our missiles were bad, and that this was the reason for this sad loss. A few days later Naji told this to President Assad. I understood*

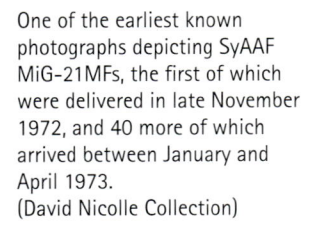

One of the earliest known photographs depicting SyAAF MiG-21MFs, the first of which were delivered in late November 1972, and 40 more of which arrived between January and April 1973.
(David Nicolle Collection)

*what he meant and turned to the president, telling him, 'This cannot be true. Over Vietnam, 97 per cent of American aircraft were shot down by missiles'. I told him it was his own pilots that did not know how to use missiles. We offered them a training plan, but no exercises were undertaken because these were too costly (one sortie within a live-firing exercise cost around USD40,000) … The president said something to Naji, and he turned red as a tomato. 'Tomorrow', he said, and went away. After four days, they came back and told me that Naji agreed with my suggestions … I flew a demonstrative mission and both of my missiles hit the simulated target. The same with guns – no miss. After that, Naji had no more questions.'*

Lacking any independent data concerning the combat deployment of MiG-21s by North Vietnam (which would actually demonstrate that Vagin's arguments were completely worthless, since North Vietnam suffered exactly the same R-3S reliability problems as Egypt and Syria), the Syrians grudgingly accepted his explanations.[5] Vagin's argumentation thus resulted in the Soviets intensifying training in use of air-to-air missiles for SyAAF MiG-21 pilots: they were granted an unlimited budget and could fire as many 'live' R-3S missiles as necessary.

## Master Plan

Throughout November 1972, Battle Days began to show its effects in Cairo. The operations were so widely publicised in the Arab media and became so popular that the position of Egyptian President Sadat in particular appeared vulnerable. Top Egyptian leaders knew their military was not yet ready to fight Israel, and they needed a calm period. Therefore, Sadat sent emissaries to Damascus, to restrain Assad through the termination of Battle Days, while simultaneously offering him reinforcement of the SyAAF through the deployment of Egyptian Air Force units to Syria, as recalled by Hussein el-Kfass:

*'As of 1972 I still served with No. 62 Squadron at Abu Hammad. Samir Farid then asked me if I would like to join him during a training tour in Libya, or if I preferred Syria again. The Syrians were fighting the Israelis almost every day and we were to reinforce them. I selected the later and thus in October 1972 I was promoted in rank to captain and assigned as number 3 to Fikry el-Gindy.*

*'We flew a lot and trained very intensively prior to our coming deployment to Syria. We also received many visits by high-ranking officers … However, a short*

Capt Hussein el-Kfas seen in the cockpit of MiG-17F serial number 2337 of the (newly established) No. 62 Squadron at Abu Hammad, in 1972. (el-Kfass Collection)

*time before our deployment I got married and thus received a month of leave. For a fighter pilot that was a feeling as if the war was over ... I returned already two weeks early. But, by the time I got back, my unit was already away, so I was reassigned to the newly established No. 62 Squadron that remained in Egypt.'*

Fikry el-Gindy completed the story of his squadron's deployment to Syria:

*'On 14 December 1972, I took my squadron from Abu Hamad AB to as-Seen AB, in Syria. I actually flew there in a MiG-15UTI, serial number 3233, but otherwise we took over Egyptian aircraft and ground equipment that were already in Syria since earlier times: only the personnel was rotated. Positioned outside Tsaykal, as-Seen was then a small air base that could accommodate only two squadrons. But at that time we were the only unit based there. We were now separated from the EAF HQs and thus became much freer: we were a completely autonomous Egyptian base with our own workshops and support equipment, but training – and often competing – with units from the Syrian Arab Air Force.'*

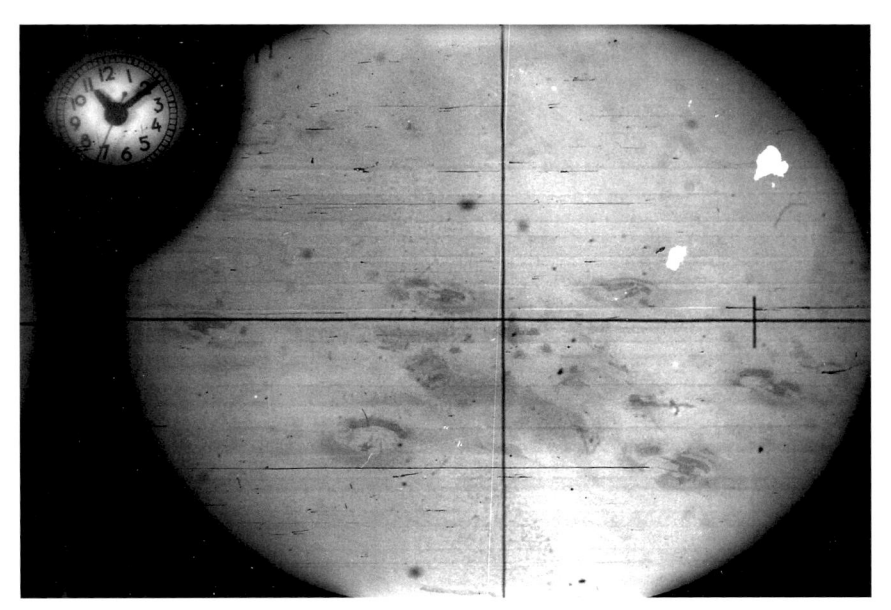

A gun-camera photo taken during one of many training sorties flown by Kfass and his colleagues from No. 62 Squadron before the war, showing a simulated attack on one of the ADC's SA-2 sites. (el-Kfass Collection)

Although subsequent negotiations between Cairo and Damascus were anything but easy, during January 1973 Egypt and Syria began to forge a new alliance. Namely, considering the sheer existence of Israel as abhorrent and rejecting the possibility of negotiations with Tel Aviv, Assad would have preferred a war with the aim of destroying Israel. However, experiences from Battle Days made him realistic enough to understand that his military was incapable of achieving this task on its own. Nevertheless, he did consider the Syrian military capable of retaking the Golan Heights and expected (incorrectly, as it turned out) that this would force Israel to surrender the West Bank.[6]

The Syrian plan for the re-conquest of Golan, Operation al-Owda, was developed entirely independently from Egypt (and Soviet advisors) by the Director of Operations of the Syrian Army, Brig Abdullah Habeisy, supervised by Chief of Staff Army Maj Gen Yusuf Chakour and Defence Minister, Lt Gen Mustapha Tlass. Al-Owda was based on relatively simple calculations. Considering that Israel would likely need between 24 and 48 hours to bring its reserve units to the Golan Heights, the Syrian attack had to secure the Golan within that period of time.

In order to slow down, and perhaps even prevent the deployment of Israeli reserves, Habeisy planned a pre-dawn infiltration of commando units behind enemy positions, to seize the crucial electronic warfare posts (especially Tel Faris in the southern Golan, Tel Abu Nida and Hermonit, both in the Kuneitra Gap, and on Mount Jebel Sheikh). Further raids by heliborne commandos were to be launched against Israeli positions on the El Al Rige, the Arik and B'not Yaacov bridges, and the Gonen and Dan roads. In that fashion, the IDF was to be left blind and blocked on the Golan, and the battlefield would be sealed from Israeli reinforcements. At first light, tactical air support would open the main attack, with subsidiary attacks against the Israeli command centre at Kfar Naffech and Mahanayim airfield. In regards ground forces, Habeisy's plan was again simple: considering the average number of Israeli tanks deployed on the Golan, he intended to deploy so many Syrian Arab Army (SyAA) tanks that Israel would be hopelessly outnumbered: regardless of the Israelis being better trained and aiming more precisely, and no matter what kind of losses they could inflict on Syria, the SyAA was to always have enough reserves to continue the advance until all Israeli armoured units were overwhelmed. This advance was to be closely supported by the SyAAF, which was planned to continue participating in combat operations whenever necessary.[7]

Al-Owda called for an advance into the Golan and liberation of the entire region, and as such stood in stark contrast to Egyptian planning. Unsurprisingly, very early during negotiations between Cairo and Damascus, Syria made it clear that if Egypt were to launch only a limited operation – anything short of an attack that would result in the recovery of the entire the Sinai – they would not go to war alongside Egyptians.[8] Furthermore, Syria wanted to attack early in the morning, when the sun would be behind them, which stood in opposition to Egypt's intention to attack in the late afternoon, for the same reason. Left with no other solution, and insisting on an alliance with Syria, Sadat and Ismail Ali then found a solution: they ordered Shazly – who by that time had completed work on The High Minarets – to further develop the plan for Operation 41/Granite 2 with an attack towards the Mitla and Gidi defiles, irrespective of how unrealistic they knew this was. This plan was then used to satisfy Assad and his generals. For all practical purposes, Cairo was thus lying to Damascus and Syria fell for the ruse. Convinced that Egypt would fight to recover the entire the Sinai, and upon Egyptian insistence, Syria abandoned the plan for al-Owda in favour of Operation Badhr.

Egypt envisaged the opening SyAAF strike being flown during the afternoon against Israeli air bases and command centres as far south as Tel Aviv, but foremost on the Golan and in the Jordan Valley. This first strike was to be followed by an advance by mechanised forces along the full length of the front. In the course of subsequent negotiations, and considering attacks on bases deep inside Israel not only too risky, but also likely to provoke a massive Israeli retaliation, Syria reduced the targeting list of objectives inside Israel to SAM sites near Kfar Giladi and Tiberias, the electronic warfare centre near Rosh Pina, and an early warning radar site outside Safad.

Finally, during the last rounds of negotiations, in August 1973, Cairo and Damascus agreed to start the war during October – a month when tidal conditions in the Suez Canal were best suited for crossing. The operation could not be delayed beyond that month because of the onset of rain and snows on the Golan Heights. Furthermore, 6 October was the anniversary of the Prophet Mohammad's victory at the Battle of Badhr, in 626, and was mid-way through Ramadan, the Muslim month of fasting, when Israel would least expect such an attack. Above all, 6 October was also Yom Kippur, the Jewish fast day, when the Israel would be guaranteed to be at its least prepared.

In summary, the plan for al-Owda was relatively simple, but was probably the best plan of attack against Israeli occupation forces in areas captured during the June 1967 War that any Arab military had ever been able to bring to the brink of execution. It was replaced by a compromise that all but precluded a favourable outcome. Namely, as subsequent developments were to show, Assad and his generals thus sacrificed not only the moment of surprise and the most promising plan for their own action, but then also squandered most of their army and air force in stubborn yet costly frontal assaults on heavily protected Israeli positions with the aim of conquering the entire Golan – in order to enable Egypt to cross the Suez Canal and secure a small bridgehead on the eastern side, and then do little else but dig in and wait for a negotiated outcome.

## EAF as of October 1973

As Egypt entered the final phase of preparations for a war with Israel, in the period 1971–1972, its air force went through several reorganisations, primarily related to keeping up with changes in other branches of the military, but also because of the need to absorb quantities of new equipment.

Because no official documentation is available, there are only rough estimates about the number of aircraft the EAF operated at the end of the War of Attrition, and how many were delivered by various sources – primarily the USSR – between August 1971 and October 1973. It is generally accepted that the EAF totalled around 23,000 personnel, of which around 5,700 were officers and 17,300 enlisted personnel. It reportedly had around 720 pilots, of which around 390 were qualified on MiG-21s and Su-7s, and 90 on MiG-17s.

In terms of aircraft, the EAF is usually assessed as being equipped with no fewer than 210-220 MiG-21s, 80-100 Su-7s, 14 Su-20s, anything between 100 and 160 MiG-15s, MiG-17s and MiG-19s, 25 Tu-16 bombers, over 160 helicopters and 70 transport aircraft, reinforced by 20 Hunters from Iraq, plus 30 Libyan Mirages.[9] Actual numbers of

Due to the lack of official documentation, precise dates of the delivery of many Egyptian MiG-21M/MFs remain unknown. Judging by their serial numbers, these two examples (serial number 8640 in foreground and 8224 in the background) probably arrived in Egypt with Soviet units deployed in the country in spring 1970. Unit insignia in the form of the head of an eagle or a hawk in dark red was used by either No. 56 or No. 82 Squadron.
(Tom Cooper Collection)

available aircraft were probably lower by a considerable degree, especially since EAF units tended to have an authorised strength of 12 combat aircraft only, compared to 16-20 in Israel or in the West, and also because no MiG-19s had been operated for some years. For example, according to Shazly, as of mid-1971, the EAF operated around 150 MiG-21s.[10] This figure included unknown quantities of:

- MiG-21F-13s (among them survivors from June 1967 War, at least six ex-Algerian aircraft and survivors of 30 Czechoslovak-built examples delivered in 1969);
- MiG-21PFS (survivors of 65 ex-VVS aircraft delivered in late June 1967);
- MiG-21FLs (a few survivors delivered before the June 1967 War and a few ex-Algerian aircraft);
- MiG-21PFMs (survivors of the June 1967 War and around 50 aircraft delivered in 1969);
- MiG-21Ms and MFs (survivors of some 20 aircraft delivered by that date).

It is unclear if Shazly included variants such as the MiG-21RF (12 of which were delivered in 1970) and MiG-21UM two-seat conversion trainers (about 30 of which were delivered starting from 1968) in his total, since neither of these were utilised for combat purposes.

Although the USSR promised delivery of no fewer than 300 additional MiG-21MFs (no other variant is known to have been delivered to Egypt after 1971) in the period

Egypt received about 30 MiG-21UM two-seat conversion trainers starting from 1968. Serial number 5654 was photographed while wearing either the insignia of the MiG-21 OTU, or a different variant of the insignia worn by MiG-21MFs of No. 42 Squadron.
(Lon Nordeen)

Patience Before Purpose

The EAF never operated as many Su-7BMKs as usually reported by foreign sources. This example – serial number 7025 – belonged to the first batch delivered to Egypt in 1967. It survived the June 1967 and October 1973 Wars, and was one of the last examples still in service as of 1981, before some 32 surviving Sukhois were donated to Iraq.
(Tom Cooper Collection)

1971–1973, exactly how many of these had reached Egypt by 5 October 1973 – and especially if any additional aircraft were delivered afterwards – remains unknown. Known serial numbers of Egyptian MiG-21Ms and MiG-21MFs indicate the arrival of at least four small batches, of which one is likely to have actually consisted of – outwardly very similar – ex-VVS MiG-21s left behind when Soviet units were ordered to withdraw, in July 1972. Namely, corresponding serial numbers – and aircraft looking more like ex-VVS MiG-21Ms than MiG-21MFs – were subsequently sighted in Egypt on several occasions. Furthermore, several reports by EAF pilots indicate deployment of R-3R (ASCC codename AA-2 Atoll) semi-active radar-homing (SARH) variant missiles during the October 1973 War: as far as is known, and despite Soviet promises, Egypt never received any MiG-21MFs compatible with such weapons, and thus the only aircraft that could use them would have been (ex-VVS) MiG-21Ms. Therefore, it is possible that the EAF might have had around 200 MiG-21s as of October 1973, some 10 per cent of which were probably held in storage, as attrition replacements.

The usually reported numbers of available Su-7BMKs are probably overoptimistic: indeed, specific Russian reports concerning delivery of no fewer than 187 Su-7BMKs to Egypt between 1966–1973 belong to the realms of fantasy. Unsurprisingly considering its lack of enthusiasm for that type, Egypt was not especially keen to order additional examples. Therefore, only one additional batch of around 20 single-seaters and a small batch of two-seaters reinforced the survivors of 41 Su-7BMKs that were available to the UARAF as of early August 1967. Considering that this fleet of – theoretically – 60 single-seaters experienced some attrition due to combat and training accidents during and after the War of Attrition, and that only one brigade with three squadrons operated this type as of 5 October 1973, it is most likely that the EAF did not have more than about 50 Su-7BMKs as of that date.

While some Russian sources cite deliveries of significant numbers of Su-7UM two-seat conversion trainers to Egypt, only four of these have been positively identified so far. Although never used in combat, they received the full coat of camouflage colours, usually applied in one of two major variants of the Nile Valley pattern.
(Albert Grandolini Collection)

Port and starboard views of EAF MiG-17F serial number 2721. Lacking more potent fighter-bomber types, Egypt was forced to retain the de-facto obsolete – but still highly popular – type in service. By 1973, most examples that were still operational wore the famous 'Nile Valley' camouflage pattern, usually applied in beige or yellow sand, green or olive green, and black-green on the upper surfaces and sides. (David Nicolle and Albert Grandolini Collections)

While it is meanwhile certain that the UARAF had no MiG-19s in service after 1970, the number of available MiG-17s is even harder to gauge. The EAF is known to have had only four operational units and one training unit operating the type in Egypt, and one in Syria. With each of the units in question having a nominal strength of 16 aircraft (plus one or two MiG-15UTIs that served as 'squadron hacks' and for continuantion training but were never deployed in combat), this would mean that about 100 MiG-17Fs were in service. Because of their heavy use in combat and in training, large numbers of MiG-17s underwent lengthy overhauls, some of these in Poland because the air force's main overhaul facility at Almazza (northeast of Cairo) was overwhelmed with demands for similar work to be undertaken on other types too.[11]

The EAF is certain to have significantly expanded its helicopter component during the War of Attrition, becaues it established a division-level unit for control of all the newly established squadrons: this 119th Helicopter Division was commanded by Col Nabil Kamil. However, the usually cited figure of 40 available Mi-6s is vastly exaggerated, considering there was only one, small unit flying 10 survivors of the June 1967 War. Most of the old Mi-1s were withdrawn from service by 1973, and the fleet of 26 Mi-4s known to have been in service as of early August 1967 was not reinforced.[12] Instead, Egypt purchased more capable and versatile Mi-8T helicopters throughout most of the 1967–1973 period, and it is possible that up to 80 of these – some of them armed with UB-16-57 pods for unguided rockets of 57mm (2.24in) calibre – entered service by

Two highly interesting views of a row of MiG-17Fs from an unknown EAF unit, seen while under inspection by FM Fawzy and AVM Mahmoud Shaker Abd el-Moneim, sometime in 1971 or early 1972. Clearly legible are serial numbers 2784, 2797, 2700 and (below) 2782. Although all painted in the same colours, not one camouflage pattern is like the other.
(David Nicolle Collection).

October 1973. Therefore, the EAF might have had a fleet of around 130, instead of the usually cited 160 helicopters available.

Similarly, although all available transport units were concentrated within the 129th Transport Division, commanded by Col Yusuf Basry, there are no indications that the fleet of 42 transport aircraft (including 27 Il-14s and 15 An-12s) operational as of early August 1967 had been significantly increased by 1973. Correspondingly, the usually cited figure of 70 transports appears unrealistic.

Pre-delivery photograph of Hunter F.Mk 59A serial number 579. Sadly, precise details about the serial numbers of IrAF Hunters deployed to Egypt during October 1973 War remain unknown.
(Albert Grandolini Collection)

A group of pilots from No. 6 Squadron with one of their Hunter F.Mk 59s (serial number 632), seen in the early 1970s.
(via Ali Tobchi)

Mohammad Naji, one of the IrAF pilots transferred to Egypt during spring 1973, has meanwhile confirmed the number of Hunters operated by Iraqi units in Egypt, as follows:

'On 18 March 1973, I found myself in a group of 35 pilots selected by Maj Yousif Muhammad Rasoul and Capt Wallid Abdul-Latif as-Samarrai to fly Hunters in Egypt … All of us had years of experience of flying Hunters, received advanced training in the UK, and additional courses from Indian instructors in Iraq. We were issued navigational maps of Saudi Arabia, with our route marked on it: Habbaniya, Taif, Tabuk, Numan Island in the Red Sea and then Luxor. Each pilot was granted permission to take one bag of personal belongings with him, which was carried by our transport aircraft that also carried spares and weapons, our technical personnel and a platoon of military police. On Friday 6 April, three groups of eight Hunters, accompanied by three replacement Hunters and four Antonov transports made the first flight to Tabuk, where we experienced significant problems while trying to land, due to crosswinds. Thank God, we landed safely and went to underground facilities to have a lunch. At 07.00 on the beautiful morning of 7 April, we took off again. Two groups proceeded with their transfer flight without problems, but one was delayed because of technical issues on one of the Hunters. The pilot changed to one of the replacement Hunters and then they followed us over the Red Sea … They caught up with us at Luxor Airport, where we all got some rest before flying to Qwaysina, following a desert road along the Nile. We passed Beni Suweif

Rather poor, but extremely rare group photograph of Iraqi Hunter pilots from No. 6 Squadron, taken during their deployment to Egypt, in mid-1973. The only officer that can be identified is Bassam Mohammed Kadoum (rear row, second from right), who later flew MiG-23BNs with No. 29 Squadron.
(via Ali Tobchi)

## Patience Before Purpose

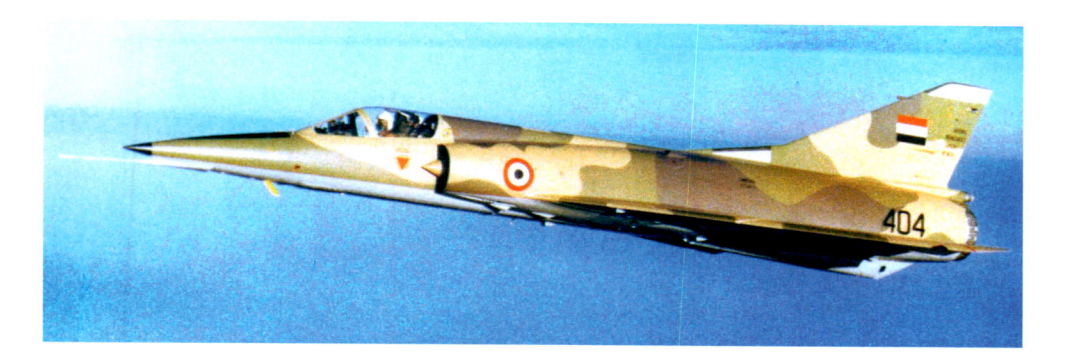

A pre-delivery photograph of Mirage 5D serial number 404. Following two years of intensive training and preparations, No. 69 Squadron EAF had 19 such aircraft in service at the start of the October 1973 War. (Albert Grandolini Collection)

*and Helwan and saw the pyramids of Gizeh. Cairo seemed huge from afar, with plenty of buildings and farms. After passing Benha, we finally saw Qwaysina along the main highway connecting Cairo with Alexandria ... Our first impression of Qwaysina was that this was a small air base near the highway, separated by a berm of sand – also as protection from surveillance from the ground. All major facilities, including our squadron ready room, were constructed underground. During the following days we found out that this was a quite new air base and some installations – like the officers' mess – were still missing. We therefore purchased all the necessary furniture and food from shops in Tanta ... Maj Gen Hosni Mubarak expected us on arrival, and after debriefing and a short conference, the Egyptians brought us to our living quarters, 2km [1.2 miles] outside the base.'*[13]

Earlier assessments concerning Libyan donation of 30 Mirages to Egypt, and reports about the transfer of no fewer than 42 Libyan Mirages to Egypt in spring 1973 (see *Volume 4*) have meanwhile been contradicted by the latest account from one of the pilots assigned to No. 69 Independent Squadron, Mohammed Okasha:

*'After some 10 months of training during which each pilot flew around 100 hours on the type, our squadron moved to Tanta AB, on 7 April 1973. We arrived there followed by several transports carrying spares and ammunition, as well as our technicians. As soon as we settled at Tanta, we started flying again, but our operations were somewhat hampered by limited amounts of ammunition and spares the Libyans provided us. As of that time, the squadron was under the command of Col Ali Zayn el-Abidine Abd al-Jawad, with 17 pilots qualified to fly ground attacks and two pilots – Abbas Shafie and Ahmed Ramzi – to fly the reconnaissance variant. We were all very experienced and nobody had fewer than 1,500 hours in his logbook. These 20 pilots had 19 Mirage 5Ds and two Mirage 5Rs at their disposal. The Libyan Mirage squadron was still working up and they were to arrive in Egypt only in November 1973.'*[14]

Furthermore, the EAF still had two small squadrons operating around 20 Il-28 bombers. Proven hopelessly obsolete during the War of Attrition, they were barely deployed in combat in October 1973. Furthermore, most available assessments have failed to take into account various other types that were in service, including 50 Helwan HA-200 jet trainers. Other assessments underestimate the numbers of operational L-29s – no fewer than 118 of which are known to have been acquired from Czechoslovakia between 1966–1968.[15] Arguably, the fleet of around 50 HA-200s saw little service even in its intended role as basic jet trainer, and it was never deployed in combat.

67

Veteran of many sorties over Yemen, and nocturnal reconnaissance missions over Israel flown in the late 1950s and early 1960s, this Il-28R – serial number 1774 – remained in service with No. 77 Independent Tactical Bomber Squadron until 1981, when it was photographed at Kom Awshim air base. (Albert Grandolini Collection)

However, two squadrons of armed L-29 jet trainers were prepared to serve during the 1973 War, as recalled by Salah Danish:

'*Early in 1973, the Air Force Academy established a squadron equipped with armed L-29s. This unit consisted of instructors and was designed to participate in minor battles. Initially it consisted of 12 aircraft and was based at Komm Awshim AB.*'

The second unit flying L-29s was established later during the same year, at Bilbeis. It consisted of additional instructors and even some of students, as recalled by Qadri Abd el-Hamid:

'*One of the pilots of that unit was Tarek Anwar Awad, my class-mate at the Air Academy, who graduated as a fighter pilot on MiG-17s before the June 1967 War. He was assigned to the Air Academy as an instructor and then to the unit equipped with L-29s. This consisted of highly experienced pilots, who trained lots of new pilots before the 1973 War. Most of them were wonderful persons that served their country in the best imaginable fashion.*'

As of October 1973, these approximately 475 combat aircraft, 130 helicopters, some 40 transports and around 150 jet trainers were based on 20 major air bases within the future combat zone, and around a dozen other air bases and airfields well away from it (including one in Libya).[16] All EAF air bases close to the combat zone were particularly well protected. Wherever possible, they had two runways, and had their taxiway, as well as the nearby highway sections, reinforced to provide emergency landing strips. Dispersed around the runways were hangars made of reinforced concrete, often covered with sand, some 500 of which were constructed during 1967–1973. These HASes had their entrances protected by massive doors and were well vented to minimise blast effects. All the operations rooms, pilots' quarters, maintenance facilities and even hospitals were also buried in concrete underground warrens. Furthermore, every base had explosive ordnance and runway repair teams.

Following all the reorganisations, re-equipment and the re-designation of various units, as of 5 October 1973 all available EAF personnel, aircraft and units were organised as follows:

## Table 1: EAF order of battle, 5 October 1973

| Unit | Base | Equipment | Remarks |
|---|---|---|---|
| C-in-C EAF: Maj Gen Mohammad Hossni Mubarak | | | |
| Deputy Commander EAF: Maj Gen Shakir Mahmoud Abd el-Moneim | | | |
| C-in-C ADC: Maj Gen Ali Fahmy | | | |
| Deputy Chief of Staff and Fighter Commander: Maj Gen Fuad Kamal | | | |
| Deputy Chief of Staff and Fighter-Bomber Commander: Brig Gen Abd el-Moneim el-Shennawy | | | |
| Chief of Operations Southern Air District: Lt Col Mohammad Abd al-Rahman | | | |
| Chief Air Operations 2nd Army: Brig Gen Fikry Abdallah el-Gahramy | | | |
| Chief Air Operations 3rd Army: unknown | | | |
| Chief of Naval Cooperations Command: Brig Gen Gabr Ali Gabr[17] | | | |
| **Direct-reporting and independent units, EAF** | | | |
| MiG-21 OTU | Beni Suweif | MiG-21UM | |
| Su-7 OTU | Jiancalis | Su-7BMK, Su-7UMK | |
| No. 6 Independent Attack and Fighter-Bomber Squadron | Kom Awshim | L-29 | CO Lt Col Nabil Ibrahim Ayyub |
| 11th Fighter Training Unit | Daraw | MiG-17F | CO Col Ahmed Saleh; Fighter Weapons School, also known as Air Brigade 139 |
| No. 16 Independent Attack and Fighter-Bomber Squadron | Bilbeis | L-29 | CO Lt Col Ahmad Maher Shehata |
| No. 55 Independent Fighter-Bomber Squadron | Jiancalis, Qutamiyah | Su-17 | CO Lt Col Farouk al-Elish<br>XO Lt Col Ahmed Abbas Mohy |
| No. 69 Independent Mirage Squadron | Tanta | Mirage 5D | CO Lt Col Ali Zayn al-Abidin Abd al-Jawad |
| No. 77 Independent Tactical Bomber Squadron | Kom Awshim | Il-28 | CO Lt Col Mohammad Gaber Hashish |
| 209th Fighter-Bomber Training Unit | Gamal Abdel Nasser (Tobruq, Libya) | MiG-15bis, MiG-15UTI, MiG-21UM | CO Lt Col Abd al-Rahim Rushdi |
| **102nd Fighter Brigade** | **Inchas** | | **CO Col Nabil Shuwakry** |
| No. 25 Squadron | Wadi Qena | MiG-2F-13 | CO Lt Col Ala'a Shakir |
| No. 26 Squadron | Inchas, Jiancalis | MiG-2F-13 | CO Lt Col Ahmad Abd al-Aziz Ahmad Nur<br>XO Lt Col Ahmad Anwar<br>Detachment of 8 aircraft at Gardeka on 6 Oct<br>Detachment of 8 aircraft to Abu Hammad on 15 Oct |
| No. 27 Squadron | Inchas, Shubrakhat | MiG-21MF | CO Lt Col Mohammad Kamal al-Sawy |
| **104th Fighter Brigade** | **El-Mansourah** | | **CO Jamal Abd al-Rahman Nassr** |
| No. 42 Squadron | Gardeka, Luxor, Saiyah el-Sharif | MiG-21MF | CO Lt Col Essam Muhammad Muqadam Sadiq |
| No. 44 Squadron | el-Mansourah, Shubrakhat | MiG-21PFS | CO Lt Col Amir Ahmad Riyadh |
| No. 46 Squadron | el-Mansourah | MiG-21MF | CO Lt Col Magdy Kamal Mahmud Sadiq |
| **111th Fighter Brigade** | **Beni Suweif** | | **CO Col Ahmad Adil Nassr** |
| No. 45 Squadron | Kom Awshim | MiG-21PFS | CO Lt Col Ahmad Muhammad Shafiq |
| No. 47 Squadron | Qutamiyah | MiG-21PFM | CO Lt Col Hisham Sayd Abduh |
| No. 49 Squadron | Beni Suweif | MiG-21MF | CO Lt Col Tamim Fahmy Abd Allah |
| No. 72 Squadron | Kom Awshim | MiG-17F | CO Lt Col Sayd Darwish |
| **123rd Reconnaissance Brigade** | **Inchas** | | **CO Col Sayd Kamal Abd al-Wahhab**<br>**XO Lt Col Nabil Hassan Kamil** |
| No. 22 Squadron | Inchas | MiG-21RF | CO Lt Col Samir Atiah |
| No. 3? Squadron | | MiG-21FL | CO Lt Col Yusuf Hassan Basri |
| No. 59 Squadron | Cairo West | Su-7BMKR | CO Maj Adil Muhammad Abd al-Fadil |

| | | | |
|---|---|---|---|
| **201st Brigade?** | | | |
| No. 66 Squadron | Qwaysina | Hunter F.Mk 59A/59B | Iraqi Air Force Unit<br>CO Maj Yusuf Muhammad Rasouli<br>XO Wallid al-Sammarai |
| **203rd Fighter-Bomber Brigade** | **Abu Hammad** | | **CO Col Tahsin Fuad Saima** |
| No. 56 Squadron | Bilbeis | MiG-21MF | CO Lt Col Mustafa Ahmed al-Hafez |
| No. 82 Squadron | Abu Hammad | MiG-21MF | CO Lt Col Munir Fahmy Barum Jirjis |
| **205th Fighter-Bomber Brigade** | **Abu Hammad** | | **CO Col Farouq Elish** |
| No. 51 Squadron | Bilbeis | Su-7BMK | CO Lt Col Hazem al-Gharby<br>CO Lt Col Jamal Muhammad Maha ad-Din Kamil |
| No. 52 Squadron | Bilbeis, Qutamiyah | Su-7BMK | COs Lt Col Osman Zaki (KIA 6 Oct)<br>Lt Col Victor Nelson Tadeus (KIA 7 Oct)<br>Lt Col Adil Abd al-Rahman Mustafa<br>XO Maj Adil al-Gradly |
| No. 53 Squadron | el-Mansourah | Su-7BMK | CO Maj Taher Mohammad Taher |
| **306th Fighter-Bomber Brigade** | **Almaza** | | **CO Col Fahmy Abbas Fahmy**<br>**XO Lt Col Hasan Fahmy** |
| No. 61 Squadron | Gardeka | MiG-17F | CO Maj Ahmad Shababi Ahmad Shababi |
| No. 62 Squadron | Abu Hammad | MiG-17F | newly established unit,<br>CO Maj Osama Hamdi, replaced by Lt Col Sharif Muhammad Arabi as-Sayd before October 1973 |
| No. 89 Squadron | Salihiyah | MiG-17F | CO Lt Col Naji Muhammad Lashin |
| **403rd Bomber Brigade** | **Aswan** | | **CO Col Osman al-Gindy** |
| No. 34 Squadron | Aswan | 7 Tu-16 | CO Col Ali Atiyah Ali Salamah |
| No. 35 Squadron | Aswan | 7 Tu-16 | CO Lt Col Ahmad Samir Ahmad |
| No. 36 Squadron | Aswan | 10 Tu-16K-11-16 | CO Lt Col Mohammad Raouf Helmy |
| **515th Transport Brigade** | **Cairo IAP** | | **CO Col Ali Abd al-Khaliq Mutawy** |
| No. 3 Squadron | Cairo IAP | Il-14 | CO Lt Col Mohammad Abd al-Rahman Fahmy |
| No. 14 Squadron | Cairo IAP | An-12BP | CO Lt Col Hamzah Kamil Abd al-Wahhab |
| No 95 Squadron | Cairo IAP | An-12BP | CO Lt Col Ali Hassan Shehata Hassan |
| **533rd Transport Brigade** | **Almaza** | | **CO Col Wafiq Abd al-Hamid Ahmad** |
| No. 2 Squadron | Almaza | An-2 | CO Lt Col Mohammad Majdi Abd al-Aziz |
| No. 15 Squadron | Almaza | An-12BP | CO Lt Col Wafiq Abd al-Hamid Ahmad<br>XO Lt Col Hassan Ismail Hassan (took over at unknown date) |
| **545th Helicopter Brigade** | **Alexandria** | | **CO Col Mohammad Jalal Muhammad al-Naji** |
| No. 11 Squadron | | Mi-8 | CO Lt Col Sayd Ahmad Zahran |
| No. 19 Squadron | | Mi-8 | CO Maj Gamal Sayd |
| No. 21 Squadron | Alexandria | Mi-4 | CO Lt Col Ad'l Hassan Sayd Ahmad |
| **546th Helicopter Brigade** | **Almaza** | | **CO Col Munir Salih Mustafa Thabet** |
| No. 7 Squadron | Almaza | Mi-6 | CO Maj Ahmad Khiry Abd al-Fatah<br>CO Muhammad Ali Hassan Masood |
| No. 8 Squadron | Gardeka | Mi-8 | CO Lt Col Mohammad Fouad Husayn Ali |
| No. 12 Squadron | Almaza | Mi-8 | CO Maj Ahmad Riyadh Ibrahim Shabarah |
| **547th Helicopter Brigade** | **Kataba** | | **CO Col Talat Tawfiq Musa**<br>**XO Col Zaki Sudani** |
| No. 9 Squadron | Ras Zafranah | Mi-8 | CO Maj Ahmad Ismail Amer Desuky |
| No. 13 Squadron | Qwaysina | Mi-8 | CO Lt Col Abdul-Hassan Abd al-Ahanin |
| No. 91 Squadron | | Mi-8 | CO Maj Sayed Abd al-Khalq<br>CO Maj Azmi Ezz el-Din Talibah |

## Patience Before Purpose

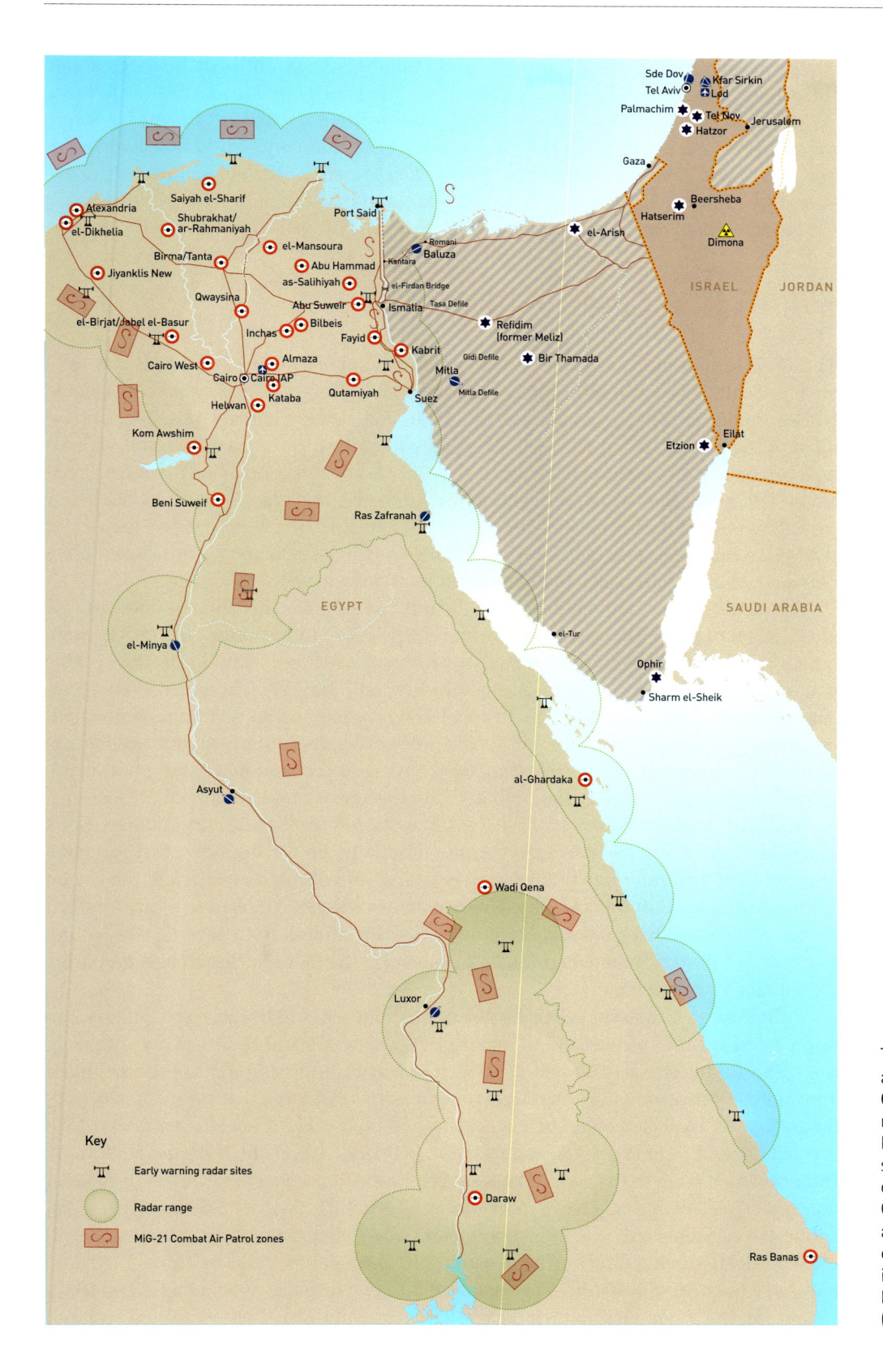

The 'blueprint' of EAF air bases and the ADC's IADS as of the October 1973 War, based on a map on display at the Military Museum in Cairo Citadel. It shows a massive concentration of early warning radars from Cairo up over the Nile Delta, along the Suez Canal down the entire coast of the Red Sea, and in the south, between Luxor and Daraw.
(Map by James Lawrence)

The reasons for interceptors and fighter-bombers from different brigades sometimes being stationed at the same air base were explained by Ahmed Abbas as follows:

*'In early October 1973, our Su-17 squadron moved back to Jiancalis, where there was also one MiG-21 squadron, and* [we were then] *ordered to redeploy half of our aircraft to Beni Suweif AB too, where they joined the MiG-21-equipped No. 49 Squadron. In this fashion our superior commanders wanted to make it impossible for the Israelis to destroy all of our brand-new aircraft with one blow.'*

## SyAAF as of October 1973

The SyAAF underwent a process of rebuilding similar to that of the EAF, but on a smaller scale and – at least initially – at a much slower pace. Syria also constructed HASes, multiple runways, and emergency landing strips wherever possible, but for most of the period 1967–1970 such attention was concentrated on expanding airfields well removed from the Israeli border. It was only from spring 1973 that facilities closer to the Golan Heights were hardened as well. Overall, and also because of the heavy losses it suffered during clashes between 1970 and 1972, the SyAAF – like the rest of the Syrian military – was only slowly expanded and even as of early 1973 lacked numbers and equipment to participate in Operation Badhr.

The situation did not improve significantly even after the Soviets delivered 40 MiG-21MFs to Syria, between Janaury and April 1973. The resulting frustration, combined with impatience and differences with Egypt over the planning for the coming war, eventually prompted Assad to visit Moscow, on 2 May 1973. In return, Soviet Marshal Gretchko visited Syria, from 10 to 14 May, and signed an additional agreement concerning military assistance. Although precise details of agreements reached on these occassions were never released, they obviously resulted in a crash programme of re-equipping the entire Syrian military, and deliveries of 40 additional MiG-21MFs, 12 Su-7BMKs and even a batch of Su-20s to the SyAAF; huge quantities of tanks, APCs and other equipment for the Syrian Army; missile boats for the Navy, but foremost enough equipment and Soviet advice to establish an entirely new branch, the Syrian Arab Air Defence Force (SyAADF). This armament was not supplied to Syria 'for free': it was made possible by a donation of up to USD100 million from Algeria, a reflection of President Houari Boumedienne's enthusiasm for the fact that Assad was preparing for a major war with Israel.[18]

Without Damascus ever releasing any official figures, and because the military certainly needed time to receive and absorb the new armament that was arriving from the USSR during the second half of 1973, it is hardly surprising that there exist quite contradictory assessments about the strength of the SyAAF at that time. Usually published figures are based on an Israeli post-war estimate, which specified a total of '338 combat aircraft', supposedly including 'up to 200 MiG-21s, 80 MiG-17s, and 80 Su-7s'.[19] Data obtained from unofficial Syrians sources and US intelligence sources is at least contradictive. Accordingly, the SyAAF operated 108 MiG-21s as of 5 October 1973, distributed – very unevenly – between no fewer than 12 squadrons, with all units operating MiG-21MFs being concentrated within one brigade, as cited in Table 2.[20] There may have been around 80 MiG-17s organised into two brigades with a total of up to six squadrons, but Egyptian reports indicate that practically all of these were concentrated

Starting in May 1973, Syria purchased large numbers of MiG-21s, including this pair of MiG-21UM two-seaters, seen at Hama air base in early 1974. (David Nicolle Collection)

at two or three air bases in the Damascus area and under the command of one brigade, indicating rather lower numbers. The number of Su-7BMKs was certainly lower than usually assessed, because the SyAAF is not known to have received more than about 20 aircraft of this type, including a handful of two-seaters, and some of these were shot down during the Battle Days. On the other hand, most available assessments ignore the – theoretically – most important reinforcement received by Syria shortly before the beginning of the October 1973 War, as recalled by Mohammad Marawy:

*'Fifteen Su-20s were delivered to Nayrab in mid-September, where they were assembled and test-flown. They arrived at T.4 only a few days before the war started, together with a sizeable shipment of [250kg/551lb] ZAB-250 napalm and OFAB-250 high-explosive fragmentation bombs. Our squadron principally included experienced former MiG-17 and Su-7 crews that underwent a conversion course in the USSR.*'[21]

As far as can be determined on the basis of the meagre evidence currently available, the aircraft in question were indeed 'genuine' Su-20s, powered by Tumansky R-29 engines. Obviously, the unit in question did not have enough time to work up to fully operational capability before the war. Not only were its pilots not entirely accustomed to the aircraft, and had received next to no combat training in the Soviet Union, but there were also the usual teething problems concerning maintenance and various related issues. Nevertheless, the squadron operating this type was to participate in the coming war, albeit not as intensively as intended.

Fascinated by Israel's deployment of helicopters during the June 1967 War, Syria purchased enough Mi-8Ts to equip three squadrons with the type by October 1973. Closely cooperating with commando regiments of the army, these units were stationed at the newly constructed Marj as-Sultan air base, in eastern Damascus, from where they could easily reach the battlefields of the coming war.

The SyAAF as of 1973 was generally assessed to have been 'very short of pilots', and the majority of those qualified to fly fast jets were neither fully trained nor experienced. Indeed, the SyAAF never put into operation a programme of intensive mass training as the Egyptian Air Force did. On the contrary, Shukri Tabet, one of a few Palestinian Arabs to join the SyAAF after the June 1967 War, recalled a relatively normal pace of training operations, lasting three years:

Shukri Tabet, seen at Gaza International Airport in the early 1990s, while serving with the small flying branch of the Palestinian Authority. (Courtesy Journal of Israel Defense Force)

'*I was born in 1946 in Beersheba. Two years later my family fled to Gaza where I finished a high school. I always loved airplanes and dreamed about becoming a pilot. I love flying. In 1964 I graduated from the high school and moved to Damascus while my family stayed in Jabalya refugee camp, in Gaza. A year later I was accepted to college and began to study law. There I learned about possibility to take pilot courses on voluntary basis. I saw my opportunity and took advantage of it. I left college and volunteered for the air force. I joined the SyAAF in 1967. The first year we did plenty of theoretical courses and flew light aircraft and L-29s. The second year we spent in Ukraine, flying MiG-21s. I was the only Palestinian around, but all my instructors treated me like everybody else. I graduated in 1969, still in Ukraine, and returned to Syria as a young MiG-21 pilot…*'[22]

Actually, and just as in June 1967, the SyAAF had enough pilots to man all of its operational aircraft, and even some in reserve. The fact that not all of these were fully qualified for all types of combat operation was related to their training system, which provided pilots with additional qualifications in only a gradual fashion. Therefore, the majority of Syrian MiG-21 pilots were not trained to fly ground attacks or by night and in bad weather: only higher-ranking pilots posessed such qualifications. However, pilots flying fighter-bombers completed very intensive exercises prior to the war and began adapting their tactics on the basis of their own, Egyptian, and even Pakistani experiences, as recalled by Fikry el-Gindy:

'*On 31 May 1973 we moved to Mazza* [colloquially known as 'Almazza' in the West and not to be mixed with Almaza outside Cairo; authors' note], *were added to a SyAAF regiment and we started flying and training with the Syrians. Our unit was officially re-designated as No. 15 Squadron, but we were nicknamed 'Saqr', meaning 'Hawk'. The CO of the Syrian regiment was Brig Subhi Haddad, and initially he had under his command only two other units, No. 5 Squadron at Mazza and No. 2 Squadron at Khelkhleh, both equipped with MiG-17Fs. We closely cooperated, sharing training experiences and flying together. The only difference was that our MiG-17Fs used Egyptian-made rockets, while the Syrians armed theirs with UB-16-57 rocket pods for S-5K rockets of Soviet origin.*

'*Our training was primarily ground-attack and close air support oriented, but included mock air combats. Hafez al-Assad attended some exercises because of his very close interest in the SyAAF. Several of our pilots were given medals or rewards as a result of these exercises at a public ceremony that was broadcast on radio and TV.*

'*Intensive training began on 5 June 1973, and I recall it as the most intensive training period ever. Our training plans were the same at both low and medium altitude, but very different at high altitude. This was where the Egyptians could learn from the Syrians – and from Pakistanis. Namely, there were two Pakistan Air Force instructors with us, both very fine men and very experienced. We used their experience a lot, in both strafing and bombing. Initially, our tactics was based on Soviet fighter-bomber tactics, adapted for MiG-17s. The basic formation was the 'finger four' – with aircraft distributed in two pairs, and with very little independence for the second pair. Only the number 1, the leader, had independence of action. In this system, the second pair was to target exactly what the first pair had already attacked, to 'finish it off'.*

'*The navigation when flying a MiG-17 was quite primitive: compass and stopwatch. The idea was to keep constant speed and heading, and at the correct moment*

Patience Before Purpose

*increase height to be able to see the target. If the target could not be seen or had moved, then there was very little the pilot could do. If pilots had to rely on compass and stopwatch alone there was great scope for error due to a slight change in speed or heading, or weather conditions. This meant that if the number 1 missed his target, or failed to find it, the entire formation repeated the failure. The Pakistani instructors showed us a new formation used by the PAF and based on the NATO system. This envisaged greater separation between the two pairs, with the number 3 – as leader of the second pair – having greater freedom of action. But, in the Pakistani tactics the second pair could see and select its own targets and would rise up before reaching the target so that it could see what was going on. We adapted that system and used it very effectively.'*

It is perfectly possible that some misinformation about the numbers and capabilities of Syrian pilots was the result of rumours purposely released by Cairo and Damascus during 1972 and 1973 in an attempt to secure surprise so that Israel would not be mobilised at the time of their attack. It is known that Egypt on several occasions launched false rumours about large parts of its military falling into disrepair following the expulsion of Soviet advisors, in the second half of 1972 and through 1973. Other possible sources of misinformation were the Soviet advisors, a fair few of whom were very critical about Syrian capabilities – while not being able to stress the importance of their presence in the country strongly enough. As in Egypt before, the lack of Soviet understanding for the Arabs, but also an inherent, and freely admitted, drawback in the Syrian character – a pride and stubborn independence, verging at times on arrogant aloofness – made it difficult for Syrians to seek or accept advice from foreigners. Col Victor K. Babich, who acted as Senior Advisor for Air Combat Tactics to the SyAAF, was one of the Soviets that had very little positive to say about Syrian pilots:

*'Syrian pilots had no tactics. They flew by intuition. We tried to organise them. We first underwent a detailed study of the enemy. This is where Libyan Mirages were so valuable, because they offered us first-hand experience with the appearance and maneuvering capabilities of the Israelis. Then we developed a training program, starting with such manoeuvres as break, reverse, slip, and the more complex ones, like high yo-yo, barrel roll and others. That way they were trained in the 'fundamentals' of air combat. Then we began training their ground controllers to direct MiGs into favourable positions before ordering them to engage. This reflected the tactics of the North Vietnamese, who did not fly straight at their opponents, but approached them from the side or from the rear.'*[23]

From spring 1973 the SyAAF began preparing for a new war with Israel. Assigned the role of close support for the Army, its MiG-17 units trained accordingly, in the course of which photographs like this came into being, showing a flight passing low over a motorised infantry unit mounted on BTR-152 APCs. (David Nicolle Collection)

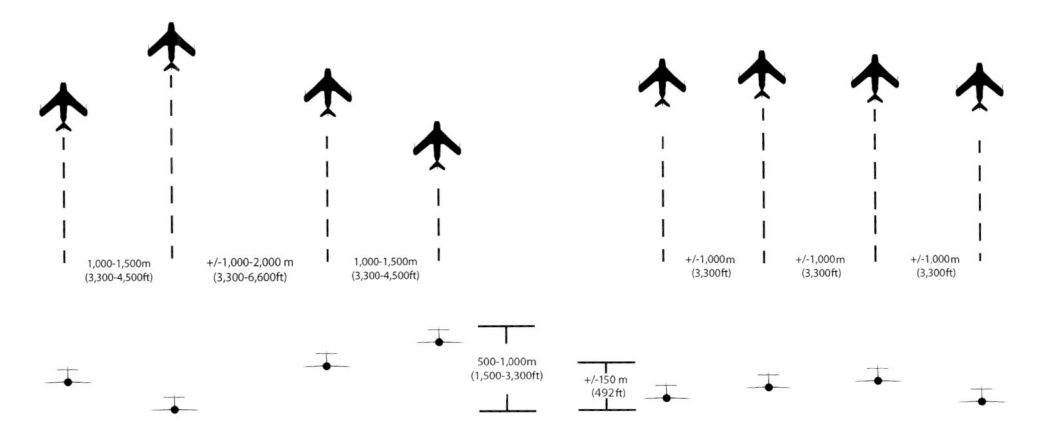

A diagram comparing the 'finger four' formation taught to the Syrians by the Soviets with the much more flexible formation known as 'combat spread' in the West, introduced to the SyAAF by Pakistani instructors prior to the October 1973 War. (Diagramm by Tom Cooper)

**Table 2: SyAAF order of battle, 5 October 1973**

| Unit | Base | Equipment | Remarks |
|---|---|---|---|
| C-in-C SyAAF: Maj Gen Naji Jamil | | | |
| **Air Brigade 7** | **Almazza** | | **CO Brig Gen Subhi Haddad** |
| No. 1 Squadron | Mazza | MiG-17F | CO Col Taher Sabbah |
| No. 2 Squadron | Khelkhleh | MiG-17F | CO Lt Col Samir Yousif Zainal (ex-IrAF) |
| No. 5 Squadron | Mazza | MiG-17F | CO Col Sharif Raya |
| No. 15 Squadron | Mazza | 12 MiG-17F, 2 MiG-15UTI | CO Col Fikry el-Gindy (EAF unit) |
| No. 18 Squadron | Blei | MiG-17F | CO Col Marwan Barsh |
| **Air Brigade 17** | **Nasiriyeh** | | |
| No. 54 Squadron | T.4 | 15 Su-20 | |
| **Air Brigade 30** | **Khelkhleh** | | **CO Brig Gen Saobaz** |
| No. 8 Squadron | Blei | 12 MiG-21MF | |
| No. 10 Squadron | Damascus IAP | 7 MiG-21F-13, 12 MiG-21MF | |
| No. 11 Squadron | Khelkhleh | 12 MiG-21MF | CO Maj Shukri Tabet |
| No. 12 Squadron | Tha'leh | 11 MiG-21MF | |
| **Air Brigade ??** | **T.4** | | |
| No. 7 Squadron | Hmemeem | 4 MiG-21F-13 6 MiG-21PFM | |
| No. 9 Squadron | Abu ad-Duhor | 7 MiG-21PFM | |
| No. 5? Squadron | Nayrab | 3 MiG-21F-13 10 MiG-21PFS | |
| No. 67 Squadron | Dmeyr | 11 MiG-21PFM 1 MiG-21UM | |
| No. 68 Squadron | T.4 | 5 MiG-21F-13 8 MiG-21PFM | |
| No. 77 Squadron | Hamah | 10 MiG-21F-13 | |
| **Air Brigade ??** | **Marj as-Sultan** | | |
| No. 25 Squadron | Marj as-Sultan | Mi-8 | |
| No. 32 Squadron | Marj as-Sultan | Mi-8 | |
| No. 37 Squadron | Marj as-Sultan | Mi-8 | |
| **Balance of SyAAF** | | | |
| No. 22 Squadron | Nayrab/Aleppo | Il-14, An-12 | |
| **Air Force Academy** | | | |
| Elementary and Basic Flying School | Nayrab/Aleppo then Kweres | de Havilland Canada Chipmunk | |
| Advanced Flying School | Kweres | L-29, MiG-15UTI | |
| Helicopter Flying School | Mennegh | Mi-2, Mi-4 | |
| MiG OCU | Kshesh | 8 MiG-21UM 4 MiG-21F-13 2 MiG-21PFS | Some single-seat MiG-21s sighted here were reportedly undergoing overhaul; 1-2 of these reportedly returned to service by the end of the war |

## Patience Before Purpose

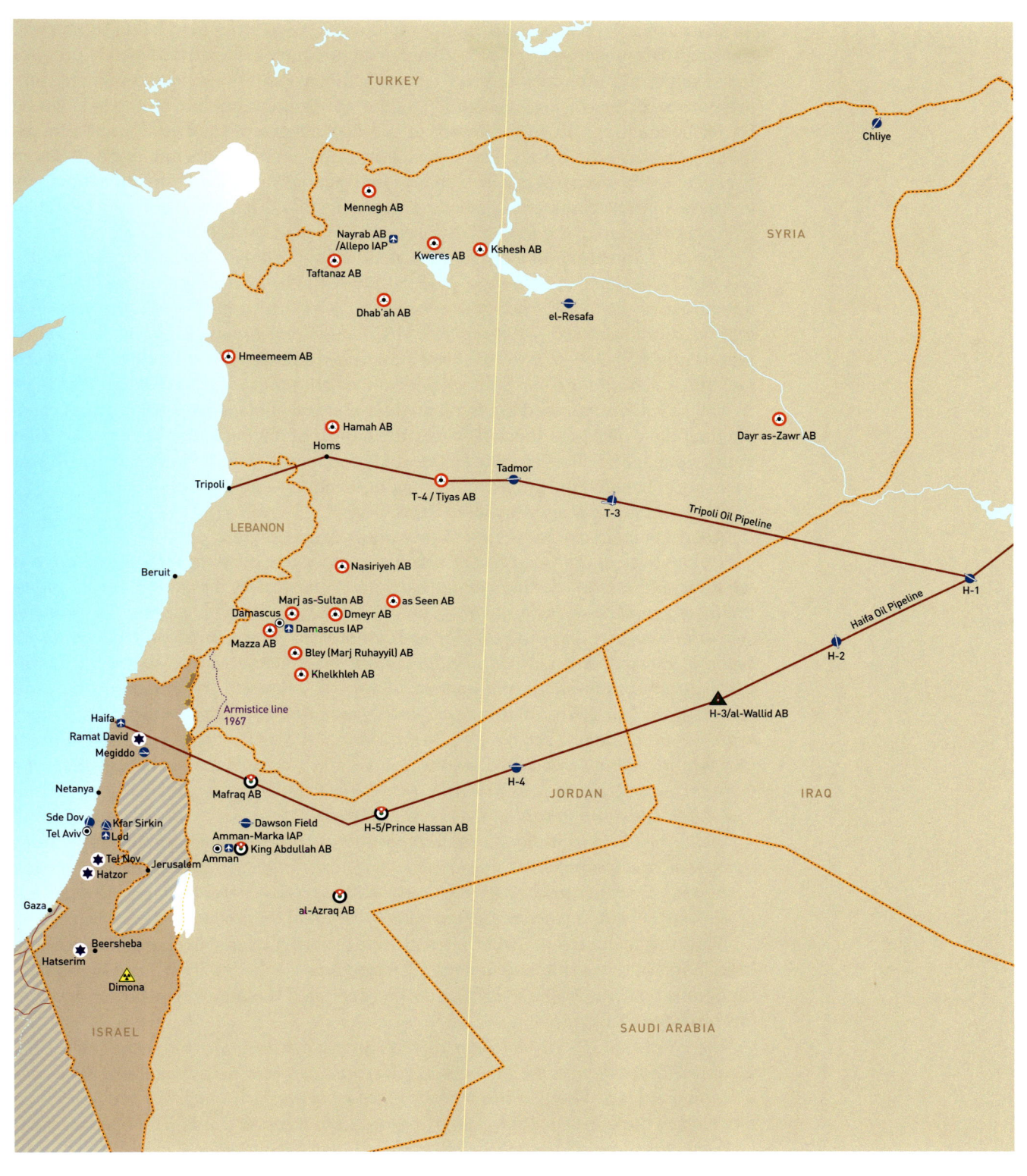

Map of major SyAAF air bases as of October 1973.
(Map by James Lawrence)

Mistrusting the Soviets, the Syrians not only imposed strict (and irritating) restrictions on their movement, but also complained that the Soviet attitude was a 'proof of indiscipline' and 'attempts to create a state within a state'. Some Syrian officers were even arrested for voicing opposition to their government's policy of dependence on Soviet instructors.[24] However, aware of the dependence of the Syrian armed forces upon Soviet arms deliveries, Assad was left without a choice: his military was forced to accept the Soviet presence in exchange for weapons provided in sufficient numbers and at favourable conditions – albeit not up to the task. This was confirmed by Tabet, who was assigned to the Khelkhleh-based No. 11 Squadron as of 1973:

*'Syrian pilots were very brave, very talented and highly trained. But their weapons and intentions were to their disadvantage … The MiG-21 was not a very good aircraft. One had to fly below the target to be able to deploy R-3S missiles, and approach to within 200–300m [656–984ft] for the gun to be effective. If one pulled more than 2.5g, the missiles did not function – and during air battles we pulled more than this all the time! Our equipment was almost at the level of World War II …'*

The Egyptians assessed the Syrian fighter-bomber pilots as only slightly less capable than their own, and those that saw them during training and in action, like Rifat Fathy – one of the pilots assigned to el-Gindy's squadron before the October 1973 War – usually concluded their commentary about them very clearly:

*'They were crazy, but very, very aggressive.'*

'Adad' summarised this period of SyAAF history as follows:

*'By the time of the October 1973 War, we undertook massive efforts to overcome the deficiencies seen during earlier wars with Israel. Our progress in air combat training was slow in the beginning, because of large numbers of new pilots joining operational units, and the heavy burden on our old pilots. But training standards began to increase dramatically in the months before the war, and so did the standards of our commanders and command staff at all levels. We ran more than 50 exercises during 1973, in which all units participated and cooperated with other branches of the armed forces. We also introduced a new system for maintenance of our aircraft, which was based on one ground crew for each aircraft, instead of one crew for each flight of four aircraft. This helped decrease the process of refuelling and rearming our aircraft to about eight minutes.*

*'With some help from Egypt, we managed to upgrade and modernise our aircraft, equipment and weapons, aiming to increase their efficiency and effectiveness through increasing the range and number of weapons they could carry, through introduction of new weapons to replace Soviet ammunition that often proved useless.'*

While the 'upgrades' to SyAAF aircraft were probably related to changes such as the installation of two additional underwing hardpoints on the Su-7BMK, and hardpoints for bombs on some MiG-17Fs, Fikry el-Gindy recalled the following as regards weapons provided by Egypt:

*'On 1 October 1973 I met Brig Haddad to explain him our anti-runway bombs made in Egypt, how to fit them to all aircraft types and help them introduce that weapon to service. These bombs were dropped from low altitude and had a parachute that slowed them into a steady vertical drop. Then a rocket would fire to wedge them deep into the ground before the bomb exploded under the surface to cause lots of damage to the runway.'*

# National markings of Egyptian and Syrian Air Forces, 1955–1973

Except for acquiring rather limited numbers of new aircraft, one of the most obvious changes the Egyptian and Syrian air forces underwent during the period 1970–1973 was that of the re-designation of official titles and the introduction of slightly adapted national markings. s.

Ever since the establishment of the United Arab Republic (UAR) including Egypt, Syria and Yemen, in 1958, the Egyptian Air Force carried the corresponding designation, the United Arab Republic Air Force, and its aircraft wore national markings that included two green stars on the white field of the pan-Arabic tricolour. As described in *Volume 2*, the Syrian Arab Air Force was disbanded during this period and had to be re-established once Syria seceded from the UAR, in 1961. While the UARAF retained its official title and markings introduced in 1958, Syria subsequently introduced slightly different markings, including three green stars on a white field. Following the agreement between Egypt, Syria and Libya to attempt the establishment of a new United Arab Republic, in September 1971, and the failure of the same, in spring 1972, Egypt altered the official designation of its air arm to the Egyptian Air Force (EAF), and introduced a new national insignia including the Eagle of Sallahaddin, applied in black, gold/yellow and red on a white field, instead of two green stars. The same emblem was not applied on the white field of the roundel: instead, this lost the two green stars. Theoretically, the SyAAF followed suit by adapting a very similar fin flash, though with the Eagle of Sallahaddin usually applied in yellow or gold only, and also removed all green stars from the white fields of its markings. Nevertheless, most photographs of Syrian aircraft during the October 1973 War show them still wearing the pan-Arab tricolour with three green stars.

In contrast, aircraft operated by the Libyan Arab Air Force received the pan-Arabic national insignia in red, white and black, but without any other details.

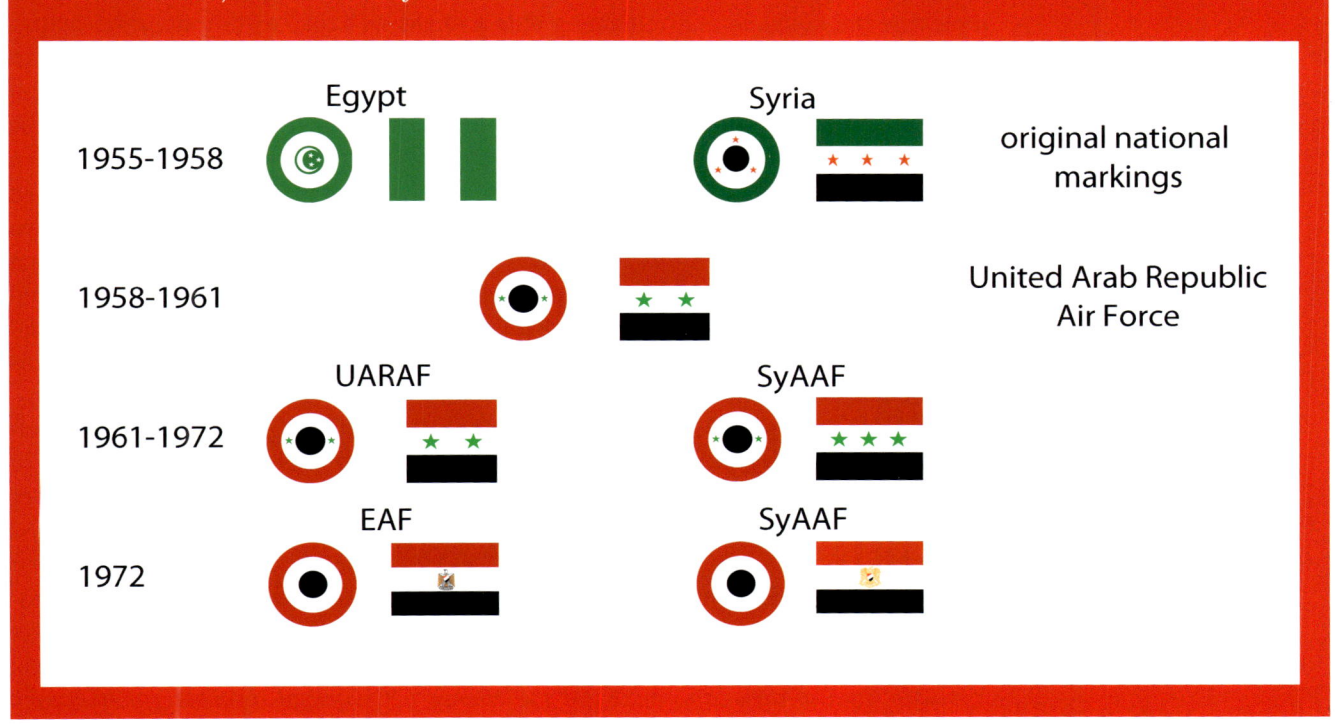

| Period | Egypt | Syria | |
|---|---|---|---|
| 1955-1958 | Egypt | Syria | original national markings |
| 1958-1961 | (UAR roundel & flag) | | United Arab Republic Air Force |
| 1961-1972 | UARAF | SyAAF | |
| 1972 | EAF | SyAAF | |

## Modus Operandi

In common with the rest of the Egyptian military, the EAF conducted an objective assessment of Israeli and Egyptian strengths and weaknesses. Supported by Military Intelligence, air force officers studied the Israeli military and strategy in general, the order of battle of the IDF/AF in particular, but also the fortifications of the Bar Lev Line, and the geography, topography, and meteorology of the Sinai. Their conclusions were sober and realistic in certain regards, and less so in others. For example, it was concluded that the EAF was the weakest branch of the Egyptian military – measured on its ability to match the IDF/AF in battle. It could not provide effective cover for ground forces while these crossed the Suez Canal or established bridgeheads on the Sinai; it could not provide full-scale close air support (CAS) for these ground forces; it could not provide rapid and accurate reconnaissance of enemy positions; and it could not seriously disrupt the work of Israeli command, communications and supply units. Egypt correctly concluded that air battles usually ended at their disadvantage since about 50 hand-picked Israeli pilots were deployed according to pre-arranged tactics to ambush EAF fighters scrambled in response and flown by 'duty roster'. Furthermore, they concluded that even the most advanced variants of the combat aircraft the Soviets were ready to sell to Egypt were no match for Israel's fighters – especially in regard to avionics, electronics, armament and payload. Egypt – probably influenced by its continual problems in training enough pilots for all its aircraft – grossly overestimated the total number of pilots available to the IDF/AF, as well as their average experience. For example, it was concluded that most Israeli pilots had logged more than 2,000 hours, which was certainly not the case.[25]

The strategy developed for the coming war by the EAF and SyAAF was thus strongly influenced by their respect for the capabilities of the IDF/AF, but also on the idea of removing the obstacle and remaining able to fight well and with honour, no matter what the result. Furthermore, contrary to earlier wars, when they had attempted to disengage whenever suffering casualties, prior to the October 1973 War Arab commanders impressed the spirit of readiness to sacrifice upon their subordinates: this was often to prove telling during the coming war.

At the tactical level, the first coordinated Egyptian and Syrian strike was designed to force a division of the IDF/AF between two fronts and in the protection of its own bases, and thus prevent it from disrupting the Egyptian crossing of the Canal, which was considered a more complex and problematic operation than the Syrian armoured onslaught into the Golan Heights. After this opening strike, it was left to the ADC and the SyAADF to maintain air superiority over the ground forces, while imposing as heavy attrition upon the Israeli forces as possible.

The EAF and the SyAAF were to assist the ADC and the SyAADF in the counter-air role as necessary, but while the EAF was to provide only the second echelon of defence, behind or in support of the SAM 'umbrella', SyAAF interceptors were very much planned to be deployed in the midst of the SyAADF's missile screen, as explained by Babich:

*'The situation in Syria was reminiscent of that in Vietnam. There was a relatively small area that was to be protected, and the MiG-21 was clearly at its advantage, possessing the necessary handling qualities. It was prudent to hide the MiG-21s during their approach, let the enemy get engaged by SAMs, then attack*

Ahmed Magdi el-Wakeel served as navigator on Mi-8s of No. 9 Squadron from Air Brigade 547 during the October 1973 War with Israel.
(Ahmed Magdi el-Wakeel Collection)

*him from the rear while he was busy. This was to become the core tactic of Syrian MiG-21 pilots during the first week of the coming war, something in which they were really in their element.*[26]

Similarly, when it came to ground-attack sorties, Egypt planned to deploy its air assets in a much more restricted fashion than Syria. The EAF was expected to primarily fly well-planned sorties against selected Israeli targets, only when no IDF/AF interceptor activity could be detected, and after Israeli ground-based air defences – foremost MIM-23 HAWK SAM sites – had been suppressed. Although not expected to leave the protection of the SyAADF's missile screen, SyAAF fighter-bombers were to be used more aggressively and also fly so-called 'free hunting' and 'armed reconnaissance' missions too.[27]

## Tactical Planning and Training

Once the strategy, equipment and orders of battle for the coming war had been crystallised, the Egyptian and Syrian Air Forces moved into the phase of final preparations. Beginning in spring 1973, both air arms commenced a series of command conferences, followed by very intensive exercises that concentrated upon coordination down the chain of command, individual and task training, accelerated maintenance of equipment and air bases, attacks upon pre-selected targets and – in the case of Syria – combined operations in support of ground forces.

Mohammad Naji recalled this period as follows:

'*Serious training of our squadron in Egypt began on Wednesday 11 April, which started with a conference with AM Hosni Mubarak. During this conference we learned that for the duration of our stay in Egypt, our two squadrons would be amalgamated and officially designated as No. 66 Independent Squadron … Six days later we also received a visit from President Sadat … On 24 April, we received a major briefing on navigation over the Nile Delta and Suez Canal by an experienced Egyptian navigator. He informed us that there were nearly 30 air bases in this area by that time, packed full of MiGs, Sukhois and Libyan Mirages. Because of this, and because Qwaysina is positioned in a densely populated agricultural area, he explained, strict control of all aircraft movements was required. Subsequently, we began preparing our training schedule, which included air combat 1-v-1 and 2-v-2, navigation at very low altitude and attacks by groups of up to four aircraft, low-altitude air combat, air-to-air and air-to-ground gunnery and deployment of unguided rockets …*

'*On 28 April, our squadron was reinforced by four additional Hunters, two of which were two-seaters, and then a decision was taken to bring our families to Egypt as well. This caused some problems, since we needed housing for our families, but the situation was eventually solved with help from President Sadat, who donated eight apartments to us for this purpose (not all of us were married; in fact, I married my Iraqi fiancée on 21 May 1973 in Cairo)… Early during our stay in Egypt we did not cooperate with any of the Egyptian squadrons, except when practicing air combats against MiG-21s. Although slower and slightly larger, during such exercises our Hunters proved much more manoeuvrable, especially so at low speeds and altitudes.*'

Targeting of such distant objectives as el-Arish, Etzion and air bases inside Israel was assigned to the two independent squadrons equipped with the longest-ranged fighter-bombers, No. 34 that flew Su-17s and No. 69 that flew Mirage 5s, as recalled by Mohammed Okasha:

*'As soon as our squadron was declared operational, we began planning an attack on Hatzor AB in Israel, envisaged to be flown on the first day of the war. Our intelligence informed us that, together with Hatzerim and Ramat David, this was one of the major Israeli air bases, that an attack on such a target would negatively affect Israeli morale, and force their air force to keep entire squadrons of their interceptors back for air defence instead of sending them to attack Arab forces on the Suez Canal and the Golan. We studied potential routes and possible weapons very carefully. We even flew several simulated sorties in the direction of the Libyan border. Eventually, we concluded that our Mirages would not be able to bomb Hatzor and return to Tanta AB, but would have to land on one of the air bases closer to the Suez Canal, or we would run out of fuel. Therefore we changed our target to Hatzerim.'*

Like the EAF fighter-bomber units, squadrons equipped with helicopters also underwent a period of very intensive training, as recalled by Ahmed Magdi el-Wakeel, who joined the air arm in 1970:

*'I was selected for the navigator course because I had very high grades in my final school exams. We were separated from the pilot trainees very early and underwent courses at Bilbeis, using an Il-14 aircraft, modified as a flying classroom with 10 positions for navigation students. Following graduation, we were employed on Il-14s, Tu-16s, Il-28s and helicopters. Helicopter pilots were not taught navigation; only to fly aircraft and deploy their weapons. Following my graduation, I was assigned to No. 9 Squadron that was part of the Kataba-based Air Brigade 547 and flew Mi-8s. Our brigade CO was Col Talaat Tewfik, with Col Zaki Sudani as his deputy; my squadron CO was Maj Ahmad Desuky, my pilots were Mohsen Hassan (first pilot) and Tahir Nur (second pilot), and we also had an engineer named Issa in our crew. We trained flying at very low altitudes over the desert and the sea, primarily over the Mediterranean, to ferry commandos, and to attack various ground targets with unguided rockets.'*[28]

After the High Command EAF received plans for missions to be flown against specific targets by different units, additional conferences took place, followed by more training, as described by Naji:

*'During the next series of conferences in May and June 1973, our squadron was assigned three targets in the Sinai, including the forward Israeli HQ at Tasa Defile, the nearby HAWK SAM site and a self-propelled artillery battery of 175mm [6.9in] calibre in the same area.*

*'The Egyptians provided each of us with two copies of the necessary maps and reconnaissance photographs, and we began preparing our mission and training accordingly… Once our plan was ready, it was provided to superiors within the chain of command and they authorised its execution. Then the plan was put into a safe to wait for a suitable moment. Additionally, we established a small intelligence centre in a room adjacent to our squadron ready room. Over time, this had its wall full of reconnaissance photographs of Israeli positions in the Sinai, taken by Soviet MiG-25s and Egyptian MiG-21RFs. We studied all of these very carefully and our morale was very high: we were sure we could reach and precisely hit every known target.'*

Patience Before Purpose

The heavily fortified centrepiece of one of the ADC's S-125 sites, with the SNR-125 (ASCC codename Low Blow) fire-control radar on the top of a mould camouflaging (and protecting) the UNK command post and other support elements of the site.
(via Tom Long)

Eventually, the High Command EAF prepared a list of targets selected to be attacked during the opening strike of the war. Top of this list were the air bases of Refidim, Bir Thamada, and Ras Nasrani in central and southern the Sinai, el-Arish in the northeast Sinai, Etzion in the eastern Sinai, Hatzor and Hatzerim in Israel. Further down the list were 10 air defence, early warning and electronic warfare sites (primarily occupied by Israeli HAWK SAMs), then four regional Israeli HQs and, finally, three large bases for ground forces. Only the operations planned by Nos 34 and 69 Squadrons continued to trouble the top EAF commanders, as Okasha concludes:

*'Our planning caused plenty of discussions in the High Command EAF. Eventually, our superiors did not let us fly that mission with the first wave. They calculated that even though we were likely to reach our target undisturbed and bomb it successfully, we would return long after other aircraft participating in the first wave of our attacks. This was likely to cause a conflict with our air defences. Instead, they decided to let us fly with the second wave and thus return to Tanta AB only minutes before the last light...'*

For similar reasons, No. 34 Squadron's plan to fly from Beni Suweif and attack Etzion was also rescheduled to the second wave of the opening attack.

Based on intelligence gathered from Israeli pilots captured during the June 1967 War, Egypt constructed several dummy airfields and SAM sites – complete with aircraft shelters, dummy aircraft, missiles, and gun emplacements – in the Western Desert. These were located at the exact distances from major air bases to the potential targets to enable air attacks to be rehearsed in their entirety, including exact timings, as described by Naji:

*'After the second series of conferences, we returned to flying and training. We were now aware of what was expected of us and thus concentrated on running some very realistic exercises. We were flying our training sorties as if at at war, against mock targets constructed at a similar distance from Qwaysina as our actual targets, only 180 degrees in the opposite direction, and including excellent replicas of not only our actual but also our alternative targets, just like the real Israeli bases.'*

Egyptian fighter-bomber units were not the only ones conducting extensive planning for the coming war. Interceptor units assigned to the ADC were planning their own operations, although these did not appear as comprehensive or potentially influential for the general flow of the war – at least not at first glance. By way of example, the staff of Air Brigade 104 was involved in planning air defence operations. This brigade operated about 30 MiG-21MFs and MiG-21PFMs (and a few MiG-21UM trainers) and was tasked with air defence of the northern coastline, support of ADC SAM units, and provision of top cover for EAF fighter-bomber units supporting the 2nd Army. Air Brigade 104 also had the special task of protecting the army's 65th Missile Brigade – the only Egyptian unit equipped with SS-1b Scud-C surface-to-surface missiles – which was based east of el-Mansoura. Should the need arise, Cairo planned to deploy Scuds for attacks on Israel from two possible positions: the Port Said area, which was the only location west of the Suez Canal from which the missiles could reach Israel; or – if there was a suitable opportunity – from the Sinai.[29]

A ZSU-23-4 'Shilka' SPAAG operated by the Egyptian Army during October 1973 War. (via Group 73)

## Expansion of the ADC

Unsurprisingly considering their inability to significantly bolster the offensive and defensive capabilities of the EAF, Shazly's staff concluded that expansion of the ADC was the only way left to match Israeli air superiority and provide at least 'adequate' air defence for the army. Therefore, between 1971 and 1973, Maj Gen Ali Fahmy, the C-in-C ADC, received almost unlimited funding and personnel.[30] Drawing upon theories from Soviet military academies, he set up an integrated air defence system (IADS) aimed at not only protecting army ground units deployed along the entire length of the Suez Canal, but also preventing Israeli aircraft from penetrating deep into Egypt, foremost over the Nile Delta and Cairo.

As of October 1973, the ADC operated no fewer than 148 battalions equipped as follows:
- 74 battalions of SA-2s (each including one site with six single-round launchers)
- 64 battalions of SA-3s (each including one site with four two-round launchers)
- 10 battalions of SA-6s (each including one site with four three-round transporter-erector-launchers)

By 1973, the ADC apparently supplanted air defence brigades and zones with five air defence divisions as its main subordinate elements. From now, all battalions were now subordinated directly to air defence divisions.

The core of the IADS – effectively a 'super SAM site' – was the 149th Air Defence Division, headquartered at Inchas. This division provided administrative and logistics control for around 25 air defence regiments, each including three to four battalions equipped with SA-2s, SA-3s and SA-6s, deployed along the western side of the Suez Canal. There the SAM sites were distributed within a relatively complex network, which resulted in overlapping engagement envelopes for their main weapons. In this way, a target that flew too low for engagement by an SA-2 could be engaged by either SA-3 or SA-6 sites nearby, and vice versa: a target that flew too high for engagement by SA-3 or SA-6 could be engaged by SA-2s. Furthermore, because of problems in detecting low-flying aircraft, each air defence regiment was assigned a battalion equipped with 23mm and 57mm anti-aircraft artillery, and teams equipped with 9K32 Strela-2 (ASCC codename SA-7 Grail) MANPADS, deployed to complement not only each other, but also to protect the dead zones of the heavy SAMs. The ADC's IADS positioned along the western side of the Canal effectively 'sealed' the zone out to around 15–20km (9.3–12.4 miles) east of the Canal to prevent operations by Israeli combat

A Syrian SA-2 SAM, as displayed at the Teshreen Panorama in Damascus (in the background is the MiG-21R described in detail in *Volume 4*). (Tom Cooper)

aircraft. For most of the coming war the Egyptian ground forces never moved out from under the protection of this 'umbrella': only a handful of ADC's SA-6 sites and some AAA units accompanied the manoeuvre forces and moved with them across the Canal.

Based on experiences from the War of Attrition, each SAM battalion was not only provided with several alternative positions, but their critical elements – including positions for command posts, fire-control systems and energy supply – were also protected by concrete bunkers, hardened to survive direct hits by bombs of up to 500kg (1,102lb). Nearly 50 per cent of ADC SAM sites would move to new positions each night of the coming war, resulting in a situation in which the IDF/AF could never depend upon intelligence on their positions from the previous day for planning the next morning. A large number of trained repair teams were positioned to quickly mend or replace damaged equipment or rebuild protection for SAM sites, in turn providing the ADC with unmatched recovery capabilities.

Separate from the 149th Air Defence Division was a group of four or five SA-2 and SA-3 SAM sites assigned to the independent military command for the Port Said Sector, an area where Egyptian Army units also operated independently from the command of the Second Field Army (responsible for the defence of the northern section of the Suez Canal). Organised according to a regimental structure, this SAM group was supported by two early warning radars, and several batteries of towed S-60 and ZU-23 AAA, as well as SA-7 teams.

Further west and providing protection for the Nile Delta and Cairo areas, and the Mediterranean coast, were units of the 139th Air Defence Division, headquartered at el-Mansourah. As in the case of the Inchas-headquartered division, the 139th provided administrative and logistics control, while operational control of units distributed in this area remained with the High Command EAF. The SAM sites in this zone were primarily deployed for the protection of the most important EAF air bases, as well as various cities and industrial facilities.

A heavily fortified SA-2 site protecting Damascus International Airport (IAP), as seen in 2009. Most such facilities were constructed during the summer of 1973. (Tom Cooper)

A third air defence division covered Egypt's Southern Air District (also known as Air Brigade South), and was unique in so far that it was the only ADC unit to exercise operational control over EAF aircraft within its area of responsibility as well. However, very little is known about the strength and composition of the ADC's Southern Air District units, or two other divisions that apparently existed around the same time.

The complementary arrangement of Egyptian SAM sites brought together different technologies to work in synergy and multiply the effectiveness of the overall defence. This IADS did not function without a proper command and control system: on the contrary, it can be said that it was heavily centralised. Its chain of command ran from ADC HQ to five divisional control centres, linked to around 50 local control centres (all buried deep under reinforced concrete and sand), supported by around 180 radar sites, primarily equipped with P-12, P-15, P-20, P-30 and a few P-35 radars. The main duty of the local control centres (similar to the HQ of an air defence brigade in other air defence forces) was to detect enemy aircraft and identify them by type and number, and then forward this information to the HQ ADC. Namely, operational control over the ADC during the October 1973 War was exercised from the HQ EAF, not from the HQ of the Air Defence Command. Except in the case of the Southern Air Division, which also exercised authority over aircraft, it was always down to the top EAF commanders to decide which SAM sites – or, alternatively – manned interceptors (MiG-21s) would engage enemy aircraft. In turn, missile battalion commanders were authorised to engage only if a target entered their area of coverage and was clearly identified as hostile.[31] This unusual control of operations was confirmed by Taher Zaki, a former MiG-17 pilot who served with the ADC for most of the War of Attrition, and who was put in charge of EAF interception operations only days before the October 1973 War:

*'A week or so before the October 1973 War, Hosni Mubarak called me and asked my advice on the Fighter Control system. He wanted to be at the Air Force HQ during the first attack, not in the ADC HQ, where he had previously sat next to Fahmy. So he selected me as his representative and put me there in the ADC HQ, promoting me to the rank of major general so that I was the same rank as the other senior officers there. My job was to advise on communications and divide responsibilities between various bases, air defence sites, and also to send our interceptor squadrons to specific missions and to decide if they were to abort the mission, and so on. I demanded from him to have direct communication to all squadron commanders and also with all the pilots in the air, to have the authority over selection of secondary targets, as well as to change missions from primary to secondary targets, or as necessary. A corresponding permission was granted and I received a 'red telephone'. This could override all other communication links, and enabled me to contact all bases, squadrons, and even pilots on alert in their HASes. In this fashion, I was able to provide them with the latest intelligence assessments, and issue direct orders.'*[32]

A ZSU-23-4 SPAAG, large numbers of which were delivered to the SyAADF and the SyAAF starting in summer 1973. (Tom Cooper)

It was not only the ADC that was vastly expanded prior to the October 1973 War. The Egyptian Army established a number of powerful air defence units of its own, too. Each of its divisions now included an air defence regiment equipped with 42 self-propelled or towed artillery pieces, primarily consisting of towed S-60 cannon, and sometimes also four ZSU-57-2s (57mm AAA on modified T-54 MBT chassis), and at least four ZSU-23-4s. Additionally, such units included a platoon equipped with six firing teams (two men with one launcher each) for SA-7 MANPADS. Finally, five independent air defence regiments were established, each of which was responsible for one of five major crossing sites, and five secondary crossing sites. Because central command and control of all of these units was not feasible, they were directed to fire at any aircraft they visually identified as hostile: obviously, the danger that friendly aircraft could be mistaken for hostile was a risk that top Egyptian military commanders were willing to accept.

# Establishment of the SyAADF[33]

As mentioned above, it was only in May 1973 that Syria started the process of establishing an air defence force as a separate branch of its military, equivalent to the Egyptian ADC. Thanks to massive deliveries of necessary equipment from the USSR between May and October 1973, the first commander of the SyAADF, Col Ali Saleh, was able to supervise the build-up of no fewer than 49 air defence battalions equipped with SAMs, of which 36 were operational at the start of the war, including 25 deployed along the Golan Heights, and 11 elsewhere around the country. The equipment of these 49 units was as follows:
- 18 battalions of SA-2s (including six operational S-75 Volga and six operational SA-75MK Dvina systems)
- 16 battalions of SA-3s (12 operational)
- 15 battalions of SA-6s (all operational)

As in Egypt, all these battalions were reinforced through the addition of batteries equipped with radar-controlled ZU-23 and ZSU-23-4 anti-aircraft guns, and MANPADS teams equipped with SA-7s. The deployment of 25 SyAADF battalions along the Golan Heights was slightly different to that of the ADC along the Suez Canal. The Syrian units were positioned in two major groups, each of which consisted of densely concentrated and overlapping SA-2, SA-3 and SA-6 SAM sites, heavily protected by AAA and MANPADS. The slightly more powerful group was deployed in the north. Headquartered at Saasa, it was responsible for protecting not only three army divisions deployed between Jebel Sheikh, Damascus and the northern Golan Heights all the way to the Rafid Gap, but also the main supply line for Syrian ground forces during the war, between Damascus and Der'a. The slightly smaller southern group was headquartered at Sheik Miskin, and covered the area between the Rafid Gap and the Jordanian border.

Overall, the SyAADF was a small and not yet coherent air defence force, covering the future battlefield, but far from all the key locations within Syria. Indeed, much less is known about the dispositions and strength of air defence units deployed away from the Golan. It seems that most air bases were protected by AAA regiments only. Namely, because of the small size of the SyAADF and the necessity to protect army units deployed on the Golan as well as a large number of newly constructed air bases, nearly all the other strategic installations in central and northern Syria were left without sufficient ground-based protection from air attacks. The units stationed in these areas usually included only anti-aircraft regiments consisting of batteries equipped with 57mm S-60 towed AAA, 37mm M1939 cannon and quadruple 14.5mm (0.57in) ZPU-4 towed machine guns.

Furthermore, being only recently established, the SyAADF relied heavily upon Soviet instruction, and nearly half of the some 2,000 Soviet advisors deployed in Syria as of summer 1973 served with air defence units. Although members of the SyAADF generally listened to their advisors, there was some friction too. Among others, the Syrians complained that they were supplied with 'only' 540 3M9 missiles for SA-6s, which they considered 'insufficient' for realistic training and subsequent combat oper-

A 5P71 launcher with two V-601P missiles of the Syrian Air Defence Force. (Tom Cooper Collection)

The crew of a Syrian S-60 anti-aircraft gun. This fearful weapon proved highly effective not only for air defence purposes, but also when deployed in a ground support role.
(Albert Grandolini Collection)

ations. However, there are indications that such opinions were based on experiences from the coming war, which have shown that because of their inexperience and due to electronic countermeasures deployed by the Israelis, the Syrians tended to fire far more weapons then envisaged by their Soviet instructors. In excitement, Syrian SA-6 operators often ripple-fired more than the usual two rounds per engagement, which was contrary to the practices taught by their Soviet advisors. This resulted not only in heavy expenditure of missiles, and their lower statistical 'probability of kill', but also in problems with re-supplies, as the logistic chain eventually proved unable to cope with the demand for reloads.

Thanks to the surge in deliveries of Soviet weapons, by summer 1973 the Syrian Arab Army (SyAA) – which relied heavily on the protection of the SyAAF's ground-based AAA units in 1967 – had significantly bolstered its own air defence assets too. Theoretically, each SyAA brigade included a battery of six ZSU-23-4s, but because the build-up was incomplete, only a total of 72 ZSU-23-4s was in service with the 5th, 7th and 9th Infantry Divisions – which constituted the first assault wave of 6 October 1973. Similarly, the build-up of the 1st and 3rd Armoured Divisions was incomplete, and these units that were expected to exploit the infantry breakthrough operated only 48 ZSU-23-4s and a similar number of towed ZU-23s. Nevertheless, and in cooperation with the SyAADF, the available Syrian Army 'Shilkas' were to cause significant problems to the IDF/AF.

## Nemesis

The fact that official Israeli doctrine – and thus the centrepiece of all of the IDF's war plans – was based on seizure of initiative and taking the battle into enemy territory (or airspace) at the earliest opportunity was well known since the June 1967 War. During that conflict, the IDF/AF proved capable of delivering decisive blows upon the Arab militaries, in turn confirming various earlier concepts. One might have expected

The F-4 Phantom II was the epitome of the 'super fighter' in the late 1960s and early 1970s. This large, yet powerful and fast fighter-bomber could outfly any MiG-21 while carrying a crew of two, was equipped with a very advanced navigation/attack suite, and carried more fuel and weapons than half a squadron of contemporary Soviet-made fighters. (IDF)

that negative experiences during the closing stages of the War of Attrition could have resulted in some reservations regarding such a posture, but this was not the case. On the contrary: Israeli military self-confidence subsequently skyrocketed beyond any reasonable levels.

Although not everybody involved felt that way, the problems the IDF/AF experienced in the face of Egyptian SAMs were considered merely an 'episode'. The general conviction was (and remains) that Israel 'won' that war, and that the IDF/AF would have destroyed Egyptian SAM sites if it had been given an opportunity to attack them in full force, as in a full-scale conflict. Correspondingly, Israel expected that – once the SAMs were destroyed – the IDF/AF would win the battle for air superiority through the deployment of superior technology in attacks on Arab bases and pre-arranged ambushes of Arab fighters. Thereafter, it would resort to the role of 'flying artillery' for its own, tank-reliant ground forces, to form the same 'invincible' combination that proved highly successful in June 1967. There is little doubt that such theories were bolstered by the availability of large numbers of highly advanced combat aircraft and weapons of US origin, and the fact that the IDF/AF regularly received more than half the national defence budget in the early 1970s. Israeli airmen did their best to exploit this great opportunity to establish a force that was technologically vastly superior to its opponents. As a result, the IDF/AF of October 1973 was an entirely different force to that of six years previous.

Considering the huge numbers of McDonnell Douglas F-4 Phantom IIs and McDonnell Douglas A-4 Skyhawks Israel acquired from the US between 1968 and 1973, but also not a little controversy surrounding their losses during the War of Attrition, it is unsurprising that there is still some uncertainitiy about the exact numbers of aircraft available to the IDF/AF at the start of the October 1973 War. Following the delivery of the first F-4Es to Israel, in September 1969, Washington granted permission for the release of four additional batches of Phantoms. Indeed, deliveries of the first batch of 44 aircraft were still incomplete (they were to last until January 1971), by the time the IDF/AF was granted six additional F-4Es as replacements for losses suffered during

Patience Before Purpose

the War of Attrition. Later in 1970, Israel was permitted to order 18 F-4Es to re-equip one of the Mirage units; in 1971 it was donated 12 F-4Es from USAF stock, and between April 1972 and October 1973 it received no fewer than 24 ex-USAF and 18 newly built Phantoms necessary to re-equip its fourth squadron with the type, and bring all units to an authorised strength of 20 aircraft. In all, the IDF/AF received no fewer than 122 F-4Es and six RF-4E reconnaissance fighters by October 1973. Given that 13 F-4Es are known to have been written off in the meantime, Israel should have had some 109 of these when the new conflict started, approximately 90 of which were operational at any given time.

The situation was even more complex in regard to the A-4 Skyhawk. Israel is understood to have ordered up to 236 of these between 1966 and 1971, of which 178 are known to have been delivered by 1972. The balance comprised 82 examples of a new, custom-made A-4N variant, ordered in 1971, but which necessitated additional research and development. It seems that only six A-4Ns had reached Israel by October 1973, since it is usually reported that Israel received 185 Skyhawks of all variants and that 13 of these were written off (to all causes) before the war began, resulting in a total of 165 remaining in service as of 5 October 1973.

Something similar can be concluded about the numbers of Dassault Mirage 5s in service with the IDF/AF. Clandestine deliveries of 51 aircraft from France were completed during 1971, but their assembly by Israel Aircraft Industries (IAI) was not entirely complete as of October 1973: 12 are known to have been introduced to service in 1971, 25 in 1972, and the last few were accepted by the IDF/AF only in February 1974.[34] Furthermore, most of the 10 Mirage 5DDs arrived only in 1974. Therefore, the usual assessment that only some 40 such aircraft were available to the IDF/AF as of October 1973 is probably too conservative, and slightly higher numbers were certainly closer to reality.

The number of Mirage IIIs available to the IDF/AF dwindled between 1967 and 1973. The IDF/AF is usually said to have ended the June 1967 War with 56 aircraft of this type (including three IIIBJ two-seaters and two IIIRJs primarily deployed for reconnaissance). The force is known to have received an additional two-seater in 1968 and IAI is said to have completely rebuilt one of the examples badly damaged before the June 1967 War. Available Israeli accounts indicate that no fewer than 18 Mirage IIICJs were written off – to all causes, including combat attrition and training accidents – by 1973 (three examples are known to have been badly damaged and completely rebuilt during the same period, usually with the help of spares and entire assemblies, foremost wings, acquired from France, but one of these was written off again). Therefore, as of October 1973, the IDF/AF should have had a fleet of 40 Mirage IIIs, including four two-seaters and two reconnaissance aircraft.

At least two Mirage IIICJs were rebuilt with the help of Mirage 5 wings delivered from France. Twenty aircraft are known to have been re-engined with more powerful and more reliable Atar 9C engines during the period 1968–1972 (the exact details about the attrition of such examples remain unknown), and one two-seater was used as a test-bed for of re-engining project. The latter aimed to provide the entire fleet with US-made J79 engines and was run by a group of engineers from the Rockwell Corporation, and was later to result in the IAI Kfir. Finally, nearly almost all Mirage IIICJs had their unreliable Cyrano Ibis radar removed and replaced with ballast in order to maintain their centre of gravity.

Comparable in size with the MiG-17F, the A-4 Skyhawk could carry nearly five time as much ordnance at the same speed over a much longer range. Relatively simple to operate, it played the role of the workhorse of the IDF/AF during the October 1973.
(IDF)

While withdrawing from service all the other older fighter-bombers of French origin – Dassault Ouragans, Dassault Mystère IVAs, and Sud Aviation Vautours – the IDF/AF still operated a small fleet of Dassault Super Mystère B2s. Twenty-six such aircraft, meanwhile renamed as the Sa'ar, were completely overhauled and adapted for the US-made J52 engine, the same unit that powered the Skyhawk. Their attrition was relatively low by 1973 and the sole unit flying them was still equipped with between 20 and 25 examples (20 were most likely operational on average).

By October 1973, the IDF/AF transport fleet included 11 Boeing KC-97 Stratocruisers, some 20 Nord N.2501 Noratlas, up to 19 Douglas C-47 Skytrains/DC-3s, 10 Lockheed C-130H Hercules and one KC-130H tanker. During the October War, the IDF/AF also requisitioned several Boeing 707 airliners of the El Al national airline, and rushed three prototypes of the IAI 101 Arava light transport into service, too.[35] A total of six helicopter squadrons operated 16 Sikorsky S-65 Stallion helicopters (18 were delivered in the period 1969–1972, but two were written off by 1971), 10 Aérospatiale SA.321K Super Frelons, up to 50 Bell Model 205s, 12 Bell Model 206s and around a dozen Aérospatiale SE.3130 Alouette IIs.

The IDF/AF's arsenal of weaponry for its combat aircraft was at least as extensive. For electronic warfare, Phantoms were equipped with AN/ALQ-71, AN/ALQ-87, and AN/ALQ-101 ECM pods that proved effective against SA-2 SAMs and moderately effective against SA-3 SAMs. Skyhawks could be equipped with a total of four Thompson-CSF Caïman standoff ECM pods (purchased before the June 1967 War and previously used by Vautours that were withdrawn from service in 1971), that proved capable of disturbing the function of large parts of the Egyptian early warning radar network. At

Significantly depleted due to earlier wars, the Israeli fleet of Mirage IIICJ interceptors had been continuously upgraded and was still the most potent air superiority weapon anywhere in the Middle East as of 1973. (IDF)

least as effective were ECM systems of US origin installed on several S-65 helicopters, known only by their Israeli designation, Katef. Furthermore, the IDF/AF operated two EC-130H electronic warfare aircraft, and several of Noratlas acted as airborne command posts and radio-relay platforms.

In terms of air-to-air missiles, the F-4Es were armed with AIM-7E Sparrow, medium-range, semi-active radar-homing (SARH) missiles. Sometime during the summer of 1973, the IDF/AF also received its first batch of the AIM-7E-2 variant, which had a much shorter minimum engagement envelope and was thus more suitable for deployment in a dogfight. Twelve such weapons are known to have been fired during the October 1973 War.

Much more importantly, in 1969 the IDF/AF had introduced two highly effective, short-range infrared-homing air-to-air missiles, including the indigenous Shafrir 2, and the US-built AIM-9D Sidewinder. Compared to the older AIM-9B Sidewinder and Shafrir 1, both weapons had a much-expanded engagement envelope, much more sensitive seeker heads with higher tracking capability, more effective warheads, and could be deployed from aircraft at much higher acceleration. Indeed, the Shafrir 2 and AIM-9D – followed by AIM-9Gs, a number of which were delivered to Israel during the October 1973 War – were to prove highly reliable, capable of very flexible deployment and murderously effective during October 1973, outmatching the Soviet-made R-3S – the only AAM in the arsenals of the Arab air forces as of October 1973 – by a significant margin.[36]

Especially since 1971, the IDF/AF had also made major leaps forward in regard guided air-to-ground weaponry. It not only acquired the above-mentioned AGM-45

Shrike ARMs (which, following the negative experience from their first deployment in 1971, the USAF and the IDF/AF upgraded to become capable of targeting SA-3 systems too), but also AGM-62 Walleye electro-optically (EO) guided bombs, followed during the later stages of the October 1973 War by the highly effective AGM-65A Maverick EO-guided missile.

As well as significant stocks of French GP bombs of 100, 200 and 400kg (220, 441 and 882lb), the IDF/AF also purchased huge numbers of US-made GP-bombs, including 500lb (227kg) Mk 82s, 1,000lb (454kg) Mk 83s and 2,000lb (907kg) Mk 84s, but also older 750lb (375kg) M117s. Furthermore, Phantoms and Skyhawks were regularly armed with US-made Mk 20 Rockeye, CBU-52/B and CBU-58/B CBUs.[37]

As of 5 October 1973, IDF/AF squadrons, aircraft and personnel were organised as follows:

**Table 3: IDF/AF order of battle, 6 October 1973**

| Unit | Base | Equipment | Remarks |
|---|---|---|---|
| C-in-C IDF/AF Maj Gen Benjamin Peled | | | |
| **1st Air Wing** | **Ramat David** | | **CO Col Arlozor Lev (until KIA on 9 Oct, then Ya'akov Agassi)** |
| No. 69 Squadron | | F-4E, RF-4E | CO Lt Col Yoram Agmon |
| No. 108 Squadron | | | |
| No. 109 Squadron | | A-4H TAAL-Crystal[38], A-4N | CO Lt Col David Itshaki |
| No. 110 Squadron | | A-4H, A-4E | CO Lt Col David Dothan (KIA in FROG-7 attack, 9 Oct) |
| No. 117 Squadron | | Mirage IIICJ | CO Lt Col Yehuda Koren |
| **2nd Air Wing** | **Sdot Micha** | | |
| No. 150 Squadron | | Dassault MD.450 Jericho | 10-13 IRBMs equipped with nuclear warheads |
| **3rd Air Base** | **Refidim** | | **CO Eliezer Cohen** |
| | | | Detachments from No. 101 and No.113 Squadrons |
| **4th Air Wing** | **Hatzor** | | **CO Col Amos Lapidot** |
| No. 101 Squadron | | Mirage IIICJ, Nesher S | CO Lt Col Avi Lanir (PoW on 13 Oct, replaced by Maj Herzel Budinger), Regular detachment at Refidim |
| No. 105 Squadron | | 26 Sa'ar | CO Lt Col Schlomo Shapira |
| No. 113 Squadron | | Nesher S | CO Lt Col Ya'akov Gal Regular detachment at Refidim |
| No. 201 Squadron | | F-4E | CO Lt Col Yiftaz Zemer (WIA 13 Oct, replaced by Maj Eitan Ben-Eliyahu) |
| **5th Air Base** | **el-Arish** | | |
| | | | No permanently or regularly attached units |
| **6th Air Base** | **Hatzerim** | | **CO Brig Gen Amihai Shmueli** |
| No. 102 Squadron | | A-4H | CO Lt Col Uri Sachar |
| The Flight School Unit (OCU) | | Fouga CM.170 Magister, A-4H, TA-4H | A-4H and TA-4H on loan from No. 115 Squadron |
| No. 107 Squadron | | F-4E, RF-4E | CO Lt Col Yiftah Spector Regular detachment at Ophir |
| **7th Air Base** | **Bir Tamada** | | |
| | | | No permanently or regularly attached units |

| 8th Air Base | Tel Nov | | CO Col Ran Ronen |
|---|---|---|---|
| Flight Test Centre | | Mirage IIIBJ, Nesher | Not involved in combat operations, but some of its aircraft distributed to combat units |
| No. 103 Squadron | | Noratlas | CO Lt Col Eli Mor, Some transports used as airborne command posts |
| No. 114 Squadron | | 5 SA.321Ka, 9 SA.321Kb, few S-65C | |
| No. 115 Squadron | | A-4N TAAL-Crystal, A-4H | CO Maj Giora Rom (replaced Lt Col Ami Goldstein, killed during training sortie on 3 Oct); only 3 A-4Hs remained operational by 8 Oct |
| No. 116 Squadron | | A-4E, A-4H TAAL-Crystal, A-4N, TA-4F, TA-4H | CO Lt Col Ehud Shelah (KIA 6 Oct) A-4Ns on loan from No. 115 Squadron, later returned; TA-4F and TA-4Hs were used as FFAC |
| No. 118 Squadron | | S-65C, CH-53A | CO Lt Col Yuval Efrat, 12 S-65C and 10 CH-53A available |
| No. 119 Squadron | | F-4E, RF-4E | CO Lt Col Eliezer Prigat F-4Es were AGM-45 compatible, regular detachments at Refidim |
| No. 123 Squadron | | AB.205A, Bell 205A | |
| No. 124 Squadron | | Bell 205 | CO Lt Col Michael Cohen |
| No. 125 Squadron | | SE.3130 Alouette II, Bell 206A/B | |
| 10th Air Wing | Etzion | | CO Col Aharon Shavit |
| No. 140 Squadron | | A-4E | CO Lt Col Dan Pesah Unit disbanded at start of the war; aircraft and personnel distributed between other units; squadron re-established only in 1978 |
| No. 144 Squadron | | Nesher S | CO Lt Col Menachem Sharon |
| 15th Air Wing | Sde Dov | | |
| No. 100 Squadron | | Dornier Do 27, Do 28, other light aircraft | |
| 21st Air Base | Haifa | | |
| IDF/AF Technical School | | | |
| IDF/AF Technical College | | | |
| 27th Air Base | Lod IAP | | |
| No. 100 Squadron | | | CO Lt Col Amnon Gilad |
| No. 120 Squadron | | 11 C-97, 9 C-130H, 1 KC-130H | CO Lt Col Yehushua Shani C-97 in process of being replaced by 707s; C-130s later transferred to No. 131 Squadron |
| No. 122 Squadron | | 19 C-47, 3 Arava | Detachment equipped with Arava deployed for medical evacuation |
| No. 131 Squadron | | C-130E | Unit created during the war to accept 12 C-130Es delivered from US |
| 29th Air Base | Ophir | | CO Yaakov Nevo Base also known as Ras Nasrani |
| | | | Detachments from No. 107 Squadron |
| 30th Air Base | Palmachim | | CO Col Uri Talmor |
| No. 200 Squadron | | Model 124I | CO Lt Col Shlomo Nir Detachments deployed in northern and southern Israel |

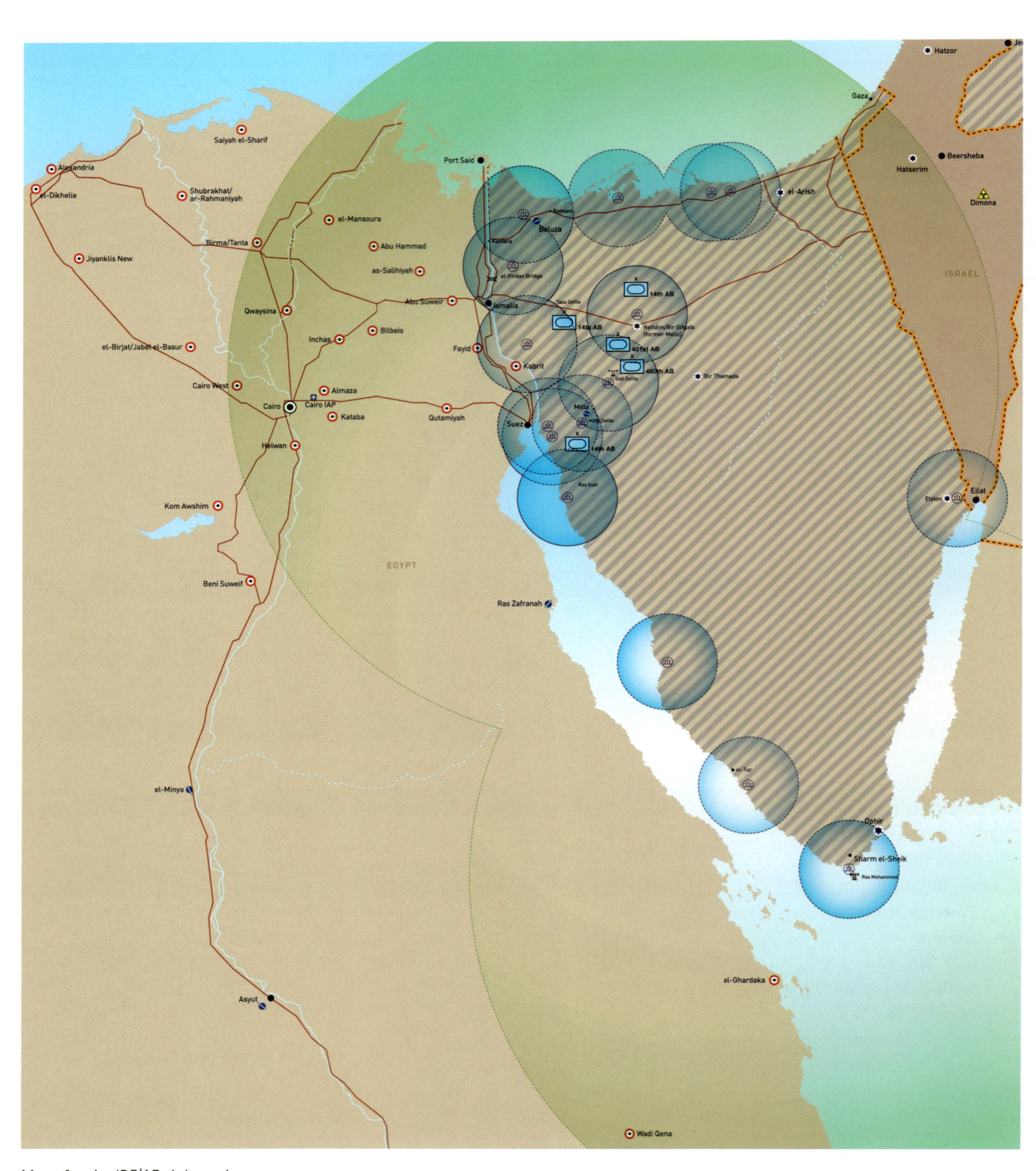

Map of major IDF/AF air bases in Israel and the Sinai. Also shown are known positions of early warning radars, HAWK SAM sites, and armour formations. (Map by James Lawrence)

Patience Before Purpose

The US-made MIM-23 HAWK SAM system (seen here) was de-facto the most advanced in the Middle East. The significantly improved MIM-23B Improved-HAWK was available in the US by October 1973, but it remains unknown if any were delivered to Israel in time to see combat during that war.
(IDF)

Except for combat aircraft, the IDF/AF operated an integrated air defence system (IADS) too. Precise details about the equipment of this IADS remain largely unknown, but it is known to have been centred around four major radar stations and control centres, including one at Mount Meron (northern Israel), one near Mitzpe Ramon (Negev Desert), one near Refidim, and one on Mount Tsafra (southern Sinai). These early warning radar stations were supported by several mobile radars deployed as 'gap-fillers' – in order to cover various 'blind spots' caused by the terrain – and they fed their information to a similar number of major ground control stations, each of which was supported by additional forward command posts.

The centrepiece of this IADS were 12 battalions of MIM-23 HAWK SAMs (each containing one site) known to have been available as of early October 1973. Five of these were deployed in the Sinai as of 6 October, including one in the Baluza area, one on Gidi Defile, one at Abu Samara, one at Ras Sudr and one at Ophir air base. An additional MIM-23 battalion – perhaps a part of US emergency provisions during the coming war – was deployed to protect the HQ and a number of major ground bases near the Tasa Defile, sometime in mid-October 1973, and it occupied a position that was constructed in the late 1960s, but vacant at the start of the fighting.

A combination of Arab and Israeli sources indicates that three MIM-23 battalions were deployed in northern Israel as of early October 1973: one near Kfar Giladi, one near Tiberias, and one at Mount Meron. Furthermore, according to Egyptian sources (see Chapter 4 for details), an additional MIM-23 battalion was deployed on the Golan a few days after the start of fighting, which was not there before the war. The last two known MIM-23 battalions were deployed deeper inside Israel: one almost certainly for protection of the nuclear complex at Dimona, and another for protection of the Tel Aviv area. Reportedly, these units could call upon a stock of about 350 missiles.[39]

Except for SAMs, the IDF/AF and the IDF also operated a mix of Soviet-made S-60 and M1939 AAA (captured from Egypt and Syria in 1967), approximately 150 Bofors L/70 AAA of 40mm calibre, and an unknown number of 20mm TCM-20 AAA installed on halftracks. While the majority of towed AAA was deployed for the defence of installations in Israel and the main bases in the Sinai, two battalions equipped with TCM-20s – the 208th and the 209th – are known to have fought in the Sinai during the October War, while another battalion was assigned to the 66th Reserve Division, on the Golan.

1 Shazly, pp172 and p198. Notably, Moscow not only repeatedly postponed, but also conditioned delivery of mentioned systems on them remaining under control of Soviet advisors in Egypt. For example, although delivering 24 transporter-erector-launchers (TELs) and related R-17E surface-to-surface missiles and helping train and establish three battalions for the 65th Missile Brigade of the Egyptian Army, these had to remain under the control of Soviet advisors. (Except for that unit, the Egyptian Army already operated the 64th Missile Brigade, which included three battalions equipped with the 9K52 Luna-M surface-to-surface missile [ASCC codename FROG-7], 288 of which had been delivered by 1972, together with 24 TELs). Deliveries of MiG-21MFs were continued only sporadically, and in very small batches through the spring and summer of 1973. Finally, the actual contract for deliveries of MiG-23s was signed only in February 1973. With Egyptian pilots and ground personnel travelling to the USSR for conversion training in May and June of the same year, there was not enough time for them to participate in the October 1973 War. Similarly, the much-promised second batch of Su-20s reached Egypt only after the end of war, and then primarily served as attrition replacement.

2 Andrey Marchenko, 'Syrian Mission', *Express Novosti*, volume 39 (319), 26 September–2 October 2003; this and all subsequent quotations from Vagin are based on a translation of the same interview.

3 'Adad', retired SyAAF Su-7 pilot, interview, May 1996 (name changed by the authors for reasons of his own safety and that of his family).

4 It is possible that not all of SyAAF pilots shot down during the Battle Day of 21 November were Syrians. According to former technician of the Hungarian Air Force and researcher Robert Szombati (interview, May 2006), there was at least one Soviet MiG-21 instructor pilot killed 'sometimes in late 1972' while flying MiG-21s in Syria. This was Captain Nikolay Pavliscuk, who is known to have served as instructor at Primorsko Atharsk AB between sometimes in 1970 and spring of 1972, and worked with several Hungarian Air Force pilots that underwent various courses there.

5 Vagin's figures are only valid because North Vietnamese MiG-21-pilots have achieved nearly all of their kills with help of R-3S. They not only operated few cannon-armed MiG-21F-13s early during the war, and mostly flew gun-less MiG-21-variants, but seldom attempted to engage with cannons too. Furthermore, Vagin certainly neither took into account that the North Vietnamese scored nearly all of their victories against non-maneuvering US aircraft, i.e. against targets 'suitable' for deployment of the R-3S, or that – even then – large numbers of missiles fired by the North Vietnamese failed to hit their targets (or outright malfunctioned). Another point to consider was the fact that the North Vietnamese MiG-21 pilots did their best to avoid entering dogfights, primarily through executing so-called 'slash' (or 'zoom and boom') attacks: generally, they tended to approach their American opponents from the rear hemisphere, at supersonic speeds, then fire R-3S missiles and disengage by diving to low altitude. Finally, although Hanoi never published specific data about R-3S-related experiences, US pilots involved in air combats against North Vietnamese MiG-21s did report a large number of missiles that missed – or failed on launch. For authoritative discussion of North Vietnamese weapons results see Mitchel, *Clashes*, pp159. Citing US intelligence reports, Mitchel concluded that the North Vietnamese were experiencing similar problems with their air-to-air missiles like Americans, and that the R-3S' in their service achieved a success ratio of about 13% at best (meaning that on average, out of 100 missiles fired in combat, no less but 87 either malfunctioned or missed their targets). Furthermore, Mitchel went as far as to conclude that actual figures were probably worse than reported, because the numbers of reported firings were only those observed by Americans: how many of North Vietnamese firing attempts were never seen by US aircrews remains unknown.

6 Burr, W., The October War and the U.S. Policy, The National Security Archive, 7 October 2003

7 Asher et all, pp62; contrary to Asher, Palit – and all of interviewed SyAAF officers, as well as EAF officers deployed in Syria during the October 1973 War – stress that the High Command SyAAF never planned to curtail its operations, or something like 'put its assets in strategic reserve', as so often claimed by various

Israeli and Western sources. On the contrary, and as described in following chapters, the SyAAF flew many more attack sorties during the war, than the EAF.

8   Shazly, pp30–37.
9   *Military Balance* 1971-72, IISS; O'Ballance, *No Victor, no Vanquished*, pp280 and others.
10  Shazly, on pp21 cites that, [in] '…mid-1971…Soviets operated around 30 percent of our MiG-21s'. Considering that the VVS deployed around 40 MiG-21SMs and Rs to Egypt in 1970, the calculation of other variants operated by the EAF as of that time is obvious.
11  The Repair Depot at Almaza was the main facility of this kind in Egypt as of that time, and responsible not only for MiG-15s and MiG-17s, but also transport aircraft and helicopters. Other similar facilities were available at Beni Suweif (Tu-16s), Cairo West (Il-28s), Inchas (MiG-21s) and Jiancalis (Su-7s).
12  Similarly, it appears that various Russian reports about deployments of Egyptian Mi-4s armed with Malyutka ATGMs belong to realms of fantasy.
13  Naji, interview to Group 73, October 2012; unless otherwise stated, this and all other quotations from Naji are based on transcriptions of the same interview.
14  Okasha, interview to Group 73, May 2008 & November 2012; unless otherwise stated, this and all other quotations from Okasha are based on transcriptions of the same interviews.
15  For precise insight – including the list of construction numbers – of L-29s delivered to Egypt, see *Volume 4*, Appendix I/B.
16  As described in Volume 4, in 1970 the Egyptians and Libyans converted the former Royal Air Force el-Adem, south of Tobruq, vacated by the RAF in early 1970, to a training centre. Re-named as Gamal Abdel Nasser Air Base (GANAB), this facility was then used by large numbers of Egyptian and Libyan aviators, supported by few Soviet and Pakistani instructors, for training in air-to-ground and air-to-air operations with MiG-15UTIs and few MiG-21UMs, as well as Libyan Mirages. Nearly all of EAF combat squadrons underwent combat training tours at GANAB by October 1973. Abdel Aziz al-Marsa provided his recollection about one of such deployments as follows:

*In spring 1972, our squadron received a batch of 'new' MiG-17s from Soviet Union and then moved to Qwaysina AB. Our new mounts were first modified with additional hardpoints for carriage of bombs up to calibre 250kg underneath the fuselage. With two such weapons and extrernal fuel tanks, the range of our aircraft at high altitude was around 340 kilometres, and around 230km at medium altitude. However, if we operated at low altitudes, as usually, where fuel consumption was much higher, our range with such load was down to only 140 kilometres….*

As soon as our aircraft were ready, we deployed to GANAB in Libya, for additional training. We returned to Egypt only in late September 1973 and I was given a vacation. By the time I returned to my unit, this was already stationed at Salihiyah AB, close to the Suez Canal, and therefore I asked our Deputy Brigade CO, Lt Col Hassan Fahmy, for permission to fly training sorties and refresh my training from Libya.

17  Gabr Ali Gabr was attached to the Egyptian Navy HQ in Alexandria since 1972, and in charge of a 'Naval Operation Command', which could call upon a Su-7-squadron specially trained for naval cooperation work. Exact designation of the unit in question remains unclear, but it is known that it was based at Jiancalis AB and might have been the Su-7 OTU. Furthermore, Gabr could call upon the Tu-16s from Bein Sueif AB.
18  Waleed Arafat, 'Syrian Military Chief Reveals the Role of Algerians on the Syrian Front', *al-Rahal* magazine (in Arabic), 14 June 2008; as the article in question reveals, Boumedienne pushed Atassi to launch a full-scale attack on Israel on 5 June 1967, supposedly demanding attacks on 'all major air force and army bases, chemical plants and the building of the Knesset in Tel Aviv', in order to reduce Israeli pressure upon Egypt. When Atassi showed himself reluctant, Boumedienne suggested deployment of 'the entire Algerian Air Force' to Syria, in order to fly these attacks. Obviously, Syria rejected this idea, and Boumedienne did not forgive Atassi for 'abandoning Nasser and Egypt and leaving Golan to the mercy of Zionists.'
19  O'Ballance, pp285

20  Data from unofficial Syrian sources (cited above and below), and US intelligence (aforementioned former DIA analyst, interviewed October 2001) is particularly conflicting in regards of the No. 5 Squadron SyAAF for period 1972-1973. According to one version, this unit became the premier interceptor outfit, equipped with MiG-21MFs. Its pilots should have claimed most of aerial victories considered as 'confirmed' during the October 1973 War. US intelligence sources generally support this version. However, other unofficial Syrian sources cite the No. 5 Squadron as one of units flying MiG-17s, and are strongly supported by Egyptian and Iraqi sources (Brig Ahmad Sadik) in this regards. The authors tend to trust the later variant primarily because Syrian and US intelligence sources also cited presence of foreign – including East German and even one British mercenary – pilots in some of SyAAF units during October 1973 War. This is not only unlikely to have been the case, but stands in strong contrast to accounts of all other Syrian, Egyptian, Iraqi, and even Hungarian sources that are known to have been in Syria at that time. Furthermore, official East German documentation that became available following the collapse of 1989, denied the presence of anything but few intelligence officers in Syria as of 1973.

21  Mohammad Marawy, interview, June 2005.

22  Lion Schlein, 'Colonel Tabet', *Journal of Israeli Air Force*, December 1999.

23  Babich, MiG-21 vs Mirage III.

24  O'Ballance, pp42; similar observations were provided by almost all of interviewed SyAAF pilots.

25  Shazly, *Return to The Sinai*, pp19-20.

26  Babich, MiG-21 vs Mirage III.

27  Palit, p156.

28  Magdy el-Wakeel, interviews with David Nicolle (March 2003) and Group 73 (November 2011); this and all other quotations from Magdy Wakeel are based on transcription of the same interivews.

29  Interview with former DIA analyst, provided on condition of anonymity, October 2001 & with various Egyptian participations of operations in this part of Egypt (see Chapter 5 for details).

30  According to Shazly, p21, '...half the engineers in Egypt were in the armed forces, most of them working on our air defences and the associated electronics, although not necessarily manning the equipment'.

31  Robert Hotz (ed.) Both Sides of the Suez – Airpower in Mideast, *Aviation Week & Space Technology*, 1975, p20.

32  Taher Zaki remained in the ADC HQ throughout the October War. Subsequently he asked for permission to retire, but President Sadat turned this request down, and ordered him to stay until the end of the Israeli occupation of the Sinai. Eventually, the former Spitfire pilot, and one of the first Egyptian pilots qualified to fly MiG-15s in 1955, continued serving until the day after the return of central Sinai under Egyptian control ('Taba Agreement') and then retired.

33  Content of this sub-chapter is primarily based on interview with retired a SyAADF officer, provided on condition of anonymity, August 2004.

34  For details on clandestine deliveries of Mirage 5s from France, see Volume 4. Notable is that – privately – the IDF veterans do not recall the use of the designation 'Nesher' (i.e. 'Nesher S' for single- and 'Nesher T' for two-seaters) as of October 1973: the type was named for what it was, a Mirage 5. The new designation should have appeared only later during the 1970s, and is – together with insistence on made by Israeli Aircraft Industries – foremost apparent in various popular printed publications.

35  Originally designed by Israelis, the IAI Arava experienced an ominous start, with the first prototype crashing due to miscalculations of its construction. It took a complete re-design of internal structure by expert US aircraft designer Gene Salvay, to make Arava an operationally-feasible aircraft. For details see Joe Mizrahi, 'The Designer of the B-1 Bomber's Airframe', *Wings*, volume 30, number 4, August 2000.

36  Authors are presently attempting to cross-examine reports related to deliveries of MiG-21Ms equipped with RP-22 radars and R-3R SARH AAMs by the USSR to Egypt before the October 1973 War, as reported in Volume 4. While there are massive doubts over this issue and most of East European sources insist that RP-22s

and R-3Rs were exported only with MiG-21bis variant (starting in mid-1977), several narratives by Egyptian MiG-21 pilots are including strong indication of R-3R's presence.

37  For details on expenditure of hundreds of US-made CBUs by IDF/AF units equipped with A-4 Skyhawks alone, see Aloni, *Israeli A-4 Skyhawk Units in Combat* and Weiss et all, *McDonnell Douglas A-4 Skyhawk*.
38  The WDNS-391 TAAL-Crystal was a navigation platform developed especially for Israeli A-4Hs, most of avionics of which was installed in a 'hump' behind the cockpit.
39  Except for Arab sources (see Fikry el-Gindy's recollections in Chapter 4), remaining information about deployment of Israeli MIM-23 HAWK SAM sites provided here was submitted by retired IDF/AF officer that used to serve with one of battalions during October 1973 War. The source provided an interview on condition of anonymity and the use of documentation officially released by Israeli Censorship only, in September 2009; unless stated otherwise, all information about activity of Israeli HAWK SAM sites during this war as provided in this book is based on transcriptions of interview with the same source.

# Chapter 3

# SEEKING REVENGE

As well as Syria's Battle Days, sporadic clashes also occurred between Egypt and Israel, in 1972, although President Sadat continuously extended the ceasefire from August 1970, every three months. However, in general, tensions between the Arabs and Israel decreased during 1973, not only because Syria was preoccupied with its own rearmament, but because relations between Assad's administration and the Palestinian Liberation Organisation (PLO) began to cool. Eventually, the PLO moved its HQ to Lebanon. A few months later, on 13 September 1973, a major air battle took place off the Syrian and Lebanese coast, in the course of which Israel claimed to have shot down 12 or even 13 SyAAF MiG-21s, in exchange for one of their own fighters. With the benefit of hindsight, some Israeli commentators have tried to compare the situation prior to the outbreak of the October 1973 War with that prior to the outbreak of the June 1967 War, since major air combats over Syria preceeded both wars. Supposedly, the air battle on 13 September should therefore have been understood as a 'warning signal' for politicians in Tel Aviv. However, as the following account of what was happening in Egypt, Israel and Syria during the following weeks will show, such efforts are actually futile: the Syrian decision to join Egypt and prepare a surprise attack on Israel was already confirmed, and this attack would have taken place with or without that air battle.

From the Israeli standpoint as of September–October 1973, there was no reason for their military and political leaders to consider the clash as any kind of 'signal'. A complicated Arab campaign of military deception had lured them into complacency: none of the information collected by their intelligence caused any sort of alert. On the contrary, the Israelis successfully convinced themselves that the Arabs were still years away from reaching the level of preparedness that would give them a hope of matching the IDF, and the IDF/AF in particular. Furthermore, even once it became clear that the Arabs were about to attack, during the last few days before the war, the US administration warned Israel from opening hostilities through any kind of pre-emptive military action. Therefore, the Arab militaries completed their preparations and then entered the countdown to the war entirely undisturbed.

Exactly how the Egyptian and Syrian air arms entered this war remains largely unknown. Although dozens of accounts of the October 1973 War have been published in the last 40 years, almost without exception, all concentrate exclusively on the Israeli side of the opening hours of that conflict. While this is understandable considering the shock the attack caused in Israel, there is not a single in-depth study of the Arab experiences, or an independent examination of losses on both sides. With this in mind, this chapter is primarily related to unravelling all the relevant developments, and detailing the EAF and SyAAF, as well as IDF/AF, operations during the first day of hostilities.

MiG-21PFS serial number 8025 was operated by No. 44 or 47 Squadron EAF during 1973–1975, and is representative of the camouflage pattern and markings applied on the aircraft flown by Ahmed Kamal el-Mansoury on 13 February 1973.
(Albert Grandolini Collection)

El-Mansoury seen later during his carrier, after conversion to MiG-21MF. Notable is the usual, 'Egyptian-style' configuration of the plane, including 'only' two R-3S missiles and two drop tanks.
(el-Mansoury Collection)

## Irritating Clashes

Despite standing orders – reinforced by Shazly – not to become involved in any unplanned combat operations, between June 1972 and October 1973 the Egyptian – and subsequently the Syrian – air arms did engage with IDF/AF fighter-bombers on a number of occasions. From the standpoint of leading Arab officers, such clashes were an irritation: they were costly in terms of pilots and aircraft, and sapped the strength of their forces at a time in which they were gearing up for a major war. The situation was all the more frustrating because a few of these air combats were caused exclusively by the aggressiveness of the Arab pilots involved, these now full of self-confidence after years of intensive training and combat operations. In his memoirs, Shazly later recalled three little-known incidents, more precise details of which remain unknown:

'On 13 June 1972, two enemy Phantoms penetrated our airspace in the area of Ras el-Esh (where there were no SAMs). Two of our MiG-21s took off from Mansourah air base and pursued the Phantoms out to the sea, only to be ambushed by eight others. (I was informed afterwards that by the time the duty controller had spotted the impending ambush on his radar, it was too late to warn our pilots.) Six other MiGs were scrambled, but when they arrived the skies were empty... On 10 October 1972, intruders approached the canal, this time in formation. Apparently, the enemy was trying new electronic measures to jam our detection radars during their approach and to jam our SAM fire-control radars while they launched their own air-to-ground missiles. Of the two missiles we launched, one hit. I felt sorry for the Israeli pilot, sacrificed for a technical exercise... At 16.12 on 28 June 1973, we shot down another Israeli aircraft...'

As usual, Israel denied suffering any kind of losses in any of these cases. Apparently unknown to Shazly was the fact that another incident where his order was disobeyed by EAF pilots occurred on 13 February 1973, when the IDF/AF sent two Mirage IIIRJs to fly a reconnaissance over el-Mansourah airfield. The ADC scrambled four MiG-21s, but the Egyptian GCI made a mistake and all interceptors ended several kilometres behind the Israelis, who were dashing away at maximum speed and very high altitude. Meanwhile, a pair of MiG-21PFS fighters was scrambled from Inchas to inter-

## Seeking Revenge

*A still from the gun-camera film of el-Mansoury's MiG-21PFS.[1] It shows an Israeli Phantom in a left turn, and a nose-up attitude. The gunsight pattern and the F-4 are blurred due to the stress caused by the MiG manoeuvring to obtain this favourable position, almost in the same plane as the target, and with the crosshairs in front of the target (the so-called 'lead'). The lead was necessary to confirm that the projectiles would reach the aiming point at the same time as the Phantom. The range to the target was around 400m (1,312ft). The 'dead zone' of the RP-21 radar was around 300m (984ft), which meant that in this case the MiG pilot would be firing his gun without a radar lock; this would explain the lack of liquid-crystal symbology – the circular, white eight-pointed star pattern). The pilot wold have led the target far enough, then fired and left the F-4 to fly through his cannon burst, which is an old procedure, used by experienced pilots who knew (from training, for example) where and how to aim, and how much to lead in front of the target, depending on the particular range, speed and relative motion of the target. (el-Mansoury Collection)*

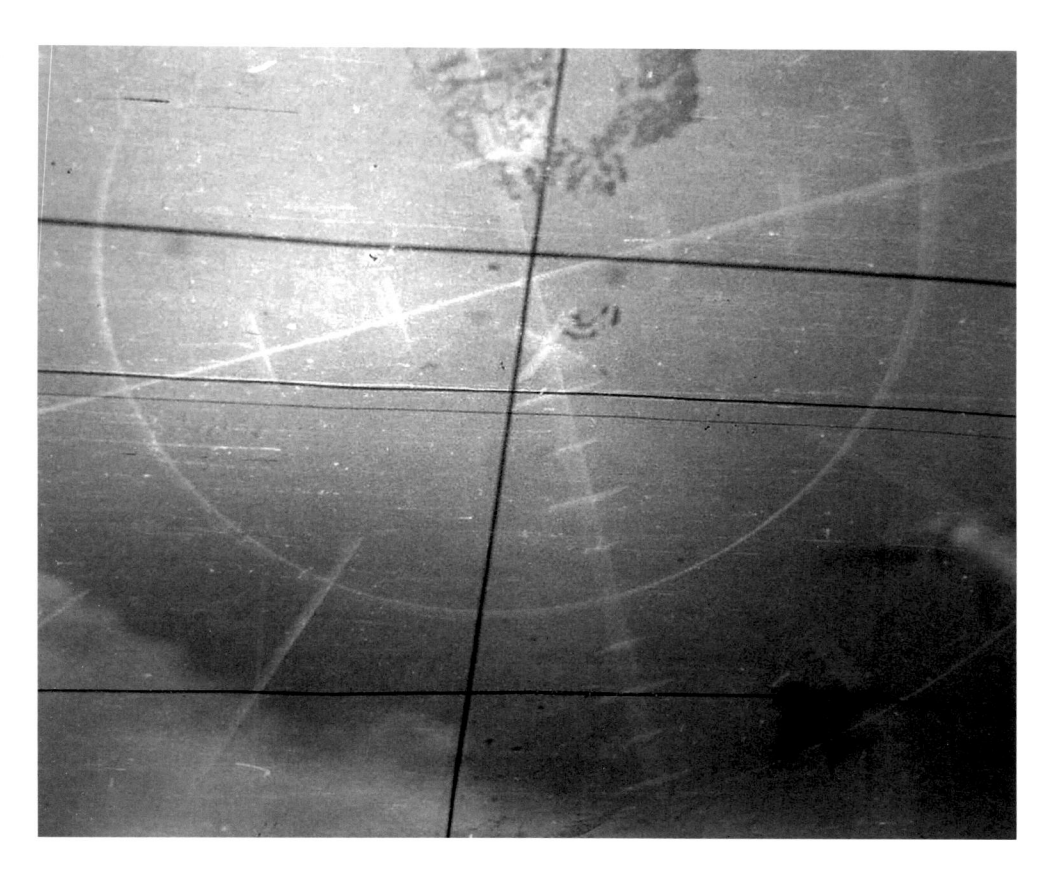

cept another pair of Phantoms that was approaching over the Gulf of Suez of Suez, as recalled by Ahmed Kamal el-Mansoury ('Jaguar Leader' during this sortie):

*'I was under way in MiG-21PFS serial number 8045, with 1st Lt Hassan Luftey as wingman. The GCI followed Shazly's order and tried hard to avoid letting us engage. We misled them, so the GCI asked, 'Who is flying over the Gulf?' He became really mad when he discovered we were about to engage. We sighted two reconnaissance Phantoms, then their protection of four F-4Es. We outmanoeuvred them easily and I attacked one Phantom and fired two missiles at it, but was not sure if they hit. I had to manoeuvre with the other [F-4E], and was trying to stay close to him, in order to deny the opportunity for a missile shot. This necessitated expertise in low-speed manoeuvring. The engagement lasted for 13 minutes, and then we ran out of fuel. I managed to return to Inchas on the last drops. Sadly, Luftey crashed and was killed.'*

Curiously, introducing a 'new pattern' in crediting its pilots with victories in air combats against Arab fighters, the IDF/AF subsequently 'confirmed' Luftey's loss to one its F-4 crews – something Israel never did in any known cases where its own pilots ran out of fuel after air battles with Arab interceptors. The reason for this decision remains unknown, but might have been based on little more than a report that one of the MiG-21s involved failed to return to its base. Certain is only that Luftey crashed well away from the scene of the engagement, while the pilot was trying to land his otherwise perfectly intact aircraft on a highway east of Abu Suweir, not because of direct action by any IDF/AF pilots.

Another still from the same film, indicating that the F-4 had only one drop tank, on the starboard side (the port outboard station is empty, with even the missile rail missing). The MiG was in a good position for opening fire with cannon, as it would be shooting in front of the Phantom with a cannon. However, el-Mansoury's MiG-21PFS was not equipped with any. Nevertheless, the port wingtip of the Phantom appears to have been damaged – either while releasing the missing drop tank or due to some kind combat damage, perhaps caused by one of Mansoury's missiles. White lines on this image belong to the so-called SETKA (Russian for 'pattern' or 'fixed grid'). The X on the sight pattern indicates the seeker boresight position of the R-3S missiles. The cannon would be boresighted to the spot where there are two large white crosses – slightly above the X. Obviously, the cannon was not selected (otherwise the symbology would be visible, as a six-sided 'diamond'). (el-Mansoury Collection)

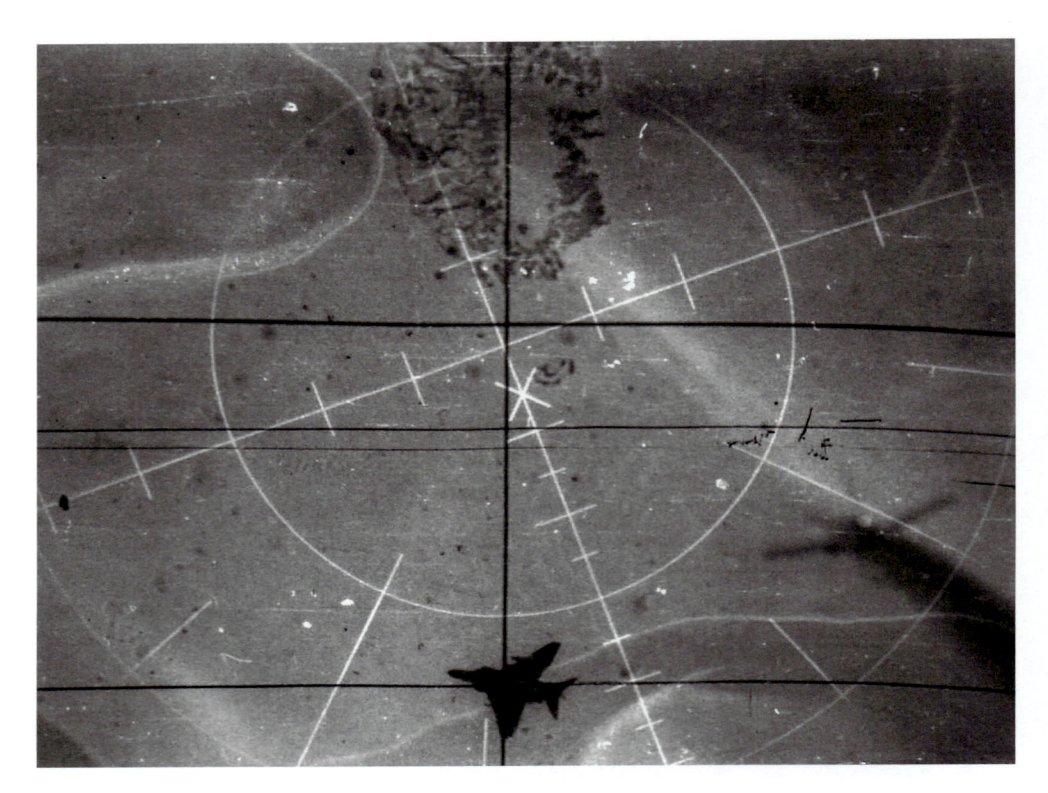

## Air Battle of Tartous

In other cases, the Arab air arms were forced to engage Israeli reconnaissance aircraft in order to prevent them from taking photographs of developments that clearly indicated preparations for the next war with Israel. The last major shipment of Soviet weapons for Syria arrived in the ports of Lattakia and Tartous in mid-September 1973, and Israel promptly dispatched its reconnaissance fighters to take photographs of the unloading process, in order to discover what type of equipment had been delivered. When the 'patrol' of IDF/AF reconnaissance aircraft approached the Syrian coast high over the Mediterranean, around 14.00 on 13 September 1973, followed by Phantoms and additional Mirages that remained at very low altitude, the High Command in Damascus put the SyAAF on alert, but ordered the SyAADF to stay out of action: there was a necessity to maintain secrecy over its new equipment and capabilities.

Four MiG-21PFMs were scrambled from Hama, followed by four scrambled from Abu ad-Duhor. Once over the coast the flight led by Capt Adeeb el-Gar bounced the Israelis. The Israeli reconnaissance fighters – apparently identified as 'Phantoms' by the Syrians – turned away, engaged afterburners and attempted to flee in a southerly direction. El-Gar was the first to reach a favourable position and he fired two missiles, one of which detonated close to its target, supposedly causing it to crash into the sea. At that moment, a flight of Mirages pounced on the Syrian formation from below, shot down two MiGs and forced el-Gar and his wingman to hastily withdraw.

Led by Capt Magar, the second flight of MiG-21PFMs engaged the Israelis off the coast near Tartus. Magar reported visual contact with MiGs and Mirages involved in

Seeking Revenge

A very rare photograph of two SyAAF MiG-21s from early 1973. The aircraft in front is a MiG-21PFM, while that in the rear is a MiG-21PFS. It seems that their camouflage colours were applied in the form of wide stripes of olive drab over orange, reaching low down along the sides. This photograph also indicates that both aircraft had roundels applied on the lower surfaces of each wing. (David Nicolle Collection)

a dogfight, but was then jumped by four Mirages himself. Two MiGs, including that flown by the formation leader, were shot down by several Israeli missiles fired at them. The remaining two Syrian jets engaged the Israelis in a dogfight and fired several R-3S missiles before one of the Syrians was shot down. The fourth Syrian pilot, Capt Esaam Hallaq, then destroyed a Mirage, the pilot of which ejected and came down in the sea off the Lebanese coast, about 600m (1,969ft) away from one of the downed Syrian pilots. Israel confirmed the loss of a Nesher interceptor, the pilot of which *'was forced to abandon his plane when the engine caught fire'*, but stressed the shooting down of nine Syrian jets in the first phase of this air battle although only eight were engaged.[2]

When the IDF/AF despatched helicopters to recover its downed pilot – and the downed Syrian nearby – additional sections of Phantoms and Mirages approached the area and the SyAAF reacted by scrambling another flight of MiG-21s, led by el-Gar on his second mission of the day. Vectored to intercept the Israeli helicopter, the Syrian flight was jumped by Israeli fighters and lost three MiG-21s, though not before el-Gar claimed another Phantom as shot down.

Eventually, Israel claimed 12 kills and one 'probable' in exchange for one loss on that day. The Israeli rescue helicopter picked up the downed Israeli pilot from the sea, and one of the Syrians. Furthermore, the IDF/AF reconnaissance aircraft apparently completed their mission, but if this was the case, they appear to have failed to bring back any useful information. For its part, the SyAAF admitted five losses, but claimed eight Israeli aircraft destroyed, including two F-4Es downed by Capt el-Gar, who was subsequently promoted and (albeit after the October 1973 War) awarded the Hero of the Syria Medal for *'destroying two Phantoms in air combat over Beirut.'*

While some Israeli sources later considered this clash as an ignored indicator of the coming war, SyAAF pilots neither drew incorrect conclusions nor gave themselves any illusions. As one of them later recalled, the chances of such air battles ending without heavy losses to the MiG-21s were minimal; the actual issue was how much damage the Syrians could cause to their opponents:

*'The Israelis always flew such missions in formations of at least four, sometimes more. We called these four formations the bait, momentum, boxer and cover. The bait formation usually consisted of only two aircraft, reconnaissance variants of the Mirage or RF-4Es. Momentum formation usually consisted of Mirage IIIs that flew behind the bait formation, outside the visual range and below our radar horizon. They were always the first to engage us in air combat and 'build the momentum'. The boxer formation was the one that delivered the main blow: it usually consisted of Phantoms and would single out and attack our scattered pilots while these were busy dogfighting Mirages, or attack any other of our formations that were sent as reinforcements. Sometimes it would start shooting Sparrow missiles from as far as 15km [9.3 miles] away, or it would suddenly appear 'out of nowhere', hit us with Sidewinders and then disappear. Finally, their cover formation served the purpose of covering all the others once they would get low on fuel and have to disengage. With this combination, the enemy could keep two to three squadrons of MiG-21s busy with just 12 of their aircraft. No matter how many formations our control brought in, they only had one chance of success: to take one of the Israelis by surprise early on. Once the dogfighting started, the chance of successfully deploying our missiles was non-existing. We matched them in maneuvering, but our missiles did not match theirs. That meant that the side that ran out of fuel first was certain*

After the October 1973 War with Israel, President Hafez al-Assad decorated Adib el-Gar with the 'Hero of Syrian Arab Republic' medal (comparable with 'Hero of the Soviet Union' in the former USSR or 'Victoria Cross' in Great Britain'), for shooting down two Phantoms during an air combat over Beirut'.
(via Amr Safadi)

This Syrian MiG-21PFM with serial number 640 was shot down in air combat with the Israelis on 13 September 1973 and crashed near Beirut in Lebanon. At least three SyAAF pilots are known to have ejected over that country during this air battle: all suffered minor injuries and were subsequently returned to Syria.
(Albert Grandolini Collection)

*to suffer losses. Because Mirages and Phantoms had a longer endurance than MiGs, and because Phantoms carried eight missiles and a gun, they could remain engaged much longer than we could. Our heavy losses were unavoidable.'*

## Mythical 'Concept'[3]

A lot has been researched, written and published – especially in Israel and the US, but also in Egypt – about how the Arabs managed to achieve strategic surprise against Israel, on 6 October 1973. This issue became the centrepiece of an extensive, official investigation run by Israel immediately after the war (the Agranat Commission), and there is also little doubt that this topic could easily fill several volumes of this size. As surprising as it might sound – foremost for most Arab readers (and especially contemporary Arab military commanders) – it seems that the issue of air superiority formed the actual core of the problem, at least in the opinion of crucial Israeli intelligence and military officers.

The Air Battle of Tartous (as this clash subsequently became known in Syria) did not cause too much concern in Israel. It rather confirmed the superiority of the IDF/AF to its major protagonists. Furthermore, during the following days Israel was proccuppied with entirely different issues. On 28 September, an Austrian-based Palestinian terror group hijacked a train carrying Jewish emigrants from the Soviet Union, and demanded the closure of Schönau Castle near Vienna, which was being used as a transit camp for Jews leaving the USSR. Despite Israeli Prime Minister Golda Meir's attempt to intervene in Vienna, the Austrian government swiftly agreed (causing much bitterness and anger in Israel). Not only did this affair draw the attention of the Israeli public during the following days, but it also made increasing concentrations of Egyptian and Syrian troops along ceasefire lines with Israel appear to be genuine 'defensive measures', prompted by concerns of the usual Israeli revenge through military means.

After supposedly 'destroying' the Arab air forces, and certainly destroying most of the Egyptian, as well as large parts of the Jordanian and Syrian armies during the June 1967 War, and after concluding that it had defeated the Egyptian Air Force during the War of Attrition, Israel became supremely confident.[4] During 1971 and 1972, Israeli intelligence assessed that the Arabs would need up to 10 years to rebuild their air power to a level where this could match that of the IDF/AF. Over time, not only the Israeli public, but also leading Israeli military commanders and politicians succumbed to this belief. Information provided by their intelligence about the Egyptian insistence on obtaining the capability to launch a massive strike against Israeli air bases, such as that flown by the IDF/AF on 5 June 1967, served only to reinforce their misconception.[5] Israel became confident that, if the Arabs ever attacked them again, they would defeat them more soundly than ever before. Israel also began to consider the issue of air superiority as so crucial, that the fundamental premise for any possible Arab attack on Israel became obvious: Egypt wanted to regain the Sinai, but would attack Israel only if it could obtain the ability to at least partially neutralise the IDF/AF (preferably on the ground, by attacks on its bases) and attack objectives in Israel with the help of MiG-23 and MiG-25 fighters; Syria would never attack Israel on its own, without Egyptian support; finally, the Arabs would only wage a war if they could achieve strategic balance and have a chance of inflicting a military defeat upon Israel.

The Israeli ELINT/SIGINT-gathering installation at Tel Faris, as seen from the Israeli (western) side of the ceasefire line on the occupied Golan Heights, in June 1991. (David Nicolle)

Thus came into being what is now known as 'The Concept' in Israel: the idea that the IDF/AF was so clearly superior to the Arab air forces that the chance of the Arabs attempting to attack Israel for a number of years was next to non-existent. Should the Arabs attempt an attack, however, Israel expected its intelligence services to remain capable of closely monitoring the work and development of enemy militaries, and in this fashion precisely predict the Arab ability to wage a war and provide a timely warning for the IDF to mobilise.

With hindsight, it is easy to conclude that – as the surprise the Arabs achieved with their attack of 6 October 1973 was to show – The Concept was based on a number of multi-facetted, yet fundamental mistakes, and no little prejudice. Although the Directorate of Military Intelligence IDF – colloquially known under its abbreviation as 'Aman' – was almost entirely aware of the Arab war plans, and the fact that the Egyptian Army possessed the necessary strength and equipment to cross the Suez Canal, because of the premises described above, it concluded that the Arabs would not go to war for several years longer. Furthermore, not only Aman but also other branches of Israeli intelligence failed to understand the new appearance and importance of Egyptian and Syrian IADS: even days after the war started, Israel remained unable to understand that its preoccupation with the projection of air superiority on to the Egyptian and Syrian skies was countered by the Arabs being content to merely negate Israeli control of the skies, rather than to dominate the skies. Before the war, the majority of Israeli strategists and analysts also failed to appreciate what a difficult, combined-arms effort would be required to suppress the Egyptian and Syrian air defences. This can be seen from a number of pre-war statements by various IDF spokespersons, the essence of which was:

*'We are convinced we have the full answer to* [the] *missiles. In July 1970, we didn't have it. Now there will be no serious problems. There will be losses, but smaller than those we sustained on the eve of the ceasefire* [that ended the War of Attrition; authors' note]. *This should be proven within the first two or three hours of war. We will overcome the whole system within two or three days.'*[6]

Much of this Israeli overconfidence was not only based on the usual means of intelligence gathering, such as extensive networks of well-positioned agents and informers in various Arab states (so called HUMINT), but in particular upon elaborate operations by the IDF's General Staff Reconnaissance Unit (Sayeret Matkal) in conjunction with Unit 848 (IDF Intelligence Corps' Central Collection Unit, which later evolved into Unit 8200 as it is known today). These operations related to the tapping of underground telephone and telegraph cables in Egypt and Syria, and eavesdropping on all other Arab means of communication.

Crucial for these espionage operations were battery-supported devices planted on telephone cables in all neighbouring countries – variously referred to as 'the special sources', 'the special means of collection', 'suspenders' or even 'Israel's insurance policy'. These enabled Israel to hear not only what was said over the telephone and telegraph lines but, supposedly, also to eavesdrop on conversations in the rooms where the telephone and telex consoles were located. At least as important was the network of observation posts (OPs) – stretching from 'Mount Hermon' (as Israel names Jebel Sheikh in the northern Golan Heights), to Umm Qashiba in the Sinai – equipped with some of the most advanced systems for electronic intelligence gathering (ELINT) and signals intelligence gathering (SIGINT) available. Indeed, constructed in 1969, the installation at Umm Qashiba – a 723m (2,372ft) hill a few kilometres north of the Gidi Defile – was a classic example of such installations. It was equipped with an early warning radar station (operated by Unit 511), tactical headquarters, and foremost an extensive electronic warfare suite equipped with receivers for data fed by acoustic, magnetic and seismic sensors deployed along the Suez Canal (Unit 545), and a small helicopter pad.

Means of electronic intelligence collection deployed at such posts proved invaluable during earlier conflicts and, in the 'worst case', were expected to provide Israel with at least 48 hours' advance warning of an Arab attack. In fact, the Israelis became so over-reliant upon them, that they never came to the idea that the Arabs might 'numb' their superior intelligence and secure strategic surprise through an elaborate deception campaign on international plan, and – foremost – frequent, large-scale military exercises.

Another Israeli ELINT/SIGINT observation post on one of the hills overlooking Qunaitra, as seen in August 1984. The IDF is heavily reliant upon such installations for a variety purposes, from providing advance warning about enemy intentions to planning its own combat operations. (David Nicolle)

## Don't Pre-empt

The military element of the Arab deception during 1973 was actually limited, although it proved to be another key feature. It consisted of the mobilisation and discharge of reservists, transport of bridging equipment and formations closer to the Canal under the guise of preparations for an exercise, shuting down and reopening of military academies, circulation of information about soldiers receiving permission to go on pilgrimage to Mecca, and creation of an 'idyllic' atmosphere along the Suez Canal.

Widely published reports in the Arab media concerning the relevant developments resulted in Israel receiving a number of signals that an Arab attack was imminent but, because of The Concept, this was misinterpreted as presenting no danger. The belief in The Concept was so strong that Israel even ignored a warning from King Hussein of Jordan – who was invited by Sadat and Assad to participate in the next war, but refused to do so – forwarded personally to Golda Meir, during Hussein's secret visit to Tel Aviv, on the night of 25 September 1973.[7]

Between 27 and 30 September, some Egyptian reserves were called up pending a week-long exercise along the Suez Canal, while the 5th, 7th and 9th Syrian Infantry Divisions completed their deployment along the ceasefire lines on the Golan. Although detecting large Syrian troop movements towards the border, as well as the cancellation of leave and the call-up of reservists in Syria, and despite corresponding warnings from the US, Israel considered this merely puzzling, rather than a threat.[8] Namely, Aman concluded that the Egyptian exercises were just that, while it 'knew' that Syria would not attack Israel without Egyptian support. Trusting the premises of The Concept, traditional Israeli ignorance of the fact that a lasting guarantee of security for Israel can only come from binding peace treaties that would reconcile the country with her neighbours, and the failure to understand Clausewitz's old postulate that 'war is the continuation of politics by other means', Israeli political leaders then unavoidably made a number of crucial mistakes. Because they made mistakes, the IDF/AF entered the coming war in an entirely unexpected fashion, resembling that of the Arab air rms on 5 June 1967: with unrealistic plans for offensive operations on hand, and forced to wait for the enemy to deliver the first blow.

It was only after Israel learned about the evacuation of the families of Soviet advisors from Egypt and Syria, during the evening of 4 October, that the situation began to look different, even though there was still no firm confirmation.[9] Even US intelligence was convinced that the probability of war was minimal – and this although a Lockheed EP-3 SIGINT-gathering aircraft of the US Navy's Patrol Squadron Two (VP-2), operating from Hellenikon in Greece, registered 'suspicious silence' while patrolling the northern coast of Egypt, on 5 October, as recalled by Lee Buchanan, its mission commander:

*'The most distinctive feature of that mission was the utter lack of electronic activity coming from Egypt. There was nothing radiating, absolutely nothing. When we called the squadron after the mission, we remarked on the complete dearth of activity'*.[10]

Actually, there was some activity: on the same day, a single MiG-17F was sent over the Sinai on two occasions, in order to provoke Israeli HAWK SAM sites into activity. This helped the crews of two Tu-16K-11-16 bombers equipped with Raisa systems to pinpoint their precise position – a measure necessary for aiming their KSR-11 missiles during the coming attack.[11]

What began to change the standpoint of the top Israeli leadership was a meeting between Mossad Director-General Zvi Zamir and Ashraf Marwan, Nasser's son-in-law with excellent connections to the top Egyptian leadership, in London, during the night of 5-6 October. In the course of that meeting, Marwan informed Zamir that an attack was imminent and would take place the next day at 18.00. Only now was Israel alerted. During the morning of 6 October, Meir met Israeli Minister of Defence and Chief of Staff IDF, General David Elazar, and Elazar advised the Air Force to make a pre-emptive strike on Syria. However, under pressure from the US Secretary of State, Henry Kissinger, and expecting that Israel could not be seriously hurt by allowing Arabs to strike first, Meir decided that Israel would not start the war, since otherwise the US would not provide assistance. Instead, a decision was taken to mobilise the entire IDF/AF and four armoured divisions and wait for the Arabs to attack.

The IDF/AF was put on alert and ordered to prepare a contingency plan for Operation Model 5, which envisaged the destruction of SyAADF SAM sites along the Golan Heights. When reports arrived of cloudy weather over the Golan, but also because it was preferable to suppress the activity of Syrian MiG-21 units and thus have a free hand to destroy the SAMs, a decision was taken to replace this with a plan named Operation Ramming, which envisaged the destruction of Syrian air bases. Operation Ramming was to see the involvement of all IDF/AF F-4E and A-4 squadrons and attacks on – among others – Khelkhleh, Damascus IAP, Dmeyr, Nassiriyah, Tsaykal and even Hamah air bases. Mid-way through the briefings for this operation, and as the ground crews were already in the process of refuelling and arming their aircraft, Meir's decision came down the chain of command: the plan for a pre-emptive strike was abandoned and the IDF/AF was ordered to stand down.

The cancellation of the attack on Syria caused no little consternation within the IDF/AF. However, the most confusing decisions came in reaction to intelligence received from Marwan Ashraf, according to whom the Arabs would attack only around 18.00. The IDF/AF was thus ordered to re-arm its fighters for air defence and be ready from around 15.00. Therefore, when the Arabs attacked, at around 14.00 Egyptian time, this came not only as a surprise, but almost a shock: not only was Israel slow to detect incoming Arab fighter-bombers on time, but also the re-armament process of IDF/AF fighter-bombers was only partially complete.

# Egyptian Countdown[12]

Meanwhile, the Arab militaries were completing their final preparations and were actually in the process of deploying for attack. Of course, the EAF and the SyAAF did not need to do much: most of their aircraft remained at their usual bases, and only some minor reshuffling of various squadrons took place during early October 1973.

On 1 October 1973 in Cairo, President Sadat conveyed his final set of instructions to the commanders of all branches of the Egyptian armed forces, explicitly stating that the strategic objective of the coming war was to smash Israel's defence doctrine by inflicting devastating losses and proving that the continued occupation of Egyptian territory would exact an intolerable price. The aim of the war was not the destruction of Israel, but a break in the diplomatic stalemate through a modest advance into the Sinai.[13]

Four days later Hosni Mubarak gathered all EAF air brigade commanders in a top-secret meeting, in order to inform them about the coming war and their tasks. Mubarak began this conference stressing confidentiality before continuing to explain that the war would start at 14.00 on 6 October 1973. He further asserted that, in order to maintain deception, all units were to continue their *'routine, peacetime exercises'* during the morning of 6 October; squadron commanders would be informed about the planned attack only on that same morning, and their pilots only during the noon-time briefing, slightly more than one hour before operation was to start. Conveying Sadat's and Shazly's messages, Mubarak explained that his commanders should expect a war of limited dimensions, primarily concentrated on crossing the Suez Canal and the establishment of bridgeheads, and that the launching of the next stage – the capture of

AM Hosni Moubarak, C-in-C EAF, seen while visiting the No. 36 Squadron, shortly before the October 1973 War. (Ahmad Keraidy Collection)

the passes – would be an entirely different type and phase of the campaign, which he did not expect would be ordered.

As the conference continued, Mubarak explained that the primary task of the EAF on the first day of the war was to execute the first, concentrated air strike against Israeli positions on the Sinai, between H-Hour minus 15 (minutes) and H-Hour plus 15. After that, all participating aircraft were to return to the western side of the Canal, and the ADC would power up its SAM shield. This first wave of the EAF air strike was planned to include a total of about 250 Tu-16s, MiG-17Fs, MiG-21MFs and Su-7s, the tasks of which included attacks on Israeli early warning sites, HAWK sites, airfields and command centres. Ninety additional MiG-17s, Su-7s and Iraqi Hunters were to hit other enemy ground bases and artillery positions. Around 40 MiG-21s were to provide top cover. Two hours after the start of the attack, between H-Hour plus 130 minutes and H-Hour plus 205 minutes, the EAF was to execute the second concentrated air strike. This time, participating aircraft were to fly along pre-determined corridors through the ADC coverage, in order to enable their positive identification. Except for aircraft that were to fly strikes against targets inside Israel, all aircraft were to be back over the western side of the canal within 30 minutes.[14] Exactly how many aircraft were to participate in the second wave remains unknown, but available information indicates that most of those involved in the first wave were to re-strike the same or similar targets again. Each air brigade commander received a thick file with all operational orders for specific units, together with related maps and reconnaissance photographs.

In accordance with Shazly's Order No. 41, Mubarak advised the ADC to expect at least 80 Israeli air strikes during the first afternoon of the war, primarily aimed at crossing points and carried out by *'two aircraft at night and four-plane formations in daylight'*.[15] No sooner was this conference over than Mubarak returned to his office and made a call to his counterpart in Libya, announcing his intention to pay an official visit to the Libyan Arab Air Force on the next day. Knowing the Israelis were listening to Egyptian telephone communications, the commander-in-chief of the EAF was insistent on maintaining deception until the last moment. Thus began the final countdown for the October 1973 War.

Samir Aziz Mikhail (second from right) and colleagues from No. 46 Squadron as seen at el-Mansoura air base shortly before the war. (Samir Aziz Mikhail Collection)

# Quiet Morning

Among the few EAF units to learn about the coming war in advance was Air Brigade 104, the pilots of which were gathered by their commander, Col Ahmed Nassr, on the evening of 5 October 1973, as recalled by Samir Aziz Mikhail:

*'Only pilots form Nos 44 and 46 Squadrons were present, because those from No. 42 Squadron were secretly transferred to Luxor. Our brigade CO told us that tomorrow there would be war, that he was perfectly comfortable with this, and then told us about our duties. After that briefing, I ordered one of our soldiers to pick up my wife from our house in el-Mansoura and bring her to Cairo.'*

During the morning hours of 6 October, MiG-21s from Air Brigade 104 were ordered into the air to continue the deception. They flew in the direction of Bilbeis at very low altitude, remaining below the horizon of the Israeli radar coverage. Once over Bilbeis, they climbed to high altitude, mimicking re-deployment of locally based aircraft away from the combat zone. The MiG-21 pilots involved were quite surprised by the order for this mission, but even more so to see fully bombed-up Su-7s on the tarmac of Bilbeis. Mikhail continued:

*'Around 11.00, they ordered us into an air combat manoeuvering training sortie, pitting pilots from No. 46 Squadron against those from No. 44 Squadron. We flew those sorties but understood they were not staged for training purposes: they were flown for the deception of the enemy.'*

The logbook of Brig Gen Abdel Moneim el-Shennawy – a veteran Su-7 pilot that meanwhile served as Deputy Chief of Staff and Fighter-Bomber Commander EAF – cites two sorties flown early on 6 October 1973, indicating that Su-7s from Bilbeis flew some training sorties that morning. Still assigned to No. 22 Squadron, the sole EAF unit flying MiG-21RFs, Mamdouh Heshmat was also airborne on the morning of 6 October:

*'Between 10.00 and 11.00 I flew a reconnaissance sortie from Salihiyah along the Suez Canal – for two reasons: we flew such a sortie every day, so it was good to keep the Israelis convinced that 'everything is as usual'. And secondly, we needed an update on Israeli positions and status of their various units. I launched from Inchas around 10.00 in the morning, and followed the usual route, taking great care to pho-*

Mamdouh Heshmat flew a very important reconnaissance sortie with a MiG-21RF during the morning of 6 October 1973, collecting valuable, last-minute intelligence concerning latest Israeli positions in Sinai. This MiG-21RF (serial number 8511) was photographed after suffering an unknown sort of landing mishap, in early 1972. (via Group 73)'

*tograph various command centres. The result of that mission was several updates of targeting intelligence for the first wave of our attacking fighter-bombers. Several other pilots from my squadron flew additional sorties, later that day, all of them returning safely. In the evening, we sat together and were in high spirits.'*

The situation was as quiet as it had been for months. Egyptian early warning radar sites did record a take-off of several Israeli aircraft from Refidim and this caused some concern, but the Israelis soon returned to their air base. From the standpoint of the EAF commander, the IDF/AF was 'sleeping'. Everything began to change around 11.30, when Mubarak entered the Operations Centre EAF.

After ensuring that everything was in place, he ordered the codeword to be passed to all air brigade commanders and air bases, and all squadron commaders, prompting them to open envelopes with their orders for the day. The battle was now about to start.

Unaware of the coming war, most Egyptian pilots pursued 'business as usual'. Hussein el-Kfas recalled that there was only one exception from routine operations on that morning:

*'On the morning of 6 October the commander of our brigade came to the officers' mess. He took a seat and drank some tea with us, joking and laughing so much we were surprised. After he left, about half an hour later, we returned to our squadron ready room and were astonished to find its walls covered with maps of the Sinai, big reconnaissance pictures of our targets, and a note that our time-on-target would be 14.00! We gathered there and wrote down all the details. I was to lead a flight including Saad Deraini as my wingman, Abdel-Aziz Ihab as number 3, and another pilot. Other three 'finger four' flights of our squadron included those led by Osama Hamdi and Jalal Zaki. While walking to our aircraft, we took a look at each other, wondering if we were ever going to see each other again…'*

At Jiancalis, Reda el-Iraqi felt ready for the war:

*'I knew the war would start on 6 October. The holy month of Ramadan began and I was fasting. At noon, our brigade commander Nabil Shuwakry collected all the pilots – even those who stood alert and were to sit in their aircraft – and told us the war would start at 14.00. He told us that our mission was the defence of Egypt, that we would be tasked with flying air defence sorties in the direction of Alexandria and Rosetta, that we would participate in the second wave through an attack on enemy*

Hussein el-Kfass with colleagues from No. 62 Squadron in front of one of their MiG-17Fs at Abu Hammad air base, shortly before October 1973 War.
(Hussein el-Kfass Collection)

*Fort Budapest near Port Said, during the second wave of the strike, and then gave us a very powerful speech that raised our morale to the heaven. He concluded by warning us that we had got only half an hour to get ready.'*

Muhammad Naji recalled the state of affairs at the Qwaysina air base:

*'The morning of 6 October was very nice and quiet, and we all gathered at our air base... Around 12.00 a small twin-engined transport aircraft arrived. An Egyptian Army officer emerged from it and went straight for our squadron ready room. He sat down and we all gathered around him: in front of him was an envelope on which it was written that we were not to open it before 12.30 of 6 October. When the time came, we opened that envelope – and it was as if lightning hit the room! There were our orders for an attack on the Israelis on the Sinai. Extremely precise, even detailing what pilot was to fly what mission. Maj Yousif Mohammed Rasoul was to lead the first formation, with Maj Walid Abdul Latif as-Samarrai as his number 3. Their objective was the Tasa HQ. Maj Mohammad Ali flew the second formation, with Mohammad Kazem as his number 3, and their target was the nearby HAWK SAM site. Flt Lt Imad Ahmed Ezzad led the third formation, with me as his number 3. Our objective was the Israeli artillery position. Each aircraft was to be armed with full load of 30mm ammunition for the ADEN cannon and 24 unguided rockets.'*[16]

Pilots assigned to units that did not participate in the strike were not even informed about the onset of hostilities, as recalled by Ahmed Abbas Faraj:

*'We were not informed that we would go to war and were thus surprised to see formations of fully-armed MiG-21s from No. 49 Squadron taking off. We learned what was going on only when they came back – and were very, very angry that we did not become involved. For our unit, 6 October was a very bad day, because we did not participate in the fighting.'*

## The Kelt Surprise

The first shot of the October 1973 Arab-Israeli War was fired by a Tu-16K-11-16 bomber from No. 36 Squadron, piloted by Maj Mohammed Abdel Wahab el-Keraidy, around 13.40. Taking off together with six other bombers from Cairo West around 13.25, Keraidy climbed over the Mediterranean Sea before releasing one KSR-11 anti-radi-

ation missile in the direction of the HQ Southern Command IDF (Unit 511), at Umm Qashiba. Keraidy's missiles were followed by several additional weapons:
- two KSR-2s fired at artillery positions near Baluza (launched by the crew of Lt Col Raouf Hilmi);
- two KSR-2s fired at the IDF armour base near Gidi Defile;
- two KSR-11s fired at the IDF/AF ground control centre near Refidim (launched by the crew of Maj Ahmed el-Gawaharegy);
- two KSR-11s fired at the HAWK SAM site near Abu Rudeis (launched by the crew of Maj Fadhil Fathi), and
- two KSR-11s fired at the southernmost IDF/AF early warning radar station and ground control station near Safra, on Ras Mohammed Peninsula south of Sharm el-Sheikh (launched by the crew of Maj George Gaoly).[17]

Cross-examination of available Egyptian and Israeli accounts about the results of these attacks reveals often-contradictory reports. One of the KSR-2s was claimed shot down by a Mirage IIICJ interceptor over Bir el-Abd area, prompting creation of a legend that this missile was fired 'at Tel Aviv', and one of the KSR-11s was downed by an F-4E while approaching Refidim.[18] Actually, not a single weapon was released in the direction of Israel and Egypt and Iraq are convinced that the KSR-11 fired at Unit 511 by el-Keraidy caused quite some damage. The effect was further increased when this highly important installation near Gidi Defile was hit by at least two 9K52 Luna-M (ASCC codename FROG-7) artillery rockets fired by the 64th Missile Brigade of the Egyptian Army.[19]

Israel confirms that the strike against Baluza hit its target, destroying several vehicles of the 9th Armoured Battalion and killing three soldiers. Similarly, the ground control station at Refidim apparently received a 'direct hit', though with unknown results. On the contrary, the result of the attack on the tank base near Gidi Defile remains unknown. Finally, the AS-5 attack on the Safra ground control station appears to have been highly successful, because even Israeli sources confirm a direct hit at the control room where three or four IDF servicepeople were killed, and a hit at the nearby ammunition depot.[20]

Mohammed Abdel Wahab el-Keraidy, the No. 36 Squadron pilot that fired the first shot of the October 1973 War, 'inspecting' the tail-gunner's position of a Tu-16 bomber together with his son Ahmad, in 1974.
(Ahmad Keraidy Collection)

Ahmed el-Gawaharegy (left) was the pilot of the fourth Tu-16 to open fire on 6 October: his two KSR-11s were aimed at the IDF/AF ground control centre near Refidim air base (formerly Bir Gifgafa/Meliz).
(Ahmad Keraidy Collection)

Seeking Revenge

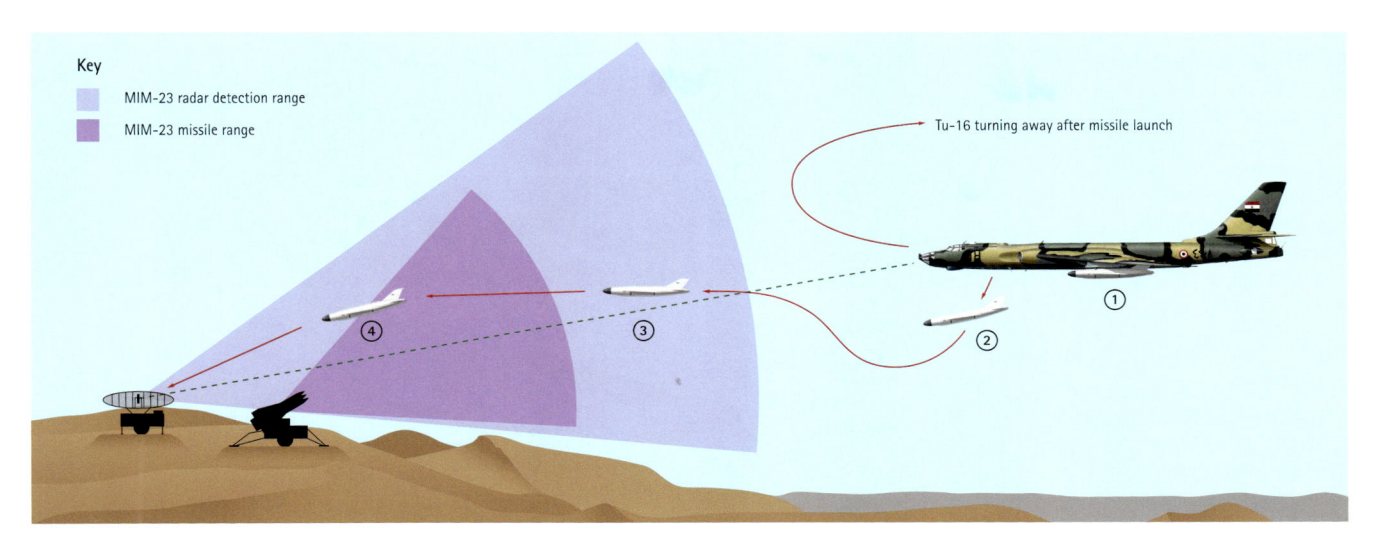

#### Guidance Diagram for KSR-11 System
1. Tu-16's Ritsaa system detects enemy radar and determines its performance and corodinates
2. KSR-11 is released, engine ignites 7 seconds later and the missile following commands from Tu-16's KS-1M station
3. during mid-course flight-phase, missile is controlled by autopilot and Tu-16's KS-1M station
4. initiating the attack phase, the missile is activating its passive seeker-head and diving at 25°

Although rocket-powered, the KSR-11 offered only a minimal increase in speed and range over the KS-1, but its guidance system homed on emissions from enemy radars, which meant that after firing it, the crew of the Tu-16 could turn away to avoid interception by enemy fighters.
(Diagram by Tom Cooper and James Lawrence)

Air and ground crew of Tu-16K-11-16 serial number 4405, piloted by Sqn Ldr Ahmed Moustafa Mohammed Hassan (who retired with the rank of major general), as seen prior to the war. Sadly, the exact target of Hassan's mission on 6 October 1973 remains unknown.
(Ahmad Keraidy Collection)

Tu-16K-11-16 serial number 4401 seen during a pre-war training flight, armed with two KSR-11 anti-radar missiles (notably, the latter were identified by individual serial number, in this case 981 and 343).
(Ahmad Keraidy Collection)

Tu-16K-11-16 serial number 4403 low over Cairo during a post-war parade. Deliveries of Tu-16s compatible with KSR-11 and KS-1 guided air-to-surface missiles remained a closely guarded secret before the October 1973 War.
(Albert Grandolini Collection)

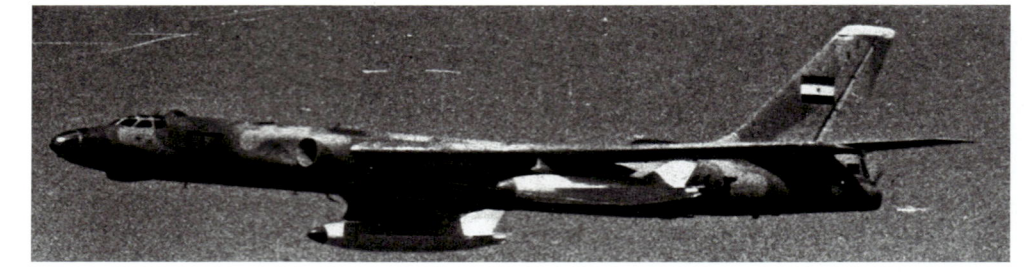

Another Tu-16K-11-16 operated by No. 36 Squadron during the October 1973 War was serial number 4404. Apparently it received an unusual camouflage pattern consisting of yellow sand and two shades of green.
(Albert Grandolini Collection)

The KS-1 (ASCC codename AS-1 Kennel) air-to-surface missile was one of three primary weapons that could be deployed from the 'new' Tu-16KSR-11s delivered to Egypt. Originally delievered to the UARAF in 1966–1967, it had a range of only 90km (56 miles) and a maximum speed of around 900km/h (559mph). It required the launch aircraft to keep the target locked-on with its own radar in order to guide the weapon, and saw relatively little service at the start and towards the end of the October 1973 War.
(via Tom Long)

The KSR-11 (ASCC codename AS-5 Kelt-B) anti-radar missile was a new weapon in the arsenal of the Egyptian Tu-16s, and was to cause quite some surprise for Israel.
(Albert Grandolini Collection)

Port profile of Tu-16 serial number 4265. As far as is known, these bombers only flew patrols in support of the Egyptian Navy during the war. (Albert Grandolini Collection)

'Vanilla' Tu-16 bombers operated by No. 35 Squadron during the October 1973 War wore markings similar to those of the Tu-16K-11-16s of No. 36 Squadron, but their serial numbers were in the 42xx range. Seen here is 4201. (Albert Grandolini Collection)

The Tu-16s fired their KSR-2 and KSR-11 missiles in such order that these crossed the Suez Canal only a few minutes before the EAF fighter-bombers did so – most of them at 14.00 precisely. For different reasons this was not always the case, however. For example, the first formation of Egyptian fighter-bombers to reach its targets – a quartet of Su-7BMKs that attacked Fort Budapest (the northernmost and strongest fortification of the Bar Lev Line) with ZAB-500-300 napalm bombs – reportedly appeared over its target around 13.57, nearly eight minutes before the planned attack. Unsurprisingly, the IDF/AF MIM-23 HAWK SAM site at Baluza did not receive permission to open fire on the Sukhois: for the Israelis, the war had not yet started.

## Operation Badhr: The First – and Only – Wave

Shortly before 14.00, the IDF Southern Command HQ at Umm Qashiba flashed a warning of an imminent Egyptian attack. In fact, an earlier warning had already been issued to all the forward positions at noon, but it forecasted the opening of hostilities for 18.00. The 'early' appearance of EAF fighter-bombers thus caught most of the Israeli garrison on the Sinai by surprise and left the local commanders with no time to react. Indeed, IDF/AF interceptors at Refidim and Ophir were scrambled only when these two bases

Hussein el-Kfass with his plane captain shortly before the next combat sortie. This young pilot got himself into a good deal of trouble early during in his career, but proved his mettle in combat.
(Hussein el-Kfass Collection)

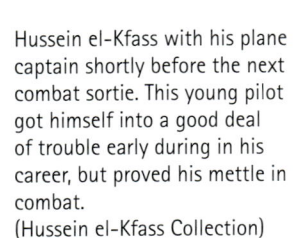

were already under attack and they failed to prevent the Egyptians from reaching their targets. Furthermore, a concern about a possible attack on air bases in Israel prompted the IDF/AF controllers to start scrambling whatever aircraft were available, no matter how were these equipped. This caused not only much confusion but resulted in a situation where most of the IDF/AF remained busy sorting itself out during the opening Arab strike: many fighter-bombers had first to fly over the Mediterranean Sea to jettison their air-to-ground ordnance and were therefore late in being vectored to intercept incoming Egyptian, Iraqi and Syrian fighter-bombers. In turn, once they jettisoned their bombs, these aircraft were useless for ground attacks and had first to return to their bases and re-arm. This resulted in a situation where for most of the first two hours of the war, very few IDF/AF aircraft were present over the battlefields.

The IDF/AF HAWK sites at Baluza and Abu Samara were among the first Israeli positions on the Sinai to come under attack, already around 14.02. The Abu Samara site was targeted by the first two flights from No. 62 Squadron. The first flight failed to find its target because its leader, Lt Col Hassan Fahmy, experienced technical problems with his aircraft. The Israelis opened fire and two HAWKs obliterated the MiG-17F flown by Abdel Hamid Hussain Zaki, who was killed. However, this revealed the SAM site's position and exposed it to attack by the remaining seven fighter-bombers, as recalled by el-Kfass:

*'Our ground crews were told that we were to fly a training sortie, so they armed each of our aircraft with two bombs and eight rockets, as usual. We took off and flew low towards a designated corridor through our SAM defences in direction of the Canal. I took a look at my number 2 only to see he had not tucked in his undercarriage! Our order was to maintain complete radio silence, so I could not warn him, and thus we crossed the Suez Canal in that configuration. Deraini could not restrain himself, and he cried loud on the radio, Allah-u-Akhbar!*

*'Our target was a HAWK SAM site. I found it and flew two attacks, first with rockets then with bombs. Out of 16 aircraft that started that mission, one failed to return: it was shot down by HAWKs. Deraini flew the whole attack with his undercarriage down. When we came back there was lots of happiness. Our brigade commander was waiting for us and I told him about our sortie, and that Deraini was*

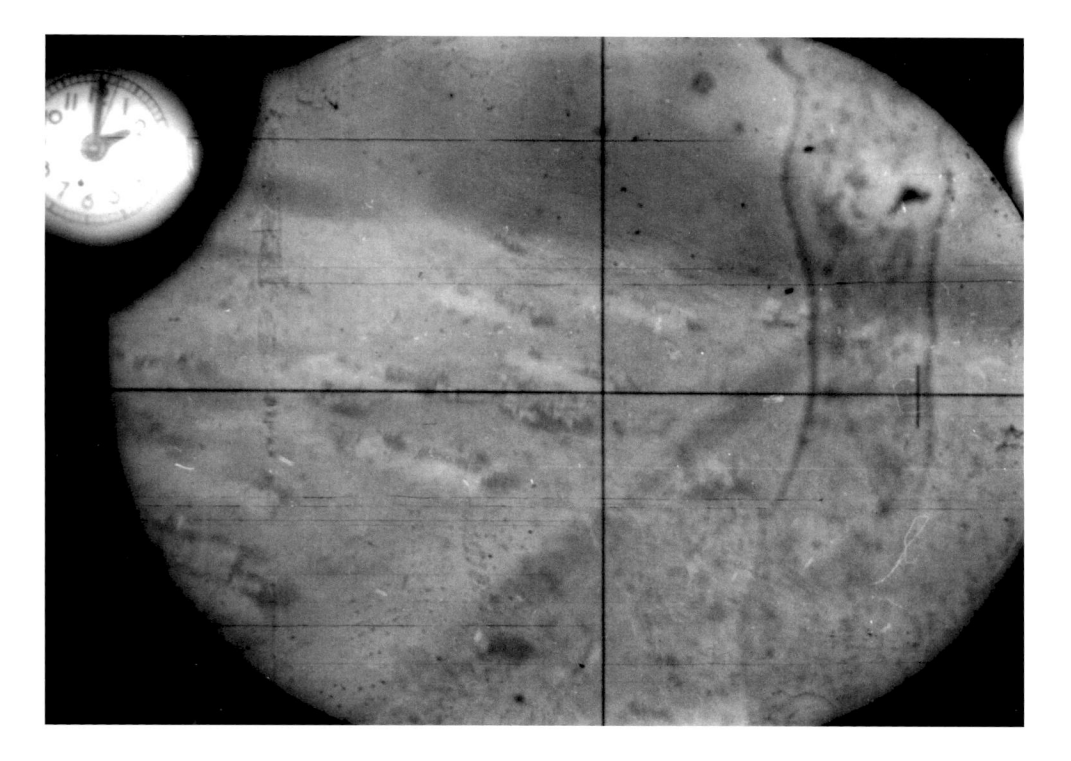

A still from the gun-camera film of Hussein el-Kfass' MiG-17F showing his attack on the HAWK SAM site near Abu Samara, around 14.00 on 6 October 1973. (Hussein el-Kfass Collection)

a hero. Deraini then passed by, sarcastically observing that something was wrong with his aircraft, that it was very hard for him to keep up with the formation: the plane was very slow...'

The HAWK site at Abu Samara had most of its early warning and fire-control radars knocked out, which rendered it unoperational for several hours. The other two flights from No. 62 Squadron attacked the HAWK site and IDF armoured base near Baluza, with unknown results.

Many of the Egyptian fighter-bombers deployed to attack Israeli positions on the northern and central Sinai crossed the Suez Canal along a corridor in the ADC's SAM belt in the Ismailia area, covered by four MiG-21MFs from No. 46 Squadron, led by Samir Aziz Mikhail:

'A few minutes before 14.00 I launched as a leader of a flight and – according to a plan developed before the war – flew very low to a position east of Ismailia where we climbed to provide top cover for the fighter-bombers attacking Israelis in that area. We remained on station slightly longer than planned: I waited for some five minutes to make sure that none of our fighter-bombers would be pursued by the enemy. Then the GCI ordered me to return to el-Mansoura, but once near our base we came under fire from our air defences, and a SA-3 detonated between me and my number 3! Once on the ground, our operations officer told us that we returned late and were fired upon by six missiles because the air defences were advised that there would be no friendly aircraft in the sky any more.'

The first attack formation to pass beneath Mikhail's flight consisted of four MiG-17Fs that attacked Fort Televizia, opposite Ismailia – apparently with negligible results. This flight was followed by several formations that converged in the direction of the major military complex that Israel had constructed within the area connecting

Hunter F.Mk 59A serial number 584 as seen shortly before the October 1973 War. Iraqi Hunters flew most of their combat sorties during that conflict in a similar configuration, carrying two 'long-range' external fuel tanks, and eight 'banks' of three unguided rockets each. (via Ali Tobchi)

the Khotmiya Defile in the north, Bir Gifgafa in the east, Mitla Defile in the south and Gidi Defile in the west. This included no fewer than three airfields near Bir Gifgafa (including the former Meliz air base, renamed Refidim by the IDF/AF, the former Bir Thamada, and a newly constructed 'satellite' airfield), and extensive command and storage facilities and bases for ground troops, all protected by several AAA batteries and three HAWK sites.

Around 14.05, four MiG-17s attacked the HAWK SAM site near Tasa Defile, but it turned out this was not occupied, and thus the pilots attacked the IDF command post nearby, with *'insignificant results'*, according to the Israelis. By 14.10, at least two flights of MiG-17s had hit the base of the 401st Armoured Brigade near Tasa Defile, reportedly damaging a number of tanks and the local HQ. Meanwhile, four IrAF Hunters had attacked the HAWK site near Gidi Defile, as recalled by Mohammad Naji:

*'Around 13.00 we went to our aircraft. Everything felt like on an exercise, because we had repeated this so often during recent months. We took off and turned in the direction of the Suez Canal, flying at less than 20m [66ft] altitude. Approaching the Canal, we saw below us lots of movement by the Egyptian Army – all heading in the same direction like us. The feeling was overwhelming. We crossed the Canal exactly as ordered, precisely at 14.00.*

*'We attacked 10 minutes later: a shallow climb, aiming for the target, a short press on the trigger and there was a series of explosions. The Israelis below us were running around in panic like sheep attacked by a wolf. We completed our attack and reformed into a formation more suitable for air combat. We were still deep over the Sinai, and there was a chance of Mirages intercepting us. Under way back to the Canal we passed several formations of Eyptian aircraft, some flying above, others below us. All 12 of us returned to Qwaysina safely, thank God, and there was a great celebration…'*

Nearby, one of two other Iraqi flights attacked an Israeli artillery battery operating 175mm (6.9in) guns and *'destroyed several of them'*, according to Israeli sources.[21] One of the pilots involved recalled:

*'We planned to approach at a very low level, then pop up to an altitude of 500m [1,640ft], acquire our target visually and fire all our rockets at the enemy. Then, we were to recover down to low altitude, make a cirucuit, pop up again and attack any vehicles that were not burning using our 30mm ADEN cannon. We assessed this would expose us not only to intercepts by Mirages, but also enemy ground fire.*

Last-minute briefing for a group of Egyptian MiG-21 pilots. Notable is that all wear orange-coloured life vests: many of the combat air patrols they flew during the October 1973 War took them over the Bitter Lakes, Suez Canal, Mediterranean or the Red Sea. (Tom Cooper Collection)

*'Eventually, none of our expectations became reality. We flew in at less than 20m [66ft], climbed, acquired our targets, fired our rockets while in a shallow dive, turned around and came back to finish the job with cannon. By that time, every artillery piece to be seen and several support vehicles were on fire. It was easier than during exercises. We returned to base while flying along the SAM corridor over Ismailia, singing all the time. No problem.'*[22]

Simultaneously, six EAF MiG-17Fs attacked the HAWK site near Mitla Defile, where Israeli defences were already on alert, as recalled by Adil Shararah:

*'My mission during the opening strike was to attack a HAWK site near the Mitla Pass. We went in with 12 MiG-17s, and I was in the second group of six, because of my rank at that time. We took off from Qutamiyah, flew low over the Suez Canal, reached our IP two minutes later and then broke into two groups. The first group suffered some losses to ground fire because they were more exposed. We then made our attack and it proved very easy, no problem to hit the target and knock out the radar and three SAM launchers. Then we returned straight back to the base.'*

This attack opened the way for two flights of MiG-17Fs from No. 89 Squadron (escorted by four MiG-21s from No. 44 Squadron) that attacked the Israeli tank base near the Mittla Defile, killing several soldiers from the 67th and 524th Armoured Battalions.

Led by squadron CO, Lt Col Munir Fahmy, 12 MiG-21MFs from No. 82 Squadron then attacked the Umm Qashiba HQ, with four jets bombing positions of the 881st Air Defence Battalion IDF, four targeting the local communication and SIGINT-gathering centre (Unit 545), and four bombing the long-range artillery battery at Ain Mussa. The IDF subsequently credited the 881st Battalion with two MiG kills. In reality, the aircraft flown by Lt Hussein Osman Beshir was hit in the cockpit area and crashed, killing the pilot. However, Lt Mohammed Najib Muhammed Najib managed to return his aircraft for a safe emergency landing back at the base, despite substantial damage to his cockpit canopy and helmet.

Ahmed el-Wakeel flew one of four MiG-21MFs from No. 42 Squadron that attacked Ras Nasrani/Ophir air base during Operation Badhr.
(Ahmed el-Wakeel Collection)

These strikes were followed by a massive effort against Israeli installations in the Bir Gifgafa and Bir Thamada areas, where Egyptian fighter-bombers were sighted for the first time around 14.08. The first formation – 12 Su-7BMKs from No. 51 Squadron led by Lt Col Hazim al-Gharby – attacked Refidim base and surrounding installations. Approaching at a very high speed and minimal altitude, al-Gharby's and the flight led by Brig Gen Abdel Moneim el-Shennawy (certainly the highest-ranking Egyptian officer to fly a combat sortie during Operation Badhr) took the Israelis by surprise and suffered no losses. The Redim runway was holed in 10 places and the control tower wrecked, and this air base was returned to service only two days later, although the taxiway remained operational and was used for take-offs and landings by IDF/AF aircraft. Also hit was the SIGINT site and the main IDF/AF ground control post (Unit 509), which lost one of its communication trucks after it received a direct hit.[23] However, the third flight from this formation – led by Capt Ahmad Ezz-el-Din – failed to find the HAWK site at Refidim and thus turned to attack the CP at Umm Qashiba, with unknown results.

Around the same time, a total of 16 MiG-21s and 24 Su-7s converged on Bir Thamada. Mustafa Hafez led his entire squadron into an attack on the local airfield:

'All 16 of our aircraft were armed with anti-runway bombs and we flew a low-level attack. On the way in I had to increase altitude at least twice because the MiG-17s were attacking the HAWK sites. I had to climb up to 150-200m [492-656ft] so as not to obstruct their attacks. With a 'dibber' bomb you don't have to aim: you just fly along the runway and let them go.'

Twenty Su-7BMKs from No. 52 and No. 53 Squadrons then attacked the Israeli air defence positions and storage depots near Bir Thamada: while missing a company of IDF tanks that had rolled out from the local base and was exposed in the open, they unleashed a total of 120 500kg (1,102lb) FAB-500M-62 bombs at various installations, causing considerable damage.

Much less successful was the last Egyptian formation to enter this area, a flight of Sukhois from No. 52 Squadron that also attacked Bir Thamada air base. The Su-7BMK flown by that unit's CO, Col Kamal Osman Zaki, was shot down and the pilot killed while approaching the target. The rest of his formation pressed their attack home and scored a number of hits on the runway and other installations. After making two passes each, two Sukhois then turned back in the direction of the Suez Canal, but Capt Mohammed Atif el-Sadat (younger half-brother of President Sadat of Egypt) then made the mortal mistake of attempting a third strafing pass: his Su-7BMK was hit by Israeli air defences and crashed, killing the pilot.

Amazingly, the IDF/AF subsequently credited no fewer than five Su-7 kills to Nesher pilots of No. 144 Squadron and one to an F-4E crew from No. 119 Squadron – in fact, these two fighter-bombers from No. 52 Squadron were the only Sukhois shot down during the entire course of Operation Badhr.[24]

## Triumph or Failure?

In addition to sending a large number of MiG-21s and Su-7s to attack the Bir Thamada area, the EAF deployed a significant force to strike Israeli positions around the southern tip of the Sinai Peninsula. This began with four MiG-17s attacking the HAWK site in Ras Sudr, around 14.05, though without much success: this unit remained operational.

Because of their fighter-bomber role, either the MiG-21MFs from No. 82 Squadron, or those from sister unit, No. 56 Squadron, wore a small black bomb as 'unit insignia' during the October 1973 War. Both of these aircraft (serial number 8611 in foreground and 8652 in the background) were marked in this fashion.
(Albert Grandolini Collection)

Almost simultaneously, eight MiG-17s from the same unit attacked the Ras Nasrani area: while four bombed and rocketed the HAWK site at Ras Nasrani and destroyed its command post and one of its radars, another flight hit the nearby ground control post (Unit 528), destroying and damaging many of the antennas in the process but apparently causing no losses in personnel.

Four MiG-17s from No. 61 Squadron attacked the HAWK site at Ras Mohammed Peninsula, about 50km (31 miles) further south, in turn opening the way for several flights of MiG-17s and MiG-21s that attacked Ophir air base. Dia el-Hefnawy flew top cover for the first wave of this mission:

*'I was with No. 27 Squadron and based at Inchas but prior to the war half of our squadron was deployed to Hurghada. On 6 October, we only got four hours' warning that the war was going to start. Our first mission was to protect MiG-17s led by Maj Sharif Arab during the attack on HAWK SAMs near Ras Nasrani airfield, called Ophir by the enemy...*

*'One of the biggest problems in the preparation of our mission was the coordination of a large number of aircraft that flew at different airspeeds, so that we would cross the Gulf of Suez and reach the target zone around the same time. MiG-21s could not fly as slow as MiG-17s carrying bombs and rockets...*

*'We launched a few minutes later than the MiG-17s and caught up with them when they were approaching the Ras Mohammed Peninsula. We saw them about 2 miles [3.2km] ahead of us and to the left, flying very low: they attacked the radar station and command centre and delivered a number of precise hits, causing large parts of the structures to fly through the sky. From anguished calls on the radio we understood that one MiG-17 had been shot down. We did not take part in the ground attack, met no opposition in the air, and flew no other missions that day.'*[25]

Ahmed Yusuf el-Wakeel was under way with one of four MiG-21MFs from No. 42 Squadron:

Front view of an EAF Su-7BMK armed with two 'dibber' runway-penetrating bombs of 100kg (221lb). These weapons were developed in Egypt with the purpose of cratering runways. During the October 1973 War, they were deployed for attacks on roads and concrete buildings too. (via Tom Long)

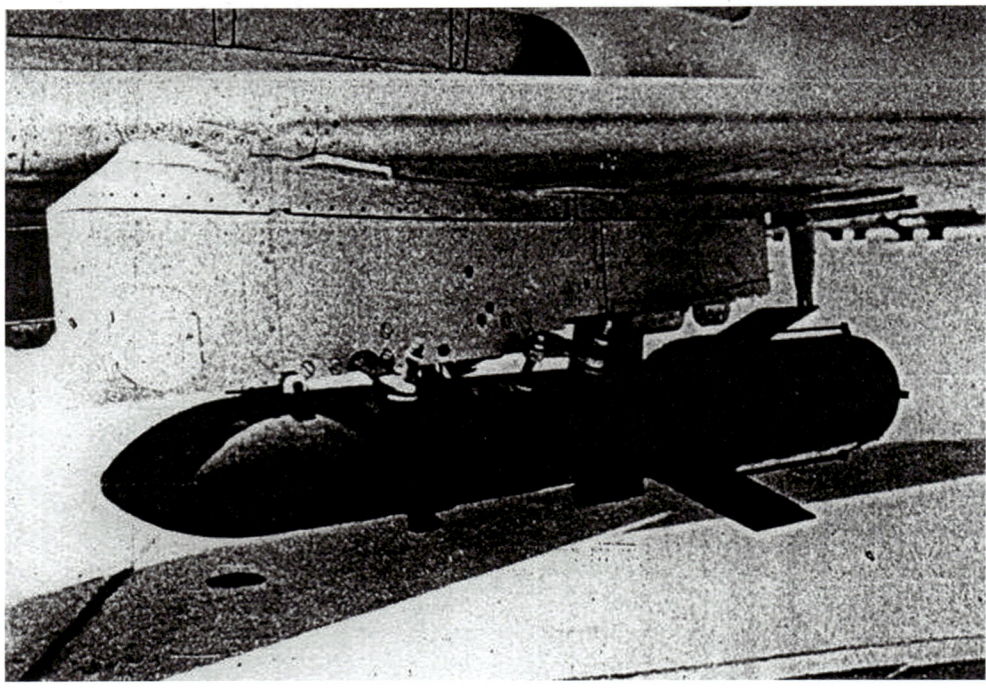

A detail view of the Egyptian runway-penetration bomb. Usually deployed from MiG-21MFs and Su-7BMKs, this weapon could be dropped from low altitude and penetrate runways up to 40cm (16in) thick, creating a 4m (13.2ft) crater and surface cracking within a radius of 270m (890ft). (via Tom Long)

*'Our task was to hit Ras Nasrani airfield with runway-penetrating bombs and we were the only MiG-21 formation to attack ground targets in this part of the Sinai. We released our bombs and made a turn, then I saw my wingman, Sobhy el-Sheikh, receiving a hit from ground fire. I think he was hit near the cockpit because Sobhy didn't eject. Instead, he directed his burning MiG into a hardened aircraft shelter that had space for three Phantoms. He crashed into that shelter, but I don't know if he destroyed any enemy aircraft there.'*[26]

According to Israeli accounts, seconds after three survivors from el-Wakeel's flight left the area, two F-4Es managed to scramble from the damaged runway of Ras Nasrani/Ophir. While making several high-speed runs on a northwest/southwest axis, their pilots enaged a number of MiG-17s and MiG-21s that were in the process of bombing Ophir, the port of Sharm el-Sheikh, the early warning radars and the HAWK site at Ras Mohammed. The two Israeli crews were credited with downing six MiG-17s and one MiG-21s, and causing another MiG to crash into the sea, and both were highly decorated. The only Egyptian MiG-21 pilot that recalled sighting any Israeli aircraft airborne over Ras Nasrani was Ahmed Yusuf:

*'I was assigned to No. 25 Squadron of Air Brigade 102. We were rotated several times between Hurghada, Wadi Qena, and Luxor during 1973 (we even staged repeated exercises combining aircraft from our units deployed at various of these air bases). On 6 October our task was to support an attack by MiG-17s on the runway of Ras Nasrani. For most of us, this mission was very similar to our training, because we had simulated this attack so often: even our target was so well known to us that it did not represent a strange sight when we arrived there. We took off in two groups from Hurghada and Wadi Qena, crossed the Gulf of Suez at a very low altitude and approached Ras Nasrani undisturbed. On arrival there, I saw a large number of Egyptian aircraft attacking. One Israeli fighter appeared, and then another one, but they kept their distance and then disappeared. Our formation made several turns above Ras Nasrani until all the MiG-17s had completed their attack and then everybody flew back, except for Sobhi el-Sheikh, who was martyred while bombing the runway. His loss was sad but we returned to Wadi Qena in high spirits.'*[27]

Similarly, while el-Hefnawy did recall one additional MiG-17 loss from the formation that attacked Ras Nasrani, he could not confirm any air combat with the Israelis:

*'The MiG-17s made repeated attack runs, bombing and rocketing as they went. They hit several hangars and caused a massive detonation in one of the hardened aircraft shelters, ripping its roof open. One MiG-17 was hit by ground fire and crashed into the sea about 2 miles [3.2km] from Ras Nasrani. Overall, we returned to our base convinced that we had caused extensive damage and thus happy about our mission. Gun-camera films shown during our post-mission debrief revealed even more precise attacks than during earlier exercises – but also the parachute of one of the downed pilots.'*

Currently available Egyptian sources do not confirm any of the seven claims credited by the IDF/AF to two Phantom crews from No. 107 Squadron: if the EAF did suffer additional losses during this mission, then these were not witnessed by the pilots interviewed so far: arguably, this could partly be attributed to the relatively limited view outside the cockpit of the MiG-21.[28]

Overall, sources differ significantly as regards the total number of EAF aircraft involved in the first – and only – wave of Egyptian air strikes against Israeli positions

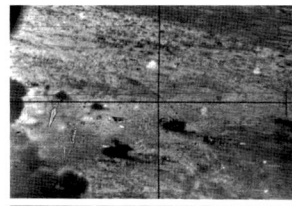

Two stills from gun-camera film of EAF Su-7s that attacked IDF depots in the Bir Thamada area on 6 October 1973. (EAF)

Capt Atif el-Sadat is known to have graduated from the Air Force Academy with Generation 25 in 1969, and is said to have flown several combat sorties during the War of Attrition. He was killed in the course of an attack on an Israeli HAWK SAM site outside Refidim airfield, while making an unscheduled, third strafing pass, during the opening strike of Operation Badhr, on 6 October 1973. His body was returned to Egypt after mediation by the Red Cross, following the war. (via Group 73)

Stills from el-Wakeel's gun-camera film taken during the pass over the runway of Ras Nasrani. According to Israeli accounts, the two black circles mark two F-4Es from No. 107 Squadron, caught by the Egyptians while still rolling for take-off. Israeli sources insist that the two Phantoms subsequently shot down six MiG-17Fs and one MiG-21, while available Egyptian sources do not recall any air combats. (EAF)

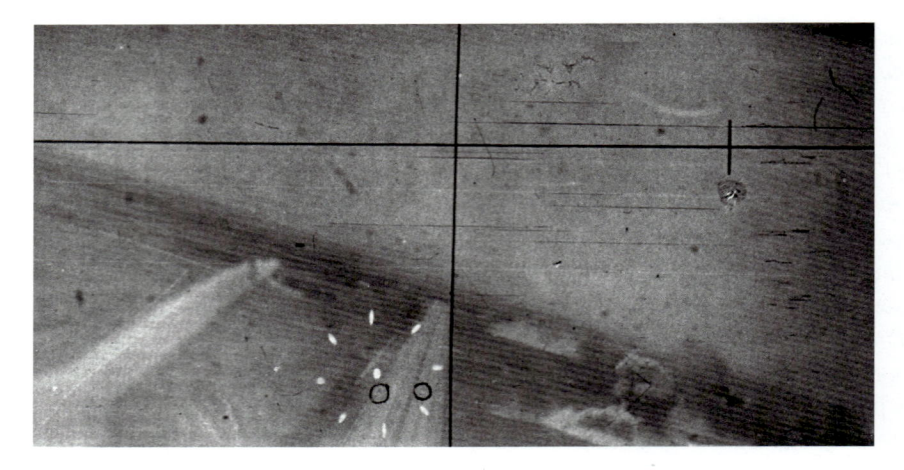

in the Sinai. While some cite as few as 128 combat sorties, Nabil Shuwarky recalled 220, and Sadat gave the figure of 222 participating aircraft. Most other quotations cite between 240 and 250 aircraft that attacked three air bases, 10 HAWK sites (although not as many are known to have been deployed on the Sinai), three major command posts and electronic warfare centres. Conducted in cooperation with Group 73 historians, our count turned up a total of seven sorties by Tu-16s, 88 by MiG-17s, 48 by MiG-21s, 60 by Su-7s, and 12 by Iraqi Hunters, for a grand total of 216 known sorties. This figure cannot be considered 'definitive' for several reasons, starting with the lack of official documentation and uncertainity about the exact number of MiG-17s involved in the attacks on Ras Sudr, Ras Mohammed and Ophir. Furthermore, it is unclear whether some Egyptian sources count other sorties known to have been flown around the same time or later during the afternoon of 6 October. For example, a quartet of MiG-21s from Air Brigade 104 is known to have been airborne west of Port Said during Operation Badhr, while Abdel Moneim el-Shennawy's pilot logbook shows three additional 'bombing' sorties flown on 6 October, but cites no targets.

There are even greater contradictions regarding the results of the Egyptian attack. Most Israeli and some Russian sources insist that Egypt inflicted only minimal, neglibile or no damage at all, that Operation Badhr resulted in a loss of about 10 per cent of the aircraft involved and thus resulted in failure (if not an outright disaster) and prompted Mubarak to cancel the planned second wave. On the contrary, most of the Egyptians involved consider it a triumph of historic proportions. Foremost, the Egyptians are extremely proud of catching the Israelis by surprise and encountering very little opposition – whether in the air or on the ground: indeed, most of the EAF pilots involved assessed their missions flown on 6 October as 'easier' than the training sorties flown before the war. Regardless of what kind of damage they might have caused, the Egyptians stress that all the formations involved managed to find, attack and hit their targets, by no means an easy feat. This is largely correct, and it should be kept in mind that such standpoints are primarily related to the deep psychological impact the entire Egyptian military experienced because of the rout of 1967. Under such circumstances it did not matter how much damage was caused, as long as the Arab attack took Israel by surprise and all the formations involved reached their targets as planned. From this point of view, there is no doubt that Egypt won its 'Battle of Revenge' and fully recovered its military pride.

Seeking Revenge

This dramatic scene was photographed during the Egyptian attack on Ras Mohammed, about 50 km (31 miles) south of Ras Nasrani, around 14.10 on 6 October 1973, and shows one of the EAF MiG-17s while being chased by one of two F-4Es from No.107 Squadron IDF/AF that was scrambled from Ophir AB. (IDF)

Finally, while Israel credited its pilots, HAWK sites and AAA with the kills of at least 10 MiG-17s, four Su-7s and up to four MiG-21s, most Egyptian sources insist on either five or six losses. Nabil Shuwarky summarised as follows:

*'During pre-war discussions regarding our planning, the Soviets estimated our expected losses at about 40 per cent. Actually, because of the determination and courage of our officers and airmen – and I know what I'm saying here, I'm responsible for my own words and ready to discuss and support them – we lost six aircraft only.'*

Cross-examination of the above-mentioned operations practically confirms Shuwakry's words, because – as far as can be said on the basis of available recollections – the EAF lost three MiG-17Fs (with two pilots killed), two Su-7BMKs (with two pilots killed), and one MiG-21MF (pilot killed). These are the same six losses mentioned by Shuwarky.[29]

Whatever actually happened, fact is that at around 14.30, the High Command EAF concluded that 95 per cent of the air raids achieved their task for a loss of less than five per cent of the aircraft involved. As a result, the second wave of Operation Badhr was cancelled.[30]

# Crossing the Canal

Immediately after EAF aircraft passed overhead on their way to targets in the Sinai, no fewer than 1,850 Egyptian artillery pieces and mortars opened up in near unison against Israeli positions on the eastern side of the Suez Canal. According to various calculations, up to 10,500 shells fell on the forts of the Bar Lev Line in the first minute of this attack, or some 175 every second. The barrage continued for 45 minutes, even after the first wave of 4,000 Egyptian infantrymen headed over the ramparts, descended to the water and began crossing the Suez Canal, at 14.20.

The first wave of 8,000 Egyptian commandos and infantrymen used about 750 rubber boats to cross the Suez Canal, supported by engineers. After scaling the ramparts they deployed one kilometre in depth, establishing ambush positions for the anticipated Israeli armoured counterattacks. The second wave then brought additional infantry and combat engineers – the latter to clear minefields around the fortifications

While claiming six EAF MiG-17Fs as shot down by Phantoms during the 'Air Battle of Ophir', the Israelis have only published photos showing the fin of one of these, although at least five should have crashed on the ground. According to available Egyptian sources, this aircraft was shot down by ground-based air defences, and the pilot killed.
(IDF)

## Seeking Revenge

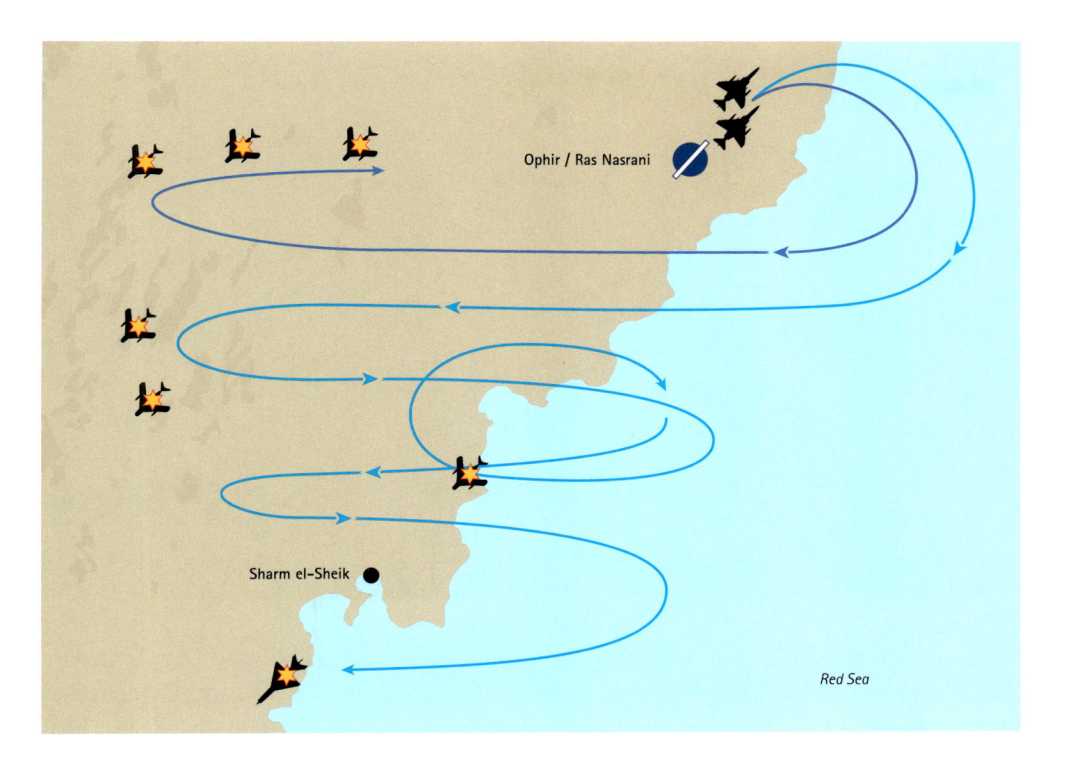

Based on an illustration published in the Hebrew-language edition of Eliezer Cohen's book *Israel's Best Defense*, this diagram shows the Israeli reconstruction of the air battle over Ras Nasrani/Ophir, on 6 October 1973. Two Israeli F-4E crews from No. 107 Squadron claimed six MiG-17s and one MiG-21 shot down in the course of this engagement, while available Egyptian sources confirm the loss of one MiG-21 and two MiG-17s only, but credit all of these to ground defences. (Diagram by James Lawrence)

of the Bar Lev Line. By the time the third wave reached the eastern side of the Canal, Egypt had a total of 2,000 officers and 30,000 troops deployed at bridgeheads that were meanwhile between 3-4km (1.9-2.5 miles) deep. Behind them, engineers began to remove the sand barrier constructed by Israel on the eastern side of the Canal using hoses attached to water pumps. The barrier was breached in about a dozen places within the following three hours – except in the sector assaulted by the Third Field Army, where clay proved resistant to high-pressure water and engineers experienced significant delays in breaching. Subsequently, the mud created during the breaching operations was emplaced by wood, rails, stone, sandbags, steel plates, or metal nets for the passage of heavy vehicles. Meanwhile, two hours after the initial landings, 10 battalions of Egyptian engineers began constructing pontoon bridges. In particular, the use of three Soviet-made PMP heavy folding pontoon bridges caught the Israelis by surprise, since they enabled construction of new bridges within astonishingly short periods of time. As well as 10 large pontoon bridges (two for each of five crossing infantry divisions), Egypt constructed a number of decoy bridges and landing sites for about 50 ferries. Although some bridges were damaged during early Israeli air strikes in the afternoon and evening of 6 October, eight were operational around midnight, when the transfer of tanks and other heavy equipment into the Sinai began.

The sudden Egyptian attack into the Sinai was opposed by an Israeli garrison of 18,000 troops. Only 16 of the forts on the Bar Lev line were occupied, by 460 reservists of the Jerusalem Infantry Brigade. The majority of IDF troops were assigned to the 252nd Armored Division, equipped with 291 M60 MBTs and 48 artillery pieces. One of its three brigades – the 14th Armored – was deployed in small groups along the Canal; the 401st Armoured Brigade was east of the Gidi Defile and the 460th Armored Brigade was to be found near Bir Gifgafa. Further south, the 35th Parachute Brigade protected

A pair of EAF MiG-17Fs returns to base at very low altitude, with all their bomb racks and rocket rails empty. (David Nicolle Collection)

the coastline and the desert between Ras Sudar and Sharm el-Sheikh. The first reaction of the Israeli commanders was to order their units into a posture of positional defence of the Bar Lev Line – which played straight into Egyptian hands. As the 14th Armored Brigade rushed its tanks forward to support the forts, these drove straight into the Egyptian ambushes, and suffered extensive losses in the process. Caught by surprise, the commanders continued ordering local counterattacks and failed to withdraw troops from the Bar Lev line, instead searching for the Egyptian main effort – of which there was none: Egyptians were attacking along the full length of the Suez Canal.

Overall, the combined surprise attack by the EAF, two Egyptian field armies (the Second Field Army north of Small Bitter Lake and the Third Field Army south of it), and forces from Port Said and Red Sea Military Districts, stunned the Israelis. Foremost, the sudden Egyptian attack – and the damage it caused to Israeli ELINT/SIGINT stations in particular – caused such shock and chaos within the IDF, that Egypt was allowed to dictate the tempo and conditions of the fighting on this frontline during the first phase of the war, and successfully concluded its crossing operation almost precisely according to plan.

## Battle for Budapest

It was only around 15.30 Egyptian time that the IDF/AF began scrambling formations of fighter-bombers with orders to attack Egyptian and Syrian ground forces assaulting IDF ground positions in the Sinai and the Golan. This decision led to the next problem: because the IDF/AF was not yet launching a battle for air superiority over either Egypt or Syria, both the Egyptian and Syrian air defence systems were fully operational and ready, in full control of the airspace over the battlefield, and waiting for the Israelis to come their way. Although having nearly a full day to get on a war footing, the IDF/AF failed to establish an effective system of forward air controllers. With ground forces demanding air support and following the motto of 'go and get them', there was no other choice: Israel launched its fighter-bombers in a haphazard fashion, pilots often not knowing what kind of target they would be ordered to hit or what kind of opposition could they expect – exactly the way so many Egyptian pilots were sent into action during the first three days of the June 1967 War. Over the front lines, the Israeli aircraft flew straight into a barrage of missiles and AAA fire, the sheer density of which inflicted havoc on their operations and resulted in most pilots jettisoning their bombs prematurely or missing their targets altogether.

Some of the first IDF/AF attacks were flown in support of Fort Budapest. Positioned 16.5km (10.3 miles) southeast of Port Fuad and thus outside the SAM coverage of Egypt's Independent Military Command for the Port Said Sector, this fortification was constructed on a narrow strip of land bordered to the north by the Mediterranean and to the south by saltmarshes. This left only one route of approach for elements of the Egyptian 135th Independent Infantry Brigade and the 128th Saiqa Group (Saiqa means 'Thunderbolt' and is used as a designation for commando forces in Egypt), supported by six old T-34/85 tanks, which launched their attack around 14.30. This faltered after three T-34s were knocked out while supporting combat engineers in breaching the 600m (656-yard) deep minefield surrounding the fort. Around 16.00, Budapest was hit by two Il-28 bombers – apparently scrambled to provide support for ground troops despite the cancellation of the second wave of EAF attacks. Their bombs killed one Israeli soldier and prompted the others to call for air support. Around 16.30, four A-4s approached the area, nonchalantly flying at 1,829m (6,000ft) altitude while searching for suitable targets and then rolling into attack – straight into a lethal combination of AAA and SA-7s. One of several MANPADS fired by the Saiqas eventually hit the number 3 in the Israeli formation, forcing the pilot to eject. The rest of the formation was forced to scatter.

While their attack on Fort Budapest thus collapsed early, Egypt was much more successful further south. Fort Orkal, 10km (6.2 miles) south of Port Fuad, was isolated by infantry of the Second Field Army very early during the crossing and eventually fell on the following day, after survivors of its garrison made a break-out attempt to join friendly forces. Fort Lahtzanit, 19km (11.8 miles) south of Port Fuad, was meanwhile successfully assaulted and was the first fortification of the Bar Lev Line to fall, around 18.00 on 6 October. By that evening, Egyptian troops had surrounded virtually all the other strongpoints, turning much of the Jerusalem Infantry Brigade into hostages requiring rescue.[31]

The IDF/AF counterattacks along the Suez Canal were closely monitored by EAF pilots on different air bases. Salah Danish recalled:

*'We learned about the start of the war from the radio and when one of the aircraft involved – a MiG-21 flown by Capt Ghoneim, a very good interceptor pilot – landed at Komm Awshim. We then gathered at the command post to follow the developments on the radio and with the help of the radar. Our operations centre was very well equipped with a big screen on which all the operations and any signs of enemy activity were plotted. The rest of the afternoon we were monitoring with great satisfaction as the Israeli aircraft would appear on on that screen – and then disappear, because they were shot down.'*

One of the Egyptian pontoon bridges laid over the Suez Canal, as seen from the Sinai side (looking back in the direction of Egypt).
(David Nicolle Collection)

The US Navy was monitoring the developing battle too – with help of the EP-3 under the command of Lee Buchanan, deployed off the coast of Egypt with the aim of recording emissions from SA-6 sites:

*'Our patrol took us just to the north of the Suez Canal, so we had a direct line of sight on several surface-to-air missile engagements. We picked up the signals from an SA-6 battery as it shot down one of the first Israeli F-4s to fall. Then we watched other SA-6 actions.'*[32]

As far as is known, no Israeli publication – regardless to what degree it is based on 'official and complete' lists of IDF/AF losses during the October 1973 War – confirms the loss of any F-4E during the afternoon of 6 October, whether over Egypt or Syria. One A-4 was hit by SAMs near the Great Bitter Lake during the afternoon, and another was shot down by SA-6s while flying a loft-bombing attack on one of the Egyptian crossing sites, after sunset on the same day (the pilot was killed). However, considering the fact that the EP-3 is a dedicated SIGINT-gathering platform, it is very hard to imagine its highly specialised and qualified crew misreading intelligence collected by their sensitive equipment and confusing the 'electronic footprint' of an A-4 with that of an F-4E – if for no other reason than because the latter is equipped with an airborne radar, while the former had none. Therefore, it is possible that Buchanan's crew monitored the loss of one of the IDF/AF Phantoms that Israel denies to have suffered.

This is not to say that the IDF/AF does not admit to have lost at least one F-4 over Egypt on 6 October. During the same evening its fighter-bombers repeatedly attacked Egyptian crossing sites on the Suez Canal. During one such mission an F-4E was hit by SA-2s around 22.00. The pilot attempted an emergency landing at Hatzerim, but one of the CBUs still hanging under the wings came loose on touchdown and detonated, destroying the aircraft and killing the crew.[33]

## Heliborne Assault

As far as is known, all Egyptian plans for a counterattack into the Sinai envisaged large-scale commando operations. Initially, most such attacks were to support advances of ground troops in the direction of the Sinai passes. However, when the plan for a limited operation was adopted instead, the majority of missions assigned to Egyptian Army commando units (Saiqa) were cancelled. Instead, relatively limited enterprises were to be undertaken, starting during the second wave of the EAF's opening strike. Even so, this was to remain a relatively large operation, including the insertion of five commando battalions with the help of nearly all available Mi-8 helicopters, and with the aim of blocking the entries and exits to the Gidi and Mitla Defiles, disrupting enemy headquarters, communications and radar bases, water and telephone lines, and supply depots. Most reports about these operations are full of doubt about their effectiveness, and available accounts indicate that nearly all of them ended in utmost disaster, causing immense casualties for no gain. This raises the question of why the top Egyptian commanders deemed such operations necessary, considering their decision not to launch any kind of an advance outside the SAM umbrella? Because the Egyptian Ministry of Defence has never published any official explanation nor released any files about the October 1973 War, the answer to this question remains unknown until today.

The five Saiqa battalions in question were to be deployed in four major areas:
- one battalion on the northern coast of the Sinai, with the aim of blocking the road connecting el-Arish with Baluza;
- one battalion in the Katib as-Sebha area, roughly halfway between Tasa and Refidim;
- one battalion on the western side of the Gidi Defile, where it was to block the exit and then wait for the arrival of the 130th Brigade of the Egyptian Marine Corps;[34] and
- two battalions were to take part in what was actually a large-scale, combined amphibious and heliborne assault on the southern the Sinai. The primary aim of one of the battalions involved was to capture the 'oil corridor', comprising oil facilities in the Abu Rhudeis and Ras Sudr area. In turn, this mission was to support the amphibious landing of another commando battalion on the evening of 6 October,

Egyptian Il-28 bombers flew some of their last combat sorties ever during Operation Badhr, when two were sent to support the failed attack on Fort Budapest, on the Bar Lev Line. This post-war photograph shows serial number 1767. (David Nicolle Collection)

EP-3As of the US Navy's VQ-2 flew a number of SIGINT-gathering missions off the Egyptian and Syrian coasts during the October 1973 War. Some of the intelligence they collected during such sorties appears to confirm IDF/AF losses denied by Israel. (US Navy)

followed by an amphibious landing by the Army's 1st Mechanised Brigade (from the 6th Mechanised Division) between Ras Malab and Ras Shargib on the evening of 7 October. These units were to create a third bridgehead on the Sinai and then advance on Ras Masala, Ras Sudar, A-Tor and in the direction of Sharm el-Sheikh.

According to Okasha, the reason that most of these operations were doomed to fail right from the start was the decision to cancel the second wave of EAF attacks:

'…*The second wave was cancelled, completely without explanation. Instead, the EAF decided to send huge formations of helicopters fully loaded with commandos over the Sinai – without any kind of protection!*'

El-Iraqi was astounded to see other aircraft take off, but to receive no orders to do the same:

'*The Tu-16s went away, followed by several flights of MiG-21s… then our time came: we were ready to attack, but received no order to launch.*'

Naji recalled that the Iraqi ground crews re-armed and refuelled the 12 Hunters that returned from the first strike '*within minutes*':

'*We took our places in our cockpits, ready to strike the same targets again. We waited… and waited… and waited… and then came a signal from General Command: the first wave had achieved its goals and there would be no second wave…*'

Mikhail was no less disappointed:

'*We spent the rest of the day sitting in our cockpits on standby, but no order came to scramble for the second wave. Later on, a few fighters were launched to fly CAPs over specific areas, but none became involved in air combats. The day ended with us sitting on the ground and watching Tu-16s launching their long-range missiles at the Israelis on the Sinai from above el-Mansoura.*'[35]

As mentioned above, the official EAF explanation for the cancellation of the second wave of Operation Badhr was that the first wave accomplished its mission and a further attack was not necessary. No matter how many Egyptian veterans of this war have been interviewed in recent years, none of them was able to provide any more expansive reason, but Mohammed Okasha left no doubts as to who was to blame for the resulting disaster:

*'It was AM Mubarak who cancelled the second wave of the opening strike, which was to have a dual purpose: delivering additional blows against targets hit in the first strike, and then covering a large-scale heliborne commando assault on the most important Israeli installations in the Sinai, and postponing the deployment of Israeli reserves towards Suez… Whether deliberately or by mistake, Mubarak made the wrong decision and cancelled this wave, thus leaving dozens of helicopters carrying hundreds of elite commando troops without the necessary protection… Instead of explaining his reasons, instead of bearing responsibility for this failure, Mubarak was made a hero and is associated exclusively with the success of October 14's air battle for el-Mansourah, as if this was solely his own achievement.'*[36]

The little that is known about the Egyptian heliborne commando operations is primarily provided by Israeli sources. For example, it remains unknown what became of most of the 183rd Saiqa Battalion deployed by helicopters in the northern Sinai. Only one company of around 100 commandos was ever encountered by the Israelis. Led by Maj Hamdi Shalabi, they blocked the road between Romani and Baluza and ambushed a column of the 217th Reserve Armored Brigade IDF that was rushing in the direction of the Suez Canal, on the morning of 7 October. Taking the Israelis by surprise, Egyptian commandos destroyed two Centurion MBTs, killed seven and injured 21 Israeli soldiers. However, another Israeli column then outflanked the Egyptian position and overwhelmed it, killing 70 commandos while losing two halftracks and 10 KIA in a series of bitter clashes.

Most available Israeli accounts usually relate to the heliborne deployment of the second Egyptian commando battalion. Although entering Israeli-controlled airspace after sunset, some 24 Mi-8s involved in this operation were left without the necessary top cover. Shortly after crossing the Canal they came under repeated attacks by Israeli F-4Es and Neshers, and were practically annihilated. Only a handful of helicopters managed to land and disembark the commandos they were carrying before all were destroyed: the sole surviving Mi-8 made an emergency landing and was subsequently captured by the Israelis. Magdi Wakeel could not say much about this mission, because he did not participate in it, but left no doubt about the fate of Nos 11 and 19 Squadrons of Air Brigade 545:

*'The air brigade from Alexandria suffered extensive losses. This was because they had to fly over the front lines on the Suez Canal and then over most of the Israeli positions beyond, and were then intercepted by Israeli fighters.'*

The only pilot from these two units the authors were able to find so far is Ahmad Badi Abu Shaba, who recalled:

*'Our squadron equipped with 12 Mi-8s transferred to Fayd before the war. At 17.00 local time on 6 October we embarked 15–18 commandos from the 183rd Saiqa Battalion – their commander was named Ibrahim – and flew in a big formation over the Suez Canal in an easterly direction. Once over the Sinai, our formation parted into three flights of four helicopters each, of which ours was to land commandos near the Gidi Defile, in an attempt to block it for the passage of Israeli reinforcements.*

*'Enemy interceptors caught us shortly after we passed by the Bar Lev fortification known to the Israelis as Lakekan. Two helicopters from the first flight crashed:*

President Sadat seen while visiting Egyptian commandos before the war. Of special interest is the Mi-8 helicopter behind them, camouflaged in Nile Valley pattern (details of this are to be reconstructed in Volume 6). (David Nicolle Collection)

*one was shot down, and one had to be abandoned by its crew after an emergency landing. The other two flights from our squadron did not suffer any other losses, but we managed to land only 50 commandos, which was not enough to block the Gidi Defile.*[37]

The ground component of this operation experienced an early debacle too. Although the 130th Marine Brigade managed to cross the Small Bitter Lake and reach the eastern shore around 14.36, one of its battalions subsequently ran into elements of the 14th Armored Brigade IDF and – according to Israeli accounts – suffered a loss of 25 tanks and APCs in an uneven battle between its lightly armoured PT-76s and much heavier and better armed M60 MBTs operated by the Israelis. Whether the loss of an IDF/AF A-4 in the Great Bitter Lake area – which is known to have occurred around 17.30 local time – was related to this clash remains unknown. The survivors of this battalion of the 130th Marine Brigade were subsequently reassigned to the 7th Division of the Third Field Army.

Highly conflicting reports are available about the activities of the second battalion of the 130th Marine Brigade. According to most accounts, its operation was cancelled immediately after the clash between the first battalion and the 14th Armored Brigade IDF: this battalion was then ordered to return to the bridgehad of the Third Army. Once there, it was assigned the duty of (northern) flank protection for the Egyptian 16th Infantry Division for the rest of the war. While there is at least one Egyptian claim that the rest of the brigade headed east and raided a radar station at Mitla Defile – or even the airfield of Bir Tamada – on the morning of 7 October, there are no known Israeli sources that corroborate this.[38]

Only somewhat confusing reports are available about the fourth commando operation launched on the late afternoon of 6 October, namely the heliborne and seaborne assault on the 'oil corridor' in the Gulf of Suez. The most likely reason for this is a number of setbacks that Egypt experienced in the course of this operation, and piecemeal reporting scattered in a number of different Israeli publications, most of which attempt to explain that this operation was over before it had even begun. Seemingly, the IDF Navy destroyed the group of boats and light launches carrying seaborne commandos; MIM-23s shot down at least two helicopters; while the 35th Parachute Brigade then swiftly overwhelmed all the Egyptian commandos, killing around 750 and capturing 330. However, when Israeli accounts are cross-examined against some of the narratives provided by participating EAF pilots, an entirely new picture emerges.

Accordingly, the seaborne landing was indeed disrupted by the Israeli Navy, prompting Egyptian commanders to cancel the transfer of the 1st Mechanised Brigade to the Sinai in this fashion. Instead, this brigade was ordered to cross the Cannal via the bridgehead of the Second Army and launch its advance in a southerly direction from there. Nevertheless, the Israeli HAWK site at Ras Sudar did not participate in the early action: although detecting and positively identifying approaching helicopters as hostile, its CO – Lt Shlomo Najari – did not receive permission to engage. As a result, the Egyptians landed unopposed, as recalled by Magdi Wakeel, who served with No. 9 Squadron:

*'On the first afternoon of the war we took off from Ras Zafranah on the Red Sea coast, from where we operated throughout the war. We first picked up commandos from a place away from the base, and then flew them over the Red Sea and to the coast of the Sinai, into the mountains. We landed without problems and these com-*

Wreckage of a Mi-8 from No. 9 Squadron, shot down by MIM-23 HAWK SAMs during the attack on Ras Sudar. The pilot and a few passengers survived the crash, though all were badly injured. (IDF)

An assault formation of EAF Mi-8s, as seen during one of many exercises held before the October 1973 War. (David Nicolle Collection)

*mandos then attacked the Israeli positions on the coast. On the way back we attacked the oil facilities, storage tanks and depots with unguided rockets.'*

Najari finally received permission to fire only when the next wave of Egyptian helicopters approached the area and ordered his operations officer, Kobi Mazor, into action. Mazor claimed one helicopter as shot down and another to have crashed when it flew into the debris of the downed Mil, but also reported that the rest of Egyptian formation landed at Sudar Junction, very close to the battery's position. Wakeel confirmed that it was only when the Mi-8s of No. 9 Squadron returned to Ras Sudar, carrying the next wave of commandos, that they encountered resistance. However, he did not recall more than one loss:

*'During our second mission one helicopter in my flight was hit by missiles which I believe were SAMs. It was hit while only 25m [82ft] ahead of our Mi-8 and crashed into the ground, spilling the crew and passengers on to the ground. The pilot and a few others survived the crash, though very badly injured, with many broken bones. They were captured by the Israelis and sent to Tel Aviv. After the war they told us the Israeli hospital facilities were so good that they recovered, whereas if they had gone to an Egyptian hospital they would have died...'*

No. 9 Squadron EAF thus continued its mission and successfully disembarked commandos between Ras Sudar and Abu Rudeis. Wakeel flew two more sorties over the Red Sea the same night:

*'During another mission the wheels of a Mi-8 flying with us hit some telegraph wires and the helicopter crashed. The pilot and crew survived unhurt and walked back to Egyptian-held territory for 17 days. During the third mission our Mi-8 was shot at by the ground defences at Ras Zafranah* [his own base; authors' note], *because the gunners thought they were under attack. Our machine was full of holes.'*

Circumstantial evidence suggests the commandos meanwhile became involved in fierce fighting with elements of the 35th Parachute Brigade IDF, which did well in preventing the Egyptians from regrouping and forced them to evade. The few scattered groups of Saiqas apparently spent the rest of the war waiting for the 1st Mechanised

Up to 25 Egyptian Mi-8s were shot down during heliborne commando assaults on Israeli positions in Sinai, on the late afternoon of 6 October 1973. This wreckage was photographed by the Israelis south of Refidim airfield. (IDF)

Brigade to arrive. When this failed to materialise, after a few days of intensive combat and evasion, most of the commandos were exhausted, killed or captured. Survivors reportedly spent the rest of the war hiding in the mountains of the southern Sinai where they were – from time to time – replenished with the help of helicopters. Egyptian accounts, however, stress that at least a company of Saiqas not only captured the Sudr Pass and kept it blocked from Israeli forces until the ceasefire of 22 October 1973, but that a few other units brought several other areas under their control too. Accordingly, the more mobile Israelis held the relatively open spaces between such positions, but could not force the Egyptians out of their hideouts.[39] No matter what side held what, the fact remains that several groups of Saiqas still maintained their positions when not only the first, but also the second and all subsequent ceasefires came into effect. Indeed, as we are to see in *Volume 6*, their continuous operations resulted in related operations by the EAF too.

Nevertheless, Mohammed Okasha's conclusion regarding the debacle of the major heliborne operations into central Sinai was particularly bitter:

*'The EAF lost 25 helicopters with most of their crews and nearly 400 commandos in that mission, while we were sitting in our cockpits, ready to take off – but not permitted to do so...'*

Almost certainly shocked by this massive loss, Egypt undertook only minor operations of this kind for the rest of the war. For example, on the evening of 7 October, six Mi-8s delivered a company of commandos to the area of the Mitla Defile, and the Israeli HAWK site near Ras Sudar claimed another Mi-8 as shot down. However, very little is known about the subsequent activities of the ground troops in question.

# Syrian Countdown

In the last few days before the attack, the SyAAF and the SyAADF underwent a similar process to the Egyptian forces, but much less is known about specific details, since next to no details have been released so far. Fikry el-Gindy, commander of the Egyptian MiG-17 squadron assigned to the SyAAF, recalled the first few days of October as follows:

'On 2 October, I was given a 'top secret' operational plan for strikes on Israeli positions on the Golan to study, and we saw heavier and heavier movement of troops between Almazza and Qunaitra. Long columns of tanks on transporters were moving towards the front, followed by artillery pieces and rocket launchers. Syrian attempts to hide these movements were rather superficial. Then suddenly a US-built C-130 Hercules transport of the Royal Saudi Air Force landed at our air base. Col Hussni came out, together with two Saudi pilots and explained to us that this was a part of a secret arrangement between Cairo and Riyadh. The plane brought with it a load of Sakr rockets from Egypt. This confirmed my thinking that the war must now be very close. Subsequently, all leave was cancelled.

'3 October began with more training, especially low-altitude exercises, but our sessions ended earlier, because we were then all sent to study a three-dimensional map of the Golan, southern Lebanon and northern Israel. We were especially curious to study northern Galilee and the routes we would follow when flying our missions. Then a second Saudi C-130 landed, this time flown by Col Hamza and bringing FM Ahmad Ismail, the Egyptian Minister of Defence. We did not know it back then, but he was on a last-minute visit to Damascus to coordinate the coming campaign with the Syrians.

'I meanwhile chatted with Hamza, who was well informed because of his senior position in the EAF Transport Command. He made it clear that the war was really imminent. Shortly after, Maj al-Maghrabi approached me with a request for leave in Egypt. I tried to explain to him that it would be better not to go, but because I knew that we were about to receive a replacement, I eventually granted him permission, and he left for Cairo on Hamza's C-130. Sadly, once in Egypt al-Maghrabi volunteered to join another unit, but was shot down and killed.'

On 4 October, IDF/AF sent two Mirage IIIs configured for reconnaissance over Syria, putting the SyAAF on alert and disrupting the training of el-Gindy's unit:

'On 4 October we continued our training, and I led two sections of four aircraft over the border to Lebanon, over the Bekaa Valley. This was strictly against the rules but I felt I had to accustomise my pilots to that area, because of the narrowness of the future front. Later the same day there was an alert because Israeli aircraft entered Syrian airspace, but they soon turned away so nobody was scrambled. Then a Soviet Antonov transport landed, carrying a number of Egyptian officers and pilots that went straight for the Syrian Supreme Headquarters in Damascus – and an additional load of anti-runway bombs.

'5 October was a Friday, and thus a weekend, but we trained and then I asked all my pilots not to go to Damascus after the end of their duty. I explained to them that I was sure the war would start the next day, and that I was very concerned that the same thing that happened in 1967 might happen again (namely, that the Israelis would attack first and try to destroy our air arm on the ground). Meanwhile, I had a meeting with Brig Haddad and subsequently we were indeed told that the hostilities would start in earnest the next day, coded Qahir 14. Thus, we went back to study the three-dimensional map as well as reconnaissance photographs of all possible targets that we expected to attack. I looked around at the faces of my young pilots and saw confidence. We were sure this time we would win.

Members of one of the Egyptian Saiqa battalions in front of an EAF Mi-8 helicopter, as seen during a pre-war inspection. Of interest is the disruptive camouflage pattern (probably in yellow sand applied over the original olive green colour) and the form and position of the markings. In contrast, most helicopters of this type seen in service since the end of the October 1973 War were painted in overall yellow sand. (Albert Grandolini Collection)

*'Later on, I began feeling feverish and cold, and after consulting our squadron doctor, Dr Zacharios (a Coptic Christian), I found out that I had a temperature of 38°C. I began to worry that I would not be fit to fly the next day. I told him to try and cure me as quickly as possible as, come what may, I was determined to lead my squadron into action. We all ended the day by going to pray and then went to sleep. Once in my room, I put all my personal effects into a small bag. Then I wrote a letter to my wife, telling her what should she do with the children and my mother in case of my death. That would serve as my will.*

*'On the morning of 6 October, there was a big conference of all the pilots from our wing, including Nos 1 (Col Taher Sabah) Squadron, 2 (commanded by Lt Col Samir Zainal, an Iraqi refugee), 5 (Col Muhammad Sharif Raya), and 18 (Col Marwan Barsh) Squadrons SyAAF, as well as our No. 15 Squadron. Col Marwan Barsh explained the operational plan, starting with a few thoughts about 1967, and how this time we are going to do it differently. Our GCI was codenamed 'Marid', meaning 'giant', while the codename of our squadron was 'Mugamar', meaning 'volunteer'.'* [40]

## Bitter Revenge

Nearly the entire SyAAF was involved in the opening strike against Israeli forces on the Golan. In the north, between 24 and 30 MiG-17s protected by MiG-21s flew CAS sorties in support of operations against the observation post (OP) on Mount Jebel Sheikh. The weather was cloudy and so it was that the first five (or more likely eight) MiG-17s that approached the IDF armour base near the Druse village of Majdal Shaams missed their target and unleashed most of their rockets and bombs upon civilians, around 13.58 local (Israeli) time. A young woman and her old baby thus became the most likely first victims of this war – while the Israelis suffered no losses in this war.[41]

Furthest to go were 24 MiG-17s that hit the HAWK sites near Kfar Giladi and outside Tiberias, as well as the EW centre of the Northern Command IDF at Rosh Pina, and a formation of 12 Su-20s (protected by eight MiG-21s) that bombed the IDF/AF control centre in Hebron on the West Bank. No accounts about the results of any of these attacks are currently available.

Additional formations including a total of about 20 Su-7BMKs and 16 MiG-17s (protected by six MiG-21s during the ingress) which then attacked nearly every single IDF base on the Golan Heights, foremost along the road between Qunaitra and B'not Yaacov Bridge. The IDF's Hushniye military camp was bombed by at least two flights of MiG-17s. Another four-ship of MiG-17s hit the air defence site protecting the armour base near Tel Abu Nida, and damaged all three M3 halftracks equipped with TCM-20 anti-aircraft cannon of the local battery from the 66th Reserve Division, rendering one inoperational[42]. Five additional flights (20 aircraft) of MiG-17s bombarded the divisional HQ at Naffekh although, according to Israeli sources, *'most of their bombs narrowly missed the camp and exploded in an unoccupied gully behind it, injuring nobody'*. Israel claimed up to eight SyAAF aircraft shot down during the opening strike of Operation Badhr, and a number of their patrols were busy searching for pilots that had ejected – primarily along the River Jordan – during that afternoon and evening.[43]

Other details about the results of Operation Badhr are unavailable. Most Israeli accounts consider it hardly worthy of mention, or declare it futile or useless; some stress that most of the SyAAF aircraft involved were either shot down or 'driven off' by anti-aircraft fire. However, other Israeli- and several unofficial Syrian sources stress that not only that these air attacks increased the chaos and confusion within the IDF, but that only one SyAAF fighter-bomber was shot down. Fikry el-Gindy's recollection of his participation indicate the high morale and extreme eagerness of the pilots involved: whether Egyptians, Iraqis or Syrians, Arab pilots in general were looking forward to extact revenge for the shame of the June 1967 War, and were thus extremely unlikely to 'flee', as explained by el-Gindy:

*'When the conference ended, we went back to our squadron ready rooms and discussed what we had heard before having lunch... We were 10 pilots in our unit: myself, Bakr Suleyman (my second-in-command), Badawi Abdul Megid Badawi, Sayf al-Islam, Yahya Abu Zaina, Yusuf, Mustafa, Naif, Hazim, and Sharif, all very keen. We had 16 MiG-17Fs at our disposal, including serial numbers 2034, 2072, 2405, 2517, 2525, 2572, 2580, 2609, 2613, 2621, 2650, 2723, 2726, 2752, 2851 and 2877. We also had two Syrian MiG-15s assigned to our unit, MiG-15UTI serial number 326 and MiG-15bis serial number 922. We agreed that we were going to call the coming war the Battle for Revenge, revenge for the cheap defeat of 1967. I did not want to minimise Israel's achievements from the last war, but we all felt that because of our bad commanders, we actually never got a chance to fight back then.'*

Indeed, el-Gindy then led his No. 15 Squadron during the opening strike, despite a fever of 37.5°C:

*'Following the noon prayers, Brig Haddad gave us a short speech talking about the day ahead. He told us the battle would start at 14.45 local time. Then a target was allocated to our squadron: a radar system in northern Israel, outside Saffad, in Upper Galilee. He saw me sweating and asked me if I was afraid. I felt the effect of the cold that had caught me the last evening, and got very angry at this question, answering in rather unfriendly terms that I was never afraid. Haddad then ordered*

Fikry el-Gindy in flying suit and with helmet, as seen at the time he commanded a squadron of Egyptian MiG-17s in Syria, in 1973.
(Fikry el-Gindy Collection)

*me not to fly, but there was nothing that would stop me from flying that day. I got angry and replied accordingly. I had been waiting for this moment for six years and would fly whatever happened. On the contrary, I then gathered my pilots and explained to them what I expected from them. In a few simple words I explained the difference between fear of taking off and anxiety about the mission.*

'*At 14.45 [Syrian time, 13.45 Israeli time; authors' note] we went to our aircraft, full of enthusiasm and shouting 'Allah-u-Akhbar'. I was to fly MiG-17F 2609, my favourite mount. Although flying all of the aircraft assigned to our squadron before the war, I tended to fly this one more often than the others. In fact, whenever I got into that plane I used to kiss it, because I liked it so much. It seemed to be able to do everything a bit better...*

'*We started our mission organised in two groups: our 10 pilots plus two Syrians, including Iraqi Col Qaisy, who flew as lead of the second group. Our plan was for us to fly towards Zahle in Lebanon, then turn south down the Bekaa Valley to Marj Ayoun, then down the Rashiya Valley in the direction of Safad. However, once airborne, we received a counter-order to change direction and head for Lake Masaada, in the northern Golan, to attack enemy ground troops there.*

'*We completed our mission without any problems, delivering our ordnance precisely on the target, and then returned to our base. I was very impressed by my pilots and the result of their training. We hadn't seen a single Israeli aircraft in the sky...*

'*But then we nearly experienced a disaster: no fewer than 37 MiG-17s arrived over the airfield all at once. Many were short of fuel and thus everybody was trying to land simultaneously. After a few tense minutes, we sorted ourselves out, letting those with less fuel in their tanks land first...*

'*Once on the ground, it was like a big celebration. We went to the side of the airfield where our ground crews greeted us. This was the first time we had hit the enemy 'in his own house', and thus they began carrying us on their hands. We never experienced such a feeling before. Gen Haddad also came and embraced me and thanked me for this achievement. Thanks to be God, it was a great day!*'

One is left to wonder why the SyAAF never attempted to attack seven bridges spanning the River Jordan between Israel and the Golan Heights, which its Su-7BMKs armed with FAB-500M-54 and FAB-500M-62 bombs could have dropped – or otherwise heavily damaged. Such an attack would have been logical considering Syrian concerns about the influx of crucially important Israeli reinforcements to the Golan, but also

Fikry el-Gindy (fourth from the left), some of his pilots and Syrian colleagues seen shortly before the October 1973 War.
(Fikry el-Gindy Collection)

in regards Hafez al-Assad's intention: it would show that Syria was only interested in regaining the territory lost during the June 1967 War. Puzzled, the authors discussed this issue with a number of Iraqi and several retired Syrian pilots, never finding a satisfactory answer: it seems that the High Command SyAAF never entertained such an idea. Indeed, one of 'most useful' answers provided by one of the Syrian pilots suggested, '...*this was beyond the mentality of SyAAF commanders.*'[44]

## Assault on Jebel Sheikh: Another Surprise

Due to the availability of the OPs at Mount Jebel Sheikh and Tel Faris, the IDF/AF received a timely warning about the incoming Syrian attack. It was already around 13.54 when the northernmost HAWK site received an authorisation to engage four SyAAF Su-7s that were heading southwest from the direction of Damascus. Israel claimed one Syrian fighter-bombers shot down and another damaged, a few minutes later, and claimed to have driven the rest of the enemy formation away from its target.

The OP at Jebel Sheikh was much more than this simple description might reveal. Constructed at a point 2,100m (6,890ft) above sea level (the peak of Jebel Sheikh is at 2,814m/9,232ft), it was actually a massive fortification made of concrete and stone, surrouned by a number of firing positions, interconnected by underground tunnels, and perfectly protected from shelling and air strikes. It also included points for visual observation, but the centrepiece was an electronic intelligence warfare centre including ELINT and SIGINT-gathering systems. The garrison of 57 soldiers – of which only 14 were members of the 13th Battalion, 1st 'Golani' Infantry Brigade and responsible for security – had only one problem: their air defence system was not yet in place.

The original Syrian plan was for the OP on Jebel Sheik to be assaulted around 12.00, Syrian time, well in advance of the opening strike and via a heliborne attack by the 500-strong 82nd Parachute Battalion (the prestigious first 'special forces' unit ever established in Syria). However, for unknown reasons, this operation was postponed and started only around 14.45, nearly a full hour after preparatory artillery shelling. According to Israeli accounts, 10 Mi-8s approached the OP flying in column formation low between the hills and through ravines, not seen – but heard – by the garrison. Syrian sources recall the involvement of only four Mi-8s, which made the main landing at the summit, some 1,200-1,300m (3,937-4,265ft) away from the Israeli fortification, but two helicopters landed their troops only 500m southwest of the site itself. The Israelis opened fire in return and claimed no fewer than eight helicopters as damaged, but it remains unclear whether their claims that one of of the Mils crashed and burst into flames (supposedly killing everybody on board except one pilot) can be considered as confirmed: available Syrian sources do not mention any such losses.[45]

The commander of the Syrian force thus had around 70 men with him when the actual assault began. Initially, these encountered only sporadic defensive fire because the shelling and air strikes forced most of the Israelis into underground shelter. Thus, the Syrians penetrated the OP around 17.00 local time. Following sporadic fighting through the night, during which 11 Israelis were able to break out, the OP at Jebel Sheikh was finally secured by 11.30 the following morning. Meanwhile, the rest of the 82nd Battalion also captured Height 1614, overlooking the road approaching the OP from the south.

A pair of SyAAF Su-7BMKs returns at low altitude from the opening strike of Operation Badhr.
(David Nicolle Collection)

Two views of EAF MiG-17F serial number 2034, as seen following its return to Egypt and an overhaul, in 1975. This aircraft was one of 16 deployed to Syria in 1972, and flown by pilots of el-Gindy's No. 62 Squadron – re-designated as No. 15 Squadron while in Syria – from Almaza airfield during the October 1973 War. (Albert Grandolini Collection)

## Armoured Juggernaut

For its assault on the Golan Heights the Syrian Arab Army deployed an imposing force consisting of three mechanised infantry divisions (each theoretically consisting of one infantry, two mechanised and one armoured brigades, but with most of these formations not operating their full complement of tanks), three armoured divisions (all at full strength), and several independent brigades (including a Moroccan Expeditionary Brigade), with about 60,000 troops. Supported by a massive barrage from about 120 artillery batteries that lasted 50 minutes, infantry formations went into action first: the Moroccans advanced along the foothills of Jebel Sheikh; the 7th Infantry Division assaulted north of the Quneitra-Damascus road; the 9th Infantry Division pushed into the Rafid Gap, while the 5th Infantry Division attacked south and east of Rafid and north of the Yarmouk Valley. Behind them, the 3rd Armoured Division was waiting to

A pair of SyAAF Mi-8s photographed while under way to deploy commandos of the 82nd Parachute Battalion for attack on the Israeli OP on Jebel Sheikh.
(IDF)

exploit the breach in the Israeli front lines near Katana and Saasa; the 1st Armoured Division did the same at Kisweh, while the Republican Guards Division was protecting Damascus.

Israel usually held elements of three regular brigades stationed on the Golan Heights, including elements from the 1st 'Golani' Infantry Brigade, 50th Paratroop Battalion, and the complete 188th Armored Brigade. Following alarming reports about the massive Syrian Army concentration on the other side of the ceasefire line, on 5 October the IDF moved the 7th Armored Brigade and some artillery reinforcements to the Golan Heights, bringing the total number of available MBTs to 177. When the Syrian attack began, the 7th Armored Brigade rushed to positions north of Quneitra, while the 188th deployed south of that town.

The assault columns of the Syrian divisions consisted of densely packed ranks of BTR-50 and BTR-60 armoured personnel carriers (APCs), supported by SU-100 self-propelled guns and T-55 MBTs.[46] Advancing over a terrain that did not favour armoured warfare, and facing murderous fire from well-positioned Israeli tanks, these fell into confusion when they reached a major anti-tank ditch and minefields in front of the Israeli defensive positions. Nevertheless, Syrian commanders and engineers managed to overcome these problems and construct at least two crossing sites opposite the 7th Israeli Armored Brigade in the north, and additional crossings in the south. Indeed, while all assaults by the 7th Infantry Division were beaten back by the Israelis, by 17.00 the 5th Syrian Infantry Division was already in the process of destroying the 188th Armored Brigade and advancing between its scattered remnants.

Under these circumstances the IDF/AF scrambled to provide support for the hard-pressed ground units. The first four Skyhawks appeared over the Golan Heights around 14.30. While under way at medium altitude and searching for suitable targets, they flew straight into the centre of the envelope put up by the southern Syrian 'super SAM site'. The lead A-4 was shot down by an SA-2 moments later: the Israeli formation leader was killed while the rest of his formation scattered. While several other flights avoided losses, around 16.00 another Skyhawk was shot down by Syrian SAMs, but its pilot survived the ejection and managed to join retreating ground troops.[47]

## Secret Weapon: SA-6 Gainful

The appearance of the 2K12E Kvadrat (SA-6 Gainful) SAM in the Arab arsenal apparently evaded the attention of Israeli intelligence. Its first deployment in combat certainly came as a nasty surprise for the IDF/AF, and this weapon rapidly earned a fearful reputation in Israel and abroad.

The original 2K12 was introduced to service by the Soviets in 1967 as a mobile, self-propelled, low-altitude anti-aircraft system to complement the much heavier and longer-ranged 2K11 Krug (SA-4 Ganef) system. Most of the equipment of an SA-6 system was installed on tracked vehicles. The centrepiece of each site was the 1S91 fire-control radar (ASCC codename Straight Flush) with a continuous-wave (CW) illuminator and an optical sight, installed on a GM-568 tracked chassis. Meanwhile, four 2P25 transporter-erector-launchers (TELs) carrying launch rails for three missiles each, were installed on GM-578 chassis. The Straight Flush radar was used for acquisition and tracking of targets, for IFF, and for illumination and missile guidance. It could simultaneously engage only one target, and guide two missiles to it.

The name Kvadrat (square) was used for the 2K12E export variant and derived from the most common arrangement pattern of the site, in which the Straight Flush was positioned in the centre, surrounded by four 2P25 TELs positioned in a square around it. The missile deployed by the Kvadrat was the 3M9E: a two-stage, solid-fuel, ramjet-powered missile weightng 630kg (1,388lb) with radio-command guidance in the first phase of the flight, and semi-active, CW radar terminal homing. It had an effective engagement range of between 6–22km (3.7–13.7 miles), and reached speeds of up to Mach 2.8. Its 57kg (123lb) warhead was detonated either by impact or proximity fuse. Contrary to some Western reports about the appearance of SA-6s in Egypt during the closing stages of the War of Attrition, the first Kvadrats entered service with the ADC only in 1971, followed by Syria in 1973.[48]

An Egyptian 2P25 TEL with three 3M9E missiles and the crew of the vehicle, seen shortly after the October 1973 War. (Tom Cooper Collection)

## Table 4: Equipment of a typical Egyptian and Syrian 2K12E Kvadrat SAM site, 1973

| Equipment and remarks | Number of items per site |
|---|---|
| P-40 Long Track EW radar (often replaced by P-15M in Egyptian and Syrian service) | 1 |
| 1S91 (Straigth Flush) fire-control radar, 25kW G/H-band, range 75km (46.6 miles) | 1 |
| 2P25 TEL | 4 |
| 2T7 (ZIL-131 6x6 truck) with three missile re-loads | 2 |

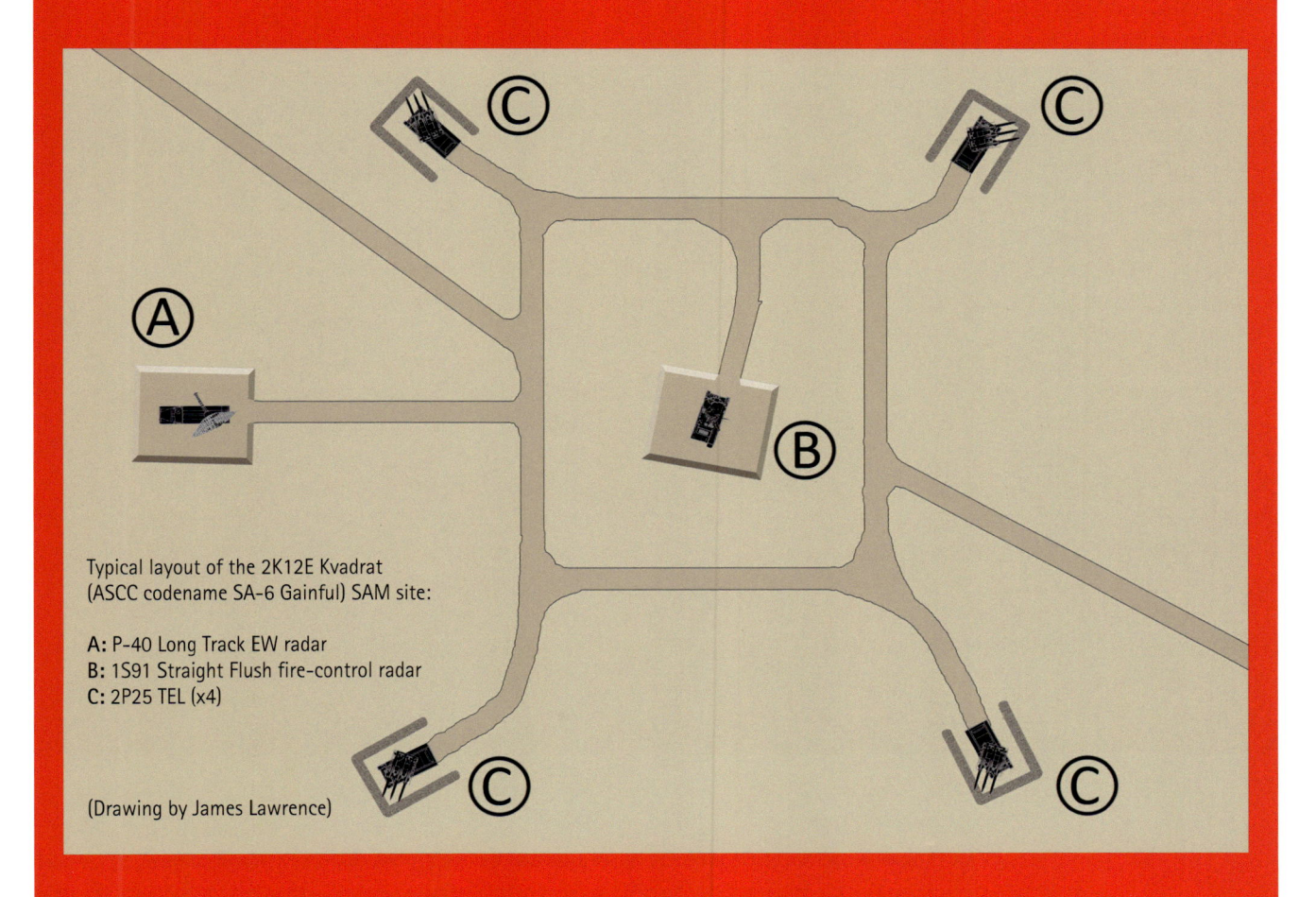

Typical layout of the 2K12E Kvadrat (ASCC codename SA-6 Gainful) SAM site:

**A:** P-40 Long Track EW radar
**B:** 1S91 Straight Flush fire-control radar
**C:** 2P25 TEL (x4)

(Drawing by James Lawrence)

After suffering severe losses to Arab air defences and especially to SA-6s in the first three days of the war (rumour has it that the IDF/AF plots dubbed it the 'Three Fingers of Death', in reference to the appearance of the TEL), Israeli representatives in the US were soon searching for a working solution, as recalled by Lt Col Dave Brog, who worked at US Air Forces in Europe (USAFE) HQ at Ramstein AB, West Germany:

*'A few days after the war began, an Israeli officer came… to talk about their problems. I called USAFE and explained what we, the air staff, were trying to do. At the start of the war the Israeli Air Force had only ALQ-101(V)6 and ALQ-101(V)8 jamming pods. We got permission to take 40 ALQ-119 pods from USAFE and fly them to Israel, together with a technical sergeant to help with installation.'*

The USAF technician helped the Israelis install the AN/ALQ-119 on their Phantoms, and the new pods proved relatively useful – albeit not against the SA-6: at that time even the US was not in possession of electronic countermeasures against that system. The US electronic warfare community had recognised that the Soviets would likely field an equivalent to the US-made MIM-23 HAWK SAM and its CW fire-control radar sooner or later, and had begun working on suitable countermeasures during the late 1960s. Their work resulted in two ECM pods (colloquially known as 'jammer pods') designated QRC-249 and QRC-335, which in turn resulted in the aforementioned AN/ALQ-119. However, the ALQ-119 proved unable to counter the SA-6, as Brog explained:

*'Above all, the Israelis wanted to know which settings we used to counter the SA-6 system. We gave them what we had, a setting for a velocity gate pull-off signal intended to distract the missile's CW seeker head. But, we did not know enough about the missile to know whether that setting would work. The Israelis decided not to use our setting. They were afraid the jamming pod would act as a beacon and they were unwilling to take the chance. So, the Israelis used the ALQ-119s to counter just the SA-2s and SA-3s, but not the SA-6.'*

The IDF/AF was thus left without the technological solutions necessary to counter the SA-6. To make matters more problematic, the new Soviet missile emitted signals that were not registered by existing RWR and RHAWS carried by Israeli fighters, meaning that the only warning of it was visual. However, the 3M9 missile was smaller than the missiles of the earlier SA-2 and SA-3 systems, and it flew on ramjet power, which left little smoke or glow. That meant that the SA-6 was extremely hard to detect, and avoid. All the IDF/AF could do for most of the war was to either take the chance, or completely avoid areas protected by SA-6s.[49]

However, early Egyptian – and especially Syrian – experiences with the SA-6 were by no means as positive as often claimed by the local media, or assumed by many foreign observers. Muhannad, a SyAADF officer and veteran of the October 1973 War explained:

*'The SA-6 was still suffering from similar problems as the earlier SA-2s and SA-3s. The Straight Flush radar suffered from ground clutter, it had poor tracking capability of targets maneuvering in the vertical axis, and required a very precise calibration – a time-consuming process – following every move. It lacked the moving-target indicator, which meant that the entire system could be easily decoyed through the use of chaff. Our combat experiences indicated two major weak spots: interruption of the wire link between the early warning radar and the command post – through combat damage, for example – or destruction or neutralisation of the Straight Flush, which rendered the entire site inoperational. Our experience with SA-6s in October 1973 was that the real killers were ZSU-23-4 'Shilka' self-propelled guns. Through integration of a 'Shilka' battery in every SA-6 site, they scored more kills than the missiles.'*[50]

1. Standard Soviet black and white gun-camera film was only 160cm (63in) long. It was activated by the pilot pressing the trigger to open fire. Two seconds of firing usually resulted in 16 to 18 frames of film. Standard Soviet films were grainy and did not react well to strong light. It seems that by 1973 Egypt had replaced them with compatible AGFA or Kodak films of superior quality.

2. Zeev Schiff, 'Israeli Air Force shoots down 13 Syrian Jets'; *Haaretz*, 14 September 1973. According to the same article, the first stage of this air battle lasted 'three to five minutes' and involved 12 Israeli Phantoms and Mirages and 16 Syrian planes. Notably, SyAAF MiG-21pilot Essam Hallaq is known to have continued a highly-successful career, reaching the rank of Major-General and serving as the C-in-C SyAAF from 2010 until 2012.

3. Largely based on Uri Bar-Joseph, 'Strategic Surprise or Fundamental Flaws' (see Bibliography for details)

4. As discussed extensively in *Volume 3*, the official Egyptian and Syrian documentation that meanwhile became available showed that the destruction of at least these two air forces during the June 1967 War was

anything but 'complete'. Much more than this, it was the shock caused by the intensive and repetitive Israeli air strikes upon Egyptian air bases, as well as incompetence of Arab commanders and general unpreparedness of all Arab militaries, that resulted in a 'clear cut' Israeli victory.

5   Asher, *Egyptian Strategy*, pp60

6   Schiff, *October Earthquake, Yom Kippur 1973*; Tel Aviv, University Publishing Projects Ltd., 1974, pp260

7   Mitch Ginsburg, 'Account of King Hussein's 1973 war warning still deemed too harmful to release', The Times of Israel, 12 September, 2013

8   For details on warnings from US intelligence see *President Nixon and the Role of Intelligence in The 1973 Arab-Israeli War* (Yorba Linda, Richard Nixon Presidential Library and Museum, 30 January 2013). Arguably, on 3 October 1973, such warnings were followed by CIA Intelligence Report titled 'Judgment that Syrian Military Preparations are Defensive in Nature', which cited a Syrian officer that expressed, 'serious fears of an Israeli attack into Syria', and that Syrians were massing their troops along the cease-fire line, 'because of our fears'.

9   Although some Soviet instructors remained in Egypt during the October 1973 War, even Israeli intelligence experts in regards of the Egyptian military confirm that none became involved in actual combat, see Asher, pp70

10  Price, pp155

11  Ahmed el-Keraidy (son of Mohammed Abdel Wahab el-Keraidy, one of Tu-16K-11-16 pilots in 1973), interview, June 2010.

12  Most of details from this sub-chapter are based on research – including numerous interviews with various participants – run in cooperation with Group 73.

13  Asher, pp61

14  Okasha, interview to Group 73, November 2012

15  Asher (citing from a captured copy of this Order), pp219

16  Note that in best tradition of applying the 'finger four' formation that was 'standard' for the IrAF as of 1973, Iraqi pilots are usually recollecting only the flight leader and his Number 3 – the leader of the second element within every flight.

17  Ahmed el-Keraidy, interview, June 2010. Similarly, using documentation left behind by his father, Ahmed el-Keraidy cited the target of his father's attack as Umm Qashiba, not 'administrative centre in Abu Rudeis', as cited by certain Russian sources recently. Furthermore, he observed that while his father used to serve on Il-28 light bombers during the Yemen War and the June 1967 War, el-Gawahergy was one of first Egyptian pilots to convert to Tu-16. He flew as co-pilot to Hossni Moubarak during the flight from Beni Suweif AB to Luxor airport, on the morning of 5 June 1967 (see Volume 3, pp51 for details). Like most of Egyptian Tu-16 pilots, el-Gawahergy has spent the following three years continuing training on Tu-16s in Iraq and then served at Inchas and Bilbeis before joining No. 36 Squadron in 1972.

18  Notable is that the Israeli sources are claiming the KSR-2 in question was fired 'at Tel Aviv', i.e. one of early warning radar stations inside Israel. From Egyptian standpoint, this was entirely out of question and not a single missile was fired in direction of Israel.

19  Many of interviewed Egyptian and Iraqi officers stressed high importance of this installation for the IDF; the only difference between their recollections about attacks on Units 511 and 545 was that the Iraqis believe these were undertaken by SS-1c Scud-Bs and considered such attacks to have been more effective than those by KSR-11s and MiGs. For example, Brig Gen Ahmad Sadik, who used to serve with the IrAF Intelligence Directorate, provided an interesting observation related to attacks on Umm Qashiba and the chaos within the IDF chain of command during the first week of the war:

*'The Israelis always lie about results of our attacks on their military, explaining little or no damage is caused, or that only civilian targets are hit...The attacks on Umm Qashiba could not have knocked out the extensive underground facilities because we were lacking suitable warheads. But post-war studies of*

*our military intelligence were perfectly clear: attacks on Umm Qashiba on 6 October 1973 have caused enough damage to put this strategically important post out of business until 13 or 14 October 1973. That meant that the IDF was blind and deaf: it could not relay on timely provision of ELINT and SIGINT intelligence. Arrogant about Arab military capabilities as they were, Israeli commanders thus lacked timely information about intentions and capabilities of Egyptian Army. They could not receive such information in advance, and thus began making the same mistakes everybody else is doing in every war'.*

Some of recently released Israeli accounts seem to confirm such conclusions. For example, Ariel Sharon's testimony to the Agranat Commission (Sharon testified on 29 July 1974) reveals that for most of the time between the moment he reached Refidim AB on the afternoon of the first day of the war and several days later, he was unsuccessfully trying to find out what was happening. Left without useful intelligence, the Israeli division commander ended doing the same most of other military commanders are doing since centuries; namely, monitoring the battlefield with his bioncular:

*'We were standing 10 or 12km km from the Canal, but we couldn't discern what was happening there. Everything was full of dust, full of smoke, and we didn't see much. Later, it turned out that there were sometimes convoys of hundreds of vehicles that the air force could have caused damage to.'*

20   Memorandum of Conversation ('Memcon'), 'Military Briefing', 22 October 1973, The National Security Archive (USA). Specifically, in the course of conversation with US representatives, the C-in-C IDF/AF Maj Gen Benjamin Peled stated:
*'The Egyptians surprised us with the Kelt missiles, which made two direct hits: Sharm el-Sheikh and Bir Gifgafa. The Kelt has 90km range against radar. We didn't know it existed. But when we did then we found a counter measure, namely shutting down the radars when the Tu-16 is in the air which is mainly at night'.*

21   Eshel, The Suez Canal Crossing 1973, Part 2, *Born in Battle*, p9.

22   Former IrAF Hunter pilot, interview provided on condition of anonymity, March 2006 (primary reason for anonymity of this source was the place where he used to live while interviewed and related concerns for his and the security of his family; readers should keep in mind that most of retired Iraqi officers that agreed to provide their full name during interviews are now living in exile and have survived assassination attempts while still in Iraq since the US-led invasion of 2003).

23   Okasha, interview to Group 73, November 2012. El-Shennawy's Pilot Log Book, kindly provided by his son Tarek el-Shennawy, cites 'bombing Refidim' for his third sortie on 6 October 1973. For Israeli account of attack on Refidim AB, see Cohen, *Israel's Best Defence* pp326-330. Notable is that Cohen grossly downplayed the results of the Egyptian raid on his command, while other Israeli sources are citing that the main runway of Refidim was repaired only rather gradually during the following days.

24   For related Israeli claims see Aloni, *Mirage and Nesher Aces*, pp67-68

25   El-Hefnawy, interview, March 2003 and el-Hefnawy, interview with Group 73, October 2011; this and all other quotations from Dia el-Hefnawy are based on transcription of the same interviews

26   Ahmed el-Wakeel, interview with Group 73, March 2010. Sadly, the interview in question was interrupted early and thus we have got no opportunity to ask a number of important questions. Nevertheless, this recollection is highly important for finally solving the mystery surrounding rumours circulating in Egypt about an unknown EAF pilot that should have crashed his aircraft into a 'row of enemy Phantoms' during the opening strike of Operation Badhr. Notable is that no Israeli account known is mentioning any of Egyptian MiGs crashing at Ophir AB.

27   Yusuf, interview with Group 73, November 2010; this and all other quotations from Yusuf are based on transcription of the same interview. Yusuf graduated at the Air Force Academy in October 1969, with Generation 25. He recalled that after graduation, his group of about 100 student pilots was split into two: while one group continued with conversion training to MiG-17s in Egypt, before moving to MiG-21s, the other group was sent to the USSR.

28 Supposedly basing their conclusions on 'official reports of the Egyptian Air Force', Russian ressearchers of the skywar.ru website are reporting that the No. 61 Squadron suffered a loss of six MiG-17s during this attack. Accordingly, although these have brought the totals for EAF losses during Operation Badhr to 11, these six losses are always omitted and only five mentioned.

29 Israeli and Western readers might find such conclusions 'amazing'. Some might even go as far as to declare them for 'Arab stories from 1001 Night'. Authors have concluded that several aspects of the situation should be kept in mind. The aim of this series is not to confirm or deny claims the IDF/AF credited to its pilots, but to find out what the pilots, officers and other Arab air forces recall about their operations and, whenever possible, collect and provide official documentation too. If three different Arab pilots do not recall to have suffered more than two losses over Ras Nasrani on 6 October 1973, our duty is to forward this information as provided, not to correct them or assume they are 'lying'.

As illustrated already in Volume 3 during the reconstruction of Egyptian experiences about Israeli attacks on UARAF air bases and resulting air combats on 5 June 1967, official documentation released by Egypt so far is showing that Israeli pilots do exaggerate with their claims by up to between 30 and 50 per cent. Whatever is causing such exaggerations, this is no exception from the rule, but rather the rule in every intensive air war in history of human kind.

Perhaps more importantly, it should be born in mind that in the Arab World it is considered noble to die for a matter like liberation of the Sinai from Israeli occupation. This is not to mean that Arab pilots were 'eager' to get killed, or undertaking 'suicide attacks', but that they were ready to pay the ultimate price for their nation's cause, and that their selfless sacrifice remains appreciated until today. Correspondingly, Arab pilots killed in action are held in high esteem and remembered by their colleagues, often so much so that pilots killed in action are better recalled than specific operations during which Arab air forces suffered no losses. In turn, this results in most of officers and other ranks interviewed in the process of this project having absolutely no problem to recall – and discuss – losses, no matter how many, when or where they occurred, or reasons why they happened. Considering that, for example, a loss of six additional MiG-17s and one MiG-21 in the course of the same air combat over Ras Nasrani would have resulted in near certain death of all seven involved pilots, their colleagues would certainly be able to recall their names. However, not only is this not the case, but multiple Egyptian pilots involved in attack on Ras Nasrani simply do not recall to have encountered any kind of opposition from Israeli Phantoms. Considering it is our intention to record their recollections, we are citing these 'as provided', without the aim of 'revising' anybody or anything. That said, readers that prefer to remain sceptical might want to compare such 'lack of recollections' with very clear and vivid recollections of surviving Egyptian Mi-8 pilots about losses suffered by their units on the first evening of the war, as provided in sub-chapter 'Heliborne Assault' (see further below). There must be more than a good reason why three pilots from three different units, interviewed entirely independently from each other on several different occasions recall the same in regards of non-appearance of the IDF/AF Phantoms and two losses the EAF suffered over Ras Nasrani; and versa-vice, there must be a good reason why other EAF pilots do recal anihiliation of two squadrons of Mi-8 helicopters over central Sinai that occurred only few hours later. The authors are confident that this stands in direct opposition to the usual Israeli and Western prejudice that 'Arabs always lie'.

30 Okasha, interview to *al-Masry al-Youm* magazine, July 2011

31 Gawrych, pp34

32 Price, pp156

33 Klein, *Israeli Phantoms*, pp65. The fact that the crew of the F-4 in question decided to fly its damaged aircraft all the way back to Hatzerim implies a question about the actual status of Refidim AB – reported as 'repaired within few hours' by Cohen. If Refidim was operational by that evening, why didn't the crew of that Phantom decide to divert their aircraft to this, much closer airfield? Notably, according to Sadik (interview

from March 2007), the Phantom in question was supposedly involved in some sort of an unsuccessful attack on Aswan Dam, in Upper Egypt.

34  Commanded by Col Mahmmoud Sayd, this brigade came into existence through reorganization of two commando battalions in 1972. They were equipped with a total of 40 Czechoslovak-made OT-62 TOPAS amphibious APCs and 20 PT-76 amphibious tanks of Soviet origin. The rest of the brigade included one anti-tank company equipped with amphibious tank destroyers based on BRDM-2 chassis. Nick-named 'Leopard' in Egyptian service, these four-wheeled light armoured cars were equipped with a retractable six-round launcher for 9M14 Malyutka (AT-3 Sagger) wire-guided anti-tank guided missiles, covered by a large lid of overhead armour. The entire 130 Marine Brigade totalled around 1,000 troops.

35  The sortie in question included just one Tu-16K-11-16, flown by Majors Mustafa Ahmed and Yusuf Rahmi, who fired two KSR-11s against the AN/TPS-43 radar at Sharm el-Sheikh. At least one of missiles hit home, completely destroying the radar and killing filling five operators.

36  Okasha, interview to *al-Masry al-Youm* magazine, July 2011; other information for this sub-chapter is from *Journal of Israeli Air Force*, October 1993 & Oleg Granovsky, *Egyptian and Syrian Helicopters in the Yom Kippur War, 1973*, waronline.org; In total, the IDF/AF credited its F-4E and Mirage/Nesher pilots with 16 kills against Egyptian helicopters on 6 October 1973. Two additional kills were credited to the MIM-23 HAWK SAM site at Ras Sudar. In early 2014, members of Group 73 attempted to interview former C-in-C EAF and former President of Egypt, Hossni Mubarak – between others with intention of asking him about reasons for cancellation of the 2nd wave of attacks, on 6 October 1973. Sadly, the interview in question was cancelled because of Mubarak's health condition.

37  Abu Shaba, interview with Group 73, February 2012; this and all other quotations from Abu Shaba are based on transcription of the same interview.

38  Bermudez, *The Egyptian 130th: the Amphibious Brigade*, pp66; later during the war, survivors from the 130th Marine Brigade were grouped together with survivors of the 25th Armoured Brigade and deployed at Kabrit AB, on the western short of the Great Bitter Lake. After the Israelis crossed the canal and advanced in direction of the Suez City, these Egyptian units formed a small bridgehead around Kabrit, which was successfully defended against all attacks until the cease-fire of 24 October 1973.

39  Hammad, pp717–722.

40  Lt Col Samir Yousif Zainal was a former Iraqi Hunter pilot, who participated in the June 1967 War, between others flying one strike against Ramat David AB, on the morning of 7 June. Zainal was forced to leave Iraq following the coup of 1969, together with between 80 and 100 other IrAF officer. He found refugee in Syria, where he joined the SyAAF. For more details about his participation in the June 1967 War, see *Volume 3*, pp159–169

41  The Sunday Times Insight Team, *Insight on the Middle East War*, pp65

42  *Journal of Israeli Air Force*, October 1992

43  Asher et all, *Duel for the Golan*, pp82-85

44  Boudros, interview, March 2007 (name changed for concerns of his and security of his family)

45  Majid Zoughby, interview, October 2008.

46  The Syrian Arab Army did receive a number of brand-new T-62 MBTs and about 30 BMP-1 infantry fighting vehicles, during the summer of 1973, but these entered the battle only at a later stage; for details, see below.

47  Aloni, *Israeli A-4 Skyhawk Units in Combat*, pp36–39

48  For details about delivery dates of first SA-6s to Egypt, see Chief Designer Ardalion Rastov, *Military Parade*, 1998-08-31; for one of several Western accounts citing their presence in Egypt at earlier dates, see Thornborough et all, *Iron Hand*, pp151-152

49  Price, *War in the Fourth Dimension*, pp156–157

50  Retired SyAADF officer, interview provided on condition of anonymity, March 2005.

# Chapter 4

# A LONG AND MISERABLE DAY

With the Arab forces having achieved such surprise on 6 October, early Israeli reactions were improvised and chaotic. From the standpoint of the IDF/AF, this was to change fundamentally from the morning of 7 October, when the Israeli Air Force began to start acting according to pre-war plans and attempt to gain air superiority over Egypt and Syria. Such planning was not only to prove arrogant and over-confident, but outright unrealistic, and this day was to result in some of the heaviest losses ever suffered by Israeli airmen. Interestingly, while Israeli accounts of the air battles on 7 October usually emphasise the 'fighter-bomber versus SAMs' aspect of the fighting, and most Western sources correspondingly barely mention Arab air forces activity, Arab accounts differ strongly, indicating hundreds of combat sorties flown and having a notable impact on the flow of fighting on the ground. The only point on which both sides agree is that most of the action was dictated by the IDF/AF. This latter was the result of its high flexibility, manoeuvreabilty, and foremost its capability to deliver much greater warloads against more distant targets than its counterparts.

## New Israeli Formations ...

During the night of 6–7 October, the IDF High Command assessed the situation on the Golan as 'stable', and thus ordered the IDF/AF to set in motion its pre-planned, 48-hour air superiority battle – Operation Challenge 4. Unable to run an enterprise involving nearly all of its squadrons on two front lines simultaneously, a decision was taken to hit Egyptian air bases in one wave first, and then to destroy the SAM belt along the Suez Canal in three successive waves, during the rest of the day. Not only did the plan for Challenge 4 prove obsolete, and its purpose completely useless, but even while the participating aircraft were still in the process of taking off, the High Command IDF recognised the severity of the crisis on the Golan Heights and the C-in-C IDF/AF, Maj Gen Benjamin Peled, then made the decision – fiercely criticised by many Israelis ever since, and often described as a 'fatal mistake' – to change the priority to a counter-air effort in the direction of Syria.

Even so, the first wave of Challenge 4 was launched and more than 100 Phantoms and Skyhawks were thus under way in the direction of Egypt, at around 07.00. Regardless of the deployment of most Israeli ground-based electronic warfare units in support of this operation, the IDF/AF was actually playing into Egyptian hands, because by attacking heavily protected and hardened Egyptian air bases deep over enemy ter-

When flown for the first time by the Israelis on the morning of 7 October 1973, the large formations of densely packed F-4Es (this trio of Phantoms from No. 119 Squadron was photographed while passing over the Dome of the Rock in Jerusalem) took Egyptian interceptors by surprise. (IDF)

ritory it was likely to suffer irreplaceable losses. Indeed, Reda el-Iraqi recalled that the Egyptians spent much of the night expecting this attack:

*'Our aircraft were not equipped for nocturnal operations but Nabil Shuwakry, our base commander, wanted to make sure that no Israelis could attack Jiancalis either. He ordered the air defences to raise a number of balloons above our base. This was a very strong means of passive defence: any incoming aircraft had to climb in order to avoid them, or risk getting cut into two if hitting the chain that tied these balloons to the ground.'*

Starting at 07.45, local time, the first wave of Challenge 4 began hitting selected Egyptian SAM sites in the Port Said area. More than half an hour later, the main wave of the Israeli attack force appeared. It consisted of F-4 and A-4 formations that attempted to reach Bani Suweif, Bir Arida, el-Mansoura, Jiancalis, Qutamiyah and Tanta.

In contrast to previous times, when the Israelis generally tended to operate in flights of four aircraft, on the morning of 7 October they began appearing in much larger groups. The Phantom units still generally operated in pairs, but single aircraft within these now flew very close to each other. The lead pair was usually about 1,300–1,500m (4,265–4,921ft) ahead of the main formation and – whenever possible – such a 'bomber' formation was followed by between two and four F-4Es armed with air-to-air missiles only, which flew about 1,000m (3,281ft) behind the rearmost pair of bomb-laden Phantoms. From such a position they were able to move forward to defend the strike group or hang

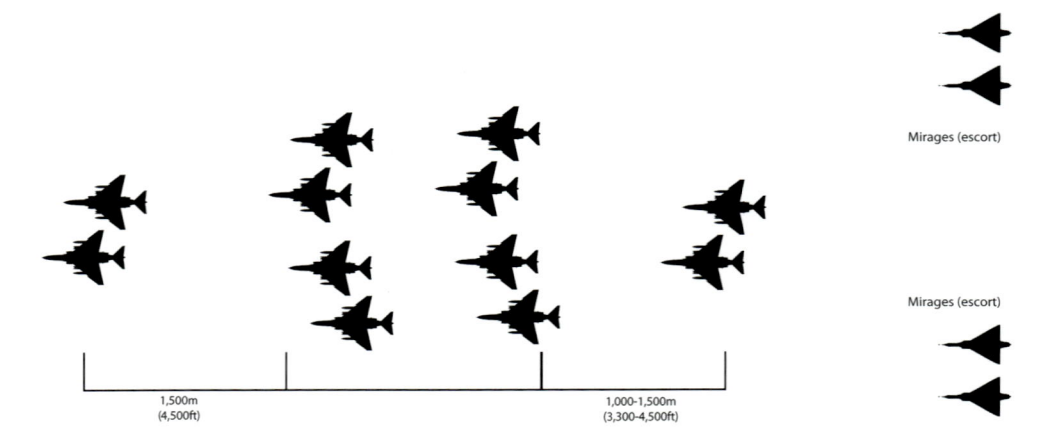

A diagram of Israeli F-4 formation as used from the early days of the October 1973 War. (Diagram by Tom Cooper)

158

back and cover them during attack runs – if not intercepted beforehand. Another characteristic of the new Israeli tactics was that the aircraft within each pair flew very close to each other: often as little as 15-20m (49-66ft). While precise data is lacking, it seems that the Skyhawks flew in similar formations but without any Phantoms behind them. What is certain is that each such formation – whether consisting of A-4s or F-4s – usually received top cover in the form of up to two flights of Mirages or Neshers, although these always remained outside the areas protected by Egyptian SAM sites.

As far as can be said about Egyptian experiences with such formations, it seems the EAF interceptors – pilots of which were used to encountering only pairs or flights of Israelis – were often taken by surprise by their new size and 'extra' members. Egyptian early warning radars usually detected each tightly packed pair as a single aircraft: correspondingly, during the first few days of the war Egyptian and Syrian pilots would frequently be advised to intercept 'a pair' or 'a flight' of Phantoms' and operate accordingly, without expecting the appearance of six or more Israeli jets. More often than not, this meant that the Arab interceptors turned from hunters into hunted in a matter of seconds after engaging their opponents.

## ... and a New Situation over Egypt

While Israeli sources stress that all aircraft reached their targets in Egypt on the morning of 7 October unmolested and bombed successfully, that they have suffered no losses, and that only the A-4 formation that attacked Shubra Kit air base was intercepted by MiG-21s (which were reportedly easily avoided by the Skyhawks escaping into clouds), Egyptian recollections of Challenge 4 tend to differ. Although the Israelis approached at a very low altitude over the Mediterranean Sea and thus 'outmanoeuvred' the massive concentration of SAMs along the Suez Canal, the extensive Egyptian Visual Observer Corps deployed along the northern coast provided timely warning of the approaching attackers. The EAF responded by scrambling MiG-21 interceptors from several bases. The first of these experienced some problems with the visual detection of well-camouflaged IDF/AF aircraft under way at low altitude and against the backdrop of the countless farms in the Nile Delta. However, they managed to intercept some of the Phantoms and force them to prematurely jettison their bombs. Indicating that he was nearly taken by surprise by the new Israeli formations, Qadri Abd al-Hamid, recalled dryly about the interception of an Israeli formation bound for el-Mansoura:

*'I was stationed at el-Mansoura. I engaged in an air combat on 7 October during the first big Israeli raid against us. My wingman shot down an F-4 which was right behind me with his cannon. The crew went to el-Mansourah hospital because they were hurt in the ejection. I also claimed a Phantom as destroyed.'*

Further west, a large formation of Phantoms was under way in the direction of Jiancalis air base, where pilots of No. 26 Squadron were waiting for their turn to participate in the action, as recalled by Medhat Zaki:

*'Our unit did not take part in the opening strike of 6 October, but we knew the Israelis would come back and we would get our opportunity. They did come back on the morning of 7 October, but the situation they found was entirely different than in June 1967... I was scrambled with Reda el-Iraqi, Mohy Fahad, and Ali to fly a CAP over Jiancalis.'*

Most Egyptian MiG-21 pilots spent the morning of 7 October sitting in their cockpits and waiting for the order to scramble. This is Medhat Zaki in one of No. 26 Squadron's mounts.
(Medhat Zaki Collection)

Reda el-Iraqi continued his recollection:

'*The ground control advised us that two formations of Israeli aircraft were approaching Jiancalis from the north. Then I heard a call from two MiGs that were airborne as they manoeuvred behind the enemy and counted 12 Phantoms before attacking them. They complained that the enemy was very hard to see because of their camouflage colours against the backdrop of many farms below...*

'*Our flight, including Medhat and me, was ordered to scramble. While accelerating, we were able to see the first two Phantoms above the end of the runway, climb-*

A MiG-21F-13 (serial number 5846) as seen inside one of the HASes at Inchas after the October 1973 War.
(David Nicolle Collection)

ing, rolling out and diving to attack as we were still on the ground but moving in their direction. Their bombs exploded next to the MiG flown by Mamdouh Monib, damaging it heavily and forcing the pilot to eject. Then the Phantoms flashed by while the rest of us quickly tucked in our undercarriage and continued to accelerate on afterburner.

'Then I saw additional Phantoms approaching from the north: realising their attack had failed and MiGs were airborne over Jiancalis, they jettisoned their bombs on surrounding farms, killing civilians and causing a large number of fires. We passed by and then turned round to start an air combat. A minute later, the airspace over Jiancalis was full of aircraft: 12 Phantoms against three, then seven of us as another flight managed to scramble (including Mamdouh, who had run to man another aircraft and scrambled within five minutes for the second time)...

'When we came back over Jiancalis, I looked upwards and saw Medhat climbing behind a Phantom, reaching a good position for a missile attack. He fired and there was a brilliant explosion but at the same time two Phantoms appeared from behind and fired missiles at him. I warned Medhat to break hard, then engaged the nearest Phantom and outturned him. Rolling out, I put my sight on him and fired a burst from my cannon. Then our AAA opened fire, and the sky was already full of smoke caused by fires from Israeli bombs that had hit nearby farms. My opponent turned away, trailing a thick trail of black smoke. Then his co-pilot ejected. I didn't see the pilot eject but I doubt he could reach Israel: he rather wanted to get away from the battle. I decided not to attack him again: after using afterburner all the time, I was short on fuel and cannon ammunition, and if approaching a slow-flying target with that much excess speed I was more likely to collide with pieces that were falling off or ingest the smoke that the Phantom was emitting than to do any harm...

Mamdouh Monib, a veteran pilot who had served with Air Brigade 102 during the War of Attrition, is known to have been shot down by nearby detonation of bombs released by Israeli Phantoms in the course of attack on Jiancalis, on the morning of 7 October 1973. Monib ejected safely and continued flying during the war. The MiG-21F-13 behind him in this photograph wore the serial number 5590. (Monib Collection)

'I returned to Jiancalis and called the tower but did not get a reply: it had suffered some damage from a bomb blast. I decided to try landing in the middle of the ongoing air combat, and through thick smoke that was now covering the entire base. Already on finals, I cleared the smoke only to see a big crater in the middle of the runway. I went around and landed on the taxiway. Medhat and others followed in the same fashion…

'Once on the ground we met Shuwarky and agreed with him to scramble again as soon as possible. It was important to show to the enemy that our air base remained operational, otherwise the Israelis would come back to hit us again and cause more damage. It was important to show them that their attack failed, too: this was very much a war of psychology.

'Shuwakry decided to make use of a stretch of highway, as planned for cases of emergency, because there were many unexploded bombs lying around the runway. Medhat and me launched again and climbed to an altitude of 6,000m [19,685ft] above Jiancalis while our engineers started the work on the runway and on removing all the bombs around it.'[1]

Eventually, pilots from Air Brigade 104 claimed two Phantom kills for no loss; pilots from Air Brigade 102 claimed two Phantom kills while losing the MiG-21F-13 serial number 5911 flown by Mamdouh Monib, while Israel claimed two MiG-21s shot down for no loss.

Contrary to 1956 and 1967, when such attacks on Egyptian air bases tended to leave them devastated and all pilots and ground personnel demoralised, excellent HASes, strong air defences and a rapid repair capability made the Israeli air strike ineffective. The damage at Jiancalis was quickly repaired, unexploded Israeli ordnance cleared, and the base was declared fully operational by the afternoon. Similarly, a flight of A-4s that managed to reach el-Mansourah air base caused no damage, as recalled by Mikhail:

A pilot from Air Brigade 102 with his MiG-21F-13 in the background. Fiercely patriotic and very well trained, the pilots of Nos 25 and 26 Squadrons looked forward to fighting the Israelis at every opportunity. (via Group 73)

*'Around 07.30 we went to our aircraft and that's when the Israeli attack came. I spent it next to my aircraft inside a hardened aircraft shelter. A fragment from one of the bombs passed next to my ear, but the only problem caused by that attack was an Israeli bomb that embedded itself next to one of the runways after failing to detonate. Squadron CO Magdy Kamal led a team that disarmed the bomb by removing the fuze, but operations never stopped: several MiGs launched to fly CAPs while that work was still going on.'*

Ahmed Abbas Faraj recalled the Israeli attack on Beni Sueif:

*'Early on the morning of 7 October we went to our squadron ready room for briefing. Then there was an air raid warning and we ran to our aircraft. Hardly had we powered up the engines of our Su-17s, when the brigade commander cancelled our scramble.*

*'Once again, we watched in frustration as MiG-21s from No. 49 Squadron took off to intercept the incoming Israelis. They did a very good job and forced the Israelis to jettison their weapons far away from our base, so we didn't even see any of our attacking enemies… but we were so frustrated that some of us began asking our brigade commander if he would permit us to at least go and join the MiG-21 squadrons at Inchas or the Su-7 brigade at Beni Suweif, so that we could fly combat sorties and reduce the burden on our colleagues. Our squadron CO called the C-in-C EAF requesting orders to attack, but none arrived until 11 October.'*

Citing from the War Diary of No. 69 Squadron, Okasha found the Israeli attack on Tanta barely worth mentioning:

*'Early that morning four enemy fighters penetrated our air defences and bombed Tanta. We were not ordered to scramble but the Israelis caused no damage and there was no interruption in normal operations.'*

The participating IDF/AF crews allegedly returned to Israel *'optimistic and reassured'*, expecting to achieve *'total supremacy'* in the air over Egypt during their next mission.[2] The reasons for such overoptimism are completely unclear, because – with the exception of the strike on Jiancalis – the Israeli attacks left next to no lasting impressions upon the Egyptians and Iraqis that witnessed them, and there are strong reasons to doubt that their reports satisfied their commanders either, foremost because most of the aircraft involved were forced to jettison their bombs prematurely. Furthermore, Challenge 4 might have resulted in the loss of two F-4Es from No. 69 Squadron IDF/AF – while causing no serious disruption to EAF operations.[3]

In contrast, the Arab response came in the form of a well-coordinated and effective two-wave strike, which began with an attack by four MiG-17Fs on the HAWK site near Baluza around 08.00. The attack was successful in opening the way for a formation of Su-7BMKs from the Bilbeis-based No. 52 Squadron. Led by Lt Col Victor Nelson Tadeus – a newly appointed squadron CO, who replaced Osman Zaki killed the day before – the four Sukhois attacked an Israeli column while this was approaching positions occupied by the Second Field Army. Tadeus ordered his pilots to fire all of their unguided rockets during the first attack, and then disengage. The formation scored a number of hits on Israeli tanks and other vehicles and then disengaged, but 1st Lt Ahmed Sayd Bakht failed to open fire during the first pass, and decided to make another attack. Tadeus returned to 'collect' his junior pilot, but then crashed, and was killed.[4] No. 52 Squadron thus experienced the misfortune of losing two squadron COs within the first 24 hours of the war.

An Egyptian Su-7BMK flashes low over Israeli positions in full afterburner following a bombing attack (note the empty underwing hardpoints). The big and fast Sukhoi could withstand a significant amount of damage, but No. 52 Squadron had the back luck of losing three aircraft – and two squadron commanders – within the first 24 hours of war. (IDF)

As far as is known, this was one of the rare occasions on which the EAF attacked one of the long columns of Israeli reservists under way along roads heading from the eastern towards the western Sinai that morning. Namely, the sudden and unexpected mobilisation of reserves and the transition from peace to war within the shortest period of time caused numerous difficulties and added to chaos within the IDF, resulting in immense traffic jams. Gen Bren Adan, CO of the 162nd Reserve Armoured Division, observed:

*'Had the Egyptian Air Force attacked our stalled convoys on the Qantara [to] el-Arish Road, I doubt that we would have escaped the same disastrous fate that befell the Egyptian forces from the Israeli air attacks on that same road in the 1956 and 1967 Wars.'*[5]

Actually, this worked both ways. While testifying to the Agranat Commission that investigated the reasons that led to the Arabs managing to achieve a strategic surprise with their attack, another Israeli general observed:

*'...I refrained from requesting aerial reconnaissance during the early days of the war because I saw that the Air Force was encountering trouble with Egyptian anti-aircraft batteries stationed along the Canal... Nevertheless, when there were convoys of hundreds of Egyptian vehicles, hundreds of tanks and hundreds of armoured*

One of the Su-7BMKs from No. 52 Squadron rolls towards its HAS at Bilbeis. (David Nicolle Collection)

A cine film still showing a pair of EAF MiG-17Fs during a pre-war exercise and demonstrating the low altitude at which the type operated for most of the October 1973 War: both aircraft are flying at less than 25m (82ft) above the ground. (David Nicolle Collection)

*personnel carriers standing bumper-to-bumper west of the Canal, this was a worthwile target to attack, and even to absorb losses... But there was a screw-up – in my view, a screw-up by the Air Force – because the information wasn't reaching it at a fast enough pace. An aerial photograph of the convoy that was standing there in the morning they would have perhaps only in the evening. They were not prepared to get this information immediately.*[6]

## Death from Below

Regardless of missed opportunities, the air war was further intensified later that morning when – as described above – the IDF/AF was ordered to switch its main effort to a counter-air enterprise against Syria. At the same time, its CAS effort was re-directed from Golan to the Sinai. Correspondingly, from around 10.00, Israel began launching a number of A-4 and Super Mystère B2 formations in a southerly direction. With Egyptian air defences remaining fully intact, most of these missions turned into costly failures: at least two A-4s and two Super Mystères were shot down by SA-6s and SA-7s between el-Firdan and el-Qantara that morning. Several additional aircraft suffered different degrees of combat damage, prompting Egypt to claim up to 20 Israeli aircraft shot down that day.

Israel did not fare any better during its counter-air effort over Syria. Relying upon plans for Operation Model 5 (or Model 5B), the IDF/AF was to open this battle with an attack on 25 SyAADF SAM sites deployed along the Golan Heights (including 15 SA-6, 10 SA-2, and five SA-3 sites). However, because the corresponding order was issued only after Challenge 4 had been launched, the units involved were left with insufficient time to prepare the mission. They launched in great haste, with some pilots receiving a briefing only once they had manned their aircraft or even when they were already airborne. Because of cloud cover, no reconnaissance sorties were flown over Syria in

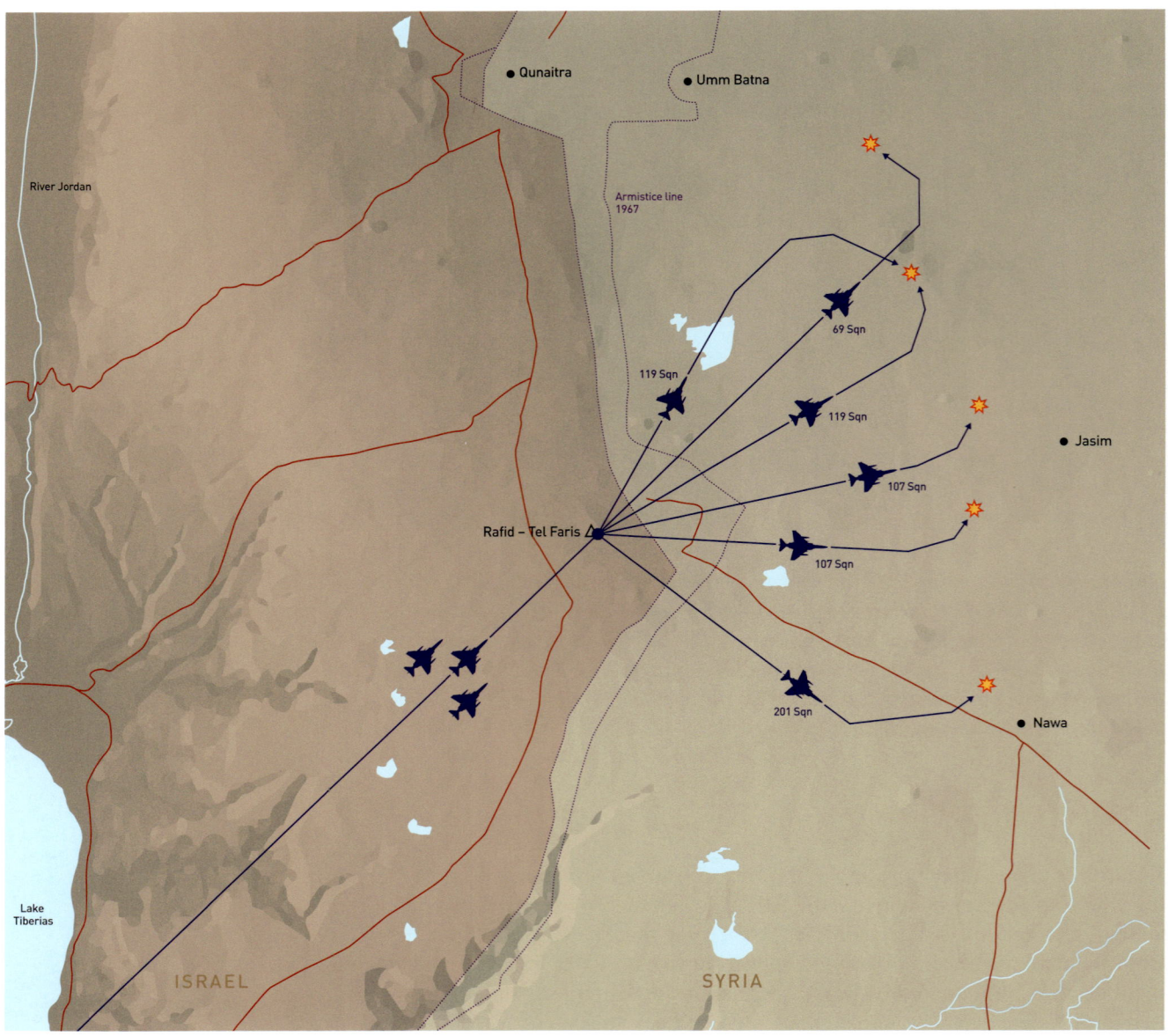

A map showing the essence of the IDF/AF's plan for Operation Model 5 (or Model 5B, according to other sources) – the attack on Syrian SAM sites on the Golan Heights, on the morning of 7 October 1973. (Map by James Lawrence)

order to pinpoint the current positions of the SyAADF SAM sites: instead, targeting data was based on positions of Syrian SAMs that were known from the days before the war. In this chaos, nobody informed the F-4 crews involved that the 188th Armored Brigade IDF had been practically destroyed and that the 5th Syrian Infantry Division was in the process of advancing deep into the southern Golan Heights.

Three squadrons of A-4s were to support the Phantoms through the deployment of eight Skyhawks armed with AGM-45 Shrike ARMs to target the fire-control radars of Syrian SAM sites, 18 armed with bombs for loft-bombing attacks on pre-selected AAA sites, and 10 armed for dive-toss attacks on additional SAM sites.

Interestingly, the planners of Model 5 envisaged the same approach route for all of the formations involved: only after reaching Tel Faris in the southern Golan was each

Crew of an Arab SA-3 site maintaining their launcher and missiles. The SyAADF was on full alert and ready on the morning of 7 October, and when the Israelis attempted to attack it, they suffered some of their worst ever losses.
(Tom Cooper Collection)

of the four F-4 squadrons involved to turn in a different direction. The first formation to fly into the combat zone around 11.30 (Israeli time) was that of No. 69 Squadron. Although flying low over the units of the 5th Infantry Division, it achieved some kind of surprise and remained undisturbed even after reaching Tel Faris and turning north – only to find no targets at the expected location. The SyAADF then went into action, shooting volleys of SAMs and opening up a massive volume of anti-aircraft fire: while trying to find an alternative target and avoid several missiles, the lead F-4E of No. 69 Squadron was either shot down or collided with the ground, killing the crew.[7] The rest of the formation failed to accomplish anything.

Next into the combat zone was No. 201 Squadron. Alerted, the Syrians reacted quickly and this formation encountered its first SAMs shortly after reaching Tel Faris and turning south. One F-4E was hit, the crew ejecting and being captured by Syrian soldiers. The next Phantom in this formation then made a combat turn north to attack the SA-6 site operated by the 2nd Battalion of the 82nd Brigade SyAADF, commanded by Capt Issam Abu Agiba, positioned outside the town of Nawa. Agiba's SA-6 site then hit that F-4E, setting it on fire: the radar intercept officer (RIO) panicked and ejected when the fighter caught fire, but the pilot remained calm and managed a safe emergency landing at Ramat David air base.[8] The next F-4E attempted to make a turn around the area where the RIO had ejected, but was then hit by two missiles, and the crew forced to eject. Seconds later, another Phantom was struck by a ZSU-23-4 from the same Syrian site and lost its right engine. The pilot managed to nurse the stricken aircraft back over Safad before the crew ejected to be picked up by a helicopter.

The third Israeli formation, consisting of Phantoms from No. 119 Squadron, fared slightly better – probably because it attacked a number of mock SAM sites north of Tel Faris. Even so, it lost one F-4E shot down and another badly damaged. No. 107 Squadron's formation returned without losses but failed to hit even a single Syrian SAM site.

A Syrian ZSU-23-4 SPAAG as on display at the Teshreen Panorama in Damascus. According to Syrian sources, the integration of 'Shilkas' into SyAADF SAM sites was the actual reason for the success during the early days of the October 1973 War: with the Israelis flying low because of the SAM threat, they frequently operated within the range of these highly mobile anti-aircraft guns.
(Tom Cooper)

Out of 36 A-4s involved, only two hit their target – the southernmost SA-3 site – and did so because the lead pilot of the rearmost pair separated from the main formation, 'cut the corner' through Jordanian airspace and approached by flying low through the Yarmouk River Valley.[9] Except for the loss of six Phantoms shot down with the loss of two of their crewmembers, the IDF/AF was forced to write off two A-4s (both pilots were killed), while six F-4Es and eight A-4s were damaged – five of them required repairs that were to last longer than a week. Nine Israeli pilots and RIOs ended up as PoWs in Syria.

The Egyptians and Syrians made extensive use of dummy SAM sites during the October 1973 War, repeatedly causing the Israelis to waste their efforts – and suffer losses – against useless targets. This simple but highly effective mock SA-3 launcher with two 'missiles' was photographed later during the war, when its 'SAM site' was overrun by advancing Israelis.
(Albert Grandolini Collection)

*A Long and Miserable Day*

Wreckage of one of the IDF/AF F-4Es shot down over Syria on 6 October 1973, as on display at the Teshreen Panorama in Damascus. (Tom Cooper)

# Battlefield Carnage

While the majority of the IDF/AF was involved in Challenge 4 and Model 5, the balance of the air arm was primarily involved in close air support operations over the Golan. These were badly needed. Namely, while top Israeli commanders convinced themselves that the situation on the Golan was stabile, the actual condition of their ground troops was bordering on catastrophe. North of Quneitra, the 7th Armored Brigade managed to repell a series of powerful attacks by the 7th Infantry Division. Although inflicting severe losses on the Syrians, the Israeli brigade lost half of its Centurion MBTs in the process. South of Qunaitra, the 5th Infantry Division destroyed most of the 188th Armored Brigade IDF during the evening of 7 October and advanced deep into the Golan Heights, followed by the 9th Infantry Division. After lengthy discussions, the General Staff in Damascus ordered the 1st Armoured Division to follow these two formations through the Rafid Gap, but instead on concentrating on the actual task and rushing towards the River Jordan, part of this unit turned north to attack the IDF HQ at Naffech: largely unscathed by earlier Syrian attacks, the Israeli OP at Tel Faris continued monitoring all of these moves and reporting on them.[10]

Meanwhile, at dawn of 7 October, two squadrons of A-4s and one of Super Mystère B2s – supported by Mirages from Ramat David air base – began launching a total of 56 sorties in the direction of Golan. Lacking reliable targeting intelligence, some pilots flew armed reconnaissance along the area from Arik Bridge towards Qunaitra and along the road to Damascus, while others operated over the Rafid Gap. With the SyAAF in full swing too, and the SyAADF in control of the skies over the Golan Heights, the skies filled with aircraft, trails of smoke and explosions, becoming a scene of murderous clashes in which at least four A-4s and one Super Mystère were shot down while attempting to support the shattered remnants of the 188th Armored Brigade in the Tel Faris area, while two additional Skyhawks were badly damaged during the first two hours of this action alone.[11] Well-informed about the movement of the 1st Armoured Division by the OP at

Arab MiGs | Volume 5

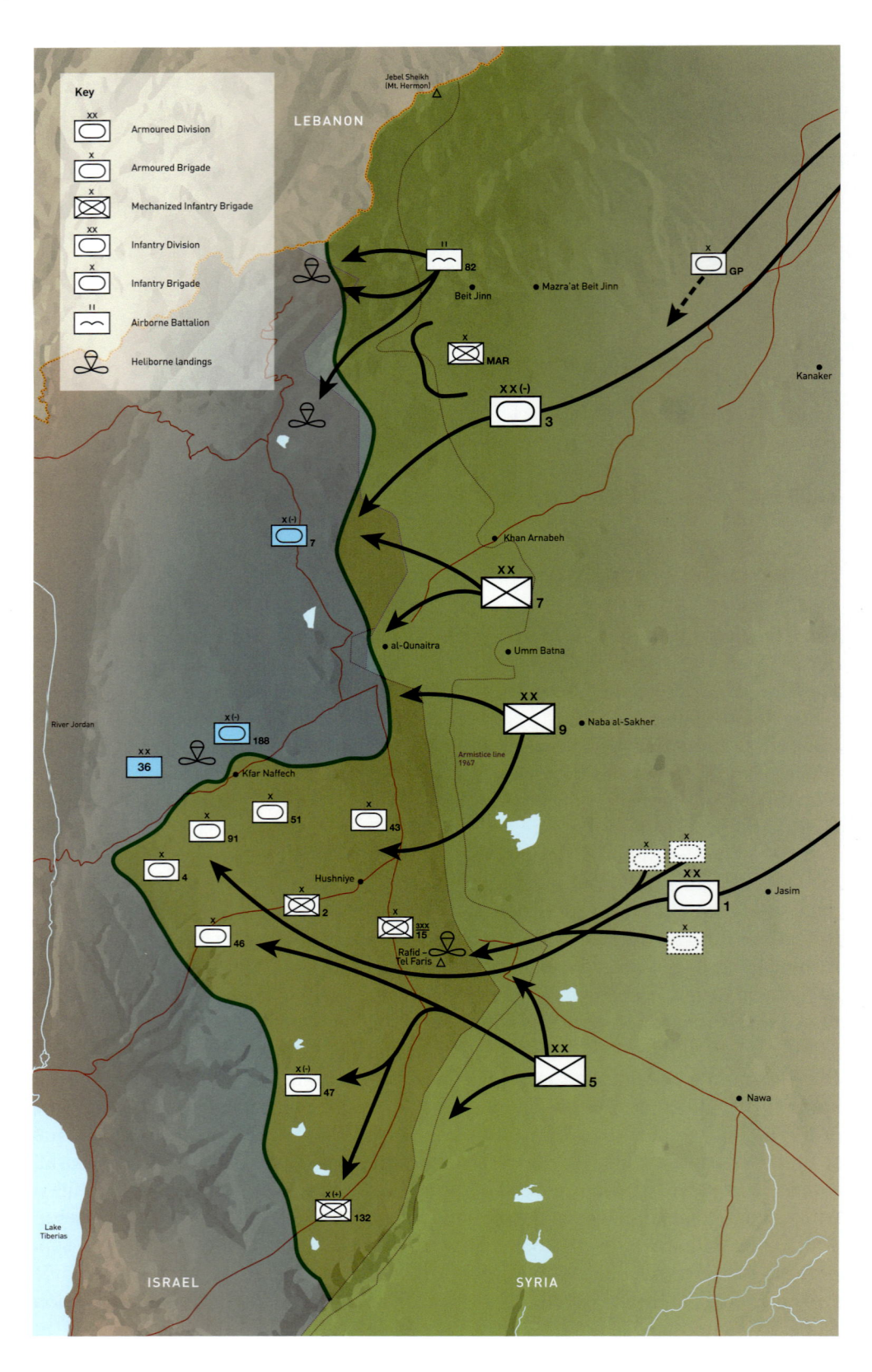

This map illustrates the deepest penetration of the Golan Heights by Syrian Arab Army units as of 7 and 8 October 1973.
(Map by James Lawrence)

## A Long and Miserable Day

Tel Faris, the IDF/AF launched a major effort against its formations in Hushniye area, starting at 07.00, local time and continuing for the rest of the day.[12]

Available Syrian and Russian sources stress intensive SyAAF activity and numerous air combats involving MiG-21s, some of which were providing top cover for friendly fighter-bombers, while others were scrambled in reaction to Model 5. Most of the interceptors in question were apparently controlled from the ground by two of the most accomplished SyAAF ground controllers: Col Akram and Lt Col Awni. Sadly, because none of the sources in question provides the precise time at which the missions in question were flown, and only somewhat rough geographic locations, and because it seems that Syrian pilots tended to call every Israeli aircraft they encountered either a 'Mirage' or 'Phantom', precise cross-examination against Israeli accounts is next to impossible.

As far as is known, the first Syrian formation to engage in air combat that morning was a flight of MiG-21MFs from No. 8 Squadron, tasked with the provision of top cover for a flight of Su-7BMKs. Following an inconclusive engagement with Mirages, the MiGs were returning to Dmeyr air base when local air defences opened fire on them: the MiG-21MF flown by 1st Lt Ahmad Sabbagh was shot down by SAMs while another – already on finals and with its undercarriage lowered – was blasted out of the skies by AAA. While the pilot of the second MiG ejected safely, Sabbagh was killed. Another flight of MiG-21s engaged two pairs of Mirages while protecting seven Su-7s in an attack on Israeli ground troops. Accordingly, Capt Sarkees separated from his wingman and sneaked up on a pair of Israelis from below and attacked one with a single R-3S fired from a range of about 1,000m (3,281ft), claiming the kill. Meanwhile, Sarkees' numbers 3 and 4 engaged a pair of Mirages in a dogfight: Capt Fayez Dawwara's R-3S fired from a distance of only 600m (1,969ft) missed, but his wingman, Capt Dibbs, then claimed a Mirage as shot down by a single missile. The two remaining Israeli fighters outaccelerated the MiGs, disengaging in a southerly direction.[13]

Another air combat over the Golan Heights on 7 October 1973 was recalled by Majid az-Zoughby:

*'That mission was a big mess. We launched from Tsaykal to provide top cover for four Su-7s that were attacking enemy ground troops. I was under way with Ala'a Addin Abdi, Ghassan Abboud, Hisham Azzawi, Ahmad Ghannoum, Osama Bahloul and Abdul Wahab al-Khattib. The GCI vectored us into a position about 1,500m [4,921ft] above and behind the Sukhois at a speed of only 850km/h [459kt]. He expected us to catch any Israelis that would attack our fighter-bombers. I think the Israelis never detected the Sukhois. Instead, they attacked us! As we were watching the Su-7s bombing, two Mirages appeared to attack me: one of them fired two missiles at me, but I flew a zero-speed manoeuvre and avoided both of them. My nose was still pointing upwards when 1st Lt Khattib, my number 3, warned me of another Mirage firing at me. As I was rolling out in the direction of a Mirage that overshot, I heard a loud bang and my plane shuddered heavily. But I remained in control and fired from a point-blank range, only some 100m [328ft] away, 150m [492ft] at most. I couldn't have missed, he was that close. I scored a few hits but had no time to follow before Khattib warned of another pair of Mirages shooting missiles at me. I broke very hard again and was now in deep trouble, at low altitude and out of speed. That was when Ghassan came in and attacked these Mirages from the rear. He fired all four of his missiles too early: none scored a hit, but they forced the Israe-*

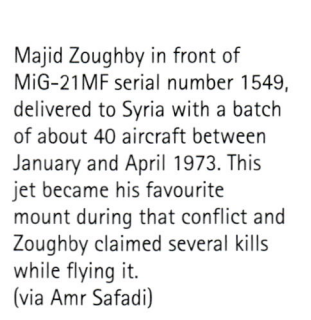

Majid Zoughby in front of MiG-21MF serial number 1549, delivered to Syria with a batch of about 40 aircraft between January and April 1973. This jet became his favourite mount during that conflict and Zoughby claimed several kills while flying it.
(via Amr Safadi)

lis to break. The Mirages tried to turn into him, but Ghassan hit one with cannon. Then the Israelis ran away and I ordered my flight back to base: we were critically short of fuel after less than one minute of air combat…'[14]

Soon after, Zogby's formation encountered the same problem as Sabbagh's, but with even more tragic consequences:

'During the transit back to Tsaykal we passed over our SAM sites and Khattib was killed. While passing Damascus, local air air defences opened fire at us too: they damaged Ghassan's plane and he was forced to make an emergency landing at Almazza. His badly damaged MiG skidded off the runway, overturned and caught fire. Ghassan died from his wounds in the hospital. Short of fuel, I decided to land at Dmeyr. That's when my plane was hit too, but I managed to land safely. Of our six MiGs, only one pair returned to Tsaykal, and we were credited with only one 'probable' against a Mirage.'

Fikry el-Gindy recalled that as the intensity of operations continued to increase, the High Command SyAAF began deploying even MiG-17Fs for combat air patrols along the battlefield.

'Early on the morning of 7 October, we went to 'the bunker', to wait for our orders for that day, and I received the order to lead the first section to take off that morning into CAS for the 5th Syrian Infantry Division. While I was preparing for that mission, Capt Abdul Majid Badawi, the leader of my second section, received reports that the enemy aircraft were about to attack our base and that he should scramble immediately. Our MiG-17s were foremost fighter-bombers; we had a secondary role in air defence, but that was primarily a job for MiG-21s.'

Meanwhile, at least one Israeli source cites a MiG-21 as shot down by TCM-20s of the 66th Reserve Division during a strike on the IDF base at Tel Abu Nida, around 10.00 – which would imply that the SyAAF had begun deploying that type for ground attack. The fighter reportedly crashed behind the Syrian front lines, after its pilot ejected.[15] Furthermore, according to el-Gindy, his squadron then suffered from additional cases of fratricide fire.

*A still from a cine film showing a SyAAF MiG-21MF armed with four UB-16-57 rocket pods. According to Israeli sources, it was on 8 October 1973 that the Syrians began deploying their MiG-21s for ground attacks too. (via Amr Safadi)*

'Unsurprisingly, that mission ended in a disaster. No sooner had Badawi's flight engaged the Israelis, they faced a number of Syrian air-to-air missiles. One hit Lt Sharif's plane: he ejected safely just a moment before his plane crashed, and was injured. The other three planes escaped, but then the Syrian SAMs opened fire again and hit the plane flown by Capt Badawi. We saw all of this from our airfield and were stunned. The plane blew up with him still inside the cockpit and Badawi was killed…

'How could such a thing happen? We had studied such cases so much before the war, in order to avoid mistakes. It was a terrible thing for my squadron to lose half a flight in just a few minutes. We were now down to eight pilots – except for me, all 1st and 2nd lieutenants.

'To make matters worse, my mission was subsequently cancelled and I went to Brig Haddad and complained bitterly about the loss of two of my pilots. He tried to offer his condolences and to comfort me, explaining we all knew such things happened in war. Then he promised this would not happen over this airfield again. We then went to action and flew a lot of sorties later that day, Syrians too. No SAMs were fired at us this time: we were very careful and kept low so they could not even target us.'

According to Syrian sources, this high tempo of operations was maintained during the late morning, too, with several flights of MiG-21s being scrambled in reaction to reports from the 5th Infantry Division about the approach of several large formations of Phantoms. Whether this action was related to Operation Model 5 remains unknown, but according to the same source the first flight to reach the combat zone was led by Maj Fayez Hegazi, with Zubair, Badawi (not to be confused with Egyptian pilot, Capt Badawi of No. 15 Squadron) and Shousha on his wing. They apparently caught a pair of F-4Es that were fleeing in a southwesterly direction low over northern Golan. Badawi hit one of the F-4Es with an R-3S missile, which knocked out one engine. Seconds later, a pair of Mirages intervened, downing his and the MiG-21MF flown by Hegazi. Both Syrians ejected safely over Syrian ground troops and – because the crew of the stricken Israeli fighter-bomber did the same nearby and was captured – Badawi was credited with a confirmed kill.[16]

A flight of MiG-21MFs led by pilot named by Russians as 'Maj Kokach' reportedly caught two F-4Es, one of which was damaged by ground fire. Kokach fired one R-3S at the Phantom that was trailing smoke, and this reportedly crashed inside Israel. Never-

*Extremely proud about their success against the IDF/AF on 7 October 1973, the Syrians put the wreckage of several downed F-4Es on display in downtown Damascus. This photograph shows pieces including the General Electric M61A1 cannon of an Israeli Phantom. (Tom Cooper Collection)*

A SyAAF MiG-21MF rolling back to its HAS following a combat sortie (note the empty launch rail for an R-3S AAM under the outboard underwing pylon). Sadly, the serial number is not entirely clear, but was probably 1581.
(via Tom Cooper)

theless, while returning to their base, Kokach's wingman was aprently shot down by two F-4Es that approached undetected from behind. Another air combat about which slightly more details are available involved six MiG-21MFs that scrambled from Dmeyr. Led by Capt Maliki, the Syrians attacked a formation of six Phantoms under way low over the Golan Heights, from above and behind, as recalled by Boudros:

'We rolled over and dove to attack. I think the Israelis saw us, since they made a u-turn to the left. Still in a dive, I followed Maliki after the two Phantoms, but we then came under attack by the rear pair of Israelis. I saw a missile approaching and broke hard left, but my plane stalled. Out of speed and at minimal altitude, I was left without a choice but to eject. Maliki's plane was then hit by a missile, but he maintained control and made a safe belly-landing back in Dmeyr. Our rear pair meanwhile attacked the two Phantoms that hit us, and fired two R-3S, downing the Israeli number 4.

'As so often during that war, the Israelis then sent another quartet of Mirages to catch the rest of our formation as this was withdrawing towards Dmeyr, short on fuel, and they shot down our number 4. The pilot ejected safely.

'Our third pair meanwhile hit and shot down the Israeli number 6, but while attempting to disengage, they passed underneath the first pair of Phantoms and our number 6 was shot down too, its pilot killed. In summary, we were credited with three 'probables' while losing three MiG-21MFs and one pilot.'[17]

In return, the IDF/AF credited its Mirage pilots with at least 10 kills of Syrian MiG-21s, for no losses to their own – at least not in air combats. Sure enough, four Mirages (and Neshers) are known to have been lost over Syria in the first three days of the war, but full details have only been provided about one of them, supposedy shot down by AAA.[18] Interviewed Syrian pilots had no doubts about their success, achieved in spite of continuous problems with their Soviet-made equipment. Boudros explained:

'Our pilots proved more skilled than the Israelis in air combat manoeuvring. Our problems were the severe limitations of the R-3S missiles and especially fuel. Most of our MiG-21s shot down by the Israelis during that war were hit while returning to base, short on fuel. The Israelis knew that Soviet-built fighters were chronically short on fuel and their bases were close to ours. Every time one of our flights turned back to base, they would send their fighters to down them on the way back to base.'

Shukri Tabet, meanwhile serving as CO of No. 11 Squadron, provided a similar observation – though with an important addition:

*'The Israelis fought better before the 1973 War. They dictated the terms every time. They were well prepared. If they decided to fight they even took the position of the sun into account… all the air battles they initiated were ambushes… In 1973 it was the opposite… there were no traps, all battles were face to face. That's where the Israelis were simply lucky: lucky to have good arms and good radars.'*

## Balance Sheet

Overall, precise figures for the losses sustained by the Egyptian and Syrian air arms on 7 October remain unavailable, while – as seen in a number of examples mentioned above – those based on Israeli claims are highly unreliable. Slightly more is known about Israeli losses. The IDF/AF has officially confirmed the loss of 23 aircraft on 7 October 1973. Unofficial lists circulating among circles of private enthusiasts and researchers cite up to 31 losses, of which 19 over Syria, and apparently including aircraft written off after making emergency landings in Israel. Except for six F-4Es and two A-4s officially cited as shot down during Model 5, such lists include two further Phantoms shot down over Syria, one of which was written off during a crash-landing at Ramat David, and two over Egypt.

While all 23 officially confirmed losses have been attributed to Egyptian and Syrian ground defences, there is little doubt that even the official Israeli documentation requires much more objective analysis than is presently possible, and preferably in the form of cross-examination against official Egyptian and Syrian documentation.

There is a lot less disagreement regarding the outcome of Operation Model 5: this was clearly the greatest catastrophe ever experienced by the IDF/AF, and it is little surprising that it was cancelled after only its first wave was flown. Not only did one of the F-4 units involved suffer extensive losses, but this failure effectively prevented Israeli air power from playing the dominat role early during this war, as envisaged in pre-war plans, and it left its mark within the ranks of the Israeli Air Force for many more years. Perhaps even more damaging was the fact that this failure of the crucial Israeli military branch occurred around the same time that the High Command in Tel Aviv finally realised the gravity of the situation on the Golan. Combined, these two blows shattered confidence within the High Command in Tel Aviv, causing some political and military leaders to make doomsday references to the 'Fall of the Third Commonwealth' and the 'Day of the Judgement'.

Air-to-Air missile envelopes at altitude of 5,000m (16,404ft) and speed of 900km/h (559mph)

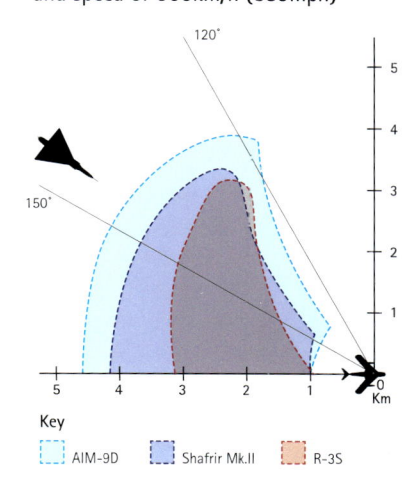

This diagram provides a comparison between the engagement envelope of the Soviet-made R-3S missile and that of the two major types of air-to-air missiles in the Israeli arsenal: the US-made AIM-9D and the indigenous Shafrir 2. It clearly shows that the Israelis could fire their missiles from longer range and at higher off-boresight angles than their Arab opponents. Furthermore, the AIM-9D and Shafir were more flexible in terms of their tracking capability, while the R-3S could not be fired at a target manoeuvring at more than 2.3g.
(Diagram by James Lawrence, based on research by Jean-Marie Langeron)

# The 'luck' factor: differences in air combat capabilities

In every armed conflict, the side capable of bringing more and heavier weapons to bear is more likely to cause heavier casualties or material damage to its opponent – and thus more likely to win. This is expressed in combat effectiveness, which in the case of the October 1973 War was nowhere more obvious than in the air. Namely, what Shukri Thabet described as the 'luck' that was on the Israeli side was one of the major reasons for the vastly superior combat capabilities of the IDF/AF in comparison to its Arab opponents: the IDF/AF was not only in possession of two new types of far more capable air-to-air missiles – the AIM-9D Sidewinder and the Shafrir 2 – which enabled them to claim a very high number of kills during the October 1973 War, but was foremost in possession of fighter-bombers that could carry much heavier warloads at higher speeds and over longer ranges than their equivalents in the Arab arsenals. The following illustration indicates the superiority of the aircraft in the Israeli arsenal in comparison to the types operated by the Arabs during the conflict, from top towards the bottom:

When configured for air combat, a single F-4E could carry four AIM-9D Sidewinder and four AIM-7E Sparrow air-to-air missiles. Its internal M61A-1 Vulcan six-barrel cannon with 640 rounds of 20mm calibre ammunition could fire at a rate of up to 5,000 rounds per minute, but was usually set for firing six one-second bursts. The Phantom's AN/APQ-120 radar was a very advanced system with nine major working modes and about two dozens sub-modes, that had a search mode capable of detecting targets 321km (200 miles) away. In comparison, the best-armed fighter-interceptor in the arsenals of the Arab air forces was the MiG-21MF, which could carry a maximum of four primitive R-3S missiles. It had one twin-barrel GSh-23 cannon of 23mm calibre, with 200 rounds, which Arab pilots characterised as 'useful for novice pilots too', but 'mediocre' in regards combat effectiveness since it 'caused insufficient damage'. Like earlier MiG-21PFS, MiG-21FLs and MiG-21PFMs (which could carry only two R-3S each and had no internal cannon), the MF was equipped with RP-21 radar with a range of 20km (12.4 miles). The oldest variant of this type, the MiG-21F-13, was equipped with the SRD-5M Kvantum ranging and gun radar only. It could carry two R-3S missiles and had an internal cannon of 30mm calibre, but this was equipped with only 60 rounds of ammunition. Obviously, the F-4E could outgun even two MiG-21MFs or up to eight MiG-21s of older variants. More importantly, as well as its superior avionics and weapons, the Phantom possessed generally similar flying characteristics and manoeuvrability, but a much superior range.

When armed as a fighter-bomber, a single F-4E could carry up to three CBU-52/Bs or CBU-58/Bs and six Mk 82s (weighing about 3,000kg/6,614lb in total), two AIM-9D Sidewinders, three AIM-7E Sparrows, and one ECM pod. This was a warload sometimes deployed for attacks on Arab air bases in October 1973. Israeli F-4 crews obviously had to jettison their bomb-loads prior to any air combat (in order to decrease the weight and increase the speed and manoeuvreabiltiy of their aircraft), but usually they could do so in good time – because their aircraft were equipped with AN/APQ-120 radar.

In comparison, the most numerous fighter-bomber in service with Egypt and Syria was the diminutive MiG-17F. The maximum warload of this type consisted of two 250kg (551lb) bombs and eight unguided rockets, a total of about 800kg (1,763lb). The MiG-17F was armed with three internal cannon (including two of 23mm calibre and one of 37mm calibre), with only 100 rounds of ammunition in total. Effectively, this meant that a single F-4E could deploy as many bombs as six MiG-17s in the course of just one sortie, and still carry at least five if not six air-to-air missiles and internal cannon for self defence. A flight of four F-4Es armed in the aforementioned fashion could saturate the same target with a total of 36 bombs weighing a total of 12,000kg (26,455lb).

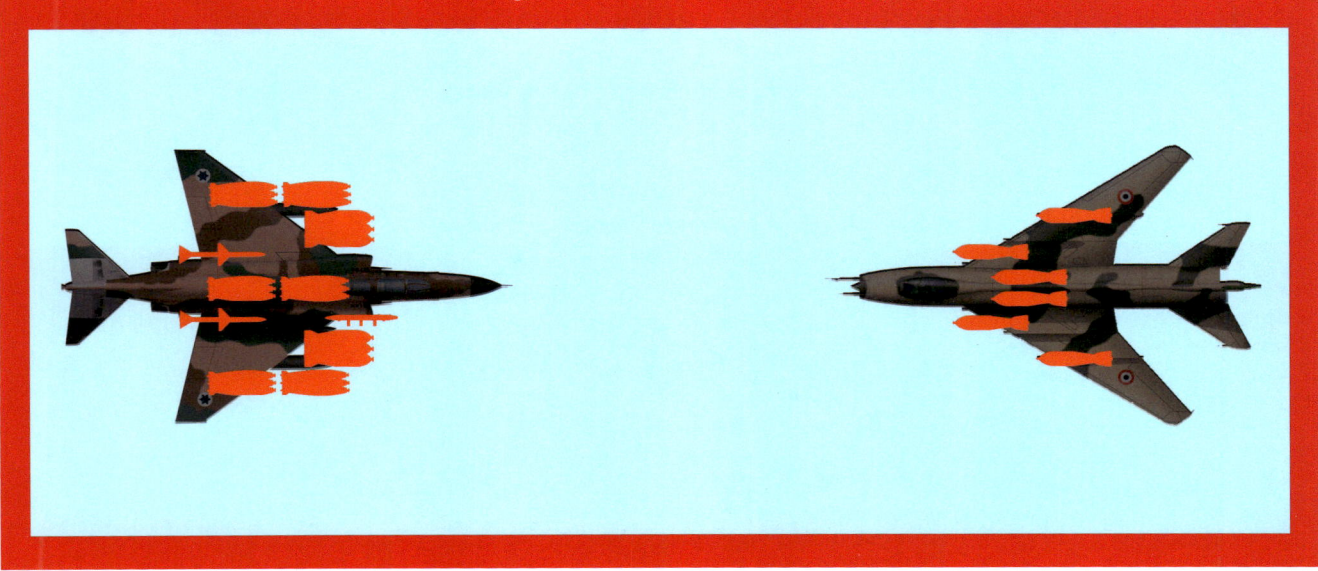

When armed as bomber, a single F-4E could carry a maximum warload of 18 500lb (227kg) Mk 82 bombs and five 750lb (375kg) M117 bombs. This amounted to a total of 6,400kg (14,110lb) of bombs that a single aircraft could deliver in the course of one mission, or 25,600kg (56,439lb) of bombs for a flight of four Phantoms. In comparison, a squadron of MiG-17s would have to fly 51 sorties to deliver the same amount of bombs on a target as a flight of four F-4Es could do on a single mission. Furthermore, the Phantom could still carry two AIM-7E Sparrow semi-active, radar-homing air-to-air missiles and an ECM pod for self protection – in addition to the internally installed General Electric M61 Vulcan cannon with 640 rounds. Even once they received the Su-17 and Su-20s, Arabs had nothing comparable. The Sukhois could be armed with up to two R-3S missiles, but when loaded with the maximum six FAB-500M-62 bombs of 500kg (1,102lb; for a total of 3,000kg or 6,613lb), they had no hardpoints left for air-to-air missiles and depended on two NR-30 cannon of 30mm calibre with a total of only 80 rounds for self-protection.

The fourth line illustrates the weapons configuration of an F-4E deployed for suppression of enemy air defence (SEAD) operations, armed with two AGM-45 Shrike anti-radar missiles (with an effective range of up to 10km/6.2 miles), three AIM-7Es and an ECM pod. In this role, the Arab air arms possessed nothing comparable: no guided missiles, no ECM pods, and – except on the latest MiG-21MFs and Su-17s – not even radar warning receivers. The MiG-17s usually deployed for SEAD operations still used their two small bombs and unguided rockets.

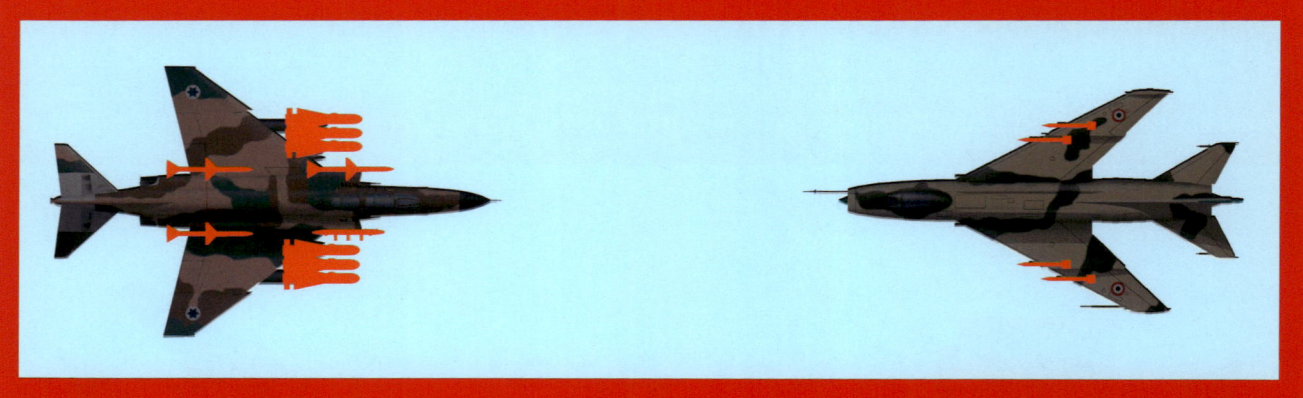

The final inset illustrates the situation towards the end of this war, when Israeli technological superiority was further increased through deliveries of US-made Hughes AGM-62 Walleye and AGM-65A Maverick electro-optical (EO) homing missiles. Although early variants of such weapons had an effective range of only a few kilometres, they belonged to the first generation of 'fire and forget' weapons, which meant that the crew only needed to lock on the seeker head at the target and fire, and could then manoeuvre freely. A single F-4E could carry a maximum of two Walleyes or up to six Mavericks (illustrated here), which proved highly reliable and extremely precise: five out of six AGM-65s usually hit their targets. In comparison, the Su-7BMKs in Arab service were still only armed with relatively light bombs (a maximum of four bombs of 500kg/1,102lb each) or, alternatively, unguided rockets – including powerful yet heavy S-24s of 240mm (9.45in) calibre. Above all, Arab-operated Su-7s almost always operated at the limits of their endurance and were thus critically short on fuel, while the F-4 could remain airborne for extended periods of time.

1. Medhat Zaki and Reda el-Iraqi, interview with Group 73, January 2010; this and all other quotations from Zaki and el-Iraqi are based on transcriptions of the same interview. Sadly, neither Zaki nor el-Iraqi could recall Ali's family name.
2. Klein, *Israeli Phantoms*, p67.
3. Different unofficial Israeli sources indicate the loss of two F-4Es from No. 69 Squadron's formation that was underway to attack Jiancalis, early on 7 October 1973. While some of these are indicating a possibility of an air combat with EAF MiG-21s, usually no reason is mentioned except for 'combat loss'. On the contrary, the official IDF/AF list of losses for October 1973 is not mentioning any kind of F-4s shot down over Egypt on that morning.
4. Tadeus' Su-7BMK is not known to have been claimed or credited to any IDF units.
5. Adan, *On the Banks of the Suez*, p4.
6. Yuval Azoulay, 'Moshe Dayan told '73 probe: I wasn't Fit for War-Time Decision Making', *Haaretz*, 10 October 2008.
7. Most of Israeli sources cite collision with the ground, for example see Aloni, *Israeli Phantoms*, p65.
8. Ibid; according to same source, this F-4E – serial number 615 – was subsequently repaired. While Israeli sources stress that the reason for RIO's ejection was an 'accident', his own account ('We were hit and I ejected'), provided by Russian sources – see article 'Dougman-5' (in Russian) on website www.skywar.ru leaves no place for doubt. The same source points out that SyAADF's Capt Agiba was subsequently decorated with the 'Hero of Syria' Medall.
9. Aloni, *Israeli A-4 Skyhawk Units in Combat*.
10. Asher et all, *Duel for the Golan*, pp184–187
11. Asher et all, *Duel for the Golan*, pp155 & Aloni, *Israeli A-4 Skyhawk Units in Combat*, pp36–39
12. Ever since, various Israeli sources – including the 'official IDF history' of this war (Aloni, *Israeli A-4 Skyhawk Units in Combat*, pp43) – are insisting that air strikes on 7 and 8 October 1973 have stopped the Syrian advance. Post-war studies have shown an entirely different picture: practically repeating Okasha's commentary about lack of precision of Israeli air strikes during the closing stages of the War of Attrition (see Volume 4, pp102-103), in his book *Arabs at War* (pp511), US military expert Kenneth Pollack added that even the IDF/AF has found that its pilots were, '...*delivering their munitions inaccurately...*' Furthermore, citing Col Trevor Dupuy (US Army, ret.), Pollack added, '...*Dupuy was able to examine many of the Syrian tanks on the Golan shortly after the war and found no clear evidence that any were destroyed by air attack. Likewise, an official US military team – allowed by the Israelis to inspect the Golan battlefield in great detail after the war – found less than five Syrian tanks destroyed by airstrikes*'. Pollack concluded:
'*While these findings must be balanced against the accounts of several observers, which indicate that Israeli airstrikes, regardless of their meagre physical effect, seemed to have a more profound psychological effect on the Syrians than on the better-disciplinned Egyptians, it is hard to make the case that the I[DF/]AF was decisive in stopping the Syrian offensive.*'
13. Babich, *MiG-21 vs Mirage III* & Konstantin V Sukhov, *Over the Syrian Front*; former fighter pilot credited with 22 victories during the WWII, Sukhov served as the chief Soviet air combat advisor in Syria, from 1973 until 1975, and was highly decorated by Hafez al-Assad, in 1989. Sadly, most of names of Syrian pilots provided by these sources stand in no relation to reality – to a degree where most of available Syrian sources have no idea where have Russians got ideas for names they have mentioned. Nevertheless, names mentioned in this paragraph have been confirmed by Syrian sources.
14. Zoughby, interview, October 2008; this and all subsequent quotations from Zoughby are based on transcription of the same interview.
15. Journal of Israeli Air Force, October 1992.
16. Names of SyAAF MiG-21-pilots involved in this air combat and their losses were confirmed by Syrian sources, although they did not mention the exact time of the day and other circumstances.

17  Boudros, interview, March 2007; this and all subsequent quotations from Boudros are based on transcription of the same interview. Notable is that while most of information about activities by SyAAF MiG-21s provided by Syrian sources differs to information provided by different published Russian sources, at least some of recollections cited here can be corroborated with details provided by Sukhov, in 'Over the Syrian Front'.

18  Aloni, in *Israeli Mirage and Nesher Aces*, pp88, is citing Ami Lahav to have flown the IIICJ with serial numer (66)32 when hit by ground fire. On pp70 of the same book, the same author is 'confirming' a loss of three *additional* Mirages (and Neshers) over Syria alone in period 6-8 October 1973, but mentions none of these in detail. Seemingly, the standpoint of certain Israeli researchers (apparently that of quite a number of IDF/AF pilots too) is that Israeli aerial supermen could not possibly get shot down by 'Arab MiGs'. If at all, such cases are not discussed in the public, as explained by one of IDF/AF veterans of the October 1973 War in an interview provided on condition of anonymity (November 2003):

*'There is no doubt that we have suffered losses in air combats; in 1973 and in all other wars. Some of our best pilots – including two of air force commanders and several 'aces' – were shot down in air combats with Arabs. Nobody can win all the time and suffer no losses. I think there is a psychological aspect of this. Whether right or wrong, we have created the myth about our invincible air force. Some officials began boasting the Israeli airspace is inpenetrable. Our public accepted this as a matter of fact. And then some of our best pilots got shot down. Nobody likes to admit he's been defeated by the enemy. Great pilots and commanders even less so. In our squadron-ready-rooms, there was no place for this: every mission was throughoutly de-briefed and there were very serious – and often enough very difficult – discussions about every single loss. Some were too ashamed to admit openly they have been beaten in air combats and then records have been adapted to 'improve stactistics for the history'...Several years later [after the 1973 War], the Air Force issued an internal booklet in which all air battles in which Israeli planes were shot down by enemy aircraft were described and analysed in great detail. Few cases were trivial, caused by pilots making a mistake and flying their aircraft into a spin, hitting the ground during hard manoeuvres, ignoring their fuel status, or ejecting before their aircraft were even damaged. But there were more serious cases too, including some of pilots insisting on denial – until today – that they have been outmanoeuvred and shot down by Arabs, and insisting they have been shot down by ground fire where there was none... That booklet remains under censorship though, and I can't discuss further details about it'.*

# Chapter 5

# HOLD THE LINE

A day after the IDF/AF experienced not only its most miserable failure on the Syrian front, but also suffered its worst single-day loss ever, it was the turn of the Israeli ground forces to endure a similar experience in the Sinai. The IDF's rushed attempt to launch a coordinated, two-division counterattack against Egyptian bridgeheads collapsed amid a series of blunders and mistakes, and only resulted in further heavy losses and consolidation of Egyptian positions in the Sinai. Ironically, with destruction of the much-expected Israeli counterattack being Cairo's principal aim of the war, and because this achievement was eventually translated into political gains on the negotiating table, it was 8 October 1973 that signalled the moment of Egyptian victory. However, not only was much more blood to be shed in a number of – de facto – completely useless operations before this fact was realised by all parties involved and the shooting stopped, but Cairo subsequently only barely avoided even this success slipping out of its hands.

Meanwhile, and much to Israel's amazement, Syria stopped its onslaught into the Golan late on 7 October and – although Damascus ordered a re-launch of its advance the next morning – the situation on the Golan began to stabilise, and then to tilt in favour of the IDF.

## Showtime

During the night of 7–8 October, Egypt consolidated its bridgeheads on the Sinai in the form of what has been described as a 'hasty defence layout'. Egypt's Second Field Army was now in control of the area between Qantara in the north and Deversoir in the south, while the Third Field Army occupied the area between the Small Bitter Lake and Port Tewfiq. A total of around 90,000 troops and around 900 armoured vehicles were concentrated within these two bridgeheads. This feat was achieved despite a massive attack by Phantoms and Skyhawks on pontoon bridges over the Suez Canal during the afternoon of 7 October. While this knocked out the equivalent of three heavy bridges, leaving Shazly with only four bridges in reserve – along with the five that were already in use[1] – and although this significantly bolstered shattered morale within the IDF/AF, Israel was slow to realise that its efforts were again completely in vain. Performing valiantly, and despite losing their commander, Brig Gen Ahmad Hamdi, in one of the IDF/AF attacks on 7 October, 15,000 Egyptian Army engineers kept the bridges and ferries operational.

Driven by the doctrine of a concentrated armoured punch and the ethos of not abandoning their fellow soldiers on the battlefield – whether dead or alive – the Southern Command IDF was eager to relieve its besieged comrades on the Bar Lev and then counter-cross the Suez Canal. The Israelis prepared a counterattack. Notably, this was prepared in complete ignorance of a number of facts: the Israeli strategy of concentration on one front in the case of a two-front war; the fact that Israeli ground troops in the Sinai could not expect to receive the necessary air support (because the bulk of the IDF/AF was still busy fighting Syrian forcess on the Golan and because the ADC had effectively neutralised the IDF/AF over the battlefield); and the latest experiences of stubborn and effective resistance by Egyptian troops (as during the aforementioned clash between the 183rd Saiqa Battalion and the 217th Reserve Armored Brigade). During the morning, Egyptian SIGINT-gathering posts and reconnaissance monitored the deployment of the 162nd Reserve Armored Division opposite to the Second Field Army, and the 143rd Reserve Armored Division opposite the northern flank of the Third Field Army. The Egyptian Army instantly called for support from the EAF and this was provided in due course, despite IDF/AF raids on at least two major Egyptian air bases. Although there are next to no accounts of this effort in available Israeli publications, Muhammad Okasha recalled:

*'Early that morning the Israelis attempted to attack Tanta AB again, but their attack was repulsed by our air defences and two Israeli Phantoms shot down.'*

Similarly, Hussein el-Kfass very clearly recalled an Israeli attack that was pressed home on as-Salihiya air base:

*'The Israelis bombed our air base on the morning of 8 October. I want to stress something here: they [the Israelis] were strong, professional pilots, flying great aircraft with excellent performance and capabilities. They really dropped many bombs and there were severe detonations going on for minutes. But, they missed all our HASes. The runway was slightly damaged by debris that was quickly swept away.'*

Within an hour of the Israeli raids, two flights from No. 62 Squadron hit the HAWK site at Abu Samara, while No. 89 Squadron launched 12 MiG-17Fs led by Lt Col Lashin into an attack on Israeli troops in front of the Third Field Army, about 20km (12.4 miles) east of the Suez Canal, where they reported the destruction of about a dozen

MiG-17F serial number 2085 seen during a post-war display with an assortment of weapons usually deployed by the type, including (from right to left): FAB-250M-46 bomb, Sakr unguided rockets, FAB-100M bomb, and another FAB-250M-46.
(Tom Cooper Collection)

A pair of Su-7BMKs from Air Brigade 205, as seen before the October 1973 War. Notable are the entirely different camouflage patterns (in yellow sand and blue-green) and the different size of serial numbers (7670 in the foreground and 7545 in the background) on each aircraft.
(Albert Grandolini Collection)

Israeli vehicles. Elsewhere, MiG-17Fs attacked the HAWK site near the Gidi Defile, clearing the way for a flight of Su-7BMKs from Bilbeis that attacked Refidim air base. By making a big circle around their target, the Egyptians took the Israelis by surprise before attacking in a westerly direction and accelerating away towards the Suez Canal. The Su-7BMKs released their bombs as a pair of Mirage 5s was in the process of taking off, and Israel claimed two Sukhois as shot down by its interceptors following a lengthy pursuit in the direction of the Suez Canal.[2]

Meanwhile, the 162nd Reserve Armored Division moved from its bivouac along the Baluza-Tasa road and attacked in the direction of Firdan and Ismailia with only two brigades equipped with Centurion MBTs: two other brigades were delayed and still en route. Due to a series of command and navigational mistakes, part of the Israeli division became entangled with Egyptian forces in the Qantara area while deploying for attack, while the other brigade made a navigational error and headed too far south, before making a sharp turn west and driving one of its battalions frontally into the centre of the Egyptian 16th Division, around 10.40. In the following minutes, Israel lost 18 tanks, with most of their crews either killed or captured. Amid confusion caused by losses and a lack of intelligence, the 217th Reserve Armored Brigade attempted another attack around 13.00. This ran straight into a trap set by the Egyptian 2nd Infantry Division with the help of SIGINT, and resulted in the loss of more than 50 Israeli tanks destroyed and eight captured.

## Scarlet Rock

While this loss of two armoured battalions caused a shock for the Israelis and forced them to comprehend the seriousness of their situation in the Sinai, 8 October was not only a bad day for the IDF/AF: the Egyptian and Iraqi air arms were to experience a spate of losses too. Namely, during the hours after the defeat of the 162nd Reserve Armored Division, Israeli ground troops found themselves on the receiving end of another surprise, caused by the Egyptian Army launching a drive to expand its bridgeheads. The most successful such attack was that by the 16th Infantry Division in the Second Field Army's sector, which reached tactically important positions on the hills named Mashchir, Televizia, Missouri and Hamutal (the last of which overlooked the juncture of the Ismailia and Artillery roads), between 14.00 and 16.30. However, the deepest penetration was achieved in the Third Field Army's sector, where the 18th Infantry Division deepened its bridgehead to 18km (11.2 miles). All Israeli countertacks

This still from a post-war semi-documentary shows an EAF MiG-17F (serial number 2205) turning around after the first attack run during which the pilot made use of Sakr unguided rockets. Two FAB-100M bombs can be made out on their bomb racks: these were about to be released during the second attack run.
(David Nicolle Collection)

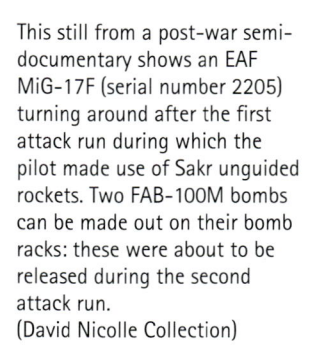

collapsed amid poor coordination and additional losses – some of which were caused by the EAF and IrAF, both of which provided support to Egyptian ground troops.

The Third Field Army continued issuing calls for CAS, and the EAF reacted by launching several formations of MiG-17Fs. One of these consisted of 12 aircraft from No. 89 Squadron, led by Lt Col Lashin and scrambled around 13.30. Arriving over the designated area slightly more than half an hour later, the Egyptian pilots found no suitable targets. Lashin therefore decided to split his formation: while his rearmost flight – led by Lt Col Mustafa Zaki el-Maghrabi – was released into a 'free hunt' mission down one of the roads in the area, Lashin led the remaining eight aircraft in the direction of the red-soiled mountains around the Gidi Defile, intending to re-attack the IDF Southern Command HQ at Umm Qashiba. This decision of the Egyptian squadron CO proved correct – in so far that it brilliantly illustrated the flexibility of air power and its potential for taking the enemy by surprise. On the other hand, it also showed the limitations of the targeting intelligence provided to the pilots involved, and exposed the fact that the MiG-17 packed too small a punch to cause significant damage. The Egyptians approached Umm Qashiba undetected and at the time Units 511 and 545 were in the process of receiving a visit by Israeli Minister of Defense Moshe Dayan, as recalled by the helicopter pilot that flew him there:

'*As I turned off my engine, I could hear aircraft approaching. Sticking out my head, I saw four MiG-17s pulling sharply upward and turning to attack us from the southwest. In less than a minute, the MiGs would shower the area with cannon fire after dropping their bombs. With my rotor still spinning, I jumped out. All my concern was focused on the Minister of Defence, who was walking slowly toward the command centre. I ran to him and pointed at the MiGs, which were already diving towards us...*'[3]

According to available Arab accounts, the MiGs dropped their bombs on the most visible target – the 'antenna farm' of the local electronic warfare station – ruining all the repairs of the last two days.[4] The Israelis reported no hits at all:

Hold the Line

A well-known still from the strike camera of one of No. 201 Squadron's F-4Es, taken during the interception of four MiG-17Fs from No. 89 Squadron near Umm Qashiba on the afternoon of 7 October 1973. It is showing a Phantom at 'deep six o'clock' of an Egyptian MiG-17F that is maneuvering in full afterburner at a very low altitude above sand dunes. Most likely the MiG in question was flown by Lt Karim al-Nasser but, contrary to Israeli claims, this was the only Egyptian fighter shot down during that action. (David Nicolle Collection)

'*...as we attempted to persuade the Minister of Defence to run for his life, the anti-aircraft cannon at Umm Qashiba proved their efficiency.*

'*The lead MiG absorbed a direct hit before completing its turn to enter attack. A large burning red hole gaped in the centre of its belly, and it did a low barrel roll and slammed into the ground before everyone's eyes. Immediately afterward, we heard another explosion above us. A second MiG began to burn from a hit by one of the L/70 cannon. It dove and crashed into the ground at the base of the cliff. The two remaining MiGs dove west of the cliff and fled.*'

Meanwhile, the second flight from Lashin's formation hit the long-range artillery battery at Ain Mana with rockets and bombs. Their attack was still ongoing when four F-4Es returning from a dive-toss attack on Suez Canal bridges appeared on the scene. Israel claimed three MiGs shot down by cannon fire, and one that crashed after its pilot lost control while in a 'scissors' manoeuvre with one of the Phantoms.[5]

As so often during the first few days of the war, it seems that Israeli methods of crediting their pilots (and air defence gunners) with 'confirmed' kills were driven more by attempts to bolster shattered morale than reality. Namely, only one Egyptian fighter-bomber is known to have been shot down during this mission. The MiG-17F flown by Lt Karim al-Nasser was hit by cannon fire from one of the Phantoms while under way at only 10m (33ft) above the desert. Nasser ejected well below the minimal safe altitude, milliseconds before his burning jet crashed, and hit the ground very hard, breaking his left arm and jaw, and sustaining numerous other injuries in the process. Despite – or perhaps because of – the immense pain, he remained conscious, buried his parachute in the sand and then started a march in a westerly direction, hoping to reach friendly lines nearly 100km (62 miles) away. Avoiding roads and evading numerous Israeli ground units, he marched until the evening then took some rest. He had only one bottle of water with him, but was experiencing immense problems alone in opening it, because of his injured hands and, while trying to drink, because of his broken jaw. Nevertheless, after countless adventures, he reached Egyptian positions late the next day. Nasser was hospitalised and needed one year of intensive treatment to fully recover, but he returned to serve with the EAF in late 1974.

## Drama at Port Said

One of the most under-reported episodes of the October War relates to the Israeli attacks on the group of SAM sites operated by the Independent Military Command for Port Said. As mentioned earlier, organised along regimental structure, this group of four SA-2 and SA-3 battalions was supported by its own early warning radars and several batteries of towed S-60 and ZU-23 guns, as well as SA-7 teams. The task was not only to protect the strategically important northern entry into the Suez Canal, or bolster defences on this exposed and – due to Lake Manzala and the extensive salt-marshes surrounding it – isolated piece of reland: the unit was also to secure launching sites for R-17E missiles of the 65th Missile Brigade of the Egyptian Army. Prior to the crossing of the Canal, Port Said was the only location under Egyptian control from which R-17E missiles could reach targets in Israel.

Starting from 8 October 1973, the IDF/AF began a series of vicious air strikes on SAM sites in the Port Said area. The first related mission saw F-4Es from No. 119 Squadron bombing the early warning radar site at Baltim and Phantoms from No. 201 Squadron hitting a similar site at Damietta, shortly after 11.00, local time. An Egyptian account of the following action described the approach of the Israeli fighter-bombers as follows:

'…*Our radar screens picked up Israeli planes approaching from the east at medium and high altitudes. Immediately, the Port Said air defence commander assigned part of his defensive effort to deal with these targets, shold they enter the operational area. At the same time he ordered the major part to be prepared to attack the planes approaching from the south and to concentrate reconnaissance efforts towards the north and west.*

'*The planes approaching from the east lost altitude to give the impression that they were about to attack. This manoeuvre deceived no one… Soon the main enemy attack was detected, approaching Port Said from the south. The planes were in two groups, one heading towards the northeast to attack the missile positions there, the other northwestward to attack the other defensive positions.*

'*Some small SA-7 personnel-borne weapons were positioned on the line of approach of the attacking aircraft. As these missiles were launched, the planes were forced to zoom up quickly, exactly as we planned. Thus, they were in the most convenient positions for our SA-2 and SA-3 batteries to destroy them.*'[6]

According to their accounts, Israelis did not suffer any losses, although the '*Port Said SAM network fired 15 missiles alone at the first Phantom from No. 201 Squadron to pop-up for its attack*'. Both sides are in agreement that Israel repeated the exercise during the afternoon, and about its results. Israeli sources cite the same two F-4 units targeting the SAM sites in the Port Said area around 16.30. The IDF/AF post-strike analysis assessed this strike as having 'inactivated' all the SAM sites in the Port Said area, and that these remained inoperational for two days, in return for no own loss.[7] The official Egyptian position largely confirms this, though differs in regards to Israeli losses:

'The Israelis sent over a total of 94 planes. Defending against such a number was beyond the capacity of our four batteries, which could face only one apiece at any one time. Any planes in addition to the four being engaged could thus bombard the missile positions and evoke no counteraction. Using these tactics, the Israelis were able to silence all four missile batteries. But in return they lost 12 planes.'[8]

Such claims were certainly exaggerated: indeed, the Israeli raid overwhelmed the capability of local ground-based air defences to such a degree that the EAF scrambled MiG-21s of Air Brigade 104 from el-Mansourah. Their appearance resulted in the Israelis rushing several flights of Mirages towards Port Said too. Samir Aziz Mikhail recalled the resulting clash as follows:

'Early that morning our squadron CO, Magdy Kamal, approached me requesting to replace him because he caught influenza and was exhausted. I accepted and took over the responsibility for our unit and his aircraft. Running the operations of our squadron, which was launching one flight after another the whole day, kept me busy, so when the time came for me to fly a mission too, I encountered a problem. Magdy Kamal was a big bloke in comparison to me, but in my rush to scramble I forgot to re-adjust my seat belts. I took off, nevertheless, together with Salah as my number 2, Qabbany as number 3 and Abdul Muneim Hammam as number 4. While accelerating and climbing, I was hoping to find a few seconds to attempt and adjust my belts, but there was no time: the GCI ordered us to accelerate towards Port Said and said the enemy was already attacking. Approaching the combat zone, I ordered my wingmen to jettison their drop tanks and prepare for combat. But, my tanks hung up because of an electrical failure. I was flying with three tanks but, since I was in the lead, I continued on... Then I saw four Mirages above us and diving towards Qabbany and Hammam. I decided to make a head-on pass and began to manoeuvre, but then four other Mirages appeared from below and behind and hit Salah. He was dead about 30 seconds later: they shot him with their cannon.

'My world darkened then: rather than entering the battle with four aircraft, we were only three, against eight enemies, two of which were coming to shoot me with their cannon. I made a very hard turn to the right, forcing them to overhoot: one of the Mirages came out in front of me and I reversed my turn to left to shoot him. I pressed the trigger, but there was no response. I tried to change to missiles, but to no avail: there was a failure in the electrical circuit for the armament. I thought, something is very wrong with my aircraft: the tanks won't separate, the gun doesn't work, and the missiles don't fire. Without armament, my aircraft was just a useless piece of iron...

'I knew they would kill me for sure; everywhere I looked I saw a Mirage. I decided to crash into one of them. If I'm sure to die, I will take one of them with me. So I tried to hit Mirages twice, but they were very clever at escaping. Qabbany and Hammam did well and fought themselves between the Israelis in my direction, forcing two Israelis to break off their attacks upon me. They all descended to very low altitude and were manoeuvring at very slow speeds. I decided to exploit this moment, made a steep dive down towards the sea to accelerate and turned in the direction of el-Mansoura. But after pulling out I said to myself, why did you leave Qabbany and Hammam alone? I made a combat turn towards them, rolled out... and then noticed a Mirage next to my right wing. Before I was able to turn left I felt an impact like a bus hitting a bicycle. A missile hit me very hard. My plane began to spin out of

Samir Aziz Mikhail as seen in 1964, shortly after his conversion to MiG-21F-13s, and while wearing the VKK-6M flight suit and GSh-4 helmet for high-altitude operations. (Samir Aziz Mikhail Collection)

Fourship of MiG-21MFs from No. 46 Squadron streaking across the skies during a post-war parade. Two (including the serial number 8444, flown by flight leader) of them still wore the 'Sand and Spinach' camouflage pattern applied before delivery, while two are already showing the Nile Valley camouflage pattern. (David Nicolle Collection)

control. While falling towards the sea, I looked into the overhead mirror and could not see the fin, while the fuselage and wings were on fire. As the aircraft began to rotate, I ejected, but felt a terrible pain in my back: my belts were not tightened and I was not in the right position to eject...

'I crashed into the water in severe pain, inflated my lifejacket and tried to remain conscious... Then I saw a fishing boat approach me quietly. It came closer and a fisherman raised a stick to hit me. I moved slightly and it fell beside me; I screamed that I was not an Israeli. They pulled me into the boat and took my gun away, then asked me if I had a belt with gold on me. I told them my rank and name and they brought me to the Coast Guard, which finally took me to a hospital... I was still in pain when several colleagues visited me, so I told them to always look behind them when entering an air combat, because the Israelis where now trying to sandwich us. Then they gave me strong sedatives and I fell asleep...'[9]

The Israelis claimed another MiG shot down during this combat (for a total of three), while grudgingly admitting the loss of a Mirage 5 (Nesher serial number 593) flown by Capt Eitan Carmi, who ejected over Lake Bardawil and was recovered by Israeli ground forces. Carmi was shot down by the Egyptian number 4, Capt Abdel Moneim Hammam.

Insistent on recovering the air defence capabilities of Port Said, Maj Gen Fahmy then ordered more of his units into the area. Ayman Sayed Ahmad Hob el-Din, then CO of 418th Air Defence Battalion ADC recalled:

'On 8 October, the enemy knocked out SAM battalions protecting Port Said and the site selected for Scud-B attacks on Israel. I received the order to mobilise my unit, *move it from its position near Cairo to Port Said, and to take over the control of local air defences.*'[10]

As we are to see in *Volume 6*, IDF/AF attacks on Port Said were to significantly increase in intensity during the following days, stunning not only most of the Egyptians involved but also their colleagues in Iraq and Syria.[11] For reasons known only to them, the Israelis have never provided a logical and working explanation for all the attacks on Port Said. One of the leading historians of the IDF/AF has attempted to offer an explanation that is characterised foremost by its understatement:

*'In itself, the Port Said SAM network was not a top-priority target. Yet it was perfect to test the new IDF/AF SEAD tactics in a sector limited to small-scale SEAD strikes…'*[12]

Following the mauling it experienced over both front lines during the first two days of the war, and considering its preoccupation with fighting on the Golan Front for the next few days, it is highly doubtful that the IDF/AF would have found the time and opportunity to deploy two squadrons of precious F-4Es and put them and their crews at risk to 'test SEAD tactics' against a 'lower-priority target'. And if the Israeli explanation is true, its commanders must have been even more arrogant and ready to gamble with the fate of the entire nation than anybody thought.

On the contrary, Egyptian sources have little doubt that this affair was linked to Israel's political leadership considering the possible deployment of nuclear weapons (to be discussed in Volume 6), and above all the possible response from Moscow, for example in the form of deployment of nuclear weapons to Egypt and their delivery into Israel with the aid of Egyptian Scuds.

A still from a cine-film showing elements of an ADC's SA-2 SAM-site on the move during the 1973 War. When the 418th Air Defence Battalion received the order to move to Port Saic, its crews could hardly imagine what an ordeal they were about to go through later during the war. (via Group 73)

Israeli sailors 'fished' the fin of the Mirage 5J/Nesher serial number 593 from the sea (unit insignia on its top is that of No. 113 Squadron IDF/AF). The plane was shot down by EAF Capt Abdel Moneim Hammam, from No. 46 Squadron during an air combat off Port Said, on late afternoon of 8 October 1973. (Albert Grandolini Collection)

189

## Tough School

The losses sustained by its own fighter-bombers during this afternoon were the probable reason for the High Command EAF to finally make use of its 'No. 66 Squadron' – Iraqi Hunters. Mohammad Naji recalled a mission flown shortly before sunset that introduced him to the realities of the modern-day battlefield:

'...*During the later afternoon of 8 October we finally received an order to go into action. We launched 12 Hunters, passed low along our SAM corridor over Ismailia, and headed for the front line. This was an important measure in order to keep us safe from Egyptian SAMs: the Egyptians flew Soviet aircraft equipped with IFF transponders that showed them on their radars as friendly. Our Hunters had no such transponders so we had to use specially designed corridors where SAM crews knew only our aircraft were flying...*

'*The first formation was led by Maj Yousif Mohammed Rasoul, with 1st Lt Amer Ahmed Qaysee, 1st Lt Wallid Abdel-Qader and another pilot. The second formation was led by Maj as-Samarrai, with 1st Lt Diah as wingman and 1st Lt Imad Ahmed Ezzat as number 3, and another pilot, and the third by Capt Salem, me as his number 3 and two other pilots. Each flight was under way in two pairs separated by nearly 3,000m [9,842ft], and with a separation of 500m [1,640ft] between the aircraft in each pair.*

'*Egyptian intelligence reported a column of Israeli armour and trucks moving along an asphalted road in the desert leading to the Tasa Defile. This would be a target easily distinguished from the air, even when flying at low level. The Egyptians warned us about a possible presence of enemy Mirage interceptors, and that we would not be provided with top cover. If we were to see any Israeli fighters in the air, it would be down to our formation leader to decide whether to proceed with the mission, engage, or run away. The Egyptians also warned us of Arabic-speaking Israeli radio operators, mimicking Egyptians to give us 'new instructions' while we were under way. Because of this we always used English for communication while under way on combat sorties. Most of us had flown together for years, and could easily recognise each other's voices. Radio silence was maintained, although the ether was full of Arabic and Hebrew chat, and we experienced a huge morale booster when we saw the Egyptian Army units battling the Israelis on the ground.*

'*We approached the target zone shortly before sunset. Maj as-Samarrai called Maj Rasoul to announce a massive volume of AAA and SAM fire ahead of us, and then the appearance of Mirages above, and suggested we to make a slight detour, but the Mirages continued circling high above us and Yusif ordered us to continue as planned. Shortly after, Samarrai's Hunter was shot down and the pilot killed. Then we reached our target and 1st Lt Diah exalted, 'Oh, my God, the junction is swarming with Israeli vehicles of all types!'*

'*We began to attack with unguided rockets, and then pumped the area with 30mm shells. I saw several fierce detonations on the ground. When the Israelis realised they were under attack, many started taking cover on the side of the road. Very few manned machine guns on their halftracks and tanks returned fire.*

'*Our intention was to make just one pass: there was serious concern that the Mirages would catch us if we remained in the target area any longer. Nevertheless, we lost the Hunter flown by 1st Lt Amer Ahmed Qaysee during that one pass.*

Major Wallid Abdul Latif as-Samarrai, deputy CO No. 66 Squadron, was one of two IrAF Hunter pilots KIA during a mission in support of The Second Field Army, during the late afternoon of 8 October 1973.
(via Ali Tobchi)

*The others broke to avoid enemy fire and managed to escape – only to come under fire from Egyptian ground forces while returning… It was sad to return missing two pilots and two aircraft: we followed our orders and completed our mission but lost two aircraft and experienced massive problems with the Egyptian air defences because we lacked the necessary IFF transponders.'*

Continuing the practice of exaggerating its claims, the IDF/AF subsequently credited two pilots from No. 101 Squadron with a total of three 'confirmed kills' against Iraqi Hunters – supposedly all scored rather easily, in the course of a *'texbook low-altitude pursuit'*.[13]

1st Lt Amer Ahmed Qaysee was the pilot of the second IrAF Hunter shot down during the late afternoon of 8 October 1973.
(via Ali Tobchi)

## Whirlpool of Death

The failure of Operation Model 5 made the Israeli situation on the Golan Heights especially desperate. The demise of the 188th Armored Brigade left the southern half of the Heights open to advances by elements of the Syrian 1st Armoured and 5th and 9th Infantry Divisions towards the River Jordan. At this critical juncture and for reasons that remain unexplained until today, one after another, all Syrian units stopped and prematurely went into a bivouac, during the late afternoon of 7 October. At the rear of brigades that stopped their advance on B'not Yaacov Bridge and El Al, other units began establishing defensive positions. Meanwhile, Israel was diverting all available reserves – including one division intended for deployment in the Sinai – to the northern sector. During the following night, they managed to push enough tanks on to the Golan that the real danger of the Syrians reaching the River Jordan passed. This meant not only that the commanders of the Syrian Arab Army had ruined their own chances of victory, but also that they managed to let the initiative slip to the Israeli side: they were never to regain it.

While continuing to maintain pressure upon the Syrian Army and the centre of the Syrian SAM umbrella further east, the IDF/AF decided to start 8 October with a concentrated counter-air campaign against Syria. Because no Syrian accounts are available, what happened when the various formations clashed can be reconstructed only on the basis of two reports, one from Russia and one from Israel.[14] While the Israelis sometimes explain this effort using understatements such as it being necessary to *'prevent annoying MiG-17 and Su-7 attacks'*[15], the number of Phantoms involved at a time the fate of the Golan Heights was still anything but certain indicates that the SyAAF's presence was strongly felt on the battlefield.

This Israeli attack began with a near-simultaneous approach of several massive F-4E formations. No fewer than 18 Phantoms from No. 119 Squadron headed via the Madar Valley in Lebanon for Nassiriyah; 16 from No. 107 Squadron followed a similar route for Tsaykal and 17 from No. 69 Squadron for Dmeyr, while 15 F-4Es from No. 201 Squadron 'cut the corner' over Jordan to approach Khelkhleh air base from the south. The 'outflanking' ingress routes failed to take the SyAAF by surprise, but the size of the Israeli formations was more than could be matched by the some 24 MiG-21s that were on patrol over southeastern Syria or on quick reaction alert (QRA) readiness that morning.

Over Dmeyr, a flight of MiG-21s from No. 69 Squadron led by Capt al-Hamidi bounced four Phantoms around 07.00 and the leader fired his first R-3S while his tar-

A SyAAF MiG-21MF (serial number was probably 1509) thunders low over Damascus, on the morning of 8 October 1973. Notable is the armament of four R-3S, as usual for Syrian MiG-21MFs: the Egyptians usually loaded only two missiles on their aircraft of this variant, with two drop tanks on the outboard underwing pylons. (Albert Grandolini Collection)

get was still under way straight and level. Hamidi's missile failed to guide. Approaching to 900m (2,953ft) distance, the Syrian fired his second R-3S as the Phantom initiated a break, and this time the missile scored a direct hit, prompting the Israeli crew to eject into captivity. Majid az-Zoughby claimed one kill during this engagement too. The IDF/AF later confirmed the loss of two F-4Es from this formation, with one 'shot down over Damascus' and another officially attributed to SA-6s over the Golan Heights, but there is little doubt that both Phantoms fell victim to Hamidi's flight.

Four MiGs were airborne over Tsaykal and four managed to scramble and engage incoming Phantoms in air combats. According to Russian sources, 'Captain Khaozhi' outmanoeuvred one Phantom and fired two R-3S in quick succession. One of the missiles went ballistic but the other hit and detonated in a brilliant fireball. Khaozhi was shot down by another Phantom shortly afterwards. Capt 'Jelyi' was with the flight that was scrambled shortly before the Israelis reached Tsaykal and attacked one of the F-4Es that was fleeing in the direction of the Lebanese border. He fired two R-3S missiles at his target, and saw one detonate underneath the F-4E which, reportedly, subsequently crashed. Short on fuel, Jelyi then attempted to land at Nassiriyah, but was shot down by Syrian SAMs and killed while attempting to eject. Israeli crews were credited with two MiG kills, while two damaged Phantoms reportedly made it back to

A view over Bley air base towards the south and the Jordanian border, some 100km away. It was from this direction that at least two formations of Israeli Phantoms arrived on their way to attack SyAAF air bases on the morning of 8 October 1973. (Tom Cooper)

Ramat David for single-engine emergency landings.[16] None of the names mentioned in related Russian reports are known in Syria. The closest match the authors were able to find was IrAF MiG-21PFM pilot 1st Lt Kamil Sultan al-Khafaji, who is known to have deployed with No. 9 Squadron to Syria during the afternoon of 7 October 1973 (see the following sub-chapter for details). Khafaji ejected safely, and was to see more action on the next day. The fact that the IrAF did not cooperate with Soviet advisors in Syria (indeed, not even with the the few Soviets in Iraq) is the probable reason for the Russians having problems recalling the names of Iraqi pilots. Of course, it does not explain why they recall Iraqi MiG-21s and their pilots as 'Syrian'.

Interestingly, while no Israeli accounts of such a mission are available, Fikry el-Gindy recalled that Mazza air base came under attack on the morning of 8 October, too:

*'On the morning of 8 October I was ordered to keep one flight back for defence of the base, while the other flight would provide air cover for the Syrian Army that repeatedly came under Israeli attacks. I flew two sorties, including one CAP and one BARCAP* [barrier combat air patrol; authors' note], *leading both of them: until I picked one of my youngsters as flight leader and instructed him appropriately, there was nobody else with enough experience.*

*'That day the Israelis bombed our airfield for the first time. They did not cause any damage but during the morning there was a lull in flying for our squadron. After a while, Syrian units continued taking off and landing. They lost two squadron leaders in combat that morning, plus one pilot injured when shot down by their SAMs. This made me restless and angry. I telephoned Brig Haddad to ask him why we were doing nothing. He said, 'Don't worry, you'll hear from us soon enough'…'*

In contrast, Mohammad Marawy recalled 8 October as one of quietest days for No. 54 Squadron at T.4:

*'We received no orders to go into action. From time to time, our Su-20s were prepared for air defence duties and armed with R-3S missiles. But we didn't get many*

1st Lt Kamil Sultan al-Khafaji seen later during his career, while flying MiG-21PFMs with No. 9 Squadron IrAF. (via Ali Tobchi)

Kamil Sultan al-Khafaji seen as a cadet at the Air Force Academy, during advanced flight training on BAC Jet Provosts. (via Ali Tobchi)

Syrian Su-7 pilot Captain Kamal Hilal Nasr was killed on 7 October 1973, during an attack on IDF HQ at Mount Meron. Reportedly, his aircraft was hit after releasing bombs, and Nasr announced on the radio he would not eject. Sadly, neither Israelis nor Syrians have ever released any other details about this mission. (via Amr Safadi)

*chances to fight any air combats: the MiG-21s based at T.4 were always faster in getting airborne and intercepting the enemy. They shot down a few Phantoms that attempted to approach our air base, and air defences did the rest, but we were not scrambled.'* In contrast, other Syrian sources recall a mission by four Su-20s against the IDF HQ at Mount Meron, near Saffad. While not mentioning results of this attack, they do recall that the formation returned without Capt Kamal Hilal Nasr, who was killed (Nasr's body was returned by Israel after the war).

Eventually, the IDF/AF attack on SyAAF air bases in the Damascus area was effective in postponing a number of sorties by Syrian fighter-bombers. Another reason for this postponement was an important change in tactics, as recalled by 'Adad':

*'I flew one ground attack on late morning that day against the enemy HQ at Naffach. On the insistence of Soviet advisors, we were ordered to fly in smaller, supposedly more flexible formations of between two and four aircraft. Instead of providing top cover by escorting us throughout the mission, MiG-21s were to fly barriers over specific areas, enabling us to reach our targets on the battlefield undisturbed by Israeli interceptors. Whenever possible, we were to operate supported by Soviet-flown An-12PP transport equipped for electronic warfare and ground-based SMALTA electronic warfare systems, which were expected to hide us from Israeli early warning radars and interceptors.'*

Majid az-Zoughby could not complain about the new tactics, since flying patrols behind the front lines offered him a rare opportunity to catch one of many Israeli Skyhawks active below:

*'We reached the designated patrol zone at an altitude of 4,000m [13,123ft] and shortly after saw several puffs of smoke, probably from anti-aircraft fire, and then two or three Skyhawks fleeing west. I dove to attack, went supersonic and caught up with the enemy very fast. I fired a missile at the rearmost Skyhawk. I doubt he ever saw me. The missile hit, several pieces fell off, then the pilot ejected.'*

Later during the day, most of the Syrian attacks on Naffach, Quneitra and in the direction of the River Jordan were beaten back with heavy losses in armour. One of these attacks, including eight Mi-8s that deployed commandos of the 82nd Parachute Battalion against the IDF HQ at Naffech around 08.00 was – at least according to Israeli sources – costly in other ways too. Three Mi-8s were claimed as shot down by ground fire and one supposedly by IDF/AF interceptors shortly after crossing the front line. While three others turned away, at least one helicopter actually managed to disembark its passengers, but most of these were swiftly encircled and neutralised by Israeli ground troops.[17] Nevertheless, the Israelis experienced an even costlier failure during their first attempt to recover the OP at Jebel Sheikh, launched around 10.00. They gave up after six hours of fruitless attacks and about 70 casualties.

Shortly before sunset the 82nd Parachute Battalion was deployed into its second operation of the day. Six Mi-4 helicopters flew one of its companies into an attack on the Israeli OP at Tel Faris. Defenders – including exhausted paratroopers of the 50th Battalion IDF, an artillery battery and some 12 tanks that were all that was left of the 188th Armored Brigade – claimed to have shot down two helicopters during their approach. Two additional Mi-4s were claimed destroyed by tank fire shortly after landing east of Tel Faris. Nevertheless, the Israelis were subsequently forced to evacuate this exposed position, which was now several kilometres behind the front lines of the Syrian Army.[18] It is possible that the attack on Tel Faris was what prompted the High Command SyAAF to finally put el-Gindy's unit on alert again:

*'At 15.45 exactly we received an order to launch two flights armed with rockets and bombs. However, by the time we were ready to take off, around 17.30, our mission was cancelled. I was angered and called Haddad again: I objected to being treated like this and started asking him questions like, 'Have you understood what I am trying to say? Have you understood my protest? Don't you think we are any good?' The chief of staff SyAAF then called me back trying to calm me down, to assure me that they considering us competent, and to say there would be special sorties for the Egyptian squadron the next day.'*

Maj Gen Naji Jamil was correct: 9 October was to prove extremely busy, for No. 15 Squadron and the entire Syrian Arab Air Force.

## From Kirkuk to Damascus

As already planned by Shazly and other leading Arab commanders during the 12th session of the Arab Collective Defence Council, in November 1971, the SyAAF was reinforced by the appearance of several units of the Iraqi Air Force, beginning on 7 October 1973.

Arguably, the outbreak of the October 1973 War could not have caught the IrAF at a worst moment: large parts of the force were involved in fighting a Kurdish insurgency in northern Iraq, while the rest was mid-way through the process of transition to an entirely new generation of combat aircraft. Many pilots and officers were scattered between conversion and combat courses in Czechoslovakia and the Soviet Union, or were completing staff courses in Iraq. Contracts for the acquisition of variable-geometry aircraft like the MiG-23MS interceptor and Su-20 fighter-bomber had been signed and their future crews were already undergoing conversion courses in the USSR.

Majid az-Zoughby, one of the most successful SyAAF MiG-21 pilots of the October 1973 War, as seen after that conflict. (via Amr Safadi)

**Table 5: IrAF order of battle and transfers to Syria, October 1973**
**(Units deployed to Egypt are marked in red, the ones to Syria in green)**

| Unit | Base | Equipment | Remarks |
|---|---|---|---|
| No. 1 Squadron | al-Hurryah (Mosul) | Su-7BMK | CO Maj Sami Hussein Alusy<br>XO Capt Khaldoun Khattab al-Bakr<br>Deployed to Damascus IAP on 8 Oct |
| No. 2 Squadron | Firnas (Kirkuk) | 4 Mi-1<br>31 Mi-4 | Slated for re-equipment with Mi-8 |
| No. 3 Squadron | Muthanna (Baghdad) | 2 de Hailland Dove, 2 de Hailland Heron, 2 Tu-124 | VIP-transport |
| No. 4 Squadron | al-Hurrya | 9 Westland Wessex HC.Mk 52<br>5 SE.316B Alouette III | CO Col Hassan Sharif<br>Slated for re-equipment with Mi-8 |
| No. 5 Squadron | al-Hurrya | Su-7BMK | CO Maj Salim Sultan Abdullah<br>XO Maj Hassan Kasim Hazem<br>Deployed to Bley on 8 Oct |
| No. 6 Squadron | Tammouz (Habbaniyah) | 12 Hunter F.Mk 59 | CO Col Adil Soleimany |
| No. 7 Squadron | al-Hurrya | MiG-17F | CO Lt Col Shehab al-Qiyasy<br>XO Capt Mohammed Omar Abdul Hadi<br>Deployed to Dmeyr on 8 Oct |
| No. 8 Squadron | Firnas | Su-7BMK | CO Capt Jawdat an-Naqeeb; unit converted to Su-7 in mid-1973 and acted as OCU for that type<br>Deployed to Dmeyr on 8 Oct |
| No. 9 Squadron | H-3/al-Wallid | MiG-21PFM | CO Maj Namik Saadallah<br>Deployed to Dmeyr and Tsaykal on 7 Oct |
| No. 10 Squadron | al-Taqqaddum (Habbaniyah) | 8 Tu-16 | |
| No. 11 Squadron | Rashid (Baghdad) | MiG-21MF | Remaining MiG-21F-13s stored<br>Deployed to Nassiriya on 12 Oct |
| No. 14 Squadron | Ali Ibn Abu Talib (Nasseriyah) | MiG-21PFM | Slated for re-equipment with MiG-21MF |
| No. 17 Squadron (OCU) | Rashid | MiG-21FL, MiG-21UM | CO Col Durhit Ibrahim |
| No. 18 Squadron | Tammouz | 12 Tu-22B, 2 Tu-22U | CO Lt Col Mahdi Mohsen Sabbagh<br>Delivered in early Oct |
| No. 23 Squadron | Rashid | 8 An-12, 12 An-2, 3 Bristol Freighter T.Mk 170 | Involved in air bridge to Syria from 7 Oct |
| No. 29 Squadron | Tammouz | 12 Hunter F.Mk 59 | CO Col Mohammed Jassam al-Jabouri<br>Slated for re-equipment with MiG-23BN |
| No. 70 Squadron | Rashid | 8-12 MiG-21R | |
| Air Force Academy | al-Sahra (Tikrit) | Zlin Z-526 (basic training), L-29 (basic jet training), MiG-15UTI (advanced jet training) | Last Hunting Percival Provosts retired from service in 1971 |
| Flying Leaders School | Rashid | 6 Hunter T.Mk 66, 17 Hunting Jet Provost T.Mk 52 | Including Weapons and Tactics School |
| SAR Flight | Firnas | 2 Mi-4 | Slated for re-equipment with Mi-8 |
| SAR Flight | Shoibiya (Basrah) | 2 Mi-4 | Slated for re-equipment with Mi-8 |

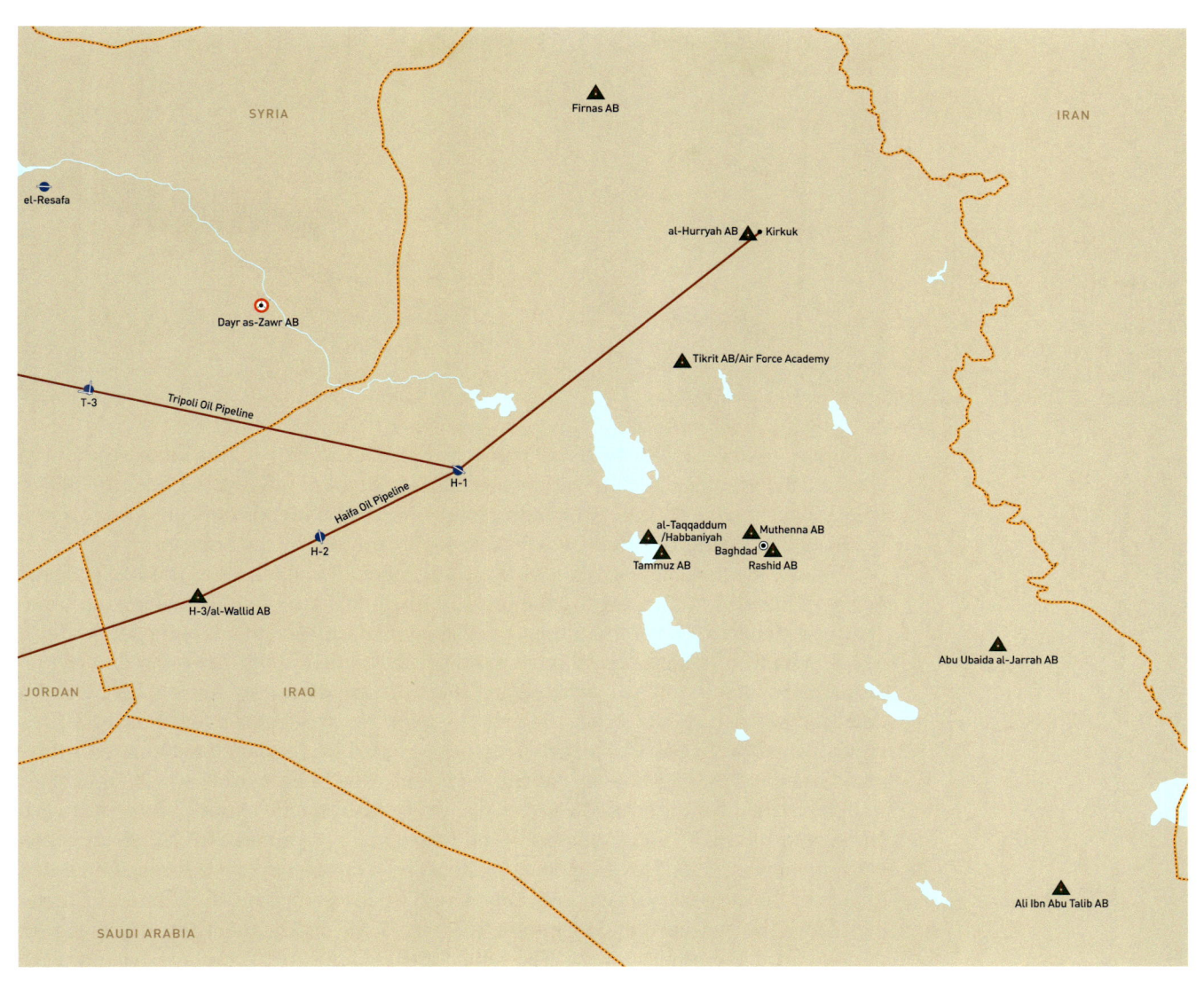

Map of major IrAF bases as of October 1973.
(Map by James Lawrence)

One of the first MiG-21MFs delivered to Iraq lands at Rashid, Baghdad, in 1971. Sadly, the serial number was obscured by the IrAF Intelligence Department. Several IrAF squadrons were in the process of converting to this variant when they were rushed to Syria in October 1973.
(Farzad Bishop Collection)

No show: although delivered in time to participate in the October 1973 War, Iraqi Tu-22s (this example wore the serial number 1114) could not go into action because the Soviets failed to deliver the necessary weapons and ground equipment. (Tom Cooper Collection)

Deliveries of MiG-21MFs were well under way but the majority of the interceptor force was still flying older MiG-21 variants. Similarly, MiG-17s – delivered back in 1958 – were still in service with No. 7 Squadron, their crews impatiently expecting conversion to MiG-23BN fighter-bombers, which were highly praised by the Soviets.

Following extensive negotiations between Baghdad and Moscow, the USSR finally began delivering 12 Tupolev Tu-22 bombers (including two Tu-22U conversion trainers), early in October 1973. Contrary to original plans, these did not enter service with No. 8 Squadron: once Iraqi military intelligence learned about Egyptian and Syrian preparations for a new war with Israel, this unit was hurriedly re-established as an OCU for Su-7s. Instead, former Il-28 crews from No. 8 Squadron and former Tu-16s crews from No. 10 Squadron that were now trained on the much-anticipated supersonic bombers established an entirely new unit, No. 18 Squadron. Fresh from their training in the USSR, Iraqi Tu-22 crews were very enthusiastic about going to war with Israel, and the IrAF High Command even began planning attacks on Israeli air bases with the new aircraft. However, such plans were scratched by the Soviets, who failed to deliver the necessary ground equipment and weapons on time. With these not arriving before the ceasefire of 24 October 1973, the IrAF Tu-22s spent the entire war on the ground at Tammouz air base. The same fate befell the Tu-16 bombers, based on the same airfield. Contrary to Egypt's Tu-16KSR-11s, these were not equipped with air-to-surface missiles. The experience of the June 1967 War had shown that sending Tu-16s via Jordan to attack heavily protected bases of the IDF/AF was practically suicidal. Therefore, no Iraqi bomber became involved in the October 1973 War.[19]

Officers and pilots of No. 11 Squadron IrAF as of December 1968, in front of one of the MiG-21FLs that unit operated at the time. (via Ali Tobchi)

Rather than bombers, the first IrAF unit put on alert for participation in the October 1973 War was No. 9 Squadron, as recalled by Ahmad Sadik (who served with the IrAF Intelligence Department in the 1980s):

*'Our intelligence had got wind about the coming war against Israel already in the late spring of 1973. Our Ministry of Defence instantly ordered the IrAF to prepare one of its units for a possible deployment to Syria. With the majority of the Air Force being busy fighting the Kurds in northern Iraq, our commanders selected No. 9 Squadron for this purpose: this unit was in the process of converting to MiG-21MFs, but this training was stopped and the squadron sent to H-3/al-Wallid AB, in western Iraq, closest to the future battlefield, still equipped with MiG-21PFMs.*

*'No. 9 Squadron was put on alert already at 16.00 on 6 October and two hours later ordered to transfer to Syria. Its aircraft, pilots and ground personnel were distributed at Dmeyr and Tsaykal, and the transfer was complete by 16.40 on 7 October 1973. The SyAAF began tasking our pilots with flying CAPs in conjunction with its own MiG-21 squadrons almost immediately, and they had their first contacts with low-flying Phantoms and Mirages during the same afternoon. Later on, they began providing top cover for IrAF MiG-17 and Su-7BMK units deployed in Syria.'*

One of the pilots assigned to No. 9 Squadron was Ma'an al-Awsi, who recalled his impressions of operations in Syria as follows:

*'Generally, the Syrian ground control was at an excellent level, and their air defence network very clear and accurate, making it possible for us to operate confidently and competently. None of our aircraft was shot down in error by Syrian SAMs, but there were some very nasty accidents with Syrian flak: their gunners were very trigger-happy.*

*'The Israelis attacked Tsaykal several times, but the Syrians had some excellent engineers and they were working at fantastic pace. The longest interruption of our operations during the war occurred later on, when the runway was closed for four hours.'*

On 8 October, two units equipped with Su-7BMKs followed, comprising Nos 1 and 5 Squadrons. Alwan al-Abossi explained the process of their transfer as follows:

*'I had meanwhile converted from Hunters to Su-7s and served with No. 5 Squadron at Hurrya AB in Kirkuk. We were involved in fighting the Kurdish Peshmerga insurgents and learned about the outbreak of the war on the radio. With Palestine being one of the central issues in the foreign policy of Iraq, and its liberation and recovery of territories lost during the June 1967 War being the major aims of our armed forces, it was clear we would become involved. Our unit was put on alert during the afternoon of 6 October, and advised to expect transfer to Baghdad, then Ramadi, H-3/al-Wallid, and Damascus…*

*'The process of transferring our aircraft to Syria began on the morning of 7 October, when 10 MiG-21s from No. 9 Squadron re-deployed to Nassiriyah and Tsaykal. They were followed by Su-7s of No.1 Squadron that moved to Damacus International on the morning of 8 October. My unit, No. 5 Squadron, flew to H-3 on the morning of 8 October. After lunch, we launched again and flew straight to Bley AB, south of Damascus. The last 200km [124 miles] we flew at only 100m [328ft] in order to avoid detection by the Israelis. There was a danger of the Israelis intercepting us while we were under way, but also of the Syrians air defences opening fire on us… Our commanders were transferred by transport aircraft before us: there was some urgency*

Pilot and ground crew of No. 5 Squadron IrAF in front of Su-7BMK serial number 769, at al-Hurrya air base, in Mosul, in the early 1970s. (via Ali Tobchi)

Hardened aircraft shelters at Damascus IAP, which during the October 1973 War served as the home base for the Su-7BMKs of No. 1 Squadron IrAF.
(Tom Cooper)

Another group of HASes at Damascus IAP that accommodated Iraqi Sukhois in October 1973. Notable are several entries to underground facilities around them.
(Tom Cooper)

in their movement, because they had to coordinate everything with the Syrian military and political leadership. We had no knowledge about Syrian air bases and had to agree everything in advance with them regarding air traffic control. Most of our ground personnel travelled by cars, buses and trucks.

'Contrary to the Syrians, we had no wing system as of that time, so we selected our top squadron commanders as representatives to superior Syrian offiers. For example, while Gen Mohammad Salman Hamad was appointed the commander of IrAF units in Syria, Maj Jassam al-Jabouri acted as liaison officer between the SyAAF and our four fighter-bomber squadrons (three units operating Su-7s and the MiG-17 squadron), while Capt Najdat an-Naqeeb did the same for our MiG-21 squadrons.

'One of the biggest issues during our expedition to Syria was to integrate the work of our ground crews with those of the Syrians, to enable a rapid flow of spares and replacements (in the case of damage). All our ammunition and nearly all of our administrative necessities, plus food, medical care and housing were provided by the Syrians: we deployed in such a rush that there was no time to take any of our stuff with us.

## Hold the Line

The October 1973 War caught the IrAF in the midst of transition to a new generation of combat aircraft. Indeed, most of its aircraft did not wear any camouflage colours, and these were applied only after their arrival in Syria. Another surprise for the MiG-17F pilots from No. 7 Squadron was that once in Syria they primarily flew CAPs, while their usual duty in Iraq consisted of flying CAS for ground troops fighting Kurdish insurgents.
(Albert Grandolini Collection).

*'The next issue was that of weapons compatibility: our Su-7s were usually armed with bombs of 250 and 500kg [551 and 1,102lb]. Alternativelly, we used ORO-57 rocket pods for four rockets of 57mm [2.24in] calibre, or UB-16-57 pods for 16 S-5K rockets of the same calibre. We did not use the older S-3Ks, which were still in Syrian service, while the Syrians were already using more modern and very powerful [9.45in] S-24s but didn't share any of them with us. Our pilots were not yet trained to use these powerful weapons.'*[20]

Muwaffak Saeed Abdullah al-Naimi recalled the situation at Bley and Damascus as follows:

*'While Damascus IAP was a high-calibre, well-protected air base with excellent facilities, Bley was little more than a forward airstrip with few HASes, little technical support and inadequate air defences. When we arrived at Bley, there were two Syrian squadrons based there, one flying MiG-17s, the other Su-7s. They were then withdrawn to other bases and only a few Syrian officers remained to introduce us to the battlefield and coordinate our operations with theirs.*

*'The Israelis easily sneaked upon it after approaching over Jordan and bombed it four times. They used the same route to attack several other Syrian air bases, further north – it was 'that good' for them. Our runway was hit on three occasions, but was quickly repaired by Syrian engineers, every time. Syrian engeineers were of very high quality. More damaging was one of their attacks – I do not recall the exact date – that resulted in the destruction of one of our Su-7BMKs inside the HAS: the ground personnel forgot to shut protective doors closed when the alert was sounded. Otherwise, the HASes proved more than viable.'*[21]

Al-Abossi continued with an explanation on the transfer of additional IrAF units:

*'The Su-7s of No. 8 Squadron and MiG-17s from No. 7 Squadron followed on 9 October. They were deployed at Tsaykal. During the transfer, all the involved units were reinforced by additional personnel reassigned from the Staff College IrAF and other training institutions, so that the ratio of pilots to aircraft was 1.5:1.'*

The last IrAF unit to move to Syria was No. 7 Squadron. The squadron CO, Lt Col Shehab al-Qaisy, was alerted by phone at dusk of 6 October, and advised to put his unit on alert for deployment to Syria. Although al-Qaisy and his staff officers were flown to Almazza in Damascus by An-24 transport the next day, the rest of the squadron followed via H-3 only on 10 October.

Once in Syria, al-Qaisy was greatly surprised when his unit was ordered to fly air defence missions. Namely, the Syrians ordered him to provide top cover for Iraqi Army units advancing on the road from Baghdad to Damascus. Furthermore, his old MiG-17s were to fly CAPs above al-Zarqa Valley and King Talal Dam on the border to Jordan, both of which were used by the Israelis to enter Syrian airspace undetected. Ma'an al-Awsy explained:

*'Our commanders were mad with the Jordanians. Although their air defences opened fire at passing Israeli planes, they never hit and anyway the Royal Jordanian Air Force was sleeping: it never scrambled a single interceptor to attack the Israelis inside their airspace, not to mention flying CAPs over the area and thus blocking this Israeli entry route into Syria.'*

1 Shazly, pp240
2 Aloni, *101: Israeli Air Force, First Fighter Squadron*, pp157
3 Cohen, *Israel's Best Defence*, pp347 & Gordon, *Thirty Hours in October*, pp469
4 Sadik, interview, March 2007
5 Aloni, *Israeli F-4 Phantom II Aces*, pp35–36
6 Badri et all, *The Ramadan War, 1973*, pp149
7 Klein et all, *Israeli Phantoms*, pp73
8 Badri et all, *The Ramadan War, 1973*, pp150
9 Samir Aziz Mikhail spent 21 days in suspension and then underwent six months of treatment before recovering completely. He returned to proudly serve with the EAF and was assigned the CO of a MiG-21-equipped air brigade at Beni Sueif AB. He retired with the rank of Major General in 1982.
10 El-Din, interview to Group 73, November 2012; this and all subsequent quotations from el-Din are based on transcription of the same interview.
11 While a handful of interviewed Egyptian officers were aware of the importance of Port Said as a possible launching site for Scud-attacks on Israel, most of interviewed Algerian, Iraqi and Syrian officers are not in posession of corresponding information until today: while all knew about these attacks and their increasing ferocity, they were unable to explain them. The following reconstruction (which is to be continued in Volume 6) became possible only through intensive search for participants by Group 73 and cross-examination of their recollections with materials provided by sources outside the Middle East.
12 Klein et all, *Israeli Phantoms*, pp73
13 Aloni, *Israeli Mirage III & Nesher Aces*, pp85 & Aloni, *101: Israeli Air Force, First Fighter Squadron*, pp158
14 Ibid, pp72 & Sukhov, *Over the Syrian Front*
15 Klein et all, *Israeli Phantoms*, pp72
16 Babich, *MiG-21 vs Mirage III* & Konstantin V Sukhov, *Over the Syrian Front*.
17 Asher et all, *Duel for the Golan*, pp 200
18 Ibid, pp 185
19 Sadik, interview, March 2007
20 Najdad an-Naqeeb served as a Hunter-pilot during the June 1967 War with Israel.
21 Al-Naimi, interview with Brig Gen Sadik, February 2007; this and all subsequent quotations by al-Naimi are based on transcription of the same interview.

# APPENDIX I

## Deliveries of MiG-21s to Arab Countries, 1961–1973

Between 1959 and 1985, three major factories in the former USSR – including the State Factory (GAZ) 21 in Gorky, GAZ-30 (also known as 'Znamya Truda Factory') in Moscow-Hodynka, and GAZ-31 in Tbilisi – manufactured 10,645 MiG-21s for Soviet service and for export (and, as mentioned in *Volume 4*, 30 additional MiG-21F-13s were delivered to Egypt from Czechoslovakia in 1969). The distribution of duties between these factories was generally clear: GAZ-21 manufactured the single-seaters for Soviet and service with allied air forces in Europe; GAZ-30 manufactured the single-seaters for export, and GAZ-31 manufactured two-seaters for both types of customer. There were few exceptions, primarily in so far that Tbilisi manufactured a small number of MiG-21Fs. Some MiG-21F-13s, MiG-21Rs and MiG-21bis were manufactured in Gorky, while production of MiG-21Us for export was undertaken by Moscow, which was also the first factory to open production of MiG-21MFs for export. One basic principle applied in all cases: export of one variant began always and only once the next variant had entered production.

While it is generally known how many different MiG-21s were ordered by major Arab air forces between 1961 and 1973, it remains unknown precisely how many were delivered. Over the years, the authors have devoted much effort to finding precise figures, but related data has proven evasive – not because of the relatively large numbers of MiG-21s that were delivered, but foremost because of a lack of original documentation. Official military archives in countries like Algeria, Egypt and Syria remain outside our reach, while the archives of the Iraqi Air Force were largely destroyed in 2002 and 2003 – partially on purpose and partially by foreign troops that invaded and occupied that country. Correspondingly, we have attempted to research with the help of former Soviet sources too. Considering the activity in the field of military aviation publishing in the Russian Federation and Ukraine since the early 1990s, and the dozens of publications authored by persons declared 'experts with approach to first-hand sources and official archives', it was quite surprising to find out that not a single publication had been released, in any language, providing a clear breakdown of specific aircraft and helicopters delivered to Arab countries. Rather than examining documents in the original archives to which they are supposed to have access, in particular the Russian researchers that publish in the English language appear to almost exclusively repeat information published in the West, or whatever they can find on the internet. Indeed, some of the publications in question are obviously lacking even the most basic research and operating rather within the realms of science fiction. Precise figures therefore remain evasive, and this is likely to remain the case for some years to come.

In response to requests from our readers, we asked Holger Müller – a former technician with the East German Air Force and meanwhile an acknowledged author on the topic of the MiG-21 – to summarise the most important data about specific variants and their production in the former USSR, and their deliveries to different Arab countries in the period 1955–1973. Because definitive figures about deliveries remain unknown, it is necessary to understand what variants and how many of these were manufactured in what period, in order to enable us to assess how many MiG-21s could have been delivered to specific Arab air forces. The first three tables provide an overview of MiG-21 production runs by GAZ-21, GAZ-30 and GAZ-31 for the period 1959–1973.

Table 6: Production of MiG-21s at GAZ-21, 1959–1973[1]

| Year | F | F–13 | PF | FL | PFS/PFM | R/RF | S | SM | SMT | MF | Totals |
|---|---|---|---|---|---|---|---|---|---|---|---|
| 1959 | 10 | | | | | | | | | | 10 |
| 1960 | 73 | 132 | | | | | | | | | 205 |
| 1961 | | 226 | 25 | 10 | | | | | | | 261 |
| 1962 | | 155 | 135 | 35 | | | | | | | 325 |
| 1963 | | | 310 | 16 | 25 | | | | | | 351 |
| 1964 | | | 47 | 52 | 320 | | | | | | 419 |
| 1965 | | | 8 | 120 | 397 | | | | | | 525 |
| 1966 | | | | | 202 | 63 | 25 | | | | 290 |
| 1967 | | | | | | 165 | 50 | | | | 215 |
| 1968 | | | | | | 79 | 70 | 30 | | | 179 |
| 1969 | | | | | | 71 | | 105 | | | 176 |
| 1970 | | | | | | 30 | | 150 | | | 180 |
| 1971 | | | | | | 40 | | 64 | 116 | | 220 |
| 1972 | | | | | | | | | 135 | | 135 |
| 1973 | | | | | | | | | 30 | | 30 |
| Totals | 83 | 513 | 525 | 233 | 944 | 448 | 145 | 249 | 281 | 0 | 3521 |

A lot less is known about specific numbers of MiG-21s manufactured at the Znamya Truda Factory, except that it launched production of MiG-21s only in 1962, and that by 1974 it had manufactured a total of 3,203 aircraft, most of which were exported. In the case of GAZ-31, only a breakdown per variant and year is available. Combined with a speculative review of the number of manufactured aircraft (which closely matches the known totals of manufactured aircraft), this is as follows:

Table 7: Production of MiG-21s at GAZ-30, 1962–1974

| Year | Variant | Number of aircraft |
|---|---|---|
| 1962–1964 | MiG-21F-13 | 23 batches of 15 aircraft each (345 aircraft in total) |
| 1964–1965 | MiG-21PF | 22 batches of 15 aircraft each (330 aircraft in total) |
| 1965–1968 | MiG-21U | 67 batches of 5 aircraft each (335 aircraft in total) |
| 1965–1968 | MiG-21FL | probably 1 extended batch of 80 aircraft |
| 1966–1968 | MiG-21PFM | 47 batches of 15 'late' FLs and PFS', and PFMs each (705 aircraft in total) |

| 1968–1971 | MiG-21M  | 39 batches of 15 aircraft each (585 aircraft in total) |
| 1970–1971 | MiG-21MT | 60 batches of 15 MTs and MFs each (900 aircraft in total) |
| 1970–1974 | MiG-21MF |  |

**Table 8: Production of MiG-21s at GAZ-31, 1957–1984**

| Year | Variant | Number of aircraft |
|---|---|---|
| 1957 | MiG-21 | 10 |
| 1959 | MiG-21F-13 | 7 |
| 1962–1966 | MiG-21U | 180 |
| 1965–1971 | MiG-21US | 347 |
| 1971–1984 | MiG-21UM | 1133 |

The next table provides an overview of MiG-21 variants known to have been delivered to Arab air forces, and their availability in the period 1961–1973:

**Table 9: Availability of MiG-21 variants confirmed as delivered to Algeria, Egypt, Iraq and Syria, 1961–1973**

| Product designation | Official designation | Description | ASCC codename | Available from | Remarks |
|---|---|---|---|---|---|
| Type 74 | MiG-21F-13 |  | Fishbed-C | July 1960 (GAZ-21) Early 1963 (GAZ-30) |  |
| Type 94 | MiG-21PFS | ex-MiG-21PF brought to MiG-21PFM standard | Fishbed-D | 1963 (GAZ-21) |  |
| Type 94 | MiG-21PFM | early MiG-21PFM | Fishbed-D | 1965 (GAZ-21) | No known deliveries to Egypt and Iraq; possibly to Syria |
| Type 77 | MiG-21FL |  | Fishbed-D | 1961 (GAZ-21) 1965 (GAZ-30) |  |
| Type 94/94A | MiG-21PFM | late MiG-21PFM | Fishbed-F | 1965 (GAZ-21) 1966 (GAZ-30) |  |
| Type 03 Type 94R | MiG-21R | reconnaissance variants | Fishbed-H | 1966 (GAZ-21) |  |
| Type 96A | MiG-21M |  | Fishbed-J | 1968 (GAZ-30) |  |
| Type 96A | MiG-21MF |  | Fishbed-J | 1971 (GAZ-30) |  |
| Type 69 | MiG-21UM | two-seat conversion trainer | Mongol-B | 1971 (GAZ-31) |  |

Correspondingly, the following can be concluded about deliveries of MiG-21MFs to Egypt – and, partially – in correction of data provided in *Volume 4*:
- The first delivery of MiG-21MFs to Egypt in March 1970 (p94), certainly included MiG-21Ms instead of MiG-21MFs, because the MF variant entered series production for export only in spring 1971.
- The MiG-21s flown by Soviet units deployed to Egypt around the same time were MiG-21Ms, not MiG-21SMs as reported (p113).

The next table provides a chronological cross-examination of the data provided in the tables above, with a summary of what is known about specific orders for MiG-21s and their deliveries to Algerian, Egyptian, Iraqi and Syrian air forces:

السعودية    الأردن    سيناء    إسرائيل    مصر

**Table 10: Chronogolical Summary of Known MiG-21-Deliveries to Algeria, Egypt, Iraq and Syria, 1961–1973**

| Date | Air force | Variant | Remarks |
|---|---|---|---|
| mid-1961 | IrAF | MiG-21F-13 | 16 aircraft ordered; all delivered by June 1962 |
| November 1961 | UARAF (Egypt) | MiG-21F-13 | 48 aircraft ordered; partially delivered by 1963 |
| June 1962 | SyAAF | MiG-21F-13 | 34 aircraft; delivered 1963-1964 |
| June 1962 | SyAAF | MiG-21U | 6 aircraft; delivered 1963-1964 |
| 1963 | UARAF | MiG-21FL | 48 aircraft ordered; about 30 delivered 1964-1966; part of order changed to MiG-21PFM |
| early 1965 | QJJ | MiG-21F-13 | 12 aircraft; most re-delivered to Egypt, June 1967 |
| late 1965 | QJJ | MiG-21FL | 12 aircraft; most re-delivered to Egypt, June 1967 |
| late 1965 | UARAF | MiG-21U | order not confirmed; no known deliveries |
| December 1965 | IrAF | MiG-21FL | 20 ordered; at least 19 delivered |
| 1965 | UARAF | MiG-21PFM | 18 aircraft; delivered instead of remaining MiG-21FLs |
| June 1966 | IrAF | MiG-21F-13 & MiG-21PFM | 35 aircraft, including at least 4 ex-V-VS MiG-21F-13s |
| July 1966 | QJJ | MiG-21F-13 | 12 aircraft ex-V-VS |
| late 1966 | IrAF | MiG-21PFM | 36 aircraft; deliveried in late 1967 and through 1968 |
| November 1966 | SyAAF | MiG-21FL | 11 aircraft; delivered 'by the end of the year' |
| June 1967 | UARAF | MiG-21PFS | 65 aircraft ex-V-VS |
| July 1967 | UARAF | MiG-21PFM | 50 aircraft, supposedly equipped with GP-9, but first confirmed deliveries of GP- pods occurred only in March 1968 |
| July 1967 | SyAAF | MiG-21PFM | 20 aircraft; supposedly equipped with GP-9, but first confirmed deliveries of GP-pods occurred only in March 1968 |
| mid-1968 | UARAF | MiG-21PFM | 20 aircraft; equipped with GP-9 |
| late 1967 | SyAAF | MiG-21 | 42 aircraft ordered |
| early 1968 | SyAAF | MiG-21PFM | 20 aircraft ordered |
| late 1968 | UARAF | MiG-21RF | 12 aircraft |
| late 1968 | UARAF | MiG-21F-13 | 30 aircraft from Czechoslovakia |
| July 1969 | UARAF | MiG-21M | 110 ordered, the first 36 delivered in 1970 must have been MiG-21Ms because MiG-21MF entered production only in 1971 |
| February 1970 | V-VS/UARAF | MiG-21MF | 40 V-VS aircraft, variously reported as MiG-21SMs but probably MiG-21MFs |
| spring 1970 | SyAAF | MiG-21M | 16 aircraft |
| mid-1970 | SyAAF | MiG-21R | 6 aircraft |
| July 1970 | UARAF | MiG-21US | 30 ordered; early examples must have been MiG-21US because MiG-21UM entered production only in 1971 |
| 1970 | IrAF | MiG-21M, MiG-21R, MiG-21US | 98 aircraft |
| 1970 | QJJ | MiG-21M, MiG-21R, MiG-21US | 52 aircraft |
| 1972-73 | SyAAF | MiG-21MF | 40-50 delivered between late 1972, through January and April 1973 |
| 1973 | EAF | MiG-21MF | delivery of four batches related to orders from 1969, 1971 and 1972 confirmed, but specific numbers unknown; total number could not have surpassed 48 because of limits related to total number of manufactured examples |
| 1973 | SyAAF | MiG-21F-13 | 11 aircraft from Czechoslovakia, delivered during October 1973 War |
| 1973 | SyAAF | MiG-21F-13 | 12 aircraft from Poland, delivered during October 1973 War |
| 1973 | SyAAF | MiG-21M | 12 aircraft from East Germany, delivered during October 1973 War |

The last table in this section offers an insight into known construction numbers and matching serial numbers of MiG-21s delivered to Algeria, Egypt and Syria from the USSR during the same period. It is organised in chronological order of production and delivery. It shows that most detail is available about the aircraft delivered to Algeria, Egypt and Syria in 1972 and 1973. Indeed, of particular interest is a number of MiG-21MFs obviously delivered to Egypt in October 1973, probably in the course of the Soviet air bridge.

**Table 11: Known and confirmed construction numbers and serial numbers of various Algerian, Egyptian and Syrian MiG-21s**[2]

| Air Force | Version | Construction Number | Serial Number | Delivery Date and Notes |
|---|---|---|---|---|
| QJJ | MiG-21U | 662320 | FC-80 | mid-1966 |
| UARAF | MiG-21U | 664318 | 5068 | August 1966 |
| UARAF | MiG-21US | 03685143 | 5624 | 1969 |
| UARAF | MiG-21RF | 94R01719 | 8501 | late 1969 |
| UARAF | MiG-21RF | 94R01720 | 8502 | late 1969 |
| UARAF | MiG-21RF | 94R01721 | 8503 | late 1969 |
| UARAF | MiG-21RF | 94R01722 | 8504 | late 1969 |
| UARAF | MiG-21RF | 94R01723 | 8505 | late 1969 |
| UARAF | MiG-21RF | 94R01724 | 8506 | late 1969 |
| UARAF | MiG-21RF | 94R01725 | 8507 | late 1969 |
| UARAF | MiG-21M | 96A1013 | | 1969 |
| UARAF | MiG-21US | 04685150 | | 1970 |
| UARAF | MiG-21M | 96A3409 | | late 1970 |
| UARAF | MiG-21M | 96A3613 | | late 1970 |
| QJJ | MiG-21M | 96A3811 | FD-26 | early 1971 |
| UARAF | MiG-21M | 96A3809 | | February 1971 |
| UARAF | MiG-21M | 96A3814 | | February 1971 |
| UARAF | MiG-21US | 03685154 | | 1971 |
| UARAF | MiG-21US | 06685154 | | 1971 |
| UARAF | MiG-21US | 07685154 | | 1971 |
| UARAF | MiG-21MF | 96A4206 | | August 1971 |
| UARAF | MiG-21MF | 96A4612 | | October 1971 |
| QJJ | MiG-21MF | 96A4702 | | Early 1972 |
| QJJ | MiG-21MF | 96A4706 | | Early 1972 |
| QJJ | MiG-21MF | 96A4712 | | Early 1972 |
| EAF | MiG-21MF | 96A4714 | | December 1971 |
| EAF | MiG-21MF | 96A5006 | | February 1972 |
| EAF | MiG-21MF | 96A5008 | 8360 | February 1972 |
| EAF | MiG-21MF | 96A6610 | | February 1973 |
| EAF | MiG-21MF | 96A6707 | | March 1973 |
| EAF | MiG-21MF | 96A6708 | | March 1973 |
| EAF | MiG-21MF | 96A6801 | | April 1973 |
| EAF | MiG-21MF | 96A6815 | | April 1973 |

السعودية   الأردن   سيناء   إسرائيل   مصر

| | | | | |
|---|---|---|---|---|
| EAF | MiG-21MF | 96A6906 | | April 1973 |
| EAF | MiG-21MF | 96A6912 | | April 1973 |
| EAF | MiG-21MF | 96A6913 | | April 1973 |
| EAF | MiG-21MF | 96A7303 | | June 1973 |
| EAF | MiG-21MF | 96A7307 | | June 1973 |
| EAF | MiG-21MF | 96A7312 | | June 1973 |
| EAF | MiG-21MF | 96A7405 | | June 1973 |
| EAF | MiG-21MF | 96A7410 | | June 1973 |
| EAF | MiG-21MF | 96A7413 | | June 1973 |
| EAF | MiG-21MF | 96A7414 | | June 1973 |
| EAF | MiG-21MF | 96A8212 | | October 1973 |
| EAF | MiG-21MF | 96A8213 | | October 1973 |
| SyAAF | MiG-21MF | 96A8214 | 1549 | October 1973 |
| SyAAF | MiG-21F-13 | 74211810 | | October 1973, ex 810, Hungary |
| SyAAF | MiG-21F-13 | 74211812 | | October 1973, ex 812, Hungary |
| SyAAF | MiG-21F-13 | 74211906 | | October 1973, ex 906, Hungary |
| SyAAF | MiG-21F-13 | 74212315 | | October 1973, ex 2315, Hungary |
| SyAAF | MiG-21F-13 | 741212 | | October 1973, ex 212, Hungary |
| SyAAF | MiG-21F-13 | 741214 | | October 1973, ex 214, Hungary |
| SyAAF | MiG-21F-13 | 741215 | | October 1973, ex 215, Hungary |
| SyAAF | MiG-21F-13 | 741222 | | October 1973, ex 222, Hungary |
| SyAAF | MiG-21F-13 | 741302 | | October 1973, ex 302, Hungary |
| SyAAF | MiG-21F-13 | 741314 | | October 1973, ex 314, Hungary |
| SyAAF | MiG-21F-13 | 741320 | | October 1973, ex 320, Hungary |
| SyAAF | MiG-21F-13 | 741324 | | October 1973, ex 324, Hungary |
| SyAAF | MiG-21F-13 | 269901 (Aero Vodochody) | | October 1973, ex 9901, Czechoslovakia |
| SyAAF | MiG-21F-13 | 269902 (Aero Vodochody) | | October 1973, ex 9902, Czechoslovakia |
| SyAAF | MiG-21F-13 | 269903 (Aero Vodochody) | | October 1973, ex 9903, Czechoslovakia |
| SyAAF | MiG-21F-13 | 360002 (Aero Vodochody) | | October 1973, ex 0002, Czechoslovakia |
| SyAAF | MiG-21F-13 | 360004 (Aero Vodochody) | | October 1973, ex 0004, Czechoslovakia |
| SyAAF | MiG-21F-13 | 360101 (Aero Vodochody) | | October 1973, ex 0101, Czechoslovakia |
| SyAAF | MiG-21F-13 | 360102 (Aero Vodochody) | | October 1973, ex 0102, Czechoslovakia |
| SyAAF | MiG-21F-13 | 460106 (Aero Vodochody) | | October 1973, ex 0106, Czechoslovakia |
| SyAAF | MiG-21F-13 | 560213 (Aero Vodochody) | | October 1973, ex 0213, Czechoslovakia |
| SyAAF | MiG-21F-13 | 560214 (Aero Vodochody) | | October 1973, ex 0214, Czechoslovakia |
| SyAAF | MiG-21F-13 | 560302 (Aero Vodochody) | | October 1973, ex 0302, Czechoslovakia |
| SyAAF | MiG-21F-13 | 74212007 | | October 1973, ex 2007, Poland |
| SyAAF | MiG-21F-13 | 74212008 | | October 1973, ex 2008, Poland |
| SyAAF | MiG-21F-13 | 74212009 | | October 1973, ex 2009, Poland |
| SyAAF | MiG-21F-13 | 74212018 | | October 1973, ex 2018, Poland |
| SyAAF | MiG-21F-13 | 74212019 | | October 1973, ex 2019, Poland |
| SyAAF | MiG-21F-13 | 74212223 | | October 1973, ex 2223, Poland |
| SyAAF | MiG-21F-13 | 74212224 | | October 1973, ex 2224, Poland |
| SyAAF | MiG-21F-13 | 740802 | | October 1973, ex 802, Poland |

| | | | |
|---|---|---|---|
| SyAAF | MiG-21F-13 | 740803 | October 1973, ex 803, Poland |
| SyAAF | MiG-21F-13 | 740805 | October 1973, ex 805, Poland |
| SyAAF | MiG-21F-13 | 740811 | October 1973, ex 811, Poland |
| SyAAF | MiG-21F-13 | 740812 | October 1973, ex 812, Poland |
| SyAAF | MiG-21M | 960403 | October 1973, ex 532, East Germany |
| SyAAF | MiG-21M | 960509 | October 1973, ex 582, East Germany |
| SyAAF | MiG-21M | 960710 | October 1973, ex 610, East Germany |
| SyAAF | MiG-21M | 962014 | October 1973, ex 402, East Germany |
| SyAAF | MiG-21M | 962015 | October 1973, ex 403, East Germany |
| SyAAF | MiG-21M | 962101 | October 1973, ex 406, East Germany |
| SyAAF | MiG-21M | 962102 | October 1973, ex 407, East Germany |
| SyAAF | MiG-21M | 962105 | October 1973, ex 412, East Germany |
| SyAAF | MiG-21M | 962107 | October 1973, ex 414, East Germany |
| SyAAF | MiG-21M | 962108 | October 1973, ex 415, East Germany |
| SyAAF | MiG-21M | 962110 | October 1973, ex 418, East Germany |
| SyAAF | MiG-21M | 962307 | October 1973, ex 424, East Germany |
| EAF | MiG-21MF | 96A8305 | November 1973 |
| EAF | MiG-21MF | 96A8310 | November 1973 |
| EAF | MiG-21MF | 96A8315 | November 1973 |
| EAF | MiG-21MF | 96A8406 | November 1973 |
| EAF | MiG-21MF | 96A8503 | December 1973 |
| EAF | MiG-21MF | 96A8513 | December 1973 |

1  Based on *MiG: Between the Past and the Future* (in Russian), a book published to commemorate the 70th anniversary of the Sokol Factory in Nizhny Novgorod (formerly GAZ-21). Notable is the fact that this factory manufactured a total of 5,765 MiG-21s between 1959 and 1985, but that it began manufacturing MiG-21MFs only in 1975 – three years after launching production of the MiG-21bis (none of which were exported before 1977).
2  The majority of Egypt-related retails herein are based on research by Dietrich Banach.

# APPENDIX II

## Deliveries of Aero L-29 Delfins to Iraq, 1968–1974

As mentioned in *Volume 3* (p121), it was in late 1966 that a delegation led by then C-in-C IrAF, Brig Gen Jassam Muhammad ash-Shaher, visited Czechoslovakia to request deliveries of Aero L-29 Delfin jet trainers and associated training. Following protracted negotiations disrupted by the June 1967 Arab-Israeli War, Contract 5279 was signed in Baghdad on 11 November 1967, which included:[1]

- Conversion training of 50 Iraqi pilots for 27 months on L-29s in Czechoslovkia (Course 264/a)
- Combat training of MiG-15 for pilots previously trained on L-29 (Contract 5279/1)
- Training of two technicians on radio equipment of L-29 (Contract 5279/2)
- Combat training of instructor pilots on MiG-15UTI and MiG-15bis (Contract 5279/3)
- Training of two aircraft commanders (both with the rank of captain) on Ilyushin Il-14 transports (Contract 5279/4)

The first L-29s reached Iraq in January and February 1968 and were initially operated by the Aviation School at Habbaniyah, pending construction of a massive new base for the Air Force Academy outside Tikrit. Subsequently, the type served with two squadrons at this air base, while one flight (including three L-29s and one spare) was regularly dispatched to fly missions of border security from airfields near Kirkuk and Mosul, in northern Iraq. Delfins serving in such operations were equipped with ASP-3MN gunsights and armed with two RB-57/4M rocket pods (each for four Soviet-made S-5M unguided rockets of 57mm calibre). The only other type of 'special' equipment installed on Iraqi L-29s was the SEMCA air-conditioning unit. In total, IrAF received 78 L-29 Delfin training aircraft.

Further negotiations in June and July 1969 resulted in additional supplements to Contract 5279, as follows:

- Completing the training on L-29 with maximum of 130 hours per pilot
- Training of 34 Iraqi students on MiG-15 for nine months with maximum of 70 hours per pilot (including 40 hours on MiG-15UTI and 30 hours on MiG-15bis (Contract 5279/6, Course 264/b)
- Training of 14 Iraqi pilots on MiG-21 for five months and 32 hours (Contract 5279/7, Course 264/c)
- Training of two groups of 10 pilots each on Su-7s for seven months and 30 hours per pilot (Contract 5279/8, Course 264/d).

Except for insisting the Czechoslovaks lower their prices as much as possible (resulting in reductions of 12 per cent for flying hours on MiG-21s and 24 per cent for flying hours on Su-7s, for example), and turning down all attempts at bribing them, the Iraqi representatives further expressed their interest in the new Aero L-39 Albatros training jet that was in the final stages of development. The IrAF thus initiated the process that was to lead to it becoming the second export customer of L-39Cs (after the former Soviet Union), and the first operator of L-39ZOs, a story that is to be told sometime in the future.

Table 12: Deliveries of L-29s to Iraq, 1968–1974

| Production batch | Construction bumber | IrAF serial number | Delivery date |
|---|---|---|---|
| 27 | 792701 | 735 | January 1968 |
| 27 | 792702 | 736 | January 1968 |
| 27 | 792703 | 737 | January 1968 |
| 27 | 792704 | 738 | January 1968 |
| 27 | 792705 | 739 | January 1968 |
| 27 | 792706 | 740 | January 1968 |
| 27 | 792707 | 741 | January 1968 |
| 27 | 792708 | 742 | January 1968 |
| 27 | 792709 | 743 | January 1968 |
| 27 | 792710 | 744 | January 1968 |
| 27 | 792711 | 745 | January 1968 |
| 27 | 792712 | 746 | January 1968 |
| 27 | 792713 | 747 | January 1968 |
| 27 | 792714 | 748 | January 1968 |
| 27 | 792715 | 749 | January 1968 |
| 27 | 792716 | 750 | January 1968 |
| 27 | 792717 | 751 | January 1968 |
| 27 | 892726 | 752 | February 1968 |
| 27 | 892727 | 753 | February 1968 |
| 27 | 892728 | 754 | February 1968 |
| 30 | 893003 | 775 | October 1968 |
| 30 | 893004 | 776 | October 1968 |
| 30 | 893005 | 777 | October 1968 |
| 30 | 893006 | 778 | October 1968 |
| 30 | 893007 | 779 | October 1968 |
| 30 | 893008 | 780 | October 1968 |
| 30 | 893009 | 781 | October 1968 |
| 30 | 893010 | 782 | October 1968 |
| 30 | 893028 | 783 | November 1968 |
| 30 | 893029 | 784 | November 1968 |
| 30 | 893030 | 785 | November 1968 |
| 30 | 893031 | 786 | November 1968 |
| 30 | 893032 | 787 | November 1968 |
| 30 | 893033 | 788 | November 1968 |
| 30 | 893034 | 789 | November 1968 |
| 30 | 893035 | 790 | November 1968 |
| 31 | 893101 | 791 | December 1968 |

| الضفة الغربية | قطاع غزة | سوريا | لبنان |
|---|---|---|---|

| | | | |
|---|---|---|---|
| 31 | 893102 | 792 | December 1968 |
| 31 | 893103 | 793 | December 1968 |
| 31 | 893104 | 794 | December 1968 |
| 51 | 395111 | 1123 | December 1973 – April 1974 |
| 51 | 395112 | 1124 | December 1973 – April 1974 |
| 51 | 395113 | 1125 | December 1973 – April 1974 |
| 51 | 395114 | 1126 | December 1973 – April 1974 |
| 51 | 395115 | 1127 | December 1973 – April 1974 |
| 51 | 395116 | 1128 | December 1973 – April 1974 |
| 51 | 395117 | 1129 | December 1973 – April 1974 |
| 51 | 395118 | 1130 | December 1973 – April 1974 |
| 51 | 395119 | 1131 | December 1973 – April 1974 |
| 51 | 395120 | 1132 | December 1973 – April 1974 |
| 51 | 395121 | 1133 | December 1973 – April 1974 |
| 51 | 395122 | 1134 | December 1973 – April 1974 |
| 51 | 395123 | 1135 | December 1973 – April 1974 |
| 51 | 395124 | 1136 | December 1973 – April 1974 |
| 51 | 395125 | 1137 | December 1973 – April 1974 |
| 51 | 395126 | 1138 | December 1973 – April 1974 |
| 51 | 395127 | 1139 | December 1973 – April 1974 |
| 51 | 395128 | 1140 | December 1973 – April 1974 |
| 51 | 395129 | 1141 | December 1973 – April 1974 |
| 51 | 395130 | 1142 | December 1973 – April 1974 |
| 51 | 395131 | 1143 | December 1973 – April 1974 |
| 51 | 395132 | 1144 | December 1973 – April 1974 |
| 51 | 395133 | 1145 | December 1973 – April 1974 |
| 51 | 395134 | 1146 | December 1973 – April 1974 |
| 51 | 395135 | 1147 | December 1973 – April 1974 |
| 51 | 395136 | 1148 | December 1973 – April 1974 |
| 51 | 395137 | 1149 | December 1973 – April 1974 |
| 51 | 395151 | 1150 | December 1973 – April 1974 |
| 51 | 395152 | 1151 | December 1973 – April 1974 |
| 51 | 395153 | 1152 | December 1973 – April 1974 |
| 51 | 395154 | 1153 | December 1973 – April 1974 |
| 51 | 395155 | 1154 | December 1973 – April 1974 |
| 51 | 395156 | 1155 | December 1973 – April 1974 |
| 51 | 395157 | 1156 | December 1973 – April 1974 |
| 51 | 395158 | 1157 | December 1973 – April 1974 |
| 51 | 395158 | 1158 | December 1973 – April 1974 |
| 51 | 395160 | 1159 | December 1973 – April 1974 |
| 51 | 395161 | 1160 | December 1973 – April 1974 |

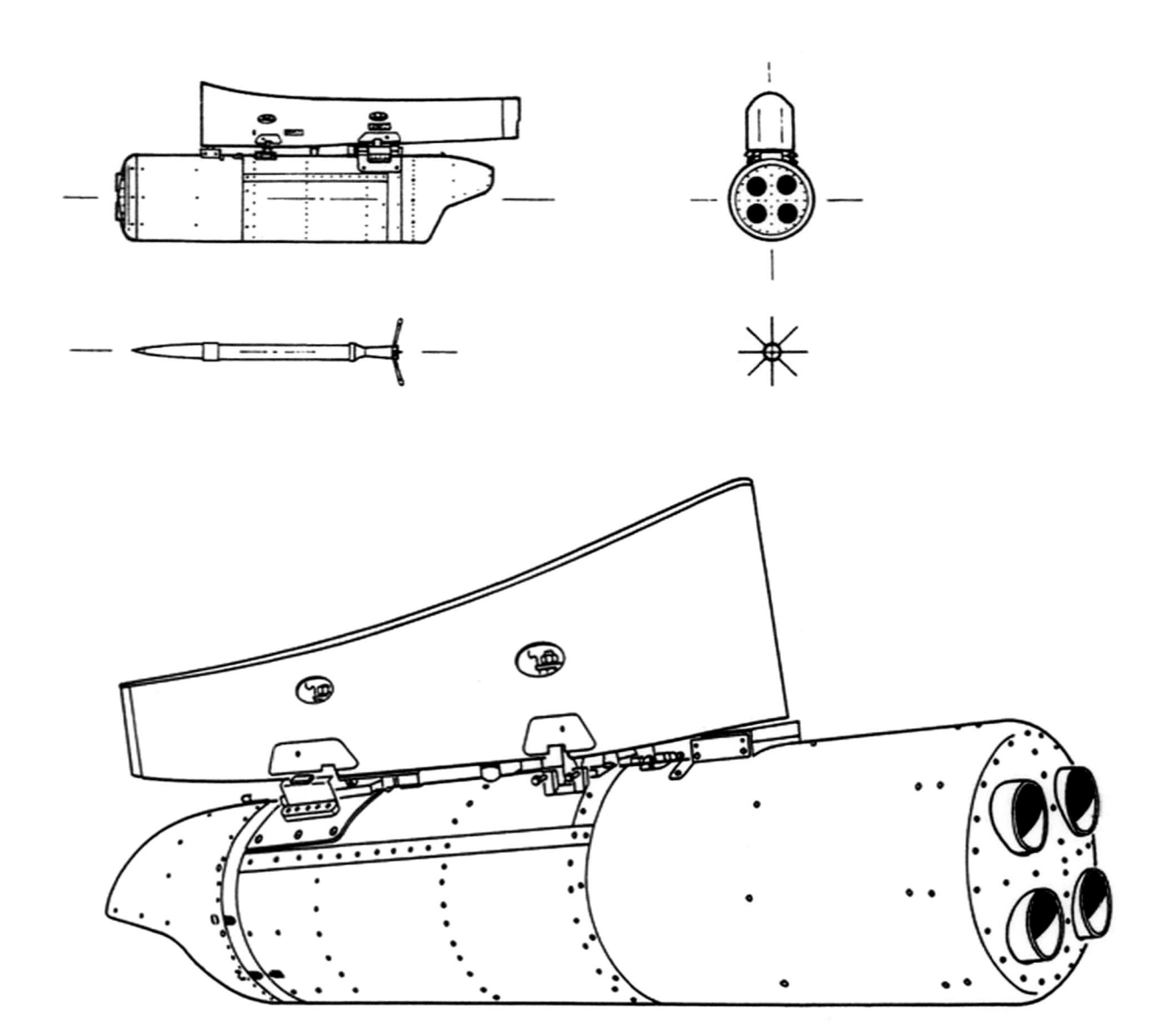

RB-57/4M rocket pod on 'universal pylon' with S-5M rocket, as installed on Iraqi L-29s for combat operations.
(Kucera et al, *Ilustrovaná historie letectví*)

1. Following sources were used for this Appendix: VÚA-VHA, MNO, 1970, SÚP, karton 139, č.j. 0152708/67, 17. 11. 1967, Zpráva ze služební cesty do Iráku ve dnech 22.10.–13.11.1967; VÚA-VHA, MNO, 1970, SÚP, karton 139, č.j. 01622063, December 1969, Výcvik iráckých pilotů; VÚA-VHA, MNO, 1970, SÚP, karton 139, č.j. 020937, date unknown, Zpráva ze služební cesty do Iráku ve dnech 22.6.–4.7.1969 from Military Archive of the Czech Republic, in Prague, and Kucera et all, *Ilustrovaná historie letectví*.

# APPENDIX III

## Logbooks of Egyptian Pilots

Because original military documentation from Arab sources usually remains well outside public reach, we use this opportunity to provide several documents that we did manage to obtain – foremost thanks to help from the historians of Group 73.

Two scans from a page of Fikry el-Gindy's logbook, detailing missions flown in Syria during October 1973. As usual, combat sorties (flown starting with 6 October) are marked in red. (David Nicolle)

### English translation

| Month | Day | Aircraft | Serial | 1st Pilot | 2nd Pilot | Duty |
|---|---|---|---|---|---|---|
| October | 6 | MiG-17F | 2609 | Self | Solo | pre-emptive strike against Israel; target enemy command centre near Prophet Joshua |
| October | 8 | MiG-17F | 2609 | Self | Solo | Interception of hostile aircraft over the airport |
| October | 9 | MiG-17F | 2609 | Self | Solo | striking enemy on the eastern slopes of Abu al-Nida Hill |
| October | 9 | MiG-17F | 2609 | Self | Solo | hit tanks near al-Farse on the Golan |
| October | 10 | MiG-17F | 2609 | Self | Solo | hit tanks west of [unreadable] and north and west of Region 17 |
| October | 10 | MiG-17F | 2609 | Self | Solo | hit tanks west of Region 17 |
| October | 12 | MiG-17F | 2609 | Self | Solo | hit tanks near al-Adssiya and fought 8 Phantom; we are four, Fikry, Baker, Sayf and Aymen; we downed 3 Phantoms, Fikry two and Aymen one |
| October | 12 | MiG-17F | 2609 | Self | Solo | hit tanks west of al-Adssiya and fought Mirage; Baker hit one |
| October | 12 | MiG-17F | 2609 | Self | Solo | hit tanks west of Saasa |
| October | 12 | MiG-17F | 2609 | Self | Solo | hit tanks 15km west of Saasa |
| October | 13 | MiG-17F | 2609 | Self | Solo | hit troops and tanks between Kfar Nassij and Khan Arnabeh |
| October | 13 | MiG-17F | 2609 | Self | Solo | hit troops and tanks near Khar Arnabeh, hit by Phantom and ejected with parachute |

السعودية   الأردن   سيناء   إسرائيل   مصر

| Year 1973 Month/Date | Aircraft Type/No. | Pilot, or 1st. Pilot | 2nd. Pilot, Pupil or Passenger | DUTY (Including Results and Remarks) |
|---|---|---|---|---|
| — | — | — | — | Totals Brought Forward |
| OCT. 2 | MIG 17F 2941 | SELF | SoLo | مراقبة |
| 2 | ~ ~ 2941 | ~ | ~ | |
| 6 | ~ ~ 2941 | ~ | ~ | ضرب مواقع صواريخ هوك أبو صمارة شمال س |
| 7 | ~ ~ 2941 | ~ | ~ | أوامر عليا (ضرب تحركات العدو شمال سيناء) |
| 8 | ~ ~ 2941 | ~ | ~ | ،، (ضرب مواقع صواريخ هوك أبو عمارة) |
| 10 | ~ ~ 2084 | ~ | ~ | ،، ضرب تحركات العدو بالطريق الشمالي |
| 12 | ~ ~ 2708 | ~ | ~ | ،، (ضرب قوات مدرعة على الطريق الأوسط) |
| 14 | ~ ~ 2941 | ~ | ~ | ،، (ضرب تحركات العدو شرق بلاح) |
| 16 | ~ ~ 2245 | ~ | ~ | ،، (ضرب مدرعات العدو شرق الدفرزوار) |
| 17 | ~ ~ 2632 | ~ | ~ | حلوان – الصالحية |
| 21 | ~ ~ 2968 | ~ | ~ | أوامر عليا (ضرب مواقع العدو في الدفرزوار) |
| 22 | ~ ~ 2597 | ~ | ~ | ،، (ضرب مواقع العدو جنوب أبو صوير) |
| 24 | ~ ~ 2941 | ~ | ~ | إختبار جوي |

Scan from a page of Hussein el-Kfass' logbook, detailing missions he flew during the month of October 1973. (Hussein el-Kfass)

**English translation**

| Month | Day | Aircraft | Serial | 1st Pilot | 2nd Pilot | Duty |
|---|---|---|---|---|---|---|
| October | 2 | MiG-17F | 2941 | Self | Solo | Interception |
| October | 2 | MiG-17F | 2941 | Self | Solo | Interception |
| October | 6 | MiG-17F | 2941 | Self | Solo | striking HAWK site in Abu Samara, North The Sinai |
| October | 7 | MiG-17F | 2941 | Self | Solo | OO (Operations Order): attacking enemy movement in Northern The Sinai |
| October | 8 | MiG-17F | 2941 | Self | Solo | OO: striking HAWK site in Abu Samara |
| October | 10 | MiG-17F | 2084 | Self | Solo | OO: attacking enemy movments on the Northern Road |
| October | 12 | MiG-17F | 2708 | Self | Solo | OO: attacking enemy armour on the Central Road |
| October | 14 | MiG-17F | 2941 | Self | Solo | OO: attacking enemy movement east of Ballah |
| October | 16 | MiG-17F | 2245 | Self | Solo | OO: attacking enemy armoured vehicles east of Deversoir |
| October | 17 | MiG-17F | 2632 | Self | Solo | aircraft transfer Helwan to Salihiyah |
| October | 21 | MiG-17F | 2968 | Self | Solo | OO: attacking enemy positions in Deversoir |
| October | 22 | MiG-17F | 2597 | Self | Solo | OO: attacking enemy positions south of Abu Suweir |
| October | 24 | MiG-17F | 2941 | Self | Solo | test flight |

الضفة الغربية     قطاع غزة     سوريا     لبنان

Three pages from Mamdouh Monib's logbook, detailing missions he flew during the October 1973 War. (Mamdouh Monib)

**Transcription**

| Month | Day | Aircraft | Serial | 1st Pilot | 2nd Pilot | Duty |
|---|---|---|---|---|---|---|
| October | 6 | MiG-21 | 5909 | Self | Solo | Operation |
| October | 7 | MiG-21 | 5911 | Self | Solo | Combat |
| October | 9 | MiG-21 | 5826 | Self | Solo | Operation |
| October | 9 | MiG-21 | 5826 | Self | Solo | Operation |
| October | 9 | MiG-21 | 5826 | Self | Solo | Operation |
| October | 10 | MiG-21 | 5918 | Self | Solo | Operation |
| October | 10 | MiG-21 | 5909 | Self | Solo | Operation |
| October | 10 | MiG-21 | 5919 | Self | Solo | Operation |
| October | 11 | MiG-21 | 5826 | Self | Solo | Operation |
| October | 12 | MiG-21 | 5826 | Self | Solo | Operation |
| October | 12 | MiG-21 | 5813 | Self | Solo | Operation |
| October | 13 | MiG-21 | 5813 | Self | Solo | Operation |
| October | 14 | MiG-21 | 5913 | Self | Solo | Combat Skyhawk |
| October | 14 | MiG-21 | 5358 | Self | Solo | Combat Skyhawk |
| October | 14 | MiG-21 | 5540 | Self | Solo | Combat Skyhawk |
| October | 15 | MiG-21 | 5540 | Self | Solo | Combat Skyhawk |

# APPENDIX IV: EAF SQUADRON COMMANDERS, OCTOBER 1973

The following gallery depicts the last-known squadron commanders of the EAF in command of specific units towards the end of October 1973 War.

MiG-21 OTU
unknown

Su-7 OTU
unknown

No. 6 Independent Attack and Fighter-Bomber Squadron
Lt Col Nabil Ibrahim Ayyub

11th Fighter Training Unit
Col Ahmed Saleh

No. 16 Independent Attack and Fighter-Bomber Squadron
Lt Col Ahmad Maher Shehata

No. 55 Independent Fighter-Bomber Squadron
Lt Col Farouq Elish

No. 69 Independent Mirage Squadron
Lt Col Ali Zayn al-Abidin Abd al-Jawad

No. 77 Independent Tactical Bomber Squadron
Lt Col Mohammad Gaber Hashish

209th Fighter-Bomber Training Unit
Lt Col Abd al-Rahim Rushdi

السعودية   الأردن   سيناء   إسرائيل   مصر

**102nd Fighter Brigade**
CO Col Nabil Shuwakry

**No. 25 Squadron**
CO Lt Col Ala'a Shakir

**No. 26 Squadron**
CO Lt Col Ahmad Abd al-Aziz Ahmad Nur

**No. 27 Squadron**
CO Lt Col Mohammd Kamal al-Sawy

**104th Fighter Brigade**
CO Col Jamal Abd ar-Rahman Nassr

**No. 42 Squadron**
Lt Col Essam Muhammad Muqaddam Sadiq

**No. 44 Squdron**
Lt Col Amir Ahmad Riyadh

**No. 46 Squadron**
Lt Col Magdy Kamal Mahmoud Sadiq

**111th Fighter Brigade**
CO Col Ahmad Adil Nassr

**No. 45 Squadron**
Lt Col Ahmad Muhammad Shafiq

**No. 47 Squadron**
Lt Col Hisham Sayd Abduh

**No. 49 Squadron**
Lt Col Tamim Fahmy Abd Allah

**No. 72 Squadron**
Lt Col Sayd Darwish

**123rd Reconnaissance Brigade**
Col Sayd Kamal Abd al-Wahhab

**Deputy CO**
Lt Col Nabil Hassan Kamil

**No. 22 Squadron**
Samir Atiah

**No. 3 Squadron**
Lt Col Yusuf Hassan Basri

**No. 59 Squadron**
Maj Adil Muhammad Abd al-Fadil

**203rd Fighter-Bomber Brigade**
Col Tahsin Fuad Saima

**No. 56 Squadron**
Lt Col Mustafa Ahmed al-Hafez

**No. 82 Squadron**
Lt Col Munir Fahmy Barum Jirjis

الضفة الغربية   قطاع غزة   سوريا   لبنان

**205th Fighter-Bomber Brigade**
Col Farouq Elish

**No. 51 Squadron**
Lt Col Jamal Muhammad Maha ad-Din Kamil

**No. 52 Squadron**
Lt Col Adil Abd al-Rahman Mustafa

**No. 53 Squadron**
Maj Taher Mohammad Taher

**306th Fighter-Bomber Brigade**
Col Fahmy Abbas Fahmy

**No. 61 Squadron**
Maj Ahmad Shababi Ahmad Shababi

**No. 62 Squadron**
Lt Col Sharif Muhammad Arabi as-Sayd

**No. 89 Squadron**
Lt Col Naji Muhammad Lashin

**403rd Bomber Brigade**
Col Osman al-Gindy

**No. 34 Squadron**
Col Ali Atiyah Ali Salamah

**No. 35 Squadron**
Lt Col Ahmad Samir Ahmad

**No. 36 Squadron**
Lt Col Mohammad Raouf Helmy

**515th Transport Brigade**
Col Ali Abd al-Khaliq Mutawy

**No. 3 Squadron**
Lt Col Mohammad Abd ar-Rahman Fahmy

**No. 14 Squadron**
Lt Col Hamzah Kamil Abd al-Wahhab

**No. 95 Squadron**
Lt Col Ali Hassan Shehata Hassan

**533rd Transport Brigade**
Col Wafiq Abd al-Hamid Ahmad

**No 2 Squadron**
Lt Col Mohammad Majdi Abd al-Aziz

**No. 15 Squadron**
Lt Col Hassan Ismail Hassan

السعودية   الأردن   سيناء   إسرائيل   مصر

| | | | |
|---|---|---|---|
| **545th Helicopter Brigade** <br> Col Mohammad Jalal Muhammad al-Naji | No. 11 Squadron <br> Lt Col Sayd Ahmad Zahran | No. 19 Squadron <br> Maj Gamal Sayd | No. 21 Squadron <br> Lt Col Adil Hassan Sayd Ahmad |
| **546th Helicopter Brigade** <br> Col Munir Salih Mustafa Thabet | No. 7 Squadron <br> Maj Muhammd Ali Hassan Masood | No. 8 Squadron <br> Lt Col Mohammad Fouad Husayn Ali | No. 12 Squadron <br> Maj Ahmad Riyadh Ibrahim Shabarah |
| **547th Helicopter Brigade** <br> Col Talat Tawfiq Musa | No. 9 Squadron <br> Maj Ahmad Ismail Amer Desuky | No. 13 Squadron <br> Lt Col Abdul-Hassan Abd al-Ahanin | No. 91 Squadron <br> Maj Azmi Ezz el-Din Talibah |

# APPENDIX V

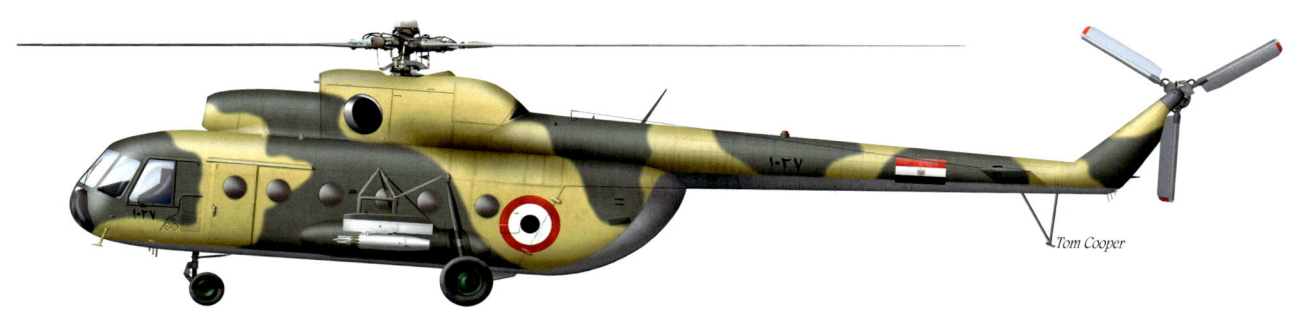

Few of early Egyptian Mi-8s went into the October 1973 War still painted in olive green and light blue colours as before delivery, but with a disruptive camouflage pattern of yellow sand applied over. Notable is very large roundel on the rear of the cabin and a fin flash on the boom – still in its original position.

Mi-8 serial number 1029 was one of few known to have been flown into the October 1973 War still wearing original colours applied before delivery – and old national markings (worn by the UARAF from 1958 until 1972). Notable is the UB-16-57 rocket pod, of which four were usually carried: Egyptian Mi-8s made extensive use of these during nocturnal attacks on Israeli positions along the coast of the Red Sea.

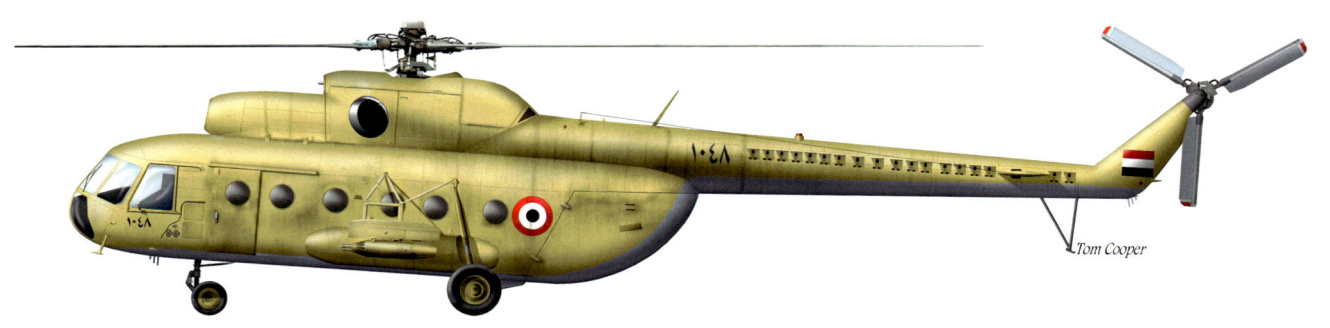

Most of EAF Mi-8s deployed during the October 1973 painted in yellow sand overall, with undersurfaces in light blue. Even wheel rims and UB-16-57 rocket pods were painted in yellow sand. Notable is that quite a few went into the war wearing only the pan-Arabic tricolore, without the 'Eagle of Salahaddin' emblem on the white field.

السعودية   الأردن   سيناء   إسرائيل   مصر

Wearing the 'negative' (also known as 'early') version of the Nile Valley camouflage pattern in beige BS381C/388, grey-green BS381C/283 and black-green BS381C/298 on top surfaces and sides, and light admiralty grey BS381C/697 on bottom surfaces, and shown armed with FAB-100 bombs and Sakr unguided rockets, the MiG-17F serial number 2084, which served with No. 62 Squadron, was one of oldest in the fleet as of October 1973.

Painted in similar fashion, the MiG-17F serial number 2609 is known to have served with No. 89 Squadron EAF. It is illustrated as when armed with FAB-100M bombs and Sakr unguided rockets. Inset is showing a reconstruction of camouflage on top surfaces: this differed from plane to plane.

MiG-17F serial number 2676 – flown by el-Shennawy in at least two combat sorties during the War of Attrition – is shown in camouflage pattern similar to that worn by one of two MiG-17Fs confirmed as lost during attack on Ras Nasrani/Ophir AB, on 6 October 1973. Except for use of green-grey and black-green, notable are undersurfaces painted in light blue, instead of usual light admiralty grey BS381C/697. The aircraft is shown armed with FAB-250M-46 bomb with locally manufactured retarding fins, in addition to usual Sakr rockets.

الضفة الغربية     قطاع غزة     سوريا     لبنان

This reconstruction of the MiG-17F serial number 2700 is based on one of photographs on page 65. The aircraft was camouflaged in Nile Valley pattern consisting of yellow sand, olive green and black-green on top surfaces, and light admiralty grey on bottom surfaces. Notable is a relatively large serial (always applied in matt black), which was sometimes repeated in much smaller digits on the rudder, underwing pylons and other parts of the aircraft.

Another of MiG-17Fs that can be seen on photographs from page 65 was serialled 2782. Painted in same colours like 2700, it is shown armed with a FAB-100M-46 bomb and Sakr rockets. Notable are stark differences in application of camouflage colours on drop tanks too: while some were left unpainted, others received most different camouflage patterns, usually in yellow sand and olive green.

The final example for one of EAF MiG-17Fs that can be seen on photographs on page 65 is serial number 2784, here shown armed with FAB-250M-46 bomb. Notable is less 'regular' application of olive green colour, applied in thinner stripes of varying width in comparison to two examples depicted above.

225

السعودية    الأردن    سيناء    إسرائيل    مصر

Although camouflaged in same colours like three examples illustrated on previous page, the MiG-17F serial number 2531 was one of aircraft that received particularly large roundels on the rear fuselage, applied directly in front of air brakes. Notable is that the drop tank of this plane was painted in beige – instead of yellow sand – olive green and black green.

Painted in this very unusual, 'broken' variant of the Nile Valley pattern in yellow sand, grey-green and black-green, the MiG-17F 2941 was favourite mount of Hussein el-Kfass, who flew five combat sorties with it during October 1973 War. 2941 survived that conflict and served until the entire fleet was withdrawn from service, in 1982.

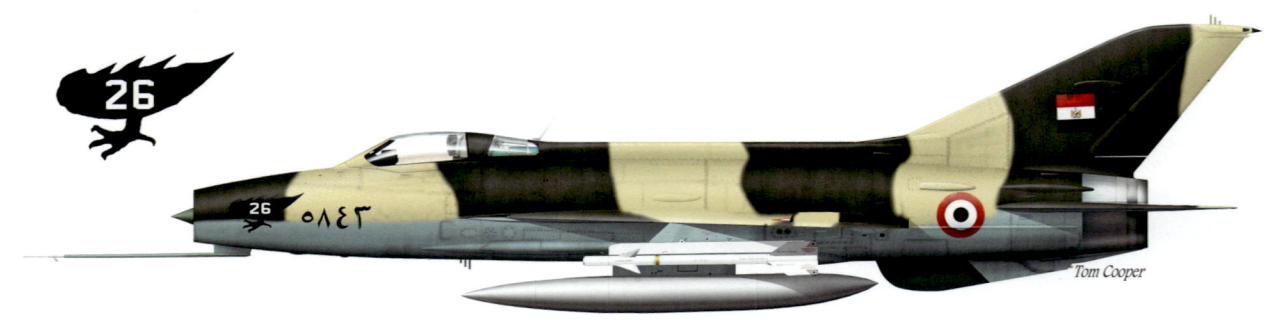

Reda el-Iraqis favourite mount, the MiG-21F-13 serial number 5843 was something like a 'flag-ship' of the No. 26 Squadron, and the only one known to have received the famous 'Black Raven' unit insignia applied on the forward fuselage. Most of MiG-21F-13s from that unit and sister-squadron No. 25 – whether manufactured in Czechoslovakia or Soviet Union, and regardless if delivered to Egypt before or after the June 1967 War – went into October 1973 War painted as shown here: in beige, olive drab BS381C/283, and light admiralty grey.

الضفة الغربية    قطاع غزة    سوريا    لبنان

Most of survivors from a batch of 60 MiG-21PFS delivered to Egypt in June 1967 were flown by No. 44 Squadron during October 1973 War. With few exceptions, all were painted in this camouflage pattern, consisting of yellow sand and dark green BS381C/641 on upper surfaces and sides, and light admiralty grey BS381C/697 on bottom surfaces. Some aircraft, including serial number 8025 shown here, wore the unit insignia on either side of the front fuselage too.

A reconstruction of the MiG-21PFS serial number 8045 flown by el-Mansoury during the clash with Israeli F-4 Phantoms over the Gulf of Suez, on 13 February 1973. As so often, the replacement cockpit frame – necessary quite often – was left unpainted. Inset is showing a reconstruction of the camouflage pattern on top surfaces.

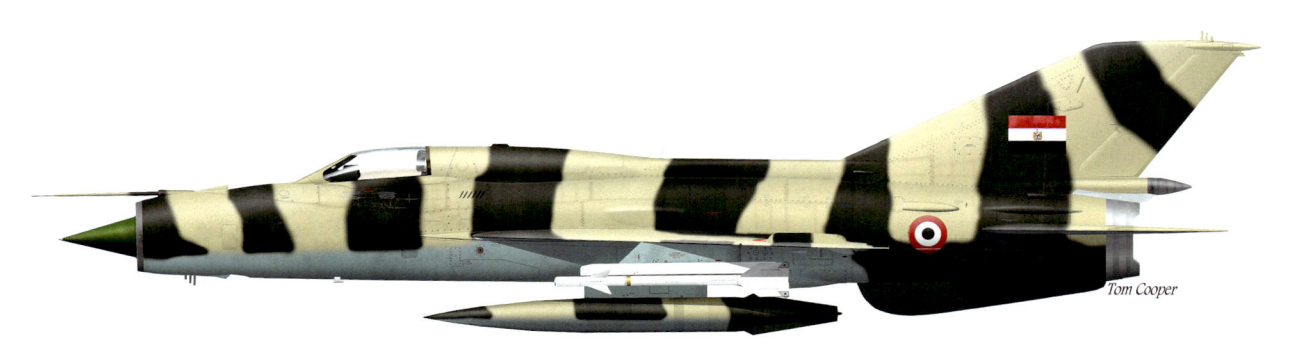

One of factories at Helwan has introduced this camouflage pattern – consisting of beige BS381C/388 and olive drab BS381C/437 on top surfaces (with the latter colour being applied diagonally across top surfaces), and light admiralty grey BS381C/697 on bottom surfaces – on all of MiG-21FLs, MiG-21PFMs and MiG-21M/MFs it has overhauled, during the 1970s and 1980s. Reason for this aircraft – serial number 6104 – having its rear lower fuselage, ventral fin, and the rear of its drop tank painted in olive drab too, remain unknown. It survived the October 1973 War.

السـعودية    الأردن    سيناء    إسرائيل    مصر

This MiG-21FL was one of quite a few survivors of deliveries from before the June 1967 War that continued serving with No. 3? Squadron of the 123rd Reconnaissance Brigade during the October War. Following an overhaul in the early 1970s, it received a 'negative' variant of Nile Valley pattern, consisting of yellow sand, olive green, black green and light admiralty grey, and is shown equipped with one of indigenous reconnaissance pods for Vinten F40 cameras.

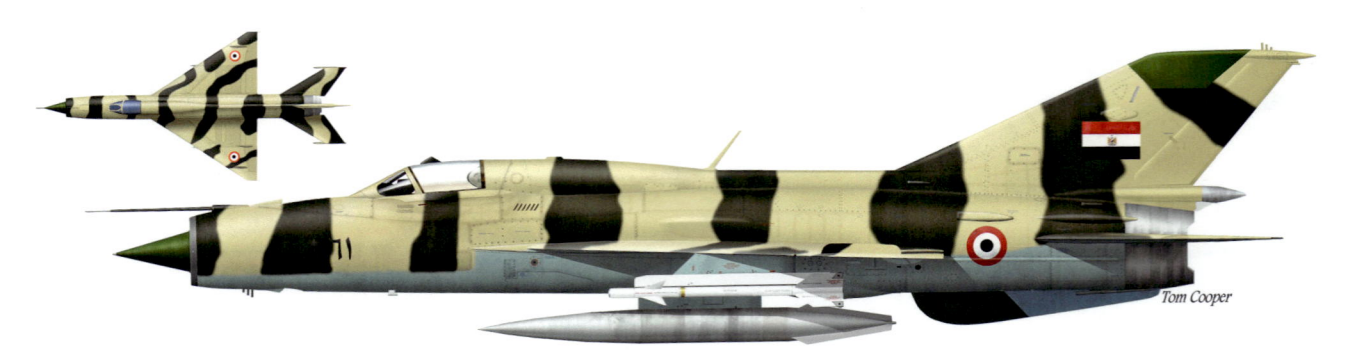

Some of locally overhauled MiG-21PFMs – including serial number 8061 shown here – have received the same camouflage pattern like various MiG-21FLs and MiG-21M/MFs, applied at one of factories in Helwan. This example was flown by No. 47 Squadron – as indicated by its ventral fin painted in light blue. Inset is showing a reconstruction of this camouflage pattern as applied on top surfaces.

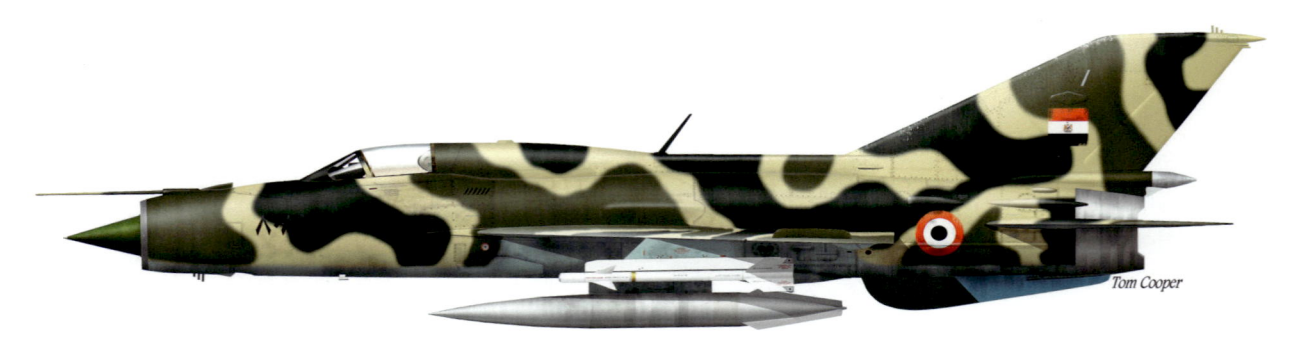

Another MiG-21PFM flown by No. 47 Squadron during the October 1973 War was this example, serial number 8081, painted in 'negative' version of the Nile Valley camouflage pattern, consisting of beige, green and black-green. It survived the October 1973 War.

الضفة الغربية    قطاع غزة    سوريا    لبنان

Many of MiG-21M/MFs delivered to Egypt in 1970 and 1971 underwent overhauls before October 1973, after which they were painted in Nile Valley camouflage pattern. Some received unit insignia too: the MiG-21M serial number 8224 wore the insignia of one of two units from the newly-established 203rd Fighter-Bomber Brigade (either No. 56 or No. 82 Squadron), applied on either side of the front fuselage.

Decorated with the same unit insignia was the MiG-21M serial number 8251 too, but that aircraft received the standardized camouflage pattern applied by one of factories at Helwan. Load consisting of two drop tanks installed on outboard underwing pylons and two R-3S missiles on inboard pylons, was typical for aircraft that stood the QRA during the October 1973 War.

While left in original 'sand and spinach' camouflage pattern applied pre-delivery (consisting of beige, olive green and light admiralty grey), MiG-21MF serial number 8437 was one of few wearing insignia of another unit from the 203rd Fighter-Bomber Brigade (either No. 56 or No. 82 Squadron). It is shown in the heaviest configuration for this variant, with three drop tanks and two R-3S missiles, used for flying CAPs. For most of October 1973 War, EAF MiG-21s were busy maintaining permanent presence on some 20 CAP-stations around the country. Inset is showing the unit insignia in black and red variants, because the exact colour in which this was applied remains unknown.

السعودية    الأردن    سيناء    إسرائيل    مصر

MiG-21MFs delivered to Egypt in early 1973 appear to have replaced older MiG-21Ms of No. 27 Squadron (the first to convert to these two variants, already back in 1970-1971). Denoting its secondary duty as 'fighter-bomber' outfit, aircraft of this unit wore a small unit insignia in form of a bomb applied in black on either side of the cockpit. 8652 is shown as configured during attack on Ras Nasrani/Ophir AB on 6 October 1973, armed with four dibber anti-runway bombs.

Shown in its original camouflage pattern applied immediately after delivery in 1970, but with national markings in use since 1972, the MiG-21RF 8506 is illustrated in typical configuration for reconnaissance operations over the Israeli-occupied parts of the Sinai. This consisted of three 490-litre drop tanks and two R-3S missiles on underwing pylons. Vinten F40 cameras were installed in the shallow 'canoe' under the cockpit and – one, looking forward – in the radome (instead of the radar).

This Su-7BMK – serial number 7242 from No. 53 Squadron – is illustrated as configured during attack on Israeli depots in Bir Thamada area, on 6 October 1973, armed with four FAB-500M-54 bombs calibre 500kg. Of interest is the use of yellow sand instead of beige colour for its Nile Valley camouflage pattern, otherwise consisting of green-grey and black-green. Heavy wear of the camouflage pattern was usually caused by their powerful Nudelman-Rikhter NR-30 cannons calibre 30mm, and very 'hot' Lyulka AL-7 engines.

الضفة الغربية    قطاع غزة    سوريا    لبنان

Most of Su-7BMKs from the last batch delivered to Egypt (sometimes in early 1973) were left in 'sand and spinach' camouflage pattern as applied prior to delivery. The aircraft illustrated here, serial number 7253, was flown by Brig Gen el-Shennawy during the opening strike on Bir Thamada, on 6 October 1973. It is illustrated as armed with four UB-16-57 rocket pods. Inset is showing reconstruction of the camouflage pattern on top sides, which was different on either side of the aircraft.

A reconstruction of a Su-7BMK serial number 7275 (operated by No. 51 Squadron) as seen on a post-war semi-documentary. The aircraft is shown as configured with four dibber anti-runway bombs, as during the opening strike on Bir Gifgafa/Refidim AB. Mustafa Hafez, veteran of the June 1967 War when he flew MiG-17PFs, led 16 similarly-configured Su-7BMKs from No. 53 Squadron into attack on Bir Thamada, on 6 October 1973.

Quite a few of Su-7BMKs from No. 52 Squadron were camouflaged like the example shown here (serial number 7655), in yellow sand and green-blue on top surfaces, and light admiralty grey on bottom surfaces. The serial number (7655 in this case) was very large and applied in rather 'untypical' fashion.

السعودية   الأردن   سيناء   إسرائيل   مصر

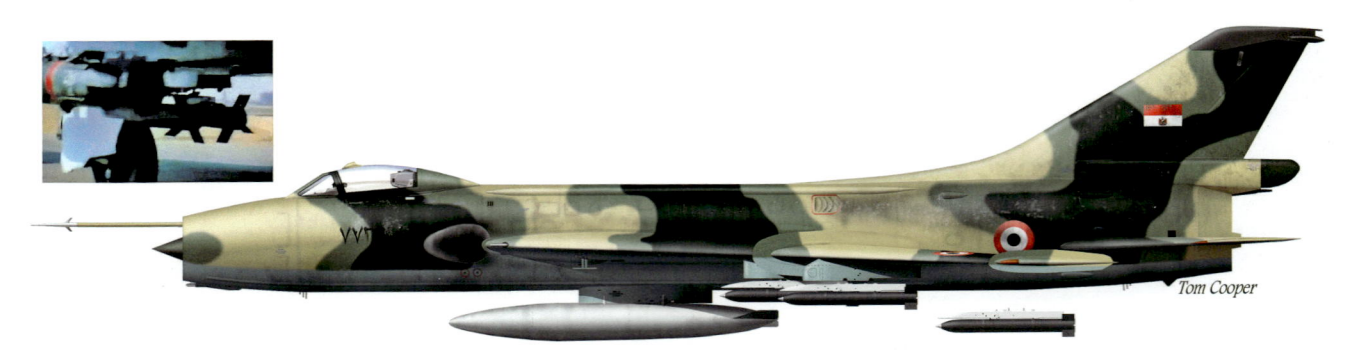

Gauging by its serial number – 7728 – this was one of last Su-7BMKs delivered to Egypt. Following a local overhaul (probably prompted by combat damage it suffered during October 1973 War), it received the Nile Valley camouflage pattern in beige, green-grey BS381C/283 and black-green on upper surfaces, and light admiralty grey on lower surfaces. The aircraft is shown armed with S-24 heavy unguided missiles: delivered only shortly before the war, these were adapted for deployment from Su-7BMKs by Egyptian technicians.

Favourite Su-17 of Ahmed Abbas during the October 1973 was painted in 'negative' version of the Nile Valley camouflage pattern (in beige, green-grey and black-green), though with undersurfaces in medium grey. Serial number 7756 did exist but remains unconfimed in relation to this camouflage pattern. Insets are showing weapons delivered with them, including (from left to right): R-3S air-to-air missiles, UB-32-57 rocket pods (on inboard underwing pylon), FAB-100-150 and FAB-250M-54 bombs, latest FAB-500M-62 bomb, RBK-250 and RBK-250PTAB-2.5M CBUs.

Remaining completely unknown in the public and usually designated 'Su-20' even by their Egyptian pilots and ground crews, the Su-17s from pre-production series operated by No. 34 Squadron were exported to Egypt only. Notable on this reconstruction of serial number 7759 are details distinguishing them from genuine Su-20s, such as the lack of inboard wing fences, cable ducts along centre fuselage, and RWR-housing at the top of the fin. Insets are showing two styles in which their 910-litre drop tanks (developed locally from smaller tanks provide by the Soviets) were painted: either left in 'bare metal overall' (left) or painted in beige and light admiralty grey (right).

الضـفة الغربية     قطاع غزة     سوريا     لبـنان

Every of Tu-16K-11-16s of No. 36 Squadron was painted in different version of the Nile Valley camouflage pattern, usually including yellow sand, green-grey and black-green at top surfaces, and light admiralty grey (shown here) or medium grey on bottom surfaces. Complete serial number (4408 in this case) were applied on the rear fuselage, with 'last two' behind the cockpit. KS-1 missiles were usually painted light blue, while KSR-2s were in white, with their own serial numbers applied in black, in very different fashion.

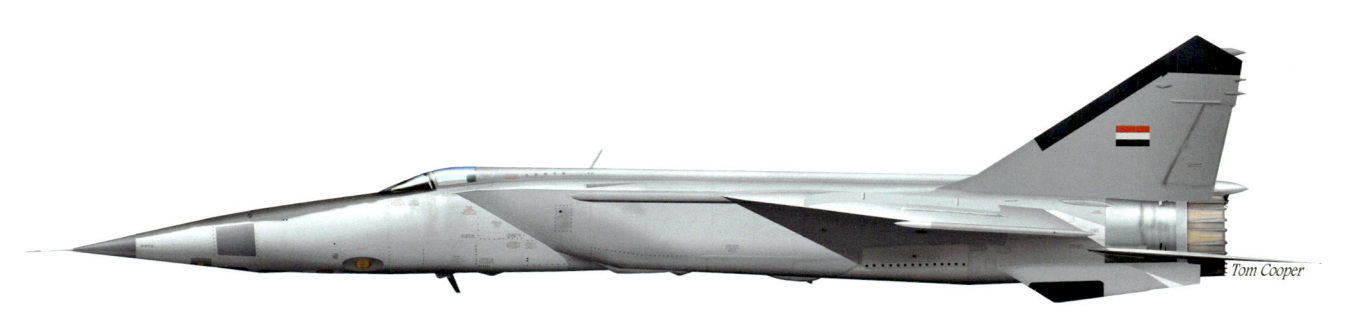

One of four MiG-25R/RBs of the 63rd Independent Reconnaissance Aviation Squadron, based at Cairo West from March 1971 until July 1972. All were painted light grey F.S.26073 overall, with all dielectric surfaces in dark gull grey F.S.26231 and the anti-glare panel in flat black F. S. 27030, although the lower surfaces and sides of the engine nacelles were left in 'neutral steel'. Egyptian national insignia was applied too, usually in six positions, though often incomplete. Roundels on the forward fuselage were always burned away during supersonic flight and had to be repeatedly over-painted.

Most of Iraqi aircraft arrived in Syria without camouflage colours and had to be painted first, before going to battle. The colours used were those meanwhile standardized by the SyAAF, namely orange and green-blue on top surfaces, and light admiralty grey or light blue on bottom surfaces. This is a reconstruction of the MiG-17F 453, known to have been flown by No. 7 Squadron in Syria during October 1973 War. The aircraft is shown armed with UB-16-57 pods for unguided rockets on detachable pylon. Insets are showing the crest of No. 7 Squadron IrAF and a reconstruction of camouflage pattern on top surfaces.

233

السعودية    الأردن    سيناء    إسرائيل    مصر

Hunters from No. 6 and No. 29 Squadrons IrAF (this is a reconstruction of the F.Mk 59B serial number 621) were operated as the No. 66 Squadron EAF during October 1973 War. They have retained their standard camouflage patterns throughout that conflict and their entire career, although some of aircraft deployed to Egypt in 1973 still had their noses and fins painted in bright red. This was a measure introduced in 1964 and described in detail in Volume 3. Inset is showing the crest of No. 6 Squadron.

Shown in the standard configuration for combat operations over the Sinai – which consisted of four banks of three 3in unguided rockets each, full load of 30mm ammunition of four ADEN cannons, and drop tanks – Hunter F.Mk 59B serial number 632 is illustrated together with the crest of No. 29 Squadron. Notable is application of the serial number on the cover of the front wheel bay.

Most of No. 9 Squadron's MiG-21PFMs arrived in Syria uncamouflaged and were hurriedly painted with standard SyAAF colours during the night from 7 to 8 October 1973. This example, serial number 857, was last seen in the 1980s, still wearing the camouflage pattern applied in Syria during the October 1973 War. Inset is showing the crest of No. 9 Squadron IrAF.

الضفة الغربية   قطاع غزة   سوريا   لبنان

A reconstruction of the IrAF Su-7BMK serial number 757, as seen on a photograph taken at al-Hurrya AB, in Mosul, 'in early 1970s'. The aircraft was painted in beige and olive green on top surfaces, and light admiralty grey on bottom surfaces. Inset is showing the crest of No. 1 Squadron IrAF, dominated by a symbolized mountain of northern Iraq.

The Su-7BMK serial number 769 was one of aircraft deployed by No. 5 Squadron to Syria, on 8 October 1973. Characteristical for Iraqi aircraft of this version as of 1973 was the lack of rear-view mirror on the top of canopy hood and only one underwing hardpoint. The aircraft is shown armed with four FAB-500M-54 bombs. Inset is showing the crest of No. 5 Squadron IrAF.

Obviously in order to bolster attack capabilities of the SyAAF, the IrAF deployed its third squadron equipped with Su-7BMKs – No. 8 Squadron, which was actually that air force's OCU for this type – to Syria too. This is a reconstruction of the aircraft with serial number 897, as seen on a bad-quality photograph taken at Kirkuk 'in the early 1970s'. Inset is showing the crest of No. 8 Squadron IrAF.

السعودية    الأردن    سيناء    إسرائيل    مصر

Similarly to the EAF, the SyAAF has camouflaged most of its Mi-8s by applying orange sand colour over the original olive green in which they were delivered. Contrary to Egyptian practice, as for 1973 Syrian helicopters of this type wore three-digit serials applied on the boom in white, with 'last two' repeated below the engine exhaust. This is a reconstruction of the serial number 285, which is known to have participated in the opening attack on Mount Jebel Sheikh – while still wearing national insignia as in use before 1972.

By October 1973, most of SyAAF MiG-17F were overhauled at 'The Factory' at Nayrab AB/Aleppo IAP, and painted in orange sand and green-blue colours introduced as 'standard' sometimes in 1971 or 1972. Bottom surfaces were painted either light admiralty grey or light blue. Many aircraft received unusually large serial numbers (1029 in this case) on the front fuselage, always repeated on the top of the fin. Inset is showing a reconstruction of the camouflage pattern on top surfaces: while this was standardized, its application on the fuselage varied greatly from aircraft to aircraft.

A reconstruction of the original look of the MiG-17F serial number 1196, put on display at the former Military Museum of Damascus in early 1974. The aircraft reportedly belonged to the batch delivered from East Germany after the June 1967 War and still wore a version of the standard camouflage pattern applied during the second half of 1967, consisting of orange sand and olive drab on the upper surfaces, and light admiralty grey or light blue on bottom surfaces. National markings were still as of pre-1972 period though there is uncertainty regarding whether the fin flash had only two or three green stars, as shown here. Meaning of the number '9' (or '29') applied on both sides of lower fuselage under the wing, remains unknown.

لبنان   الضفة الغربية   قطاع غزة   سوريا

SyAAF MiG-21F-13s that survived the June 1967 War and the War of Attrition were overhauled and painted in 'sand and spinach' camouflage pattern, similar to that applied on newly-delivered MiG-21MFs. This is a reconstruction of the serial number 1302, as seen on a post-October 1973 War semi-documentary. Notable is absence of roundels on the rear fuselage, which is traditional practice for all Syrian MiG-21s until today.

Another variant of the same camouflage pattern as applied on the MiG-21F-13 serial number 1315. Originally delivered to Syria in 1964, about 19 of these aircraft remained in service by early October 1973, and a handful is known to have survived the next major conflict with Israel too. The only details of the camouflage pattern as applied on top wing surfaces that have been recognized so far are that the serial number 1302 received diagonal stripes, while the serial number 1315 seems to have received more usual 'horns' of olive drab.

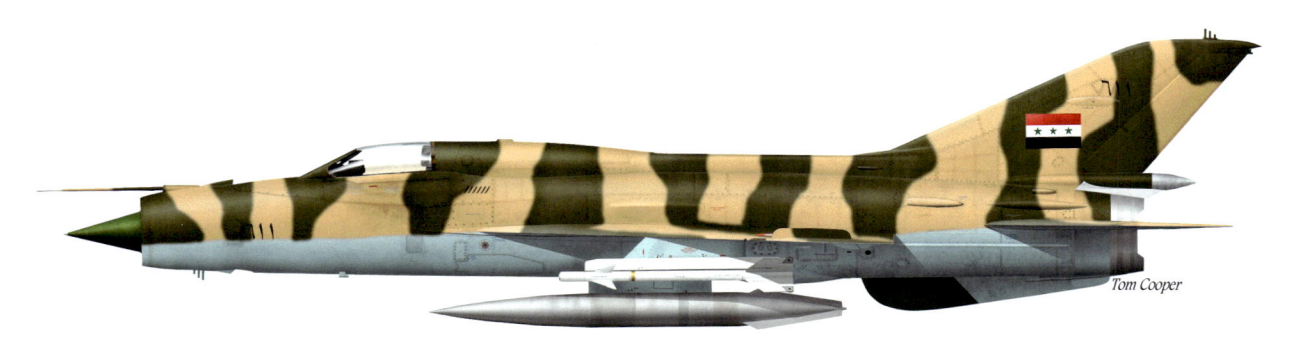

Included in the batch of about 20 MiG-21PFMs Soviets have supplied to Syria to replace losses of the June 1967 War were few MiG-21PFS. This is a reconstruction of one of aircraft in question, based on several different photographs the quality of which is too poor for reproduction. Camouflaged at the same time like MiG-21PFMs from the same batch, it was painted in orange sand and olive drab on top surfaces, and light admiralty grey on bottom surfaces.

237

السعودية   الأردن   سيناء   إسرائيل   مصر

A reconstruction of one of few MiG-21FLs – serial number 1421 – delivered to No. 67 Squadron SyAAF before the June 1967 War and still in service as of 1972-1973. It was last sighted sometimes 'in the early 1970s', while still painted in colours used by Syrians from July 1967 until sometimes in 1971 or 1972.

Some of Syrian MiG-21FLs were overhauled and re-painted by 'The Works' at Nayrab AB either shortly before or immediately after the October 1973 War, and thus saw the introduction of new colours in form of orange sand and green-blue on top surfaces. Notable is how high the light admiralty grey colour used to paint bottom surfaces was applied to the sides of the fuselage. This aircraft was withdrawn from service sometimes in the 1980s and ended as a 'gate guard' in front of Kweres AB, in northern Syria.

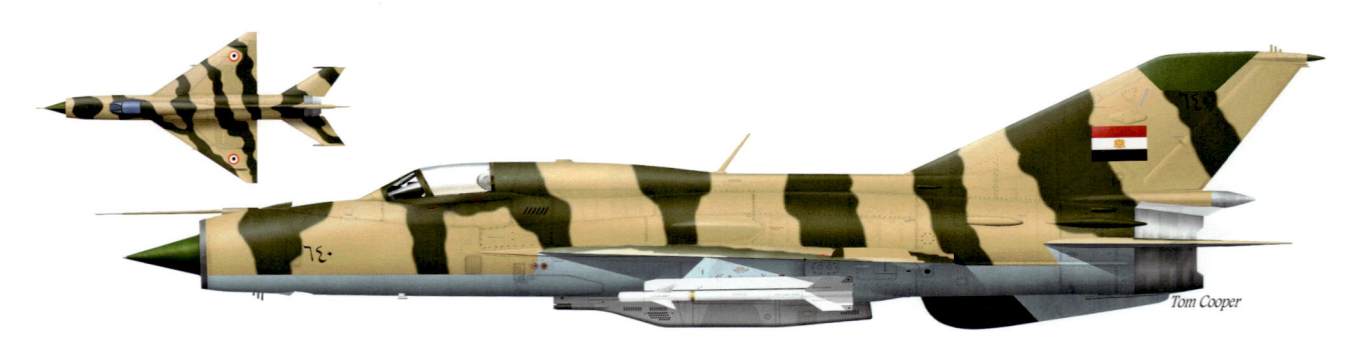

Based on photographs (and gun-camera stills) of several different Syrian MiG-21FLs and MiG-21PFMs, this is a reconstruction of the MiG-21PFM serial number 640, which was shot down and crashed on a beach near Beirut during the air battle of 13 September 1973. Delivered to Syria in late June 1967, 640 was camouflaged about a month later in orange sand and olive drab on upper surfaces. Inset is showing reconstruction of the camouflage pattern as applied on top surfaces.

الضفة الغربية        قطاع غزة        سوريا        لبنان

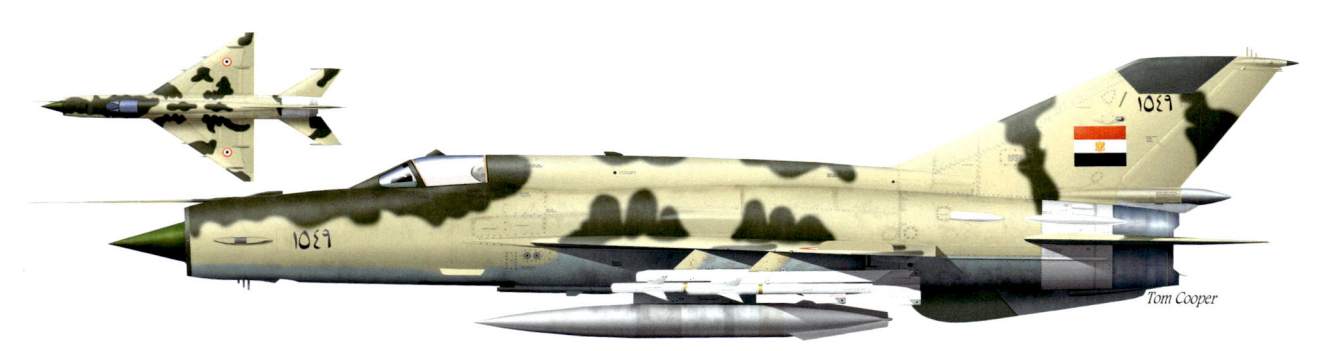

Long time thought to be serialled 1949, it was only shortly before this book went to press that the correct identity of Majid Zoughby's favourite MiG-21MF was established as serial number 1549. Zoughby claimed most of his seven kills while flying this plane. Notable for the 'sand and spinach' of these early MiG-21MFs is that most of them had their rear fuselage – right in front of afterburner 'can' – and auxiliary intake in front of the same, painted in aluminium-silver.

The MiG-21MF serial number 1554 belonged to the first batch of this variant delivered to SyAAF. It was camouflaged in 'sand and spinach' already before delivery, survived the October 1973 War, acted in a post-war semi-documentary, and was last seen abandoned at D'haba AB (outside al-Qusayr, in western Syria), when this was overrun by insurgents, in early 2013.

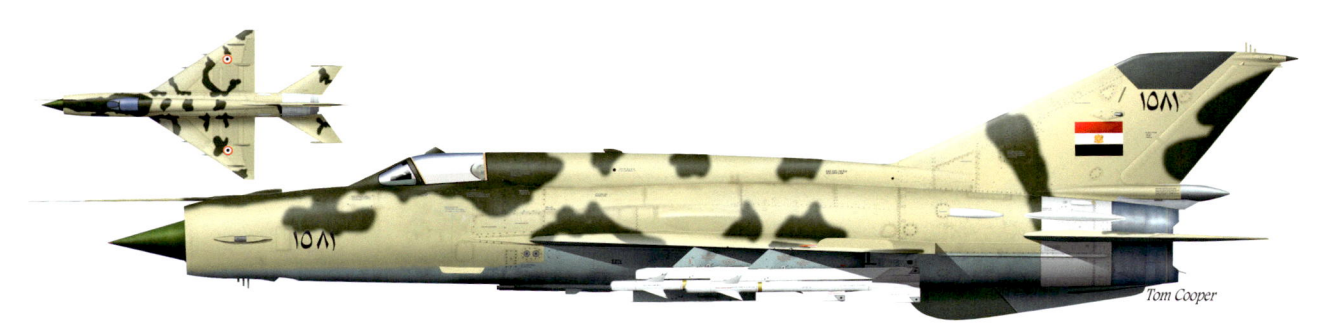

A reconstruction of the camouflage applied on the port side and top surfaces of the SyAAF MiG-21MF 1581, based on photographs of several different aircraft. The aircraft is known to have survived the October 1973 War. It is shown in usual combat Syrian configuration for this variant during that conflict, including four R-3S AAMs (centreline drop tank with capacity of 490-litre was usually jettisoned on initiation of an engagement).

السعودية    الأردن    سيناء    إسرائيل    مصر

This is a reconstruction of a MiG-21MF serial number 1941, as seen on a photograph too poor for reproduction, published in one of rare official publications of the Syrian Ministry of Defence. Belonging to a number of MiG-21MFs Soviets rushed to Syria during the October 1973 War, it had its rear fuselage (in front of afterburner 'can') painted in beige and light admiralty grey – which was unusual for aircraft of this variant in service with SyAAF at the start of this conflict.

Another Syrian 'survivor' from all the battles of the early 1970s was this Su-7BMK, serial number 813 (or 1813), put on display at the Military Museum of Damascus in the mid-1970s. One of less than 30 aircraft of this type acquired by Syria starting in 1970, it was painted in orange-sand and green-blue in similar camouflage pattern like that usually applied in the USSR prior to delivery. Notable is that it was modified through addition of a rear-view mirror on the top of the cockpit and four underwing pylons – like Egyptian, but unlike Iraqi Su-7BMKs.

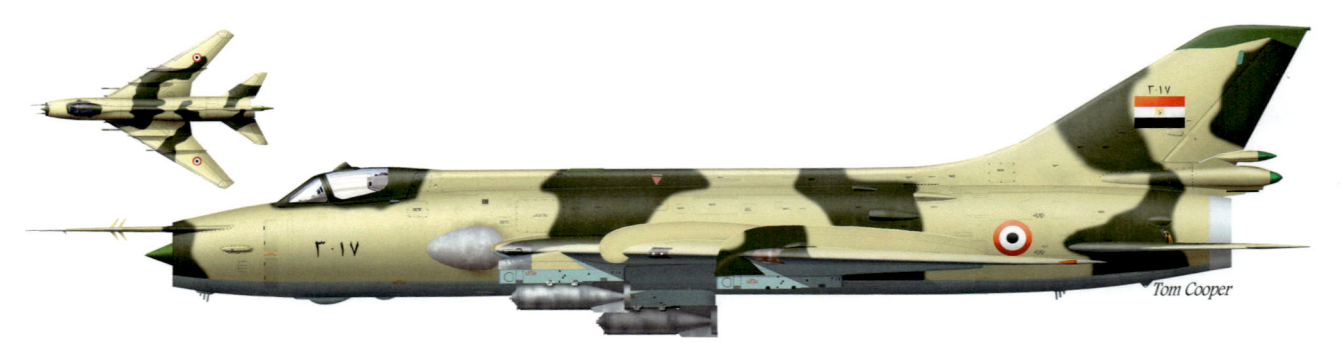

A reconstruction of one of 15 Su-20s delivered to Syria just months before October 1973 War, and operated by No. 54 Squadron from T.4 AB, based on a semi-documentary often shown on Syrian National TV in the 1990s and 2000s. The serial number (3018) remains unconfirmed, but details of the 'sand and spinach' camouflage pattern (and RBK-250 CBUs, which arrived in Syria together with these aircraft) are accurate.

# BIBLIOGRAPHY

All titles are presented in English though some sources were originally published in other languages, as noted below

Adan, Avraham (Bren), *On the Banks of the Suez* (Novato: Presidio Press, 1991) ISBN 0-89141-043-0

Aloni, S., *101: Israeli Air Force First Fighter Squadron* (Bet-Hafer: IsraDecal Publications, 2007), ISBN 965-7220-08-4

Aloni, S., *Israeli A-4 Skyhawk Units in Combat* (Oxford: Osprey Publishing, 2009) ISBN 978-1-84603-430-5

Aloni, S., *Israeli Mirage and Nesher Aces* (Oxford: Osprey Publishing, 2004) ISBN 1-84176-653-4

Aloni, S., *Israeli F-4 Phantom II Aces* (Oxford: Osprey Publishing, 2004), ISBN 1-84176-783-2

Aloni, S., *Israeli Air Force 107 Squadron: The Knights of the Orange Tail* (Erlangen: AirDOC, 2005), ISBN 3-935687-60-5

Aloni, S., *Israeli Air Force Tayeset 119: Ha'Atalef – The Bat Squadron* (Erlangen: AirDOC, 2007), ISBN 978-3-935687-62-1

Asher, D., *The Egyptian Strategy for the Yom Kippur War, An Analysis* (McFarland & Co Inc., 2009), ISBN 978-0786442539

Asher, J. S., and Hammel, E., *Duel for the Golan: The 100-Hour Battle that Saved Israel* (Pacifica: Pacifica Military History, 1987), ISBN 0-9355553-52-5

Babich, Col V., Egyptian Interceptors in War of Attrition, *Istoriya Aviaciy Magazine* (in Russian), Vol. 3/2001

Babich, Col V., Egyptian Fighter-Bombers in War of Attrition, *Aviaciya i Vremya Magazine* (in Russian), unknown volume

Babich, Col V., *MiG-21 vs Mirage III*, *Aviaciya i Vremya Magazine* (in Russian), unknown volume

Babich, H. el-, Magdoub, T. el-, Zohdy, M. D. el-Din, The Ramadan War, 1973 (Dunn Loring, T. N. Dupuy Associates, 1978), ISBN 0-8824-460-8

Bar-Joseph, U., Strategic Surprise or Fundamental Flaws? The Sources of Israel's Military Defeat at the Beginning of the 1973 War, *The Journal of Military History*, Volume 72, Number 2, April 2008 (pp 509-530, article)

Blum, H., *The Eve of Destruction: The Untold Story of the Yom Kippur War* (HarperCollins Publishers, 2003), ISBN 0-06-001400-8

Carlowitz, D., *Egypt at War* (Publishamerica, 2007), ISBN 978-1604411058

Centre for Military Studies, *The History of the Syrian Army* (in Arabic), (Damascus, 2001–2002)

Cohen, Col E., *Israel's Best Defense* (Shrewsbury: Airlife Publishing Ltd, 1993) ISBN 1-85310-484-1

Cull, B., Nicolle, D., And Aloni, S., *Spitfires over Israel* (London: Grub Street, 1994) ISBN 0-948817-74-7

Cull, B., Nicolle, D., And Aloni, S., *Wings over Suez* (London: Grub Street, 1996) ISBN 1-898697-48-5

Dunstan, S., *Israeli Fortifications of the October War 1973* (Oxford: Osprey Publishing Ltd, 2008), ISBN 978-1-84603-361-2

Dunstan, S., *The Yom Kippur War (1): the Golan Heights* (Oxford: Osprey Publishing Ltd, 2003), ISBN 1-84176-220-2

Dunstan, S., *The Yom Kippur War (2): the Sinai* (Oxford: Osprey Publishing Ltd, 2003), ISBN 184176-221-0

Dupuy, Col T. N. and Blanchard, Col. W., *The Almanac of World Military Power* (2nd Edition), (London: Arthur Barker Ltd, 1972), ISBN 0-213-16418-3

Efrati, Y., *Colors & Markings of the Israeli Air Force* (Bat-Hefer, IsraDecal Publishing, 2005), ISBN 965-7220-03-3

Farr, W. D., *The Third Temple's Holy of Holies: Israel's Nuclear Weapons* (Air War College, USAF Counterproliferation Center, Counterproliferation Paper No. 2, 1999)

Fawzy, Maj Gen M., *The Three-Years War* (in Arabic), (Beirut: Dar Mustakbal al-Arabi, 1998)

Flintham, V., *Air Wars and Aircraft: A Detailed Record of Air Combat, 1945 to the Present* (London: Arms and Armour Press, 1989), ISBN 0-85368-779-X

Gamasy, FM M., A., G., el-, *The October War: Memoirs of Field Marshal el-Gamasy of Egypt* (Cairo: The American University of Cairo Press, 1993)

Gawrych, Dr. George W., *The 1973 Arab-Israeli War: The Albatross of Decisive Victory* (Combat Studies Institute, US Army Command and General Staff College)

Gindy, Fikry, el-, *Egyptian Eagles over the Golan* (in Arabic), (Cairo: al-Hay'ah al-Misriyah al-'Ammah lil-Kitab, 1992)

Glassman, J., D., *Arms for the Arabs: The Soviet Union and the War in the Middle East* (Baltimore: The John Hopkins University Press, 1975), ISBN 0-8018-1747-1

Gordon, S., *Thirty Hours in October* (Tel Aviv: Ma'ariv Book Guild, 2008)

Green, S., *Living by the Sword: America and Israel in the Middle East* (Brattleboro: Amana Books, 1988), ISBN 0-9155957-60-8

Haloutz, D., *Straightforward* (in Hebrew) (Miskal, Yedioth Ahoronoth Books and Chemed Books, 2010), ISBN 978-965-482-870-3

Hammad, G., *Military Battles on the Egyptian Front 1973* (in Arabic, Cairo: Dar al-Shuruq, 2002), ISBN 0-8129-0567-9

Heikal, H. M., *The 30 Years War* (in Arabic), (Cairo: el-Ahram Publishing & Translation Centre, 1990), Reg. No. 5063/1990

Insight Team Of The London Sunday Times, *The Yom Kippur War* (Garden City: Doubleday, 1974), ISBN 978-0-385-06738-6

Iraqi Ministry Of Defence, *History of the Iraqi Armed Forces, Part 17; The Establishment of the Iraqi Air Force and its Development* (in Arabic), (Iraq: 1988)

Jawadi, Dr. M. al-, *In Between the Catastrophe: Memoirs of Egyptian Military Commanders from 1967 to 1972* (in Arabic), (Cairo: Dar al-Khiyal, 2001)

Klein, A., And Aloni, S., With Weiss, R., De Haven, L. R., And Myasnikov, A., *Israeli Phantoms: the Kurnass in IDF/AF Service, 1969-1988* (Erlangen: Double Ugly Books, 2010), ISBN 978-3-935687-81-2

Konzelmann, G., *Damaskus: Oase Zwischen Hass und Hoffnung* (Frankfurt/Main: Ullstein Buch, 1996), ISBN 3-548-35588-9

Kotlobovskiy, A. B., *MiG-21 in Local Wars* (in Russian) (Kiev, ArchivPress, 1997)

Kucera, Hurt, Z., & Chalas, O., *Ilustrovaná historie letectví – deHavilland Tiger Moth Avia/Letov C-2, Aero L-29 Delfín* (in Czech), (Prague: Nase vojsko, edice Triáda, 1992), ISBN 80-206-0219-4

Labib, A. M., *The Third Arm: A History of the Egyptian Air Force* (in Arabic), Volumes 7 to 9

Michel, Marshall L., *Clashes: Air Combat over North Vietnam, 1965–1972* (Naval Institute Press, 1997), ISBN 1-55-750-585-3

Moneim el-, A. A., *Lieutenant Colonel Salah Danish: the Only Egyptian Pilot captured in June 1967* (in Arabic), online article

Moneim el-, A. A., *Wolf in the Sun's Disc* (in Arabic), (Cairo: 1988)

Moukiiad, Maj Gen M. A., *My Life* (in Arabic), (Damascus: al-Zakhira, 2005)

Mustafa, Gen H., *The June War, 1967, Part II* (Lebanon: Establishment for Arab Studies and Publication, 1970)

Newdick, T., *Modern Israeli Air Power* (Houston: Harpia Publishing LLC, 2013) ISBN 978-0-985455-2-2

Nicolle, D., And Cooper, T., *Arab MiG-19 and MiG-21 Units in Combat* (Oxford: Osprey Publishing Ltd, 2004), ISBN 1-84176-655-0

Nordeen, L., *Fighters over Israel*, (Guild Publishing, 1991)

O'Ballance, E., *The Electronic War in the Middle East, 1968-1970* (London: Faber and Faber Ltd, 1974), ISBN 0-208-01469-1

O'Ballance, E., *No Victor, No Vanquished: The Yom Kippur War* (Presidio Press, 1996), ISBN 978-0-89141-615-9

Okasha, Maj Gen M., *Soldiers in the Sky* (in Arabic) (Cairo, Ministry of Defence, 1976)

Omar, Maj Gen K. K., *Memoirs of the Iraqi Air Force CO* (unpublished document in Arabic)

Ovendale, R., *The Origins of the Arab-Israeli Wars* (Harlow: Longman Group UK Ltd, 1984), ISBN 0-582-49257-2

Palit, Maj Gen D. K., *Return to The Sinai: The Arab Offensive, October 1973* (New Delhi: Lancer Publishers & Distributors, 1974, reprtinted 2002), ISBN 81-7062-221-2

Peled, Gen. B., *Days of Reckoning* (Moshav Ben-Shemen: Modan Publishing House, 2004)

Pollack, K. M., *Arabs at War: Military Effectiveness* 1948-1991 (Bison Books, 2004), ISBN 0-8032-8783-6

Price, Dr. A., *War in the Fourth Dimension: US Electronic Warfare, from the Vietnam War to the Present* (London: Greenhill Books, 2001), ISBN 1-85367-471-0

Riad, M., *The Struggle for Peace in the Middle East* (Consett: Quartet Books, 1981), ISBN 978-0704322974

Sa'adon al-, M., *Pilot Memoir* (privately published document, 2005)

Sadat el-, A., *In Search of Identity* (Harper & Row Publishers, Inc., 1977) ISBN 0-060137428

Sadik, Brig Gen A., And Cooper, T., *Secret Helpers in Yom-Kipur War* (in German), *Fliegerrevue Extra* Vol.13, May 2006

Sadik, Brig Gen A., And Cooper, T., *Iraqi Fighters, 1953–2003: Camouflage & Markings* (Houston: Harpia Publishing, 2008), ISBN 978-0-615-21414-6

Shazly, Sa'ad el-, *The Crossing of the Suez* (San Francisco: American Mideast Research, 2003), ISBN 0-9604562-2-8

Sheif, Z., *The Israeli Military Encyclopaedia* (Amman: 1st Arabic Edition, translated into Arabic and published by Dar el-Jaleel For Publishing, Research & Studies, 1988)

Shevchuk, D., *The Soviet-Israeli War* (in Russian; unpublished manuscript)

Stafrace, C., *Arab Air Forces* (Carrolton: Squadron/Signal Publications Inc., 1994) ISBN 0-89747-326-4

Sokolov, A, 'PVO in Local Wars and Armed Conflicts: The Arab-Israeli Wars', *VKO*, No. 2 (2), 2001

Sokolov, A., 'The Arab-Israeli Wars', *VKO*, No. 2 (5), 2002

Sukhov, K. V., *Over the Syrian front* (in Russian; unpublished manuscript)

Tessler, M. A., *A History of the Israeli-Palestinian Conflict* (Bloomington and Indianapolis: Indiana University Press, 1994)

Vyhlidal, M., *Československá pomoc při výstavbě vojenského školství v arabském světě v letech 1948–1989* (in Czech), (Brno: Filozoficka fakulta Masarykovy university, 2010. 100 s. Magisterska diplomova prace, 2010)

Weiss, R., And Efrati, Y., *McDonnell Douglas A-4 Skyhawk* (Bat-Hefer: IsraDecal Publication, 2001), ISBN 965-7220-00-9

Zaloga, Steven J., *Red SAM: The SA-2 Guideline Anti-Aircraft Missile* (Oxford: Osprey Publishing Ltd, 2007), ISBN 978-1-84603-062-8

Zolotaryov, Maj Gen V. A., *Russia in Local Wars and Military Conflicts in the Second Half of the 20th Century* (in Russian), (Moscow: Institute of Military History, Ministry of Defence of the Russian Federation, 2000)

Various volumes of *Armed Forces Magazine*, published by the Egyptian Ministry of Defence, 1950s and 1960s; *El-Djeich* (official publication of the Algerian Ministry of Defence), various volumes from 2007 to 2012; various magazines and journals published by the Iraqi Air Force and the Iraqi Ministry of Defence, 1970s, 1980s and 1990s; various volumes of the *Vyesnik Vozdushno-Kosmicheskaya Oborna ('VKO')* magazine, from 2001-2005 (see endnotes); various volumes of *AirInternational* and *Aircraft Illustrated* magazines, 1973-1991; interviews with various Algerian, Egyptian, Iraqi, Syrian and Soviet Air Force officers, pilots, and ground personnel (see Acknowledgments and Footnotes), and personal notes of all authors

# INDEX

**Aircraft**
A-4  90
Boeing KC-97G  34, 90
EC-130H  53
F-4E  90, 105, 106, 158 (formations), 176–178 (war loads)
F-14A  53
F-15A  53
HA-200  67
Hunter  66
Il-28  67
L-29 deployment in Nigeria  24, 68
L-29 deliveries to Iraq  211–213
MiG-17 formations  75
MiG-17 versions, equipment, modifications and performances  64, 72, 177
MiG-19 deliveries to Egypt  16
MiG-19 deliveries to Iraq  15
MiG-21 versions, equipment, modifications and performances  47-50, 62, 105,106, 176
MiG-21 summary of all deliveries 1961–1973  203-209
MiG-23  48 (to Egypt), 195 (to Iraq)
MiG-23 (wrong designation for MiG-25, often cited in the West of the early 1970s)  41
MiG-25  37–41, 233
Mirage III  90
Mirage 5  67, 90
Model 124I (UAV)  40, 53
Su-7 versions, equipment, modifications and performances  63, 72, 178
Su-7 deliveries to Syria  72
Su-7BMKR (Egyptian variant for reconnaissance)  34
Su-17 (in Egypt)  30
Su-20 armament and war load  177, 178
Su-20  31 (in Egypt), 73 (in Syria), 193
Tu-16  118–121
Tu-22 deliveries to Egypt  50
Tu-22 deliveries to Iraq  198

**Air defence armament (SAMs) and related equipment**
MIM-23 HAWK  97
NRZ-1, 12, 15, 20 IFF systems  20, 21
P-12, P-14, P-15, P-18, P-19, P-30, P-37 and P-40 radars  21
SA-3 (S-125 Pechora)  20, 32, 33
SA-6 (2K12 Kvadrat)  41, 48, 150–152

**Armament**
9K72 Elbrus (SS-1c Scud-B)  55, 186
AGM-45 Shrike anti-radar missile  36, 93, 166
AGM-62 Walleye air-to-ground missile  94
AGM-65 Maverick air-to-ground missile  94
AGM-78 Standard anti-radar missile  41
AIM-7 Sparrow air-to-air missile  39–41
AIM-9 Sidewinder air-to-air missile  93, 175
KSR-2  51, 118–120
KSR-11  51, 117–120
RS-2US (AA-1 Alkali) air-to-air missile, deliveries to Iraq  15
R-3S (AA-2 Atoll) air-to-air missile, Iraqi conversion to air-to-ground missiles  16, 58, 175
Sharfir Mk.II air-to-air missile  93, 175

**Egypt**
Abbas, Ahmed (EAF pilot)  72
Abbas, Nabil (EAF/UARAF pilot)  96
Abduh, Hisham Sayd (EAF/UARAF pilot)  69, 220
Abdul-Jawwad, Ali Zien al-Abideen (EAF/UARAF pilot)  200
Abdullah, Samir (EAF/UARAF pilot)  73
Abdullah, Tameem Fahmy (EAF/UARAF pilot)  69, 220
Ahanin, Abdul-Hassan Abd al- (EAF/UARAF pilot)  70, 222
Ahmad, Wafiq Abd al-Hamid (EAF/UARAF pilot)  70, 221
Ahmad, Adil Hassan Sayd (EAF/UARAF pilot)  70, 222
Ahmed, Abbas (EAF/UARAF pilot)  42, 43, 49, 75, 76
Air Defence Command (ADC)  31, 84–86 (order of battle)
Ali, Ahmed Ismail (Egyptian Minister of War)  42
Ali, Mohammad Fouad Husayn (EAF/UARAF pilot)  70, 222
Anwar, Ahmad (EAF/UARAF pilot)  69
Atef, Ahmed (EAF/UARAF pilot)  47
Atiah, Samir (EAF/UARAF pilot)  69, 220
Ayman, Ahabadin (CO 414th Air Defence Battalion)  34
Ayyub, Nabil Ibrahim (EAF/ARAF pilot)  69, 219
Aziz, Mohammad Majdi Abd al- (EAF/UARAF pilot)  221
Badawi, Badawi Abdul Megid (EAF pilot)  145

247

Baghdadi, Air Marshal Ali (C-in-C UARAF) 42
Bakht, Ahmed Sayd (EAF pilot) 163
Barakat, Alaa (EAF/UARAF pilot) 29–31, 41, 67, 74, 77
Basri, Yusuf Hassan (EAF/UARAF pilot) 69, 220
Beshir, Hussein Osman (EAF pilot) 125
Break with Moscow 48-51
Danish, Salah (EAF/UARAF pilot) 30, 32–34, 68
Darwish, Sayd (EAF/UARAF pilot) 69, 220
Desuky, Ahmad Ismail Amer (EAF/UARAF pilot) 70, 222
Din, Ayman Sayed Ahmad Hob el- (CO 418th Air Defence Battalion ADC) 188, 189
EAF (formerly UARAF)
EAF Air Brigades
    Air Brigade 102  47, 51, 69, 129, 162
    Air Brigade 104  69, 84, 115, 162, 187
    Air Brigade 111  69
    Air Brigade 123  69
    Air Brigade 201  69
    Air Brigade 203  69
    Air Brigade 205  69
    Air Brigade 206  22
    Air Brigade 306  69
    Air Brigade 403  69
    Air Brigade 515  69
    Air Brigade 533  69
    Air Brigade 545  69
    Air Brigade 546  69
    Air Brigade 547  69, 80
EAF Commands
EAF/UARAF deployment to Syria  21
EAF heliborne assault on the Sinai  137–142
EAF national markings  79
EAF order of battle  69–71
EAF units
    Air Force Academy  30, 32, 33, 43, 68, 76
    Fighter Weapons School  69
    MiG-21 OTU  69
    No. 11 FTU  69
    No. 209 FTU  69
    No. 2 Squadron  70
    No. 3 Squadron  70
    No. 6 Squadron  69
    No. 7 Squadron  70
    No. 8 Squadron  70
    No. 9 Squadron  70, 140
    No. 11 Squadron  70
    No. 12 Squadron  70
    No. 13 Squadron  70
    No. 14 Squadron  70
    No. 15 Squadron  70
    No. 16 Squadron  69
    No. 19 Squadron  70
    No. 21 Squadron  70
    No. 22 Squadron  69, 115
    No. 25 Squadron  69, 129, 226
    No. 26 Squadron  34, 47, 69, 159–162, 226
    No. 27 Squadron  69, 127, 230
    No. 34 Squadron  69, 70, 83, 232
    No. 35 Squadron  70
    No. 36 Squadron  70, 117
    No. 42 Squadron  69, 115, 126, 127
    No. 44 Squadron  69, 104, 115, 125, 227
    No. 45 Squadron  69
    No. 46 Squadron  69, 115, 123
    No. 47 Squadron  69, 104, 228
    No. 49 Squadron  69, 72
    No. 51 Squadron  70, 126, 231
    No. 52 Squadron  30, 70, 126, 163, 231
    No. 53 Squadron  30, 70, 126
    No. 56 Squadron  70, 127, 229
    No. 59 Squadron  69
    No. 61 Squadron  70, 127,
    No. 62 Squadron  22, 58, 70, 122, 182, 226
    No. 66 Squadron (designation for Iraqi Air Force units in Egypt)  67, 69
    No. 69 Squadron  67, 69, 83, 163
    No. 72 Squadron  69
    No. 77 Squadron  69
    No. 82 Squadron  70, 125–127, 229
    No. 89 Squadron  22, 70, 125, 182, 185, 224
    No. 91 Squadron  70
    No. 95 Squadron  70
    Su-7 OTU  69
Elish, Farouk (EAF/UARAF pilot)  69, 70, 219
Ezz-el-Din, Ahmad (EAF pilot)  126
Fadil, Adil Muhammad Abd al- (EAF/UARAF pilot)  69, 220
Fahad, Mohy (EAF pilot)  159
Fahmy, Maj Gen Mohammed Ali (C-in-C ADC)  31, 188
Fahmy, Fahmy Abbas (EAF/UARAF pilot)  70, 221
Fahmy, Hassan (EAF/UARAF pilot)  70, 122, 221
Fahmy, Mohammad Abd ar-Rahman (EAF/UARAF pilot)  221
Fahmy, Munir (EAF/UARAF pilot)  125
Faraj, Ahmed Abbas (EAF pilot)  30, 51, 117, 163
Fatah, Ahmad Khiry Abd al- (EAF/UARAF pilot)  70
Fathy, Rifat (EAF pilot)  78
Fawzy, Mohammed (Egyptian Army General)  29, 30
Fuad, Tahsin (EAF/UARAF pilot)  77
Gabara, Mohammed (UARAF pilot)  32
Gabr, Gabr Ali (EAF/UARAF pilot)  69, 99
Gamasy, Mohammed Abdel Ghani el- (Egyptian general)  42
Gahramy, Fikry el- (EAF/UARAF pilot)  47, 68
Gaoly, George (EAF/UARAF pilot)  118
Gawaharegy, Ahmed el- (EAF/UARAF pilot)  118
Gharby, Hasem (or Hazem) al- (EAF/UARAF pilot)  30, 70, 126
Ghema, Mustafa Mohammad (UARAF pilot)  99
Gindy, Fikry el- (EAF/UARAF pilot)  58, 59, 74, 78, 142–146, 172, 173, 193–195, 215
Gindy, Osman al- (EAF/UARAF pilot)  70, 221
Gradly, Adil al- (EAF/UARAF pilot)  70
Hafez, Mustafa Ahmed al- (EAF/UARAF pilot)  55, 67, 70, 126, 220
Hafrush, Farid (EAF/UARAF pilot)  47–49
Hamdi, Osama (UARAF/EAF pilot)  70
Hamid, Qadri Abd el- (EAF/UARAF pilot)  68, 159

248

Hashish, Mohammad Gaber (EAF/UARAF pilot)  69, 219
Hassan, Ahmed Moustafa Mohammed (EAF/UARAF pilot)  119
Hassan, Ali Hassan Shehata Hassan (EAF/UARAF pilot)  221
Hassan, Ismail Hassan (EAF/UARAF pilot)  221
Hefnawy, Dia el- (EAF/UARAF pilot)  47, 127
Heshmat, Mamdouh (EAF/UARAF pilot)  115
Hilmy, Mohammad Raouf (EAF/UARAF pilot)  118, 221
Hinnawy, Air Marshal Shalaby el- (C-in-C UARAF)  43
Husni, Hassan (EAF/UARAF pilot)  143
Ibrahim, Muhammad al- (EAF pilot)  31
Iraqi, Reda el- (EAF/UARAF pilot)  45, 116, 138, 158-161
Islam, Sayf al-  (EAF pilot)  145
Ismail, Hussein (EAF/UARAF pilot)  47
Jawad, Ali Zayn al-Abidin Abd al- (EAF/UARAF pilot)  69, 219
Jirjis, Munir Fahmy Barum (EAF/UARAF pilot)  70, 220
Kamal, Fuad (EAF/UARAF pilot)  69
Kamal, Magdy (EAF/UARAF pilot)  163, 187
Kamil, Jamal Muhammad Maha ad-Din (EAF/UARAF pilot)  70, 221
Kamil, Nabil Hassan (EAF/UARAF pilot)  220
Keraidy, Abdel Wahab el-  22, 51, 117, 118
Kfass, Hussein el- (EAF/UARAF pilot)  21, 58, 116, 122, 182, 216
Khalq, Sayed Abd al- (EAF/UARAF pilot)  70
Lashin, Naji Muhammad (EAF/UARAF pilot)  70, 182, 184, 185
Luftey, Hassan (EAF pilot)  105
Lufty, Ahmad Samir Muhammad (EAF/UARAF pilot)  221
Mansoury, Ahmed Kamal el- (EAF pilot)  104
Maraghy, Mortada el- (UARAF pilot)  32
Maghrabi, Mustafa Zaki el- (EAF/UARAF pilot)  184
Marsa, Abdel Aziz al- (EAF/UARAF pilot)  43
Masood, Muhammad Ali Hassan (EAF/UARAF pilot)  70, 222
Mikhail, Samir Aziz (EAF/UARAF pilot)  13, 123, 138, 162, 163, 187, 188
Mohy, Ahmed Abbas (EAF/UARAF pilot)  69
Moneim, Air Vice Marshal Mahmoud Shaker Abd el- (Deputy C-in-C EAF)  43-45, 69, 217
Monib, Mamdouh (EAF pilot)  161
Mubarak, Hosni (EAF/UARAF pilot, later Egyptian President)  42, 43, 69
Musa, Talaf Tawfiq (EAF/UARAF pilot)  70, 222
Mustafa, Adil Abd al-Rahman (EAF/UARAF pilot)  70, 221
Mutawy, Ali Abd al-Khaliq (EAF/UARAF pilot)  70, 221
Naji, Mohammad Jalal Muhammad (EAF pilot)  70, 222
Najib, Mohammed Najib Muhammed (EAF pilot)  125
Nasser, Gamal Abdel (Egyptian President)  27, 28
Nasser, Karim al- (EAF pilot)  185
Nassr, Ahmad Adil (EAF/UARAF pilot)  220
Nassr, Jamal Abd al-Rahman (EAF/UARAF pilot)  69, 220
Nur, Ahmad Abd al-Aziz Ahmad (EAF/UARAF pilot)  69, 220
Okasha, Mohammad Abdel-Moneim Zaki (EAF/UARAF pilot)  21, 43, 67, 82–84, 138, 142, 163
Randopolo, Tanashi (US spy in Egypt)  48
Riyadh, Amir Ahmad (EAF/UARAF pilot)  69, 220
Rushdi, Abd al-Rahim (EAF/UARAF pilot)  69, 219
Sabry, Ali (Egyptian Vice President)  29
Sadat, Anwar el- (Egyptian President)  28, 48
Sadat, Mohammed Atif el- (EAF/UARAF pilot)  126, 129
Sadek, Mohammed Ahmed (Egyptian Minister of War)  41
Sadiq, Essam Muhammad Muqadam (EAF/UARAF pilot)  69, 220
Sadiq, Magdy Kamal Mahmud (EAF/UARAF pilot)  69, 220
Saima, Tahsin Fuad (EAF/UARAF pilot, ex-RJAF)  70, 220
Sakr, Dorry Riyad (UARAF pilot)  22, 23
Salamah, Ali Atiyah Ali (EAF/UARAF pilot)  70, 221
Saleh, Ahmed (EAF/UARAF pilot)  69, 219
Sawy, Mohammad Kamal al- (EAF/UARAF pilot)  69, 220
Sayd, Gamal (EAF/UARAF pilot)  70, 222
Sayd, Sharif Muhammad Arabi as- (EAF/UARAF pilot)  70, 221
Shaba, Ahmad Badi Abu (EAF pilot)  139
Shababi, Ahmad Shababi Ahmad (EAF/UARAF pilot)  70, 221
Shabarah, Ahmad Riyadh Ibrahim (EAF/UARAF pilot)  70, 222
Shafiq, Ahmad Muhammad (EAF/UARAF pilot)  69, 220
Shakir, Ala'a (EAF/UARAF pilot)  69, 220
Shararah, Adil (EAF pilot)  125
Shazly, Sa'ad el- (Egyptian Army General)  29–32, 41, 42, 104
Shehata, Ahmad Maher (EAF/UARAF pilot)  69, 219
Shennawy, Abdel Moneim el- (EAF/UARAF pilot)  30, 42, 51, 69, 126, 130
Shuwakry, Nabil (EAF/UARAF pilot)  69, 131, 158, 162, 220
Sidki, Abdul Rahman (EAF/UARAF pilot)  30
Sudani, Zaki (EAF/UARAF pilot)  70
Suleyman, Bakr (EAF pilot)  145
Tadeus, Victor Nelson (EAF/UARAF pilot)  70, 163
Taher, Taher Mohammad (EAF/UARAF pilot)  70, 221
Tala'at, Abdul el-Hamid (EAF/UARAF pilot)  60
Talibah, Azmi Ezz el-Din (EAF/UARAF pilot)  70, 222
Thabet, Munir Salih Mustafa (EAF/UARAF pilot)  70, 222
Wakeel, Ahmed Magdi el- (EAF pilot)  80, 82, 140

Wakeel, Ahmed Yusuf el- (EAF pilot)  126–129, 139
Wagedy, Ali (EAF/UARAF pilot)  47
Wahhab, Hamzah Kamil Abd al- (EAF/UARAF pilot)  221
Wahhab, Sayd Kamal Abd al- (EAF/UARAF pilot)  69, 220
Yusuf, Ahmed (EAF pilot)  129
Zaghloul, Sa'ad (EAF/UARAF pilot)  30
Zaina, Yahya Abu (EAF pilot)  145
Zahran, Sayd Ahmad (EAF/UARAF pilot)  70, 222
Zakaria, Kamal (EAF/UARAF pilot)  30
Zaki, Abdel Hamid Hussain (EAF pilot)  122
Zaki, Medhat (EAF/UARAF pilot)  34, 45, 49, 159, 160
Zaki, Kamal Osman (EAF/UARAF pilot)  70, 126, 163
Zanaty, Safay el- (EAF/UARAF pilot)  47

**Iraq**
Abdel-Qader, Wallid (IrAF pilot)  190
Abossi, Alwan al- (IrAF pilot)  199–202
Diah (IrAF pilot, first name unknown)  190
Ezzat, Imad Ahmed (IrAF pilot, first name unknown)  190
Hamad, Mohammad Salman (IrAF pilot)  200
IrAF deployment to Egypt, 1973  66, to Syria 196–200
IrAF MiG-19 deal  15
IrAF order of battle for September 1973  196
IrAF Units
    Flying Leaders School  196
    No. 1 Squadron  196, 199, 235
    No. 2 Squadron  196
    No. 3 Squadron  196
    No. 4 Squadron  196
    No. 5 Squadron  196, 199, 235
    No. 6 Squadron  66, 196, 234
    No. 7 Squadron  16, 196, 201, 202, 233
    No. 8 Squadron  196–198, 235
    No. 9 Squadron  16, 196, 199, 234
    No. 10 Squadron  196–198
    No. 11 Squadron  16, 196–198
    No. 14 Squadron  196
    No. 17 Squadron  196
    No. 18 Squadron  196–198
    No. 23 Squadron  196
    No. 29 Squadron  196, 234
    No. 70 Squadron  196
Jabouri, Jassam al- (IrAF pilot)  200
Khafaji, Kamil Sultan al- (IrAF pilot)  193
Naimi, Muwaffak Saeed Abdullah al- (IrAF pilot)  201
Naji, Mohammad (IrAF pilot)  66, 81–83, 89, 117, 124, 137, 190, 191
Naqeeb, Najdat an- (IrAF pilot)  200
Qaysee (or Qaisy), Amer Ahmed (IrAF pilot)  190, 191
Qaysee (or Qaisy), Shehab (IrAF pilot)  201
Rasoul, Yousif Muhammad (IrAF pilot)  66, 70, 190
Sadik, Brig Gen Ahmad (IrAF Intelligence Department)  15, 199
Samarrai, Wallid Abdul-Latif as- (IrAF pilot)  66, 190, 191

Shaher, Jassam Muhammad ash- (C-in-C IrAF)  121, 122
Windawy, Munthir al- (IrAF pilot)  16

**Israel**
Adan, Bren (IDF General)  164
Bar Lev Line  62–64, 67
Carmi, Eitam (IDF/AF pilot)  188
IDF/AF electronic countermeasures  92, 93, 151, 152
IDF/AF interception attempts of Soviet MiG-25s  38–41
IDF/AF order of battle  94
IDF/AF units
    Flight School Unit  94
    No. 69 Squadron  94, 167, 191
    No. 100 Squadron  95
    No. 101 Squadron  94
    No. 102 Squadron  94
    No. 103 Squadron  95
    No. 107 Squadron  94, 129–133, 167, 191
    No. 108 Squadron  94
    No. 109 Squadron  94
    No. 110 Squadron  94
    No. 113 Squadron  94, 189
    No. 114 Squadron  95
    No. 115 Squadron  95
    No. 116 Squadron  95
    No. 117 Squadron  94
    No. 118 Squadron  95
    No. 119 Squadron  95, 126, 167, 191
    No. 120 Squadron  95
    No. 122 Squadron  95
    No. 123 Squadron  95
    No. 124 Squadron  95
    No. 125 Squadron  95
    No. 131 Squadron  95
    No. 140 Squadron  95
    No. 144 Squadron  95, 126
    No. 150 Squadron  94
    No. 200 Squadron  40, 95
    No. 201 Squadron  94, 167, 185, 186, 191
Najari, Shlomo (IDF)  140
Peled, Benjamin (C-in-C IDF/AF)  94, 157

**Operations**
Air Battle of Tartous  106
Battle for Fort Budapest  134
Operation 41 (Egypt)  41, 60
Operation 'Challenge 4' (Israel)  157–159, 165
Operation Badhr (Egypt)  61, 72, 121–131
Operation Badhr (Syria)  144–148
Operation 'Model 5' (Israel)  113, 165–167, 175
Operation '(al-)Owda' (Syria)  60
'Plan 200' (Egypt)  29
'Plan Granite' (Egypt)  29, 41
'Plan Granite Two' (Egypt)  41, 60
'Plan The High Minarets' (Egypt)  41, 60

**Soviet Union**
47th Independent Guards Reconnaissance Aviation Regiment  37
63rd Independent Reconnaissance Aviation Squadron  37, 233
135th Fighter Aviation Regiment  38

Babich, Viktor K. (V-VS pilot, instructor in Syria) 80
Borshov, Nikolay (V-VS pilot) 37
Chudin (V-VS pilot, first name unknown) 37
Gordienko, Viktor (V-VS pilot) 37
Grechko, Andrey Antonovich (Marshal of the Soviet Union and Minister of Defence) 46
Marchenko, Yuriy (V-VS pilot) 37
MiG-25 operations over Sinai 38, 39
Petrov, Vyacheslav (V-VS pilot, instructor in Egypt) 47
Stogov, Nikolay (V-VS pilot) 37
Uvarov, Vladimir (V-VS pilot) 37
Vagin, Alexander G (V-VS pilot, instructor in Syria) 56

**Syria**
Adad (SyAAF pilot, name withheld) 56, 194
Assad, Hafez al- (Syrian President) 55
Badawi (SyAAF pilot, first name unknown) 173
Barsh, Marwan (SyAAF pilot) 76, 144
Boudros (SyAAF pilot, name withheld) 156, 174
Chakour, Maj Gen Yusuf (Chief of Staff Syrian Arab Army) 60
Dakkar (first name unknown; SyAAF General) 20
Dawoud, Mohi ad-Din Kamal (SyAAF pilot) 180
Gar, Adeeb el- (SyAAF pilot) 106, 107
Habeisy, Brig Gen Abdullah (Director of Operations Syrian Arab Army) 60
Haddad, Brig Gen Subhi (SyAAF pilot) 76, 143-145
Hamidi, al- (SyAAF pilot, first name unknown) 191, 192
Hegazi, Fayez (SyAAF pilot) 173
Jamil, Naji (C-in-C SyAAF) 57, 76, 195
Jazeera, Hassan el- (SyAAF pilot) 31
Kallas (SyAAF pilot, CO Nayrab AB) 20
Lagamy, Yunus Abdulla al- (SyAAF pilot) 184
Mansour, Fayez Hafez Ashraf (SyAAF pilot) 25
Marawy, Mohammad (SyAAF pilot) 193
Nasr, Kamal Hilal (SyAAF pilot) 194
Raya, Sharif (SyAAF pilot) 76, 144,
Sabbah, Taher (SyAAF pilot) 76
Sabbah, Brig Gen (SyAAF pilot, first name unknown) 76, 144
Sabbagh, Ahmad (SyAAF pilot) 171
SyAADF 87–89
SyAAF air bases
  Abu ad-Duhor 76
  Aleppo/Nayrab 76
  Almazza/Mazza 21, 76
  Bley/Marj Ruhayyil 76
  Damascus IAP 113
  Dmeyr 76, 113
  Hamah 76, 113
  Hmemeem 76
  Jarrah/Jirah/Kshesh 76
  Khalkalah/Khelkhleh 76, 113
  Lattakiya (Basil al-Assad)/Hmemeem 172
  Marj as-Sultan 76
  Mennegh 76
  Nasiriyeh 76, 113
  Rasin el-Abboud/Kweres 76
  Suwaiyda/as-Suwayda/Tha'leh 172
  T.4/Tiyas 76
  Tsaykal /Seen 113
SyAAF national markings 79
SyAAF order of battle 76, 77
SyAAF units
  Air Brigade 7 76
  Air Brigade 17 76
  Air Brigade 30 76
  Air Force Academy 76
  AAA Regiment 72 171
  AAA Regiment 725 171
  Air Force Academy 171
  No. 1 Squadron 76
  No. 2 Squadron 76
  No. 5 Squadron 76
  No. 7 Squadron 76
  No. 8 Squadron 76, 171
  No. 9 Squadron 76
  No. 10 Squadron 76
  No. 11 Squadron 76
  No. 12 Squadron 76
  No. 18 Squadron 76
  No. 22 Squadron 76
  No. 25 Squadron 76
  No. 32 Squadron 76
  No. 37 Squadron 76
  No. 54 Squadron 76, 193, 240
  No. 67 Squadron 76, 238
  No. 68 Squadron 76
  No. 77 Squadron 76
  MiG OCU 76
Tabet, Shukri (SyAAF pilot) 73, 78, 174
Tlass, Lt Gen Mustafa (C-in-C Syrian Arab Army) 60
Zainal, Samir Yousif (SyAAF pilot, ex-IrAF) 76, 144
Zoughby, Majid az- (SyAAF pilot) 171, 192, 194

**Others**
Boumedienne, Houari (Algerian President) 189
Bouziane, Abbdesalam (FARM pilot) 14
Bozroub, Brig Gen Mohammed Taher (C-in-C QJJ) 21
Buchannan, Lee (USN pilot) 112, 136
Johnson, Lyndon B. (US President) 27
King Hussein of Jordan 27
Kissinger, Henry Alfred (US Security Adviser) 112
Klootwyk, Ares (South African mercenary in Nigeria) 24
Nixon, Richard B. (US President) 27
No. 66 Squadron, Royal Air Force (UK) 20
Rogers, William P. (US Secretary of State) 27
SAVAK (Iranian Organization for Intelligence and National Security) 15
United States Air Force (USAF), deployment to Saudi Arabia, 1963-1964 14
United States Military Advisory Assistance Group (MAAG) in Iran 15
VP-2 Squadron, USN 112

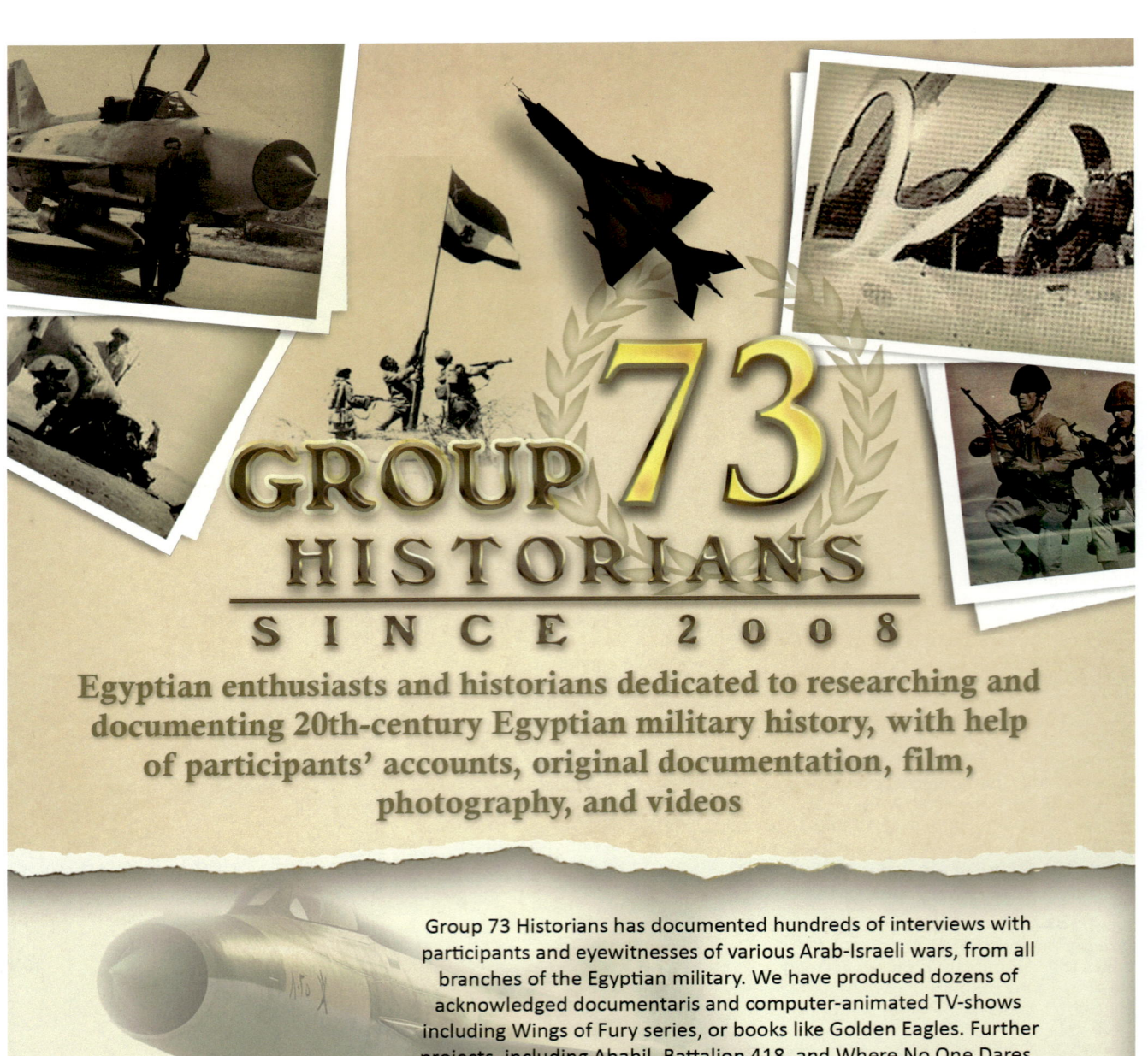

# GROUP 73 HISTORIANS

## SINCE 2008

Egyptian enthusiasts and historians dedicated to researching and documenting 20th-century Egyptian military history, with help of participants' accounts, original documentation, film, photography, and videos

Group 73 Historians has documented hundreds of interviews with participants and eyewitnesses of various Arab-Israeli wars, from all branches of the Egyptian military. We have produced dozens of acknowledged documentaris and computer-animated TV-shows including Wings of Fury series, or books like Golden Eagles. Further projects, including Ababil, Battalion 418, and Where No One Dares, are in the process of coming into being.

Join us at our website and Facebook page:

**www.group73historians.com**
**facebook.com/Group73Historians**

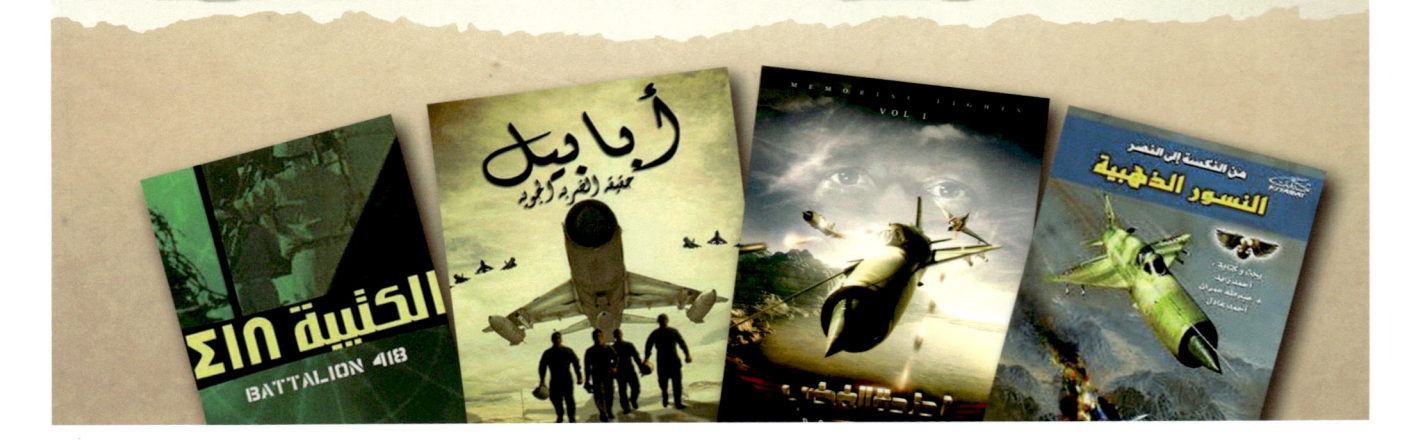

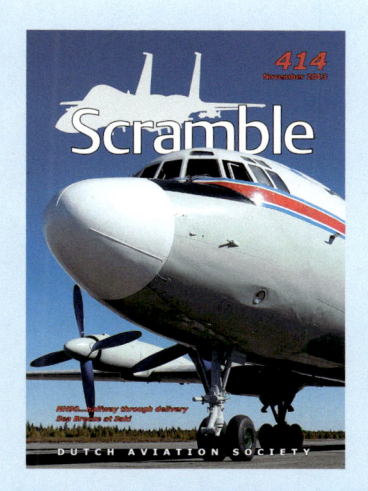

Read all the latest Civil & Military aviation news in **Scramble Magazine**

Also for Smartphone & Tablet

starting at only $2,75 a month

**Visit www.scramble.nl for air force overviews, serial rundowns and more**

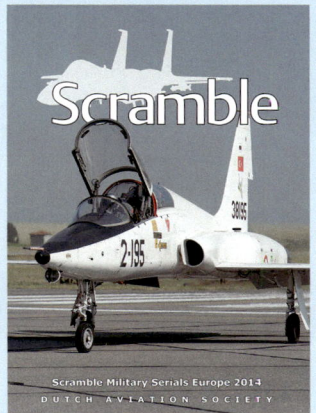

### Military Serials Europe 2014
Included in the 2014 edition are European (except Russia) and permanently stationed Singapore and United States military aircraft in Europe. For every country, all types are listed that have at least one aircraft of that type active as of 1 February 2014, not including those only used by technical schools

### Military Serials North America 2014
After seven years of absence, we are pleased to introduce a new edition of the SMS North America. This 223 pages book includes an Order of Battle containing a rundown on where all USAF, US Army, US Navy, USMC, NASA & Coastguard aircraft and helicopters are based

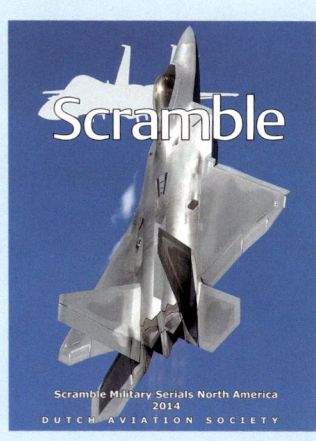

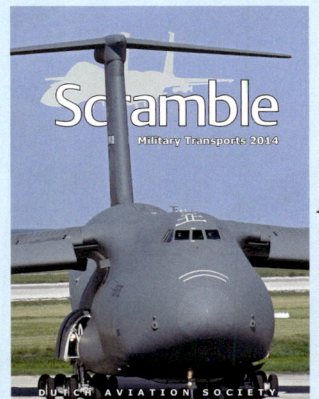

### Military Transports 2014
New in our inventory is the Scramble Military Transports 2014. The book covers all active transport, tanker, maritime patrol, liaison and training aircraft of the world's armed forces, as well as government operated aircraft

The 'must have' during your trips:
**The Scramble database app**
With unlimited database searches & saves

Available on the App Store
ANDROID APP ON Google play

Visit: www.scramble.nl/shop

**DUTCH AVIATION SOCIETY**

# ACIG

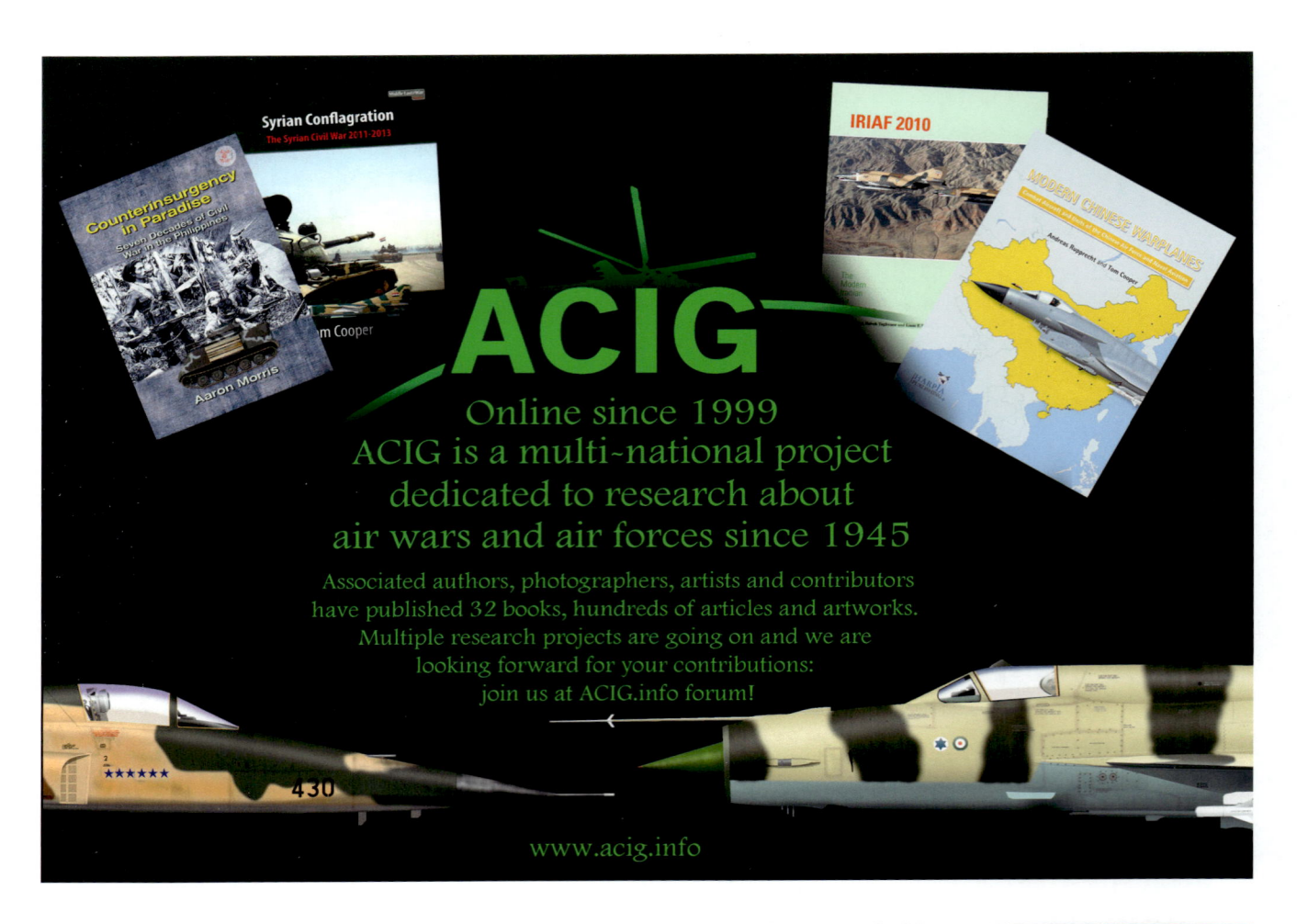

Online since 1999
ACIG is a multi-national project dedicated to research about air wars and air forces since 1945

Associated authors, photographers, artists and contributors have published 32 books, hundreds of articles and artworks. Multiple research projects are going on and we are looking forward for your contributions: join us at ACIG.info forum!

www.acig.info

www.aviationgraphic.com
We are on FACEBOOK
Join our community!

# HARPIA PUBLISHING

## Glide With Us Into The World of Aviation Literature

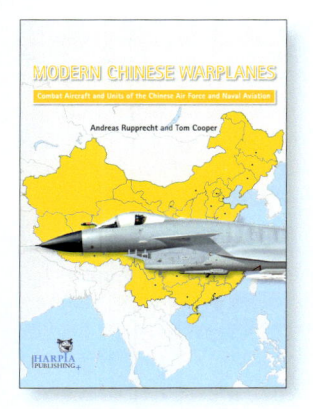

### Modern Chinese Warplanes
### Combat Aircraft and Units of the Chinese Air Force and Naval Aviation
Andreas Rupprecht and Tom Cooper
256 pages, 28 x 21 cm, softcover
35.95 Euro, ISBN 978-0-9854554-0-8

Much of the fascination that Chinese military aviation holds for the analyst and enthusiast stems from the thick veil of secrecy that surrounds it. This uniquely compact yet comprehensive directory serves as a magnificently illustrated, in-depth analysis and directory of modern Chinese air power. It is organised in three parts: the most important military aircraft and their weapons found in Chinese service today; aircraft markings and serial number systems; and orders of battle for the People's Liberation Army Air Force and Naval Air Force.

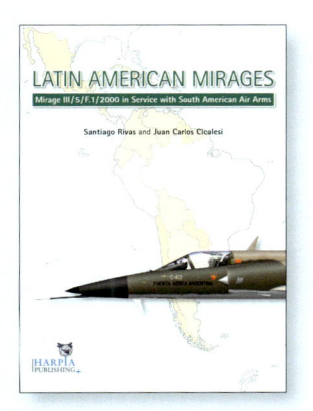

### Latin American Mirages | Mirage III/5/F.1/2000 in Service with South American Air Arms
Santiago Rivas and Juan Carlos Cicalesi
256 pages, 28x21cm, softcover
35.95 Euro   ISBN 978-0-9825539-4-7

For more than four decades, different versions of the classic Dassault Mirage fighter have served as one of the most potent combat aircraft in Latin America. Equipping seven South American air forces in significant quantities, the delta-winged jets have seen action in various different wars and internal conflicts, and they continue to fulfil their mission with a number of operators. This book tells the story of all the members of the Mirage family in service with Latin American air arms, with individual histories of the air arms and their constituent units that have operated the Dassault-designed fighter, as well as its Israeli and South African derivatives. The volume provides a comprehensive collection of colour photographs and profile artworks that cover all the variants, plus maps, and tables that illustrate the individual stories of all the aircraft, their units and their various weapons.

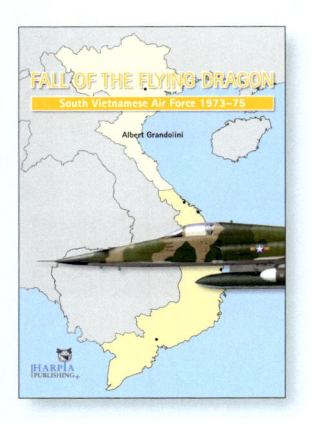

### Fall Of The Flying Dragon | South Vietnamese Air Force 1973–75
Albert Grandolini
256 pages, 28 x 21 cm, softcover
35.95 Euro, ISBN 978-0-9825539-7-8

Compiled with extensive help from previously unavailable documents that have emerged from official Vietnamese archives, and also with the assistance of narratives from dozens of participants and eyewitnesses, this volume reveals that air warfare over Vietnam did not end when the US pulled out of Southeast Asia.

---

THE AVIATION BOOKS OF A DIFFERENT KIND
**UNIQUE TOPICS I IN-DEPTH RESEARCH I RARE PICTURES I HIGH PRINTING QUALITY**

www.harpia-publishing.com

# HARPIA PUBLISHING

**Glide With Us Into The World of Aviation Literature**

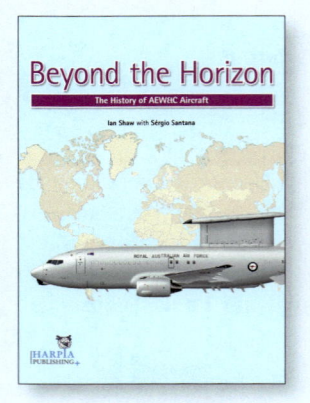

### Beyond the Horizon: The History of Airborne Early Warning
Sérgio Santana and Ian Shaw
256 pages, 28 x 21 cm, softcover
35.95 Euro, ISBN 978-0-9854554-3-9

No modern air force would contemplate a critical air operation without the involvement of some kind of airborne early warning component. For the first time, Harpia Publishing presents the full history of the airborne early warning mission and its various aircraft, from these first tentative steps in World War II up to the present day, and the use of AEW and control (AEW&C) platforms as a familiar 'force multiplier' in modern air warfare. Detailed, precise and accurate, Sérgio Santana and Ian Shaw draw upon a myriad of technical data, archive material and extensive interviews with the personnel who have operated AEW&C aircraft throug the years. As well as detailing the development of technology and daily operations of the airborne early warning community, attention is also given to the deployment of these capabilities in combat, from World War II, via Korea and Southeast Asia to the various Arab-Israeli Wars, Operation Desert Storm and more recent campaigns.

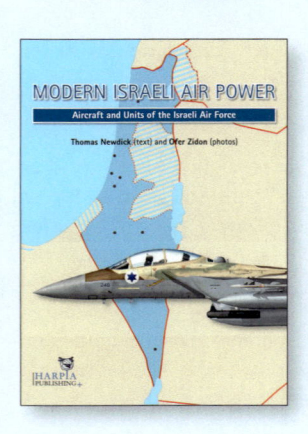

### Modern Israeli Air Power
### Aircraft and Units of the Israeli Air Force
Thomas Newdick (text) and Ofer Zidon (photos)
256 pages, 28 x 21 cm, softcover
35.95 Euro, 978-0-9854554-2-2

Israel remains the cornerstone of Middle East conflicts and tensions, and the spearhead of Israeli military might remains the Air Corps (Kheil Ha'Avir) of the Israeli Defence Forces. Renowned for its continuous efforts to maintain dominance in every dimension of air warfare, improve its capabilities, and outsmart its opponents, the Israeli Air and Space Force has recently been moving away from preparations for interstate wars towards improving its potential to wage asymmetric conflicts, counter-insurgency campaigns and special operations.

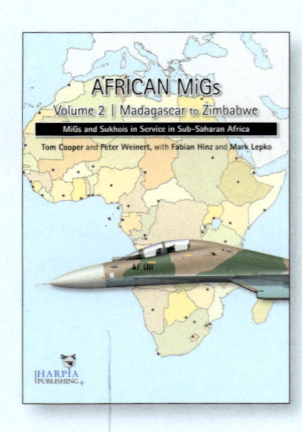

### African MiGs, Volume 2 | Madagascar to Zimbabwe,
### MiGs and Sukhois in Service in Sub-Saharan Africa
Tom Cooper and Peter Weinert, with Fabian Hinz and Mark Lepko
256 pages, 28 x 21 cm, softcover
35.95 Euro, ISBN 978-0-9825539-8-5

Completing an in-depth history of the deployment and operations of MiG and Sukhoi fighters (as well as their Chinese-built Chengdu and Shenyang variants) in sub-Saharan Africa, Volume 2 covers 11 additional air forces, from Madagascar to Zimbabwe.

This encyclopaedic account is so far the only one of its kind to provide detailed analysis of aerial conflicts including those waged between Ethiopia and Somalia, Tanzania and Uganda, and in Sudan.

---

**THE AVIATION BOOKS OF A DIFFERENT KIND**
UNIQUE TOPICS I IN-DEPTH RESEARCH I RARE PICTURES I HIGH PRINTING QUALITY

www.harpia-publishing.com

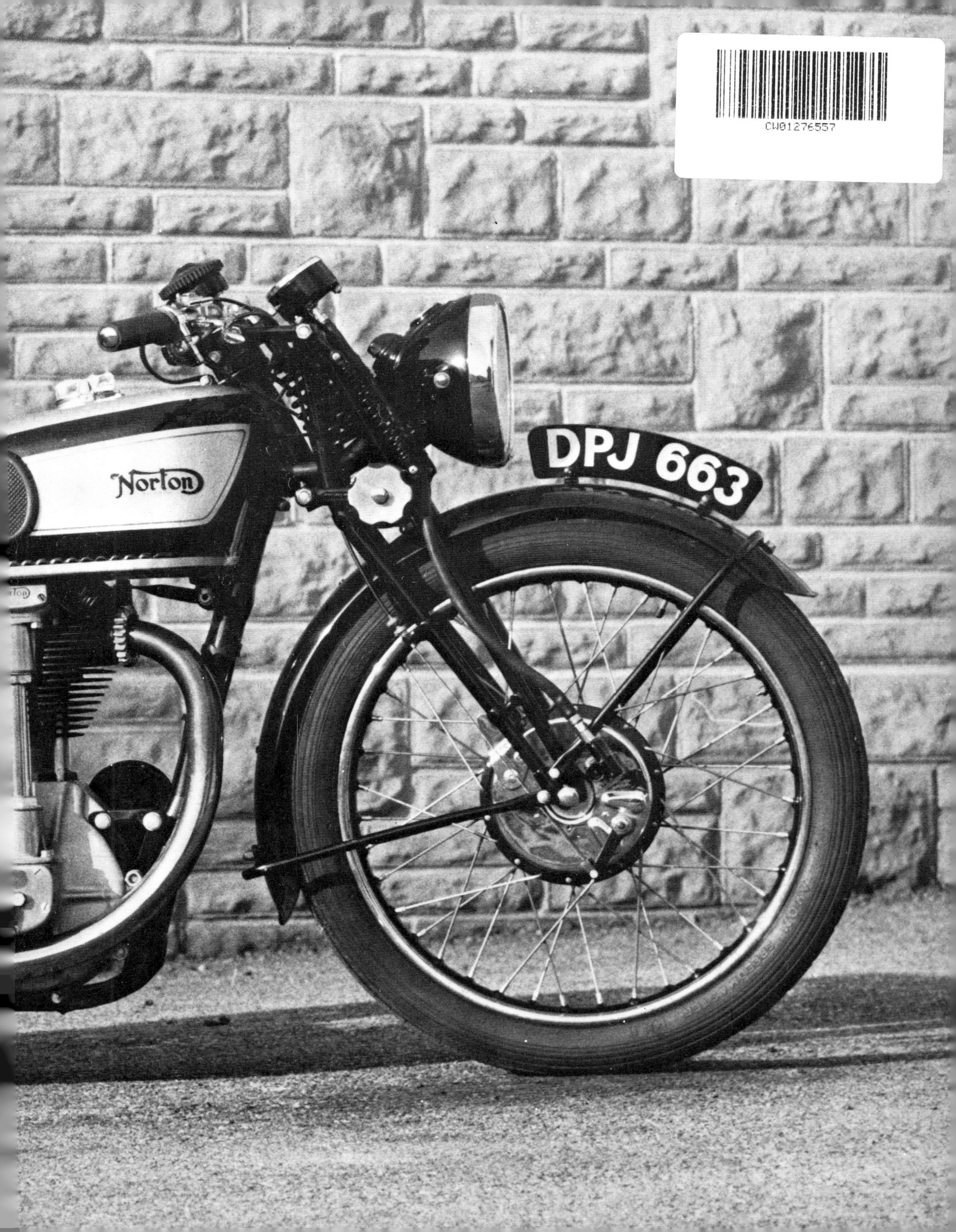
Norton
DPJ 663

# INTERNATIONAL NORTON

C. J. Ayton

## CONTENTS

| | |
|---|---|
| FOREWORD | 4 |
| HISTORY | 5 |
| EVOLUTION | 8 |
| SPECIFICATION | 13 |
| ROAD TESTS | 15 |
| OWNER'S VIEW | 21 |
| BUYING | 25 |
| CLUBS, SPECIALISTS & BOOKS | 27 |
| PHOTO GALLERY | 28 |

Foulis

Haynes

ISBN 0 85429 365 5

A FOULIS Motorcycling Book

First published 1985

© Haynes Publishing Group

All rights reserved. No part of this book may be reproduced or transmitted in any form or by any means, electronic or mechanical, including photocopying, recording or by any information storage or retrieval system, without written permission from the publisher.

Published by:
Haynes Publishing Group
Sparkford, Yeovil,
Somerset BA22 7JJ

Haynes Publications Inc.
861 Lawrence Drive, Newbury Park, California 91320, USA

British Library Cataloguing in Publication Data

Ayton, C.J.
  International Norton super profile. — (Foulis super profile series)
  1. Norton motorcycle
  I. Title
  629.2'275  TL448.N6

ISBN 0-85429-365-5

Library of Congress Catalog Card Number 85-060138

*Dust jacket design:* Rowland Smith
*Jacket colour illustration:* The 1937 International Norton of Les Thomas photographed by Andrew Morland
*Page Layout:* Mike King
*Photographs:* Andrew Morland
*Road Tests: The Motor Cycle,* and *Motor Cycling* courtesy of EMAP National Press Ltd
*Printed in England by:*
J.H. Haynes & Co Ltd

Titles in the *Super Profile* series

Ariel Square Four (F388)
BMW R69 & R69S (F387)
Brough Superior SS100 (F364)
BSA A7 & A10 (F446)
BSA Bantam (F333)
Honda CB750 sohc (F351)
Matchless G3L & G80 (F455)
MV Agusta America (F334)
Norton Commando (F335)
Sunbeam S7 & S8 (F363)
Triumph Thunderbird (F353)
Triumph Trident (F352)
Triumph Bonneville (F453)
KSS Velocette (F444)
Vincent Twins (F460)
AC/Ford/Shelby Cobra (F381)
Austin-Healey 'Frogeye' Sprite (F343)
Chevrolet Corvette (F432)
Ferrari 250GTO (F308)
Fiat X1/9 (F341)
Ford Cortina 1600E (F310)
Ford GT40 (F332)
Jaguar E-Type (F370)
Jaguar D-Type & XKSS (F371)
Jaguar Mk 2 Saloons (F307)
Jaguar SS90 & SS100 (F372)
Lancia Stratos (F340)
Lotus Elan (F330)
Lotus Seven (F385)
MGB (F305)
MG Midget & Austin-Healey Sprite (except 'Frogeye') (F344)
Mini Cooper (F445)
Morris Minor Series MM (F412)
Morris Minor & 1000 (ohv) (F331)
Porsche 911 Carrera (F311)
Rolls-Royce Corniche (F411)
Triumph Stag (F342)
Bell U-H1 (F437)
B29 Superfortress (F339)
Boeing 707 (F356)
Grumman F8F Bearcat (F447)
Harrier (F357)
Hawker Hunter (F448)
MIG 21 (F439)
Mosquito (F422)
Phantom II (F376)
P51 Mustang (F423)
Sea King (F377)
SEPECAT Jaguar (F438)
Super Etendard (F378)
Tiger Moth (F421)
Vulcan (F436)
Great Western Kings (F426)
Intercity 125 (F428)
V2 'Green Arrow' Class (F427)

# Super Profile

## FOREWORD

However many grands prix the Japanese go on to win, Nortons will not be forgotton. The name is part of racing history — more particularly, of Isle of Man racing history. It is for their racers that Nortons will be remembered. At times, it may have appeared that the road bikes suffered from the attention Bracebridge Street gave to TT replicas. In the 1930s roadsters bearing the name were noisy, old-fashioned and none-too-cheap. But worthy. Shamelessly, they coasted along on glory borrowed from the racers.

The situation was rather different in the case of the Internationals, subject of this profile. For a few years, soon after birth in 1932, Inters were in fact *racing* Nortons, detuned for the road. Strictures applying to lesser models in the '30s ranges cannot, in fairness, be levelled at the Models 30 and 40, for there appeared to be no intention on the part of management to market them other than as out-and-out sports bikes, with no pretensions to gentlemanly behaviour.

Perhaps — unknowing — Nortons were rather clever in their treatment of the Inter. A more go-ahead manufacturer might have improved it, and thereby fudged that precious link with the racers. As long as the International continued to be (mechanically) noisy, oily and chronically overgeared, kinship with the racers was irrefutable. Smooth out the ragged edges, make it more tractable, pleasant and traffic-amenable, and it would have lost much of its — the word has to be used — *charisma.* Ordinary chaps fulfilling a life's ambition to own an Inter thundered along on the new arterials of the '30s and imagined they were chasing Woods and Guthrie in the IoM. A quiet, civilised bike would not have done at all. On the other hand, a modicum of development might have been appreciated by Inter veterans who had fallen out of love with oil-sprayed knees (from that 'open' cambox), rattling tappets and — would you believe? — rather indifferent performance.

It would have required fine judgement for Nortons to trade off some part of that charisma for practicality. Unsurprisingly, no such judgement was made — the matter was probably given very little thought — and Inters, unchanged, rattled down through the years, steadily becoming more dated in comparison with the 'opposition' while acquiring immortailty and, lately, eyebrow-raising value.

An Inter was the Sheene or Roberts replica of its day. I owned an Inter, and even (confession time) lost my licence speeding in unsuitable circumstances on one. I wish I had an Inter now.

In compiling this book I would like to thank Les Thomas, Len Crane and John Frith for making their respective machines available for photography and for answering my many questions.

I thank too the respondents to the owner's view section, C.E. Allen and F.P. Heath, for their help. Additionally, I take an opportunity to apologise for (presumably) the strain of the interviews which, combined with a selfless determination to keep their voices in bell-like condition, so that I should miss no part of their reminiscences, caused both to imbibe several pints of brown liquid — cool, frothy and Burton-born in one case, scalding-hot and high on the tannin scale in the other — during the course of our conversations. It might be useful to medical science, if strictly beyond the bounds of this motorcycling book, were I able to point to an astounding difference in the general condition of these two enthusiasts, and attribute it, one way or the other, to their respective addictions (I exaggerate, Phil), which each has indulged for rather more than 50 years. However, the fact is that both appear to be in first-class nick and, unless they are sharing another elixer which the world should know about, I am inclined to ascribe their well-being to exposure over the years to the "cool breezes and thorough oxygenation" that *Ixion,* that masterful commentator, perceived long ago as exclusive benefits of motorcycling and, hence, prime reasons for a motorcyclist's abundant good health. Well, it's a thought.

Cyril Ayton

# Super Profile

# HISTORY

Nortons in their heyday enjoyed a reputation that transcended an antiquated factory, sometimes shaky finances and a production run that was, by (for example) BSA standards, neither large nor various. Enthusiasts revered — but usually did not buy — them. Ride-to-work men on humble two-strokes dreamed of them. In the 1950s even British women had heard of them (credit for this unique achievement belonging to the young Geoff Duke who, within months of first straddling a racing Norton, impressed motorcycle sport on the national consciousness in a way that was never to be repeated, even in Barry Sheene's palmiest days).

In motorcycling circles, both before and after the 1950s, Nortons achieved and maintained fame through racing successes that were relentlessly publicized in the specialist press. The instrument chosen for these successes, in the overwhelming majority of cases, was the classic single-cylinder engine with valve operation by overhead camshaft(s). In a history that began at the turn of the century and ended, so far as the manufacture in quantity of big-engined, 'conventional' motorcycles is concerned, 75 years later, the overhead-camshaft models were in production for rather less than half that time. But it was their achievements which gave the marque its enviable standing among contemporary manufacturers who, though often wealthier and better-selling, were unable to match the single-minded dedication to racing that was the hallmark of Norton Motors for three decades. The successes of the racing Norton are legion and deserve (and presumably will have) a separate account in this series. What is significant here is that during the first several years of their existence racing and roadster ohc Nortons were basically identical and shared the name of International (which was often, understandably, abbreviated to Inter).

Although the first ohc Norton to be given the Inter title was not made available to the public until 1932, its antecedents date back to before 1927. Anybody perusing Nortons' Isle of Man record may note Senior race victories in 1924 and 1926 and conclude, on a superficial reading, that the lapse in the intervening year was attributable as much to Alec Bennett's crash, and subsequent slowing, while leading on a Norton, as to Howard Davies' estimable handling of his winning HRD-JAP. TT Nortons at that time had pushrod-operated overhead-valve engines; the 1924 Senior was the first TT victory for the firm since Rem Fowler's outing in the original Tourist Trophy meeting of 1907. In the mid-20s, therefore, the ohv Nortons were seasoned and successful. On the face of it, there seemed to be little reason for change. But in 1926 Alec Bennett, the firm's number-one rider, disturbed Nortons' management by a runaway win in the Junior TT on a brand-new Velocette with an overhead-camshaft engine. Clearly his ohc mount was much faster than Jimmy Simpson's 'traditional' Big Port ohv AJS. It could only be a matter of performance difference between the two machines. Nobody, certainly not Bennett, would seriously claim to be 10 minutes 25 seconds faster than the dashing Simpson over $264\frac{1}{4}$ miles of the TT course.

In the Senior, Bennett's Norton slowed with clutch trouble, and he retired. It was left to Stanley Woods, having his first TT outing on a Norton, to save the reputation of the firm; he did so with a winning margin of four minutes over second man Walter Handley, on a vee-twin Rex Acme. It was a decisive victory. But to William Mansell, the director most concerned with Nortons' competition activities following the death of James Lansdowne Norton in 1925, the showing of the Junior-winning Velocette two days earlier had been more conclusive.

A talented designer, Walter Moore, had spent much time since 1924 in developing Pa Norton's overhead-valve engine to TT-fitness. He was in Douglas during the 1926 TT. It is interesting, and surely not entirely fanciful, to speculate that he discussed with Bill Mansell the outlook for Norton's continuing involvement in racing. Moore was a convert to having the camshaft on top of the head long before Velocette's Junior race foray. He had designed an overhead-camshaft layout in 1925 on hearing rumours (slow to materialise) that Sunbeams were to produce ohc engines. All his design work was done in his own time, he was to maintain later.

Early the following year the motorcycle press said that Moore's overhead-camshaft Norton was ready. It was not entirely a new engine. Crankcase, bottom-end assembly, barrel and piston were much as before, in the ohv models. Bore and stroke, at 79 x 100mm, were identical. The offside (timing side) had been altered to accommodate an enclosed vertical shaft taking drive from the main-shaft through a pair of bevels to a single camshaft set across the head in a separate box and operating the valves through two-piece rockers. Below the bottom bevel housing was Moore's 1925-designed oil

5

# Super Profile

pump of high capacity, with an external control to vary the amount of oil remaining in the crankcase and picked up by the return side of the pump.

The valves were closed by coil springs, following the pattern of the pushrod models. Ignition was provided by a rear-mounted magneto driven by chain from the left-hand end of the mainshaft. This, too, was an ohv precedent, as was siting the single exhaust pipe on the left.

The engine was mounted in a frame having a reinforced steering head and a steel forging joining the front down tube with the seat tube, to form a low-slung cradle. Previously, the Norton frame had been of diamond type, with the crankcase forming the connection between front and rear sections. Extra lateral stiffness was provided at the rear by a middle set of tubes arranged horizontally between the usual seat and chain stays and contributing, at their forward extremities, to a mounting for the freshly designed bottom-pivoted, foot-controlled, three-speed gearbox. It was a long, tall frame — tall because the 100mm-stroke engine, with cambox atop the head, was even loftier than its ohv forbears — and it became more renowned for steadiness at straightline speeds than for nimbleness in the turns.

The forks were of Webb pattern, introduced in 1925, complete with friction shock absorbers and a steering damper. The brakes, at 8in diameter, rivalled in size those fitted to Norton's grand-prix rivals, Rudge-Whitworth.

In the hands of Stanley Woods and Bennett the ohc Nortons dominated the 1927 Senior race in the Isle of Man. One, ridden by Woods, eventually succumbed to clutch failure after more than 150 miles at record speed; which left Bennett, a master tactician, to time his winning ride to come home eight minutes ahead of Jimmie Guthrie on a New Hudson.

Unbeatable speed in one machine, speed plus reliability in the other; it amounted to an unarguable demonstration of superiority for the ohc engine. It was this engine that was progenitor of the 1932 International; though there were, as will be made clear, a few significant changes made along the way.

For 1928 Nortons followed their policy of offering to the public production versions of the previous season's factory-restricted models. Thus the first ohc Nortons went on sale. They were little changed from 1927. The lower bevel box had been cleaned up a little, the shape of the oil tank altered. They were catalogued as the CS1, and sold at £89.

In TT practice in 1928 Joe Craig, then more notable as a Norton factory rider than for his work in the firm's test shop, where he assisted Walter Moore, appeared on a 350 ohc model. Its engine was a scaled-down version of the 500, fitted in a frame lightened by omission of the middle chain stays. Soon he was joined by other members of the team on similar machines. On race day not one of them finished. And the Seniors fared little better. Woods was the best-placed Norton man, at fifth. Craig retired after briefly getting into the lead on the third lap. A very competent rider (four times a class winner in the Ulster GP), he recognised his on-the-road limitations in the company of racing giants such as Woods, and Simpson, and Guthrie. When he retired in the 1928 Senior he gave up race-riding altogether. Nortons were soon to benefit from the undivided attentions in the test shop of the man who later earned the title — half humorous, wholly respectful — of 'Wizard of Waft.'

In 1929 the ohc 350 was sold as the CJ1 (Camshaft Junior). It was not a good year, in racing, for Nortons. There was a dismal showing in the TT, salt being rubbed into Norton's wounds by the crushing superiority shown by rival ohc designs from Velocette and AJS, in the Junior race. On the Continent the best result was a lone 500 GP win, by Tim Hunt. Boardroom spirits in Bracebridge Street were further depressed by Walter Moore's departure — defection, it was called — to work for NSU in Germany. His cammy engine might have been going through a sticky patch, but it was the only one fit for a racing motorcycle that Nortons had; and now Moore, the ingrate, was off to foreign parts and making clear that he would be designing a similar engine for his new employers. There was no question of preventing him, of invoking copyright protection on the CS1, for Moore was not slow to point out that the design had been evolved at home, in his own time.

But bad times are not uniformly black.

It was at this point that Craig showed his worth. Elevated to seniority on Moore's departure, he winkled out one Arthur Carroll from the 'design department' — in reality, a corner of the test shop where Craig passed his days — and took him to see Bill Mansell, by then Managing Director. It was agreed that Moore's design could stand improvement. Mansell said that Moore's work had been unduly influenced by Chater Lea, and that the design for the ohc Norton should have reflected more of a 'Velocette' approach. Arthur Carroll, promoted to Chief Draughtsman, went to work. The measure of his success is that thereafter the ohc Norton was known as the Carroll engine. This is reasonable, because it had a career lasting almost 30 years whereas the original, Moore engine existed for no more than three. However, both engines, retaining the long-established 79 x 100mm configuration, had the camshaft driven by a vertical shaft, with bevels top and bottom, on the offside; to say that Carroll's was a completely new design, as many have done, is to stretch the facts.

Carroll was influenced not merely by the Managing Director's opinions but by the more practical consideration of turning out a engine which would serve both in an out-and-out racer and in a roadster; as the CS1, of course, had done. It could not, therefore, be too radical. Among rival makes there was no design that better demonstrated fitness for this dual role than Velocette. (AJS was a possibility but the break with precedent, however brief, in changing to a *chain* -driven camshaft was unacceptable.)

So Carroll went for the Velocette look — beefed up a little, of course, for Nortons had none of the Goodman family's purist approach to engineering that demanded that structure echo purpose; Bracebridge Street tradition decreed plenty of inbuilt strength, with a margin allowed for unexpected stress and strain. If the result tended to be massive, and a trifle overweight, that was not seen as a drawback.

Carroll dispensed with Moore's drive shaft, reciprocating oil pump and the clean, cricket-bat-like exterior of the lower timing case. Instead, in authentic Velocette style, he had a centre shaft vertical drive with Oldham couplings, a gear-type oil pump, and an offside magneto-drive case, all working from a square timing box cast in to the side of the crankcase. The cambox, too, followed Velocette pattern in being vertically split with rockers poking through slots to operate exposed valve stems; and, just like the original, it worked well at the expense of an incurable weakness for leaking oil.

At this point we have arrived at a recognizably 'International' engine. It appeared in the showrooms, though not as an International (the CS1 being still the only ohc 500 on sale to the public), in the spring of 1931, following a so-so first year of racing, with factory backing, in 1930.

In 490cc form it had a left-hand exhaust pipe, as had all the previous Moore-designed engines. The 348cc CJ1 had a right-hand pipe; by the following year, and from then on, all the camshaft engines were thus equipped. The CS1's frame was of triple (more accurately, six) stay type, in contrast to the CJ1's conventional layout. Here, too, the 350 set the pattern for ensuing years for by 1932, when the International made its bow, the extra stays were part of history.

1931 was a great year for Norton's factory racers, with a shoal of wins at home and abroad. What more fitting than to celebrate with a new-name model?

# Super Profile

# EVOLUTION

The 1932 490 and 348 cc Internationals were, as indicated, TT replicas, equipped for the road.

In greater detail, their Carroll engines may be described thus ... A tall, well-ribbed crankcase, larger than that of the ohv models, carries the crankshaft in three ball bearings, two on the drive side, on of the timing side. The connecting rod runs on a caged roller big-end, with the crankpin pulled up against shoulders by nuts. The small-end has a plain bush; the flat-top piston, with valve cutaways and slipper skirt, has two compression rings, one scraper. The cast-iron cylinder is deeply spigoted into the crankcase mouth and retained by four long bolts screwed into the crankcase and passing up through the barrel and head into sleeved nuts, which are shouldered and internally threaded at their upper ends to support and retain the cambox by a further set of bolts.

The cambox, like the crankcase, is split vertically, on the longitudinal line, with a ball race in each half to support a single shaft on which is keyed the exhaust cam with, on the left (near side) of it, and pinned to it by roller, the cam for the inlet valve. A selection of holes to take the roller, in the circumference of the cams, allows for a variation in timing between the valves, while the bevel at the right (offside) end of the camshaft, meshing with the top bevel of the vertical driveshaft, has a similar vernier arrangement: all of which makes for relatively quick adjustment of valve timing, when required.

Rockers pivoting on spindles in plain bushes in the fore-and-aft extremities of the cambox halves take cam movement into the open, and to the valves through threaded adjusters.

In early Inters the valves had coil springs, CS1 fashion.

The vertical shaft, jointed top and bottom by Oldham couplings and supported by a pair of widely separated bearings, spins inside a chrome-plated tube bolted at its lower end to a box cast-in to the crankcase wall. It is this, so much more Velocette than CS1, that basically identifies a Carroll engine from the earlier design; and underlines the difference by carrying — also in Goodman fashion — the casing for the chain drive to the rear-mounted magneto.

In the box, together with the bevel gear driving the vertical shaft from the mainshaft, is a gear-type oil pump, cylindrically housed and pressed into a hole in the crankcase side. Oil ... and now I draw heavily on the clean-cut prose of an old maintenance manual ... is pumped from the tank, to the sump, and thence, by way of a tell-tale just to the rear of the vertical-shaft base, to the big-end bearing; to the rear wall of the cylinder; to the cambox; to the pressure release valve.

Oil is taken along the timing side mainshaft and through the flywheel and into the crankpin, the rear of the cylinder wall being fed via an adjustable screw in the end of the hollow rear crankcase bolt; correct adjustment of the adjuster is between a half to three-quarters of a turn from the fully open position, or until a faint smoke haze appears in the exhaust during acceleration. The cambox receives oil through the external pipe behind the vertical shaft tube. Early Inters rely on the supply dropping on to the cams; later models enjoy a more scientifically devised feed via the camshaft to the flanks of the cams.

In 1933 the pressure-release valve in the bevel chamber, previously non-adjustable, was replaced by an adjustable valve positoned at the rear of the crankcase, behind the magneto-chain cover; among other functions (such as, when at fault, contributing to the Inter's notorious weakness for allowing oil to drain into the crankcase!) the valve influences the supply, and pressure, of oil fed to the cambox. Small external pipes, with a threaded sleeve at one end and relying on a simple push fit at the other, transfer lubricant in a rather hit-or-miss manner from the cambox to the valve guides.

The engine looked, somehow, marvellously right, in a way that the Moore design, though full of merit, did not. More to the point, it performed well from the outset and was much admired throughout a long life by those who maintain that in engineering there is a concordance between looks and performance. This is a shaky proposition; but nobody would deny that the Inter makes a good case for its advocates.

In its first year the International was catalogued without lights. The intention was to emphasise its sporting, near racing character. The CS1/CJ1 line was there to cater for the man who had no ambitions to go racing but wanted to indulge in fast road work. The reception given to the Inter was so enthusiastic — and not merely from the racing fraternity — that Nortons were forced to think again. From 1932 the CS1, with ES2-size petrol tank, horizontal inlet and touring wheels, was obviously going to be overshadowed by its more expensive (for the 500s, in the order of £90 to £75) stablemate. Fortunately, the early catalogue, while picturing the Internationals without lighting equipment, listed a Lucas Magdyno as replacement for the standard ML magneto. Thereafter the Inter was projected as a fully equipped sports roadster, with a variety of aids to fast motorcycling available as optional extras, or replacements.

In 1932 the Inter's engine, sparked by ML magneto, was installed in a frame shortened and lowered following a change introduced in the similar CS1 frame during the previous year. The forks were of Norton manufacture, following years of loyalty to Webbs. It is said that a race crash which caused a disturbingly easy warping of the Webbs precipitated the change; this may be so but it is clear that Nortons themselves were anxious to take over as much work in design and manufacture as possible, as a way of reducing costs. It was in 1931 that the Roadholder tag was first used. The Sturmey-Archer gearbox was a four-speeder with foot control and — in non-racing form — a kickstarter. It followed the pattern of the one fitted to the 1931 racers, with close ratios. The change lever operated via a positive-stop mechanism enclosed in a pressed-steel case and tacked on above the box. Working through external rods, it gave a long movement that with age, and increasing wear at the clevis pins in the rods, became even longer, and more sloppy. The gearbox however, was virtually unbreakable.

The wheels were quickly detachable and shod with (in later terminology) a 3.00 x 21in ribbed tyre at the front and a 3.25 x 20in block-pattern at the rear. The qd fitting and brakes were of Carroll design, and Norton manufacture, the former following the usual layout of three studs to hold the hubs, by their flanges, to the brakes. The brakes, on the near side in both wheels, measuured 7in x 1¼in, with shoes of cast-alloy mounted on individual anchor posts. Road-test reports of the day praised Inter braking power, and spoke of halts in under 30ft from 30 mph. Owners have been puzzled, not to say sceptical, about these claims down the years. The front brake, especially, while adequately large in diameter, was a lightweight pressing more akin to a cocoa tin. (The description is not mine. It was offered by someone who, fifty years on, vividly recalled moments of anguish in attempting to slow the progress of a 100 mph Inter in the early 30s). The front fork, Nortons' own, as previously mentioned, was a trifle narrower than those fitted to the ohv/sv models. The mudguards were of skimpy section on tubular stays that, in the case of the one ahead of the front fork, was of extended U-form and taken over, and bolted to, the top of the mudguard: a sporting fashion of the days that managed also to be both neater and stronger than the dual-stay arrangement favoured for the lower end of the range. The long, narrow fuel tank, finished either in race style, with black lining extending front to rear on a silver base, or with lined panels on chrome, was decorated with the chunky George Dance kneegrips, named after the great hill-climb specialist, who had devised them as an additional way of glueing himself to a speeding Sunbeam. An André steering damper was anchored to the tank top.

Exhaust silencing — to be a preoccupation of Nortons through the 30s — was entrusted in the first year to a rather shapely canister ending in a fishtail. Petrol was fed to an Amal TT carburettor via flexible pipes fitted with racer-style lever taps.

When bought for racing, usually without lights, the International could be fitted with a nearside filler for the oil tank. The factory's claim was: 'In every single respect they [the Inters] are identical to those which have been so successful in every road race in 1931'. Prices were £90 for the 490cc Model 30 and £82 10s for the 348cc Model 40. The CS1 and its 350 lookalike, the CJ1, with the ohv/sv cycle parts, sold at £79 10s and £72 respectively.

Once launched, the International(s) went through the 1930s largely unaltered. Certainly, few changes were made to the engine, and at the end of the decade the running gear remained, visually at least, much as it had been in 1932.

In 1933 check springs (an earlier race fitting) were attached to the front-fork links and the intake side of the cylinder was redesigned for appreciable downdraught. Prices remained at 1932 levels. Sales were none too buoyant. This was not unexpected. The International was, after all, something of a flagship for the range and priced a little high for the average motorcyclist.

The following year, transmission came in for attention. On the gearbox the positive-stop mechanism was improved, and hidden by a smaller, neater cover. The clutch was changed. In previous years Sturmey-designed, with Ferodo inserts and six-spring operation, it had a cush-drive arrangement in the sprocket. Although it worked well enough, manufacturing costs were high. The trend, in any case, was to more completely in-house production. The replacement Norton clutch, with three springs and rubber shock absorbers, was so efficient that it continued without major modification until long after the war. As the new clutch was introduced, so the face-cam shock absorber on the mainshaft was abandoned. The primary case, while remaining outwardly much as before, was redesigned internally to incorporate a rubber band as a seal between the halves of the case, compressed on tightening a single nut. Simple and effective, this too was to endure throughout the International's life (and was only replaced, on the ohv machines, twins and singles, after Nortons passed into AMC ownership in the 1950s). The front hub lost its qd facility. This was not a great loss. It had been simpler and quicker, in

9

# Super Profile

any case, to ignore the qd bolts and remove the wheel by slackening the spindle nuts. The hub and brake drum (now on the right) were modified to the narrow, one-piece construction featured on works racers in earlier years. With stiffening provided by the spoke flange around the drum, the brake showed some improvement, with less belling-out of the drum on heating-up during use.

A further minor, internal, improvement for 1934 was the fitting of a sludge trap in the crankcase. More obvious was a new T-shaped Lucas battery, fitted when lighting equipment was specified. The cylinder head could be obtained in light-alloy, at an extra charge of £3 10s 6d.

In 1935 gearbox manufacture was taken over by Nortons, with help from Burmans, as Sturmey-Archer withdrew from their suppliers role to concentrate on production of the new Raleigh three-wheeler. This was the year when the distinctive George Dance kneegrips gave way to ½in-thick grips, and one of the periodic rethinks in the design department led to adoption of a barrel silencer incorporating spiral baffles. Coil springs at the valves were replaced by racer-style — more reliable — hairpins. Both Models 30 and 40 could be bought as out-and-out racers having hand-built engines with light-alloy head, straight-through exhaust pipe, close-ratio gearbox and 4½ gallon petrol tank.

The following year, 1936, the hairpins were modified to permit rotation of the valves. The front section of the engine cradle was rounded, and raised, to improve the minimal ground clearance, and the anchor for the André steering damper moved from the tank to the steering column. When head and barrel in light-alloy were specified, the additional charge was £14.

In 1938 Nortons' plunger rear springing, based on that used on the previous year's works machines, was made available as a £15 extra. While conferring some welcome comfort to the hard-riding owner, the new layout effectively spoilt the symmetry, and strength, of the solid frame. An unwelcome phenomenon from that time on was seat-tube breakage. With rear springing, the rear wheel lost its qd fittings. Other changes included a smoother look for the magneto chaincase cover and, more controversially, a new silencer of flattened aspect ending in two small-bore pipes, one above the other. Known at the works as the 'cow's udder' silencer, it was claimed to be supremely efficient. It was also a mistake, on two counts. Full of spiral baffling and perforated tubes, it reduced an Inter's exhaust boom to an asthmatic snuffle which emphasised the rattle of exposed tappets running at a generous 10 and 20 thou clearance. And its looks, of course, were an unmitigated disaster. Self-respecting Inter men in 1938 had little choice but to find extra money, to buy a Brooklands can. By 1939 the 'cow's udder' had been replaced by a conventional single-exit barrel silencer.

In 1939, with world war threatening, an International to full sports specification was a very different proposition from the standard model. Sports as a description is hardly adequate; these were virtually full-blown racers to the standard of, say, the 1936 works machines used by the likes of Frith and Daniell. In 1939 an International for racing, ordered from a rider-agent, would be fitted with plunger springing (as an individual item now priced at £7 10s), straight-through pipe, or megaphone, conical hubs, bolt-through tanks — with the oil container's filler on the nearside — Elektron crankcase and large, square-finned cylinder head. No ordinary Inter, this ... The price, too, was far from ordinary, at around £125.

From the perspective of the 1980s such figures may appear grotesquely low. They take on significance when it is realised that reasonable family cars — the Montegos and Cavaliers of their day — then cost no more than £140. More importantly, in the 1930s, a period of financial stability — sometimes financial depression — for manufacturers and consumers alike, prices remained constant, indeed often dropped, through the decade. Thus a 500 Inter in standard trim began, in 1932, at approximately £90 and ended its pre-war life within a £ or two of that figure. This, alone, was reason enough for tiny sales during years when sporting Ariels and BSAs were available at two-thirds of an International's price. The difference is quoted as a percentage because, try as one may, it is difficult nowadays to imagine oneself living in a world where petrol cost no more than 5p a gallon and £20–£30 represented the difference, in 1980s terms, between a 650 Honda and a Ducati desmo 900!

Production of civilian motorcycles ceased in 1940. This was the year when the split was planned to take place between Inter as road bike and Inter as racer: the latter to be known as the Manx, when it would have been equipped with the telescopic front fork pioneered by the factory racers in 1938, and a 499cc engine. The telescopic fork was to be available as an extra on the roadster, and there was talk of a new end cover to integrate selector mechanism and gearbox proper. In the event, these developments had to wait six years.

Internationals did not reappear until 1947. When they did, it was in strictly sports-roadster form. From this time on the racing Norton became the specialist Manx model, as envisaged for 1940. The C models were dropped. The Inter had, as standard, plunger springing and a telescopic Roadholder fork with one-way damping. The rear plungers had been tidied up, and lightened, from pre-war style, and were also featured on the top ohv model, the ES2. The engine was

10

firmly back to all-iron specification, under a tank of pre-war shape but uniformly finished in chrome, with panelling, and deprived of those once-distinctive wavy-edge soldered seams. The André steering damper had gone too. Apart from its racy looks, the André's chief merit had been that, mounted above the steering head, it operated free of the grease that usually filtered down from head bearings into the leaves of the typical under-head damper. Now the Inter was fitted with an ordinary damper, controlled by a suitably ordinary disc on the steering column. The small rubber saddle — in its 1930s life not, perhaps, universally admired but, again, a mark of the special attention Bracebridge Street had devoted to the Inter — was no more. In its place was a mundane, but possibly more comfortable, fabric Terry's. Another downmarket move was the use of sensibly wide mudguards. The rear one, especially, struck a dull note in the way it was carried farther down at the back, in marked contrast to the skimpy, yet elegant, pre-war guard (that must, admittedly, have sent a spume of rainwater over any following vehicle in inclement weather!).

The bars were wider and higher than before. The Inter man now rode a little taller in the saddle than his 30s counterpart. It was, though, still a very good riding position, with the incomparably narrow tank and lengthy footrest hangers giving near-perfect control.

As a competition motorcycle, the Inter's days were almost over. A brief swansong not devoid of glory occurred in the Clubman's TT races, first included in the TT programme in 1947. Even in these races, however, intended primarily as an Island baptism for clubmen new to racing, the prizes went to those who — quite reasonably — were canny enough to avail themselves of the advantages offered in the small print of the regulations. Thus it was that both Eric Briggs and Denis Parkinson, winners of Senior and Junior Clubman's respectively, rode 1939 Inters. They reasoned, accurately, that the very complete, mainly light-alloy, engine specification of the old model, with its greater tolerance of 1947 70-octane petrol, was a very good trade-off against the superior tele forks of the brand new, all-iron (and definitely slower) post-war version.

Later, Inters of the 1940s became available to special order with a light-alloy engine and bolt-through fuel tank, but with nothing else of the near-racer equipment that had been on offer in the 30s. However outdated the International was becoming in the post-war world of Tiger 100s and Gold Star BSAs, it proved good enough, in plunger-frame form, to be the chosen mount of five Clubman's TT winners, including the 26-year-old Geoff Duke, in 1949.

From 1947 to 1953 nothing occurred to disturb the Inter's sales life; certainly nothing in the way of improvements. No whisper of valve-spring enclosure was heard; no rumour of another camshaft, for double-knocker action. Annual notes on modifications, sometimes far-reaching, to the remainder of the range, usually concluded in this sort of manner: 'The ohc Models 30 and 40 continue unchanged'. Occasionally, as forelock-touching to a game old warhorse, there might be some fairly meaningless line about '— the race-bred cammy models beloved of the hard-riding enthusiast'.

In 1953, however, the Inter was given a kiss of life. The engine was installed in the new twin-loop Featherbed frame. Not the iron engine, but one with light-alloy head and barrel. The Featherbed frame, first used for works racers in 1950, then with the Dominator twin in 1952, is too familiar, too much a part of motorcycling history, to merit detailed description here. What it did for the Inter was to give the venerable banger a superb send-off, with a final Clubman's win in 1953, into oblivion.

Fitted with new-style gearbox (the old one laid horizontal and in a smaller casing) having a short, precise gear-change movement, and single-side brakes in 19in wheels, the Inter now had a frame that, for the first time, outperformed the engine. Previously the engine, particularly in the pre-war solid frame but even later, when part of the 'Garden Gate' springer, had been powerful and vibratory enough — especially on open pipe — to highlight steering and other deficiencies. Strong men had been lifted off racing Inters, after a punishing race, as numbed and enfeebled caricatures of their vigorous selves. This did not happen in the Featherbed era. Now, with the traditional problem of an over-effective silencer — in the case of the Featherbed, an unlovely pear-shaped device — fighting valve overlap, the Inter could appear as definitely short of power.

Production continued at a very low ebb while the price, contrariwise, maintained a steadily rising path, from £246 (for the 500) in 1953 to just over £300 in late 1957. This reflected the early stirring of inflation, that now all too familiar background to UK life and times — plus, perhaps, a management policy calculated to depress incipient demand for a costly-to-produce — maybe downright *uneconomical* to produce — motorcycle.

What is quite clear is that price increases were not accounted

# Super Profile

for by an accompanying run of improvements to the product. There were very few of these. In 1955 the rear sub-frame was welded to the main frame, instead of being bolted on, and the brakes (the front one having been increased to 8in diameter in the first Featherbed year) were enclosed in full-width light-alloy hubs. And that is about all. By 1956-57 the Inter – when it was mentioned at all in Nortons' plans for the coming year – had slipped from the 'no change' category to a chilly 'to special order'. In 1958 perhaps 12 were made, with rather flashy chrome-plated panels on the petrol tank. They were the last and the brightest – if not the most memorable – of a line of fabled motorcycles. They had first appeared 14 years after the end of the first world war, and they died 14 years after the second. There is almost certainly no significance in the fact ....

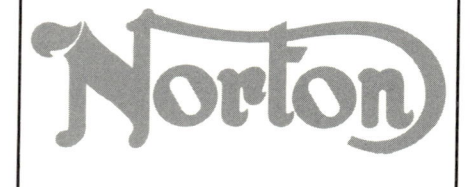

# SPECIFICATION

| | | |
|---|---|---|
| Model | 30 | 40 |
| Bore and stroke (mm) | 79 x 100 | 71 x 88 |
| Cubic capacity (cc) | 490 | 348 |
| Compression ratio | 7.23:1 | 7.33:1 |
| Bhp | 29½ | 24½ |
| Ignition timing  BTDC | 42½° | 42½° |
| Valve timing | | |
| Inlet opens BTDC | 47½° | 47½° |
| Inlet closes ABDC | 70° | 70° |
| Exhaust opens BBDC | 85° | 85° |
| Exhaust closes ATDC | 42½° | 42½° |
| Tappet clearance (in) | | |
| Inlet | 0.010 | 0.010 |
| Exhaust | 0.020 | 0.020 |
| Carburettor | Amal TT | Amal TT |
| Choke (in) | 1 5/32 | 1 3/32 |
| Main jet | 310 | 260 |
| Gear ratios | | |
| 4th | 4.64:1 | 5.15:1 |
| 3rd | 5.1:1 | 5.66:1 |
| 2nd | 6.18:1 | 6.85:1 |
| 1st | 10.8:1 | 12:1 |
| Suspension | | |
| Front | Girders (1932-39) Telescopic (1947-58) | Girders (1932-39) Telescopic (1947-58) |
| Rear | Solid (1932-39; plunger optional '38, '39) Plunger (1947-52) Pivot-fork (1953-58) | Solid (1932-39; plunger optional '38, '39) Plunger (1947-52) Pivot-fork (1953-58) |

| | | |
|---|---|---|
| **Brakes (in)** | 7 x 1¼ front and rear (1932-52) | 7 x 1¼ front and rear (1932-52) |
| | 8 x 1¼ front, 7 x 1¼ rear (1953-58) | 8 x 1¼ front, 7 x 1¼ rear (1953-58) |
| **Fuel tank capacity (gal)** | 3¾ | 3¾ |
| **Oil tank capacity (pt)** | 6; 7 from 1953 | 6; 7 from 1953 |
| **Dimensions (in)** | | |
|    Wheelbase | 54½ | 54½ |
|    Ground clearance | 4; 5½ from 1953 | 4; 5½ from 1953 |
|    Seat height | 28; 30 from 1953 | 28; 30 from 1953 |
|    Overall width | 29; 27 from 1953 | 29; 27 from 1953 |
|    Weight (lb) | 380 approx; 420 from 1953 | 380 approx; 420 from 1953 |

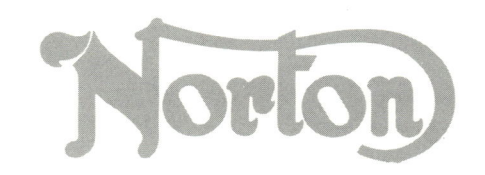

# Super Profile

MotorCycling SPORTS MODEL ROAD TESTS   11

The 490 c.c. o.h.c. Model 30

# NORTON "INTERNATIONAL"

Impressions of the Fully-equipped Version of a World-famous Racing Machine

## ROAD TESTS

FULLY equipped replica of a road-racing layout which has well-nigh dominated the circuits of the world since the late summer of 1930, the 490 c.c. Model 30 "International" Norton is justly regarded as the ultimate in single-cylinder performance.

Not only in the matter of speed has this sturdy bevel-driven overhead-camshaft engine commanded respect—it possesses a reputation, underlined by continual success, for outstanding reliability in all conditions of racing. Yet all this has been achieved without resort to a freakish design.

Within the confines of a 79-mm. bore and 100-mm. stroke the "International" possesses a measure of urge which has brought envy and despair to many would-be copyists. If the foregoing were all that could be credited to the Norton it would be sufficient cause for proud boasting—but super engines demand equally high standards of hairline steering and roadholding—yet another feature of the famous Bracebridge Street products.

Remembering these facts brought a keen sense of anticipation when we took over an example of the latest "International" for test. Here was a specimen of race breeding in the true sense of that much-abused term. This was the machine which set a standard in high-speed handling, complete with the recently developed "Roadholder" forks and the rear springing incorporating the crystallized experience of first-class racing men.

Once astride the "International" there can be no doubting its ancestry: the rider is poised above the job and footrests are set to give that braced, taut position so necessary in high-speed road work. Yet the 28¾-in. saddle height will permit even a five and a half footer to place a toe on the ground without effort. The bars are adjustable for height and angle to reasonable limits, the gear-change lever can be operated without removing the foot entirely from its rest and the rear brake pedal is correctly set with an adjustable stop.

Following a short experience with the particular machine on test, starting became a surprisingly easy matter. With a cold engine it was advisable to put the model onto its central stand so that a hand over the air intake could accompany the necessary swinging kick. Failure to set the ignition control at half-retard would bring a hefty reminder, whilst care had to be taken

*(Above) On its own stamping ground, taking a fast curve while trying out the Norton on the T.T. course.*

*Apart from its pictorial attraction, this view gives an excellent impression of the businesslike appearance of the Norton "International."*

to avoid overflooding the downdraught T.T.-type carburetter. The air control could be practically forgotten in the warm weather which accompanied the testing period.

Some clutch drag was experienced, however, and engagement of bottom gear was liable to produce a decided "clonk," although once on the move no further trouble occurred and there was no tendency to "creep" during traffic halts with the clutch held out.

In view of the standard high bottom gear (10.8 to 1) it was, perhaps, just as well that the clutch was more than up to its job, as despite frequent trips through heavy traffic no untoward slipping was evidenced.

Changing from bottom to second gear (6.18 to 1) demanded intelligent use of the clutch to avoid transmission snatch, for there is an appreciable difference in ratio. Nor is slow marching in the 4.64 top gear a practice to be recommended on a machine

Reprinted from the 3rd July 1947 issue of Motor Cycling.

12   MOTOR CYCLING SPORTS MODEL ROAD TESTS

so obviously suited to hard and fast motoring, but it was easily possible to dawdle at 22 to 23 m.p.h. with the ignition one-third retarded before a drop into third was indicated.

With T.T. coverage requiring the tester's presence in the Isle of Man during temporary ownership, what better place to assess the abilities of this thoroughbred road-burner? Accordingly HOE 445 became a very useful means of locomotion, more than capable of making up for the usual delay when a tired tester wished to reach distant parts of the course to witness early morning practising!

It was selected without hesitation as the means for transporting *Motor Cycling's* Junior T.T. pictures, etc., from Liverpool to London—a 205-mile trip accomplished with an ease which almost amounted to scorn. Incidentally, on this longish trip fuel consumption worked out at nearly 70 m.p.g. despite lengthy periods of 75 m.p.h. cruising on the open stretches.

*(Above)* The nearside of the machine shows how compactly everything about it fits into place. It is, in every sense, a mount to make the enthusiast's mouth water. The price, equipped as shown, is £252. 2s. 0d. including purchase tax.

*(Right)* The wonderful 490 c.c. o.h.c. engine developed from experience gained in road races all over the world.

**TESTER'S ROAD REPORT**
MODEL 1947 490 c.c. "INTERNATIONAL" NORTON

**Maximum Speeds in:—**

| | | | Time from Standing Start |
|---|---|---|---|
| Top Gear (Ratio 4.64 to 1) | 97 m.p.h. | 5782 r.p.m. | 44⅘ secs. |
| Third Gear (Ratio 5.1 to 1) | 91 m.p.h. | 5962 r.p.m. | 29⅘ secs. |
| Second Gear (Ratio 6.18 to 1) | 83 m.p.h. | 6590 r.p.m. | 20 secs. |

**Speeds over measured Quarter Mile:—**
Flying Start 94.71 m.p.h.   Standing Start 56.01 m.p.h.

**Braking Figures On** WET TARRED **Surface, from 30 m.p.h.:—**
Both Brakes 31 ft.   Front Brake 40 ft.   Rear Brake 56 ft.

**Fuel Consumption:—** ALL IN 58 m.p.g.

**Oil Consumption:—** 1360 m.p.g. (CASTROL "R")

**WEIGHT:—** 390 LBS. APPROX.

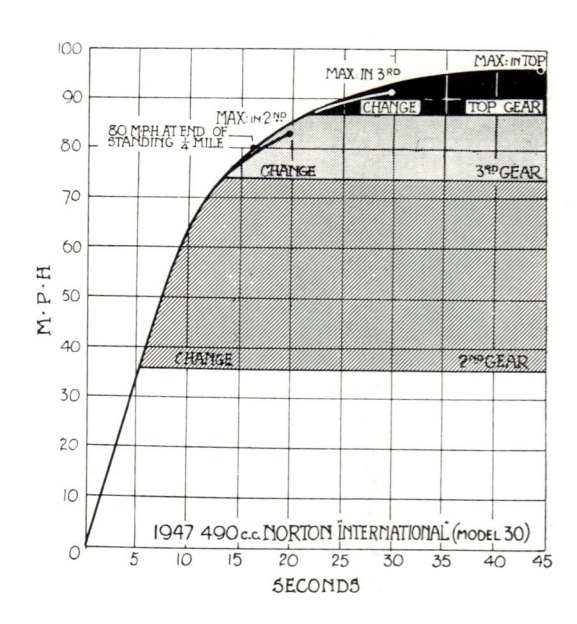

1947 490 c.c. NORTON INTERNATIONAL (MODEL 30)

## MotorCycling SPORTS MODEL ROAD TESTS

Vibration was just noticeable when pulling hard between 58-60 m.p.h. and there was a tendency for the 3¾-gallon fuel tank to "drum" at very high speeds—especially when the level was somewhat low. This criticism, however, was offset to a large degree by the dynamo-like smoothness of power delivery at abnormally high cruising speeds. At a maintained 70 or 75 m.p.h. on the main trunk routes there was scarcely a tremor to denote the activity of a healthy motor and it would hold this near half-throttle gait without effort.

With so much power available, high averages become a routine affair—aided by acceleration which brings a 75 m.p.h. reading from a 40 m.p.h. dawdle in a matter of 6.4 seconds. With three top ratios ideally close, the "International" simply asks to be driven by the man who understands and appreciates full use of such a gearbox.

Braking was adequate for all ordinary conditions of fast travel over main and country roads, but a little more "bite" on the front anchor would have been appreciated. There was a decided "sponginess" to this control—yet the full braking figure of 31 feet at 30 m.p.h. on a wet tarred surface was very good for a machine scaling 390 pounds.

Unusual on a machine of this type, yet a point worthy of mention, is the extent of the mudguarding whereby the front blade is carried low, enabling short rides to be tackled over wet roads without need for waders. Even long, fast runs under such

*(Above) Steering to a hairline is second nature to the Model 30—another feature developed in a long series of T.T. successes.*

The new Lucas head lamp, of 8-inch diameter, enabled speeds in the region of 60-65 m.p.h. to be maintained during the dark hours.

A slight oil leak from the bottom bevel housing caused a small smear to appear on the exhaust pipe but, generally speaking, the unit retained its lubricant well and a check over of the offending nuts following the initial 500 miles minimized the trouble considerably. Here it should be noted that the standard and recommended oil is Castrol "R"—somewhat difficult to obtain in these austerity days.

Mechanical noise was much in evidence until the engine was fully warmed up—it could hardly be otherwise with exposed tappets set at 10 and 20 "thou" cold clearance, but after two or three miles it diminished until, at speeds above 45 m.p.h. with a warm unit, there was a just-discernible tapping.

conditions brought surprisingly little backwash and the engine unit remained free from mud.

During the first 200 miles the rear springing felt "hard" in action, a trait which is quite in order, for with nearly 800 miles recorded it was doing its job splendidly and roadmenders' vicious cross-gullies could be tackled without grip-easing. No comment is needed on the telescopic "Roadholder" forks—they did their job with an unobtrusive efficiency which earned respect.

Maintenance and accessibility brought no unexpected problems, although such matters hardly attain paramount importance on such a machine as this. The provision of a very reasonable tool kit with the triangular seat stay container, in conjunction with a new and simply worded construction book, meant that every "rider's job" could be tackled with confidence.

There is little need to dwell upon the finish and appearance of this latest "International." It looks right and every hard rider, whatever his ultimate choice, will inevitably harbour a covetous regard for that impressively deep tank, with its silver, red and black motif. It is a motorcycle which offers vivid performance with a standard of safe handling difficult to express in words.

*(Right) One of our testers whips the Norton past "The Highlander," whilst en route to Crosby.*

### BRIEF SPECIFICATION

**Engine:** Single-cylinder; 79 mm. bore by 100 mm. stroke=490 c.c.; compression ratio 7.12 to 1; bevel driven overhead camshaft with valves operated by hairpin springs; dry-sump lubrication; crankshaft carried in one ball and one roller bearing on drive side and ball bearing on timing side; triple row roller big-end bearing with light-alloy cage; Amal T.T. 36 type carburetter, 1 5/32-in. bore; Lucas Magdyno ignition; large-capacity silencer with fishtail exit.

**Transmission:** Four-speed gearbox with positive-stop foot control; solo ratios, 4.64, 5.1, 6.18 and 10.8 to 1; sidecar ratios, 5.16, 5.67, 6.85 and 12.02 to 1; primary chain ½ in. by .305 in., running in oil bath; five-plate clutch with Ferodo inserts and incorporating vane-type shock absorber; rear chain ⅝ in. by ¼ in.

**Frame:** Full cradle type incorporating Norton plunger springing to rear wheel; central spring-up stand; integral lugs for pillion rests.

**Front Forks:** Norton "Roadholder" telescopic, with automatically controlled hydraulic damping and built-in lamp brackets.

**Wheels:** Fitted with Dunlop ribbed 3.00-in. by 20-in. front and Dunlop Universal 3.25-in. by 20-in. rear; one security bolt per wheel; brakes fitted with 7-in. by 1¼-in. shoes; finger adjustment.

**Tanks:** All welded steel petrol tank, capacity 3¾ gallons, incorporating built-in rubber kneegrips; saddle tube fitting oil tank, 6 pints capacity.

**Dimensions:** Wheelbase, 54¾ in.; overall length, 85 in.; overall width, 30 in.; saddle height, 28½ in.

**Weight:** Approximately 390 lb., fully equipped.

**Finish:** Chromium-plated tank with matt silver panelling lined in black and red; wheel rims and oil tank chromium with black and red lining; frame, mudguards and usual accessories in black.

**Equipment:** Lucas 6v. Magdyno lighting with automatic voltage control; electric horn; 8-in. head lamp; Smiths rear-wheel-driven speedometer, flush mounted in top fork bridge and internally illuminated.

**Price:** £247 0s. 4d. (including £52 10s. 4d. purchase tax), plus £4 (plus £1 1s. 8d. p.t.) for 120 m.p.h. trip speedometer.

**Tax:** £3 15s. 0d. per annum (£1 1s. 8d. per quarter).

**Makers:** Norton Motors Ltd., Bracebridge Street, Birmingham, 6.

# Road Tests of 1935 Models

## THE 490 c.c. o.h.v. NORTON

### A Mount which Justifies a Fine Reputation

*(Top, left) A handsome, speedy looking mount, the C.S.1 Norton is comfortable to ride. (Above) The "engine-room" of the machine, clearly showing its relationship to the world's most famous racing motorcycle. (Right) Great attention has been given to ease of control, the steering being typically race-bred, and the brakes exceptionally good, as witness the sensible pedal shown.*

WELL is the Norton called by its makers "The Roadholder." The C.S.1 model, which is the subject of this test, has as a motor the celebrated 490 c.c. overhead camshaft engine, in a form suitable for fast touring and general road work. In consequence, it is almost superfluous to say it had a fine performance, and was capable of putting up high average speeds.

### Steering

Excellent though the performance of this splendid unit undoubtedly was, it is none the less true to say that the first and most lasting impression which the machine made was in respect of its steering and brakes. The navigation in general was delightful. The machine could be taken into bends at speeds which, even in these days of highly developed design, are truly remarkable, to say the least. Even when flat out the use of the steering damper was quite unnecessary.

Many people are apt to think of the camshaft Norton as being a big machine as well as a powerful one. It is, in point of fact, particularly compact and of such moderate weight, compared, at any rate, with many other machines of the same cylinder capacity, that until one has had the opportunity of opening the taps, one might be excused for judging it to be a "350," so handy is it with its controls and steering. This is high praise, but fully merited. Moreover the convenience in handling does not have to be paid for by any sacrifice in comfort or general road worthiness.

The machine held the road splendidly and was particularly free from any tendency to pitch or bucket on poor surfaces. It was a mount which asked to be driven, and driven fast, all day long.

To complete the confidence which these qualities quickly engender in the rider, there is a pair of really "super" brakes. It is not often that it is possible to say that the two brakes on a machine are of equal excellence, but this is emphatically the case of the Norton. The gentlest of pressure either on handlebar lever or pedal produced instantaneous and rapid deceleration, the quickness of which was at first quite difficult to appreciate owing to the complete absence of any effect which it had on the steering and handling generally.

*August 14, 1935.*       MOTOR CYCLING       551

# MODEL C.S.1

## Brief Specification

**Engine:** Norton single-cylinder, bore 79 mm., stroke 100 mm., 490 c.c. Overhead valves and camshaft, driven by vertical shaft and bevel gears, single-port exhaust system with special Norton tubular type silencer, dry sump lubrication by gear pumps, pressure feed to bearings and piston, valve guide lubrication incorporated, separate oil tank. Amal carburetter with twist grip throttle control. Compression ratio 6½ to 1.

**Gearbox:** Norton four-speed. Solo ratios 4.44, 5.37, 7.85 and 13.2 to 1. Positive stop foot control (hand control optional), multi-plate clutch incorporating vane-type rubber block transmission shock absorber.

**Transmission:** Renold chains, front enclosed in oil bath case with inspection cover, rear covered by guard with extension to protect lower run.

**Frame:** Cradle type, adjustable foot rests and handlebars with special flexible mounting. Detachable rear mudguard, spring-up rear stand, prop stand and usual type front stand. Norton front forks with rebound springs and hand adjustable shock absorbers and steering damper.

**Brakes:** Internal expanding, 7 ins. in diameter, 1¼ ins. wide.

**Wheels:** Quickly detachable and interchangeable Magna pattern hubs, chromium-plated rims. Tyres 26 ins. by 3.25 ins.

**Petrol Tank:** Approximately 2 gallons capacity, chromium-plated and fitted with knee grips.

**Equipment:** Flexible top saddle, all-metal tool box with lock, complete tool kit.

**Dimensions:** Overall length, 85 ins.; overall height, 37½ ins.; overall width, 30 ins.; wheelbase 54½ ins.; ground clearance, 4¼ ins.

**Weight:** Approximately 354 lb.

**Price:** £75.

**Extras:** Lucas Magdyno lighting set, solo £5 10s.; stop light, 5s.; tank instrument panel, 10s.; Lucas "Altette" horn, £1 5s. 6d.; Smith Trip speedometer, 120 m.p.h., £2 16s.; oversize tyres, 26 ins. by 3.5 ins., 12s. 6d.; 27 ins. by 4 ins., 17s.; 3-gallon petrol tank, £1 10s.; Petroflex oil and petrol pipes, £1; pillion seat, 12s. 6d.; pillion footrests, per pair, 6s. 6d.

**Makers:** Norton Motors, Ltd., Bracebridge Street, Birmingham 6.

**Tax:** £2 5s. per annum.

**Insurance:** Under a *Motor Cycling* policy, per annum; solo, London Postal Area and Glasgow, fully comprehensive £11, third-party only, £4 10s. London Metropolitan Police Area (excluding the Postal Area) and Lancashire south of the Ribble, comprehensive £9 10s., third-party £5 15s. Elsewhere, comprehensive £9 10s., third-party £5. Where a sidecar is permanently attached to the machine a deduction of 40% may be made from these premiums.

**Note:** Price of machine, as tested (complete with trip speedometer, Lucas Magdyno lighting and electric horn and tank-top instrument panel), £85 1s. 6d.

*In the top of the Norton's petrol tank is a handsome instrument panel housing a speedometer, ammeter, lighting switch and filler cap. Note also the rubber-mounted bars.*

m.p.h., on a level stretch of road, was the excellent one of 32 ft., and this performance was repeated four times without there being any appreciable variation in the distance.

That these fine qualities have a pronounced effect on the average speed capabilities was strikingly demonstrated when, soon after taking over the machine, a journey of some 92 miles was undertaken. Owing to the fact that things were still just a trifle stiff, a maximum speed of 50 m.p.h. was rigidly adhered to, and no hard driving up hills was indulged in. Despite the fact that the 92 miles included the negotiation of three largish towns and two smaller ones, the inclusive average speed for the trip worked out at 38.7 m.p.h. —pretty good going for a journey in which both machine and rider were definitely "taking it easy." With a fully run-in engine and the wick really turned up very high averages were possible and 45 miles of ordinary going could be covered quite easily within the hour.

Such a performance indicates that the Norton is a machine capable of putting up a remarkably good average speed even having regard to the presence of 30 m.p.h. limits in quantities.

## On the Rough

Colonial sections and rough stuff generally offered no difficulties. The Norton is, of course, popular with trials men, and it certainly handled excellently both in muddy and rocky going: moreover, the engine pulled well at low revs., and this made it possible to pick one's way in difficult circumstances, where a less flexible engine would have necessitated a rush of the do or die order. The Norton forks, with their cleverly arranged rebound springs which go into tension whichever way the forks move from their normally loaded position, were found to function admirably, even with the friction dampers slackened right off. Correct weight distribution obviously was not the only secret of Norton steering.

The overhead camshaft engine is a most imposing

This held good whether the machine was travelling fast or slowly, on the straight, or round a bend. Using both brakes together, the stopping distance from 30

A25

## ROAD TESTS OF 1935 MODELS (Contd.)

unit to look upon, and the cylinder is provided with particularly large and deep cooling fins. Clean in design and splendidly finished, it was completely oil tight, a virtue which was still apparent at the end of the test. The dry sump lubrication system is very efficient, oil being fed to all the main bearings, the piston, and the overhead valve gear. A separate lead is carried to each valve guide. Oil consumption worked out at approximately 1,900 m.p.g.

Although the valve gear could be heard quite clearly at low speeds, it quietened down at about 25 m.p.h. and thereafter was inaudible from the saddle. As a whole, the engine must rank as above the average for mechanical silence.

### Speed

Maximum speeds obtained on a level road, in top, third and second gears, were 85 m.p.h. (5,040 r.p.m.), 73 m.p.h. (5,200 r.p.m.) and 57 m.p.h. (5,970 r.p.m.). When it is borne in mind that these highly satisfactory figures were obtained with the very moderate compression ratio of 6¼ to 1, something of a true appreciation of the excellence of the design will be gained. Obviously in the C.S.1 there has been no question of increasing the compression to obtain the performance. The performance is intrinsically the result of careful design, both thermally and dynamically and, in consequence, a moderate compression ratio has been quite practicable and has combined to produce a unit which is pleasantly docile and possessed of real punch at low r.p.m. Its performance on the road is a splendid example of the manner in which the lessons gained from successful racing can be applied to the standard production article.

A certain amount of vibration, or rather torque reaction, could at times be felt, though, considering the engine's robust performance, it would be unfair to offer this as a serious criticism. The exhaust note, though a trifle loud on wide throttle openings, was pleasantly deep and not at all offensive.

Passing on to the transmission, this was particularly smooth and the gearbox, on all four of its ratios, was one of the quietest we have had to handle. Really quick changes were possible at any speed and the clutch, though completely innocent of any trace of slip or drag, was smooth and progressive. There was no sound from either the primary or final chains, both of which, without adjustment, remained at a satisfactory tension.

The petrol consumption of 74 m.p.g. also must be regarded as satisfactory, as it covered a mileage which included a large amount of high-speed travel. Ethyl seemed to suit the engine very well and using this fuel it rarely showed any tendency to detonate. As already stated, flexibility was very good and this, coupled with the excellent rubber-block transmission shock absorber incorporated in the clutch, resulted in a minimum speed of 17 m.p.h. being quite comfortably maintained in top gear with the ignition two-thirds retarded. In third and second the lowest non-snatch speeds were 12 m.p.h. and 7 m.p.h.

Starting was quite easy, one or at most two kicks almost always securing the desired response, provided the air lever was closed and the carburetter slightly flooded if the engine was cold.

On the machine tested, a neat tank-top instrument panel housed the lighting control switch, ammeter, speedometer and petrol filler cap. Dynamo charging rates at 30 m.p.h. on top gear were "Charge" 4 amps. and "Dim" 3 amps. With the switch in the "Bright" position the lamps' requirements were exactly balanced. Although the speedometer is no doubt better protected from damage in the instrument panel than on the fork head, some riders would probably prefer it in the latter position.

### Equipment

The equipment is complete and a commendably comprehensive tool kit is housed in an all-metal lock-up box. One would like perhaps to see the three-gallon petrol tank (at present listed as an extra) standardized. Both wheels are detachable and interchangeable without the necessity for disturbing the transmission, and a portion of the rear mudguard comes away easily to facilitate the operation. In addition to the prop stand already mentioned there is a spring-up rear stand and one of the ordinary type at the front.

The C.S.1 Norton is not, of course, cheap to buy, but it represents none the less real value at the catalogue price, as it is a true thoroughbred, a delight to handle, and the finished performance and equipment reach a very high standard.

*The off side of the model C.S.1 Norton, a fast motor listed at £75 with lights.*

# Super Profile

## OWNER'S VIEW

My enthusiasm for Inters was kindled as a teenager by occasional – very occasional – sightings of the bikes, and by reading about them. They were, I thought, the best-looking motorcycles on the road. I still think so. And for quite a while I was convinced that their performance matched their looks. I no longer think so. Disillusion did not come quickly, or easily. My first extended experience of an International was with a 1938 model with all-iron engine and solid frame. A perfectly standard Inter, in fact – even to having an all-chrome tank. It was *all* chrome because the painted panels had been petrol-washed and rubbed away over the years. We sent the tank to Bracebridge Street, asking for it to be refinished as the experts thought fit. It came back, after a couple of months, carefully packed in a wooden box and painted silver, with black and red lining, in the racing style. There was a bill for £6. It seemed good value. We left the oil tank in chrome and painted on new lining. It went very well with the petrol tank.

It had been used for 24,000 miles, and vibrated more than a little. The head steady was missing, so we made one and fitted it; the vibration remained much the same. The steering was light and very precise, I remember. Once a little incident occurred on the road which made us think there might be something in the idea of 'race-breeding'. Somebody was riding it on icy roads and balancing a crate of oranges on the tank. I cannot recall now, after 30 years, why he was carrying a crate of oranges, although possibly it was because it had fallen off the back of a cargo ship, and time was pressing. At any rate ... descending a steepish hill, he touched the rear brake, which resulted in a broadsiding skid that took him and the Norton (and the oranges) through 360 degrees before he was able to resume forward progress. We said it was the Inter's breeding showing, and had he had been riding a BSA there would have been no hope of getting out of the skid.

Now I am not so sure. He was lucky, or perhaps a better rider than he knew. He might even have managed it on a BSA.

I had read road-test reports in *The Motor Cycle* and *Motor Cycling,* dismissing the former because it credited the Inter with a top speed of no more than 88 mph. It was Charlie Markham's report in the Green 'Un that took my attention, and respect. He had managed 97 mph, though it took a long, long time to get there. I write from memory, without reference to the fascimile report that appears elsewhere in this book: my recollection is that Mr Markham was in the saddle for 44 seconds from standstill to 97 mph. This is not so much a tribute to tenacious memory as to the indelible nature of early impressions.

With hindsight, I now believe both reports and ascribe the difference in speed to the better – ie, non-silencing – silencer fitted to the Markham bike. Inters with their valve timing designed for an open pipe, were always at the mercy of a law-abiding silencer. Well baffled, they were no match in speed for a quiet, gentlemanly Tiger 100.

Many years later I bought another Inter, a 1950 springer with something of a pedigree. It had been used in the Clubman's TT, though not to any great effect. It came into the hands of C.E. (Titch) Allen who had the all-alloy engine rebuilt by a Norton man. Taller and heavier than the 1938 version, with TT-style bolt-through tank, the bike was authentically oily and noisy though not, as it turned out, much of a goer. Perhaps, even as long ago as 1950, 'Friday afternoon' bikes were being turned out at Bracebridge Street. Or perhaps Titch's engine builder had had his mind on other things. Whatever the reason, this Inter was a disappointment. It oiled up, internally as well as around the cylinder head and back on to the oil tank (and thereafter, of course, my right leg), whenever it was pushed along at 85 mph. Consumption, of oil and petrol, was heavy. Handling was mediocre. Top speed? A little over 90. On a straight road in the Fens I had to bid farewell, though at the time I was too busy to wave, to David Minton who was supposed to be keeping me company on his Comerfords-prepared 1939 Tiger 100. The Triumph had 5 mph over the Inter. Defeat rankled. Even in those days Minton was younger and braver than me, which may have had some bearing on our respective speeds, but at the time I blamed the Inter. I still do. There was, obscurely, solace in a further defeat, later in the day, at the hands of a well-prepared *250* Suzuki which passed the Inter only seconds before screaming past Minton's Triumph. Jointly humbled, we gazed almost fondly at the flower of pre-war British motorcycling. Twin and single seemed tired; the Inter rather more so than the Triumph. And oilier. We turned towards London in reflective mood. I was prepared to believe the day of the old-style crackling big single was over.

But what a looker the Inter was!

This section is not intended for reminiscences of this sort, I suppose. Current owners must have their say. I went to Phil Heath,

21

# Super Profile

of Leicester, one-time road-racer — on ohc Nortons, of course — and a prominent member of the VMCC.
*CA:* When did you have your first ride on an Inter?
*FPH:* Oh. many years ago. It was, let me see ... 1932. I didn't actually ride it. I was on the pillion. It belonged to one of our crowd.
*CA:* 1932. You'd have been very young.
*FPH:* I was 17. I'd just left school and I had a 350 Matchless. It was ohv, but horrible! The Inter was wonderful. The best-looking bike I'd ever seen. It was their first year, and of course I knew all about them from reading the weekly papers — I mean, magazines.
*CA:* Was this chap, the owner, the local big noise? Financially.
*FPH:* Yes, he had to be because Inters cost a lot of money. £100, the price new, was as much an many people earned in a year. Everybody envied him.
*CA:* Why, wasn't there anything to compare with the Inter? I know it was the latest thing, but surely there were others ...
*FPH:* Well, there was the CS1, of course. *That* had been around for a year or two. But it wasn't the same. The tank was like any other Norton's. Not that I'd seen more than a couple of CS1s, come to that.
*CA:* So there you were, on the pillion, with this well-heeled bloke out to show you what one of the new Inters was like ...
*FPH:* Yes. I remember so well. Maybe not like yesterday, but at any rate like last week. The speed in the gears, that was what impressed me.
*CA:* It was the same with me. It's only now, thinking about it, that I realise that an Inter's gear speeds were so impressive mainly because the *ratios* were so high.
*FPH:* Of course; and they were close ratios, too, like a racing bike. I looked over his shoulder and saw the needle past 90. We must have got near to 100.
*CA:* What sort of silencer?
*FPH:* It made plenty of noise! It was rather like a small Brooklands can, with a fishtail, or rather, a kind of fantail. It suited the bike, I think.
*CA:* And the tank, how was it finished?
*FPH:* In chrome, with panels.
*CA:* When did you have your first *ride?*
*FPH:* Probably ... yes, I think it wasn't till after the war, though I'd owned an ES2. It would have been 1947. I bought a new one — well, it was in my name in the book, though it was a complicated deal and Jim Ferriday put up the money to buy it from Humphrey and Andrews. I had it to ride in the first Clubman's TT. When I first rode it, in Leicester, I was disappointed. The silencer took the edge off the performance. It wasn't till we went to the Island and changed to a straight-through pipe that it got some speed, and seemed something like that first one, in '32. It had an iron engine. I was lying third on the last lap when the tank split and lost petrol. I freewheeled and pushed downhill from the Bungalow, and finished. The tank was welded up then, not soldered, like the pre-war tank.
*CA:* Was the '47 bike very different from the earlier ones?
*FPH:* No, hardly different at all. It was rear-sprung, of course -- but you could have springing on an Inter in '38 and '39, though the frame and plungers were heftier then. It had hairpins, as they'd had from 1935, and the rockers and spindles were a little bigger than in '32; but, no, it was basically the same — though probably a little slower, because of the awful Pool petrol.
*CA:* Going back to 1932 — surely the Inter wasn't the only sporting bike around?
*FPH:* No, of course it wasn't. But it was certainly the best. I've mentioned the CS1, a sort of sub-Inter. Someone in our crowd had a Model 90 Sunbeam, but it didn't compare with the Norton. There were TT replica Rudges, but I never fancied them. And there was the B14 Excelsior. That's about all.
*CA:* Do you remember the road tests of the '40s bikes in the weeklies?
*FPH:* Very well! I helped Charlie Markham do the *Motor Cycling* report.
*CA:* When was a bolt-through tank made standard?
*FPH:* Robin James, that very good restorer in Leominster, says 1950. He's doing a big job on what's claimed to be Geoff Duke's 1949 Clubman's TT winner.
*CA:* I know you've come up to date with Inters. What about your Featherbeds?
*FPH:* I love them. The Featherbed Inter is everything I've ever wanted in a road bike. All the stamina of the cammy engine, plus marvellous handling. Who could want anything better!
*CA:* Well, some people might want something that didn't sling oil —
*FPH:* That's a drawback, I'll admit. Mine's oily, but I don't worry too much till I see some other people's Inters, which can be spotless.
*CA:* I used to think it was all to do with those felt pads on the rocker bosses compressing and wearing and letting oil through ...
*FPH:* They were changed from felt, you know, in about '39 to a composite material, rubber and fabric. Those let oil through, too ... But if you were going to say it's not just the pads that can be at fault, you're correct. Pressure build-up can be too much. You have to set the adjuster behind the mag. case just right. It's a tricky job. You need a co-operative, trained snake to help! Have you seen what the manual says on the subject? It advises you, quite simply, to send the cambox back to the factory for adjustment.
*CA:* Here's a rotten question. If things turned really tough and you had to restrict your riding — all right, let's say your riding of *Inters* — to either Garden Gate or Featherbed models, which would it be?
*FPH:* (instantly): The Featherbed!
*CA:* That shows, I think, that you're a practical kind of motorcyclist. A lot of these so-called enthusiasts,

22

# Super Profile

collector-maniacs, would go for a Garden Gate or a pre-war rigid job, just because they're antique, uncomfortable and rare.
*FPH:* I'd rather ride my Featherbed than the Commando I have. It's lighter, a better roadholder, and not so thirsty.
*CA:* How would you define the difference between the Featherbed Inter and the earlier models?
*FPH:* I tend to think of them in a racing context. They were basically the same, Inter and Manx, as you know, though post-war the private-owner Manx was far superior as a power-producer. The Garden Gate's handling was — well, *interesting*. They would roll, especially on fast, bumpy bends. Nothing ever happened; they'd always pull out of it, even with a broken frame, which was not uncommon, because of vibration. But some bends, and situations, needed a determined hand and — well, I suppose you'd say guts. The Featherbed was a revelation. At Floreffe in Belgium, where I used to race, there was a series of right- and left-hand bends on a fast downhill section. On a Garden Gate you could, I suppose, go through them flat in third. But it called for a lot of physical effort. On a Featherbed it was much easier ...

As for the engine, I've always thought it was the best on offer to the ordinary road rider. I'm talking about the Inter now. Not the 350, though. *That* was always undergutted. The 500 is tireless. Performance never goes, even when the engine's worn out.
*CA:* Worn out?
*FPH:* When the cams and bearings are going, when it's rattling.
*CA:* Yes, I think it's fair to say you're an Inter enthusiast. What's the 'strength' now?
*FPH:* You remember some occasions, some rides, for ever. For instance, just after the Clubman's I was talking about, I rode the same bike down to Torquay. I was working for *Motor Cycling* then. I left Birmingham at five on a Friday evening and went to Torquay at 80-90 mph. Had a wonderful weekend. I'd gone there to see a girl — and left Torquay early on Monday morning to get to the office by nine. I'm sorry — you were asking about my 'stable'. Only two now, though of course there are plenty of bits and pieces around the place. I sold my 350 Featherbed. Too Slow. There's the 1949 Garden Gate bike, the ISDT one, ex-Bill Stone [one-time works manager, Norton Motors]; and my '58 Featherbed, which I have in this slightly off, green-grey shade which the purists complain about as being non-original. I like it, though. I like the bike ...

My second, final, interview was with C.E. (Titch) Allen who, on learning that I was seeing Phil Heath, said that in the interests of impartial reportage I ought to put on record the other side of the Inter picture. FPH, declared Mr Allen, was besotted by cammy Nortons, could admit of no imperfection in a design which the young Arthur Carroll had committed to the drawing board more than — did I realise? — half a century ago. Titch Allen, founder of the VMCC, historian of the motorcycling scene, owner of some of the most interesting motorcycles in the country, occasional sidecar racer — when a passenger is available — and everyday motorcyclist: why didn't he like Inters?
*TA:* I don't say I don't like them. But they're over-rated. It's the bike every enthusiast wants — till he's got one. Mind you, the situation now, as I see it, is pretty well ideal: Inters in the '80s are owned by people who don't ride them but stand around and drool over them. That's fine. That way, you're not disappointed.

Still, one has to be fair to Nortons. They never tried to sell the Inter. It didn't pay. There couldn't have been any profit in them. The factory used to discourage ordinary people from buying Inters for the road. You can imagine it. Crowds of disappointed Inter men coming to Bracebridge Street, complaining they hadn't been able to do 95. And there would have been warranty problems — though they didn't use the word then, of course — with such rarified machinery in the hands of people raised on sv bangers.

Racing men, though, did not expect any kind of guarantee. So most Inters were sold for racing. That suited Nortons fine.
*CA:* Come on, *some* road people must have bought Inters.
*TA:* Well, yes, there have always been tough types who liked that kind of bike. The people who turned to Gold Star BSAs later on. Masochists. The questions a would-be Inter owner had to ask himself were: Am I man enough? Am I prepared to go out and find a bike with a pool of oil underneath?
*CA:* Man enough? So you admit it's a good performer.
*TA:* Not really. With an ordinary silencer, it's hopeless. Markham's test in '47 doesn't prove a thing. Charlie could always screw 2-3 mph more out of a bike than any other press man; and that silencer certainly wasn't standard. No, to be an Inter rider — note that I say rider, not merely an owner — you have to be rugged. Inter riding acquaints you with the slings and arrows of motorcycling.
*CA:* All right, so why did *you* buy an Inter?
*TA:* The one I sold to you? I'd always had the good sense not to fall for an Inter. I did my admiring sensibly, from the sidelines, so to speak. But then fate took a hand and put 'our' Inter my way. It had a history. It was, after all, an ex-Clubman's bike, not that dear old Willie [Wilshere; who died, still a great motorcycle enthusiast, at 80? in 1984] ever set the racing world alight with it. Wasn't it *disappointing!*
*CA:* Yes ...
*TA:* Truth is, Nortons never developed the Inter. It was a good bike in '32. But to be using the same engine 25 years later — Well!
*CA:* Did you have anything to do with Inters pre-war?

23

# Super Profile

*TA:* No. I never knew anybody who had one — at least, for use on the road. Nortons never advertised them, they were never seen in dealers' showrooms. If you wanted one, it was a case of 'to special order'. You see, they just weren't practical. In those days the clubman used one and the same bike for riding to work, for weekend trips, for taking his bird out, grass-track racing ... The Inter wasn't versatile enough.

*CA:* What about rivals for the Inter in the early days?

*TA:* I have to admit that the Inter stood alone. Rudges were getting past it. So were Sunbeams. Though I must say that, being more antiquated, at least they didn't have the oil-spewing habits of the Norton — there was, of course, no automatic oiling for *their* rockers, hence no oil to leak!

It was 1935 before a rival came along. In my view, the Vincent-HRD 500 was a better bike than the Inter. It had about the same performance, but was altogether more civilised. And it didn't require an open pipe to crack 90 mph.

*CA:* What should Nortons have done with the Inter?

*TA:* Most importantly, after a year or two, they should have enclosed the valves. Jack Williams — who, I ought to explain, is not AMC's Jack Williams ...

*CA:* — you don't need to explain. If he's to do with Nortons, this Jack Williams must be the Cheltenham Flyer. Right?

*TA:* Yes, well — as I was saying, Jack Williams had a works bike with complete valve enclosure — of *coil* springs, mind — in about 1937. It was an Edgar Franks idea. But that was about the only sensible development of the single-cam engine in a quarter-century.

Why wasn't something done about the oil pump? It seems to me that Carroll copied the cammy Velo wholesale — which was mostly a good thing but in one or two instances, like the oil pump, was downright stupid. You need an absolutely tight fit for the pump body in the crankcase, which means that it has to be pressured in, and then getting it out is a hell of a job, with heating of the case, and so on. It was an impractical design for a production bike. Franks' arrangement for the ohvs was much better, and cheaper.

*CA:* (rather depressed): At least, you have to admit it's a great-looking bike.

*TA:* Yes — but ask yourself why. It's that *tank!* Take the tank away, or fit an ordinary 2½ gallon ohv tank on an Inter, and you've lost all the charisma people rave about.

*CA:* (suspicious): Why are you anti-Inter? Nortons ...

*TA:* — whats wrong with a good ohv Norton? That's what we're racing these days. I mean, all you have to do to get Inter performance from an ES2 or Model 18 is build up the cams and grind them to Inter form, for ohc overlap, raise the compression ratio, put on a big-bore carb — And it won't sling oil.

*CA:* Oh.

After the interview Titch Allen had to prepare his ohv Norton for Cadwell Park. What would he be doing after that? 'Well, I have this project ...' We went into the workshop. A tank had been superbly painted, ready for fitting. And a frame. Forks, brakes and other running gear, checked and, where necessary, exchanged in the interests of authenticity, were waiting. He was full of enthusiasm. Old photographs and press clippings were produced.

What was the bike? One of the very earliest Inters! Odd people, motorcyclists.

# Super Profile

## BUYING

An International is a bankable asset. If the asking price is not outrageous, anybody fortunate enough to be presented with the opportunity of buying one would be a fool not to do so. It is no function of this book to advise on pricing. If you want an Inter, and you have found one, and the price seems at all right — buy it!

As for authenticity, this is something of a grey area. The items that especially distinguish a pre-war Inter are — obviously — engine and tanks; the wheels are distinctive, too, but mainly because they happen to be of larger diameter than those fitted to the rest of the range. The gearbox has close ratios. What this means is that the frame can be 'bodged' from a late ES2, and the wheels made up on appropriate rims. If you are not familiar with the correct gearbox, an ES2's would be convincing. Ironically, it would in any case be rather more serviceable, having a sensibly lower first-gear ratio than the Inter's, which can make hill-starts a clutch-glazing ordeal. But all this, of course, is heresy. Authenticity — particularly if a 'cheque book' purchase is at stake, to swell a (usually non-riding) collector's stable — can be everything.

Post-war, in the Featherbed era, there is greater scope for mixing-and-matching. The frame is that used in far greater number for the Dominator twins, and the wheels and brakes are much the same as those fitted to any of the lesser Featherbed models. It is up to any potential buyer to determine how important authenticity and originality is to him.

There are, of course, some points to watch when buying, which may be used as a lever to bring down the asking price. In the case of a pre-war model, spindle wear in the links of the girder front fork can be a time- and cash-consuming business to rectify. Oddly, though, even appreciable slop in the fork, which may seem horrendous during a static examination, appears to have little effect on an Inter's manners on the road. Since the advent of fast Japs it has become fashionable to talk of the necessity for pluperfect adjustment of steering head bearings — for precisely the 'right' size, profile, tread, balance and inflation of tyres — for the correct type and setting of suspension systems. On an Inter, however, going fast seems to be mainly a matter of having enough petrol and oil and, ideally, getting rid of exhaust baffling.

'Bottom-end' construction of the engine is immensely strong — second only to that of the specialised Manx, from 1947 on — and gives very little trouble. Piston slap can be difficult to detect, aurally, on account of tappet cacophony but will reveal itself, in equally time-honoured fashion, by a smoky exhaust. Here, though, it may be difficult to distinguish between wear and over-oiling for the rough-and (sometimes too)-ready valve-guide lubrication from the cambox can lead to a very oily combustion chamber and furry valves.

A head steady was a standard fitting, but over the years may have disappeared. Whether the steady is on or off, there seems to be little difference in vibration levels which, though not low, remain quite tolerable at other than near-maximum rpm, when such items as the horn bracket may be in some danger. Of rather more point as a vibration-beater, at least to the rider, is the presence or otherwise of solid brass plugs in the handlebar ends of pre-war Inters. If these have been removed, in a misguided operation involving a change of handlebar, a damping effect will have been lost and the bar will transmit unnecessary tremors to the rider. Post-war, with a different frame and bar, the end plugs were omitted.

Ignition and lighting throughout the International's lifespan were (usually) the responsibility of Mr Lucas, and accordingly display all the qualities associated with that famous name and encountered in any one of dozens of British motorcycles of the times. Nothing peculiar to Nortons, or the International, was ever enacted with Lucas equipment; except, possibly, progressive displacement of the voltage-control unit from seat stay to under-saddle to sheltered nook inside the capacious toolbox of the post-war model.

Sticklers for authenticity who, looking at a 1939 or '46/47 Inter's primary chaincase, may accuse an owner of over-generous chroming, should think again, for extra brightwork here, along with the customary black enamel, was a factory foible for a while. Farther back, the guard over the rear chain should be (on pre-Featherbed machines) of straight-line form, along the upper edge, with none of the wrap-round over the sprocket

# Super Profile

that occurred with sv/ohv models. And though fuel taps almost invariably were of racer type, with levers swinging through 90 degrees (unless, as is not uncommon, they have seized up), for a year or two in the late '40s ordinary push-pull taps were fitted to that lordly tank.

In the earlier, vertical gearbox, with or without the single end cover, linkage wear was inevitable and was translated via the long control lever into unacceptably lengthy movement on gear-changing. Unkind folk reared on clickety-click Triumph gearboxes and the like said that Norton riders had to watch out for knee-to-chin contact during a smart change-down (though they might, if fair-minded, admit that the changes, either way, never missed and seldom 'scrunched'). The remedy, of course, involves new pins and bushing and careful resetting. Sometimes — rarely — the lever on early models will show a reluctance to return to the middle position, caused by breakage of the hairpin spring in the control box. In 1939, and for some, though not all post-war Garden Gate models, a downcurved lever was fitted to the gearbox in an effort to keep the rider's right foot in reasonable proximity to the footrest during gear-changing. It is debateable whether this lever is more effective than the shorter, straight lever usually fitted.

# CLUBS, SPECIALISTS & BOOKS

## Clubs

*Membership of the Norton Owners Club* is definitely a good thing. Though mainly, it seems, devoted to the interests of Dominator and Commando owners, the NOC includes ohc specialists and there is a general body of knowledge of all things Norton within the club that can only benefit Inter men.

Total membership is around 3,000. There are branches throughout the UK and valuable links exist with Norton owners worldwide. A lively and useful magazine, *Roadholder,* appears bi-monthly. Applications for membership should be addressed to the PRO, John Evans, Polgarth, Commercial Street, Cheltenham, Glos. Cammy matters are best taken up with NOC specialist Andrew Savage, 5 Beryl Grove, Hengrove, Bristol, England. (Bristol 779870).

## Specialists

Single cylinder spares at reduced NOC prices are handled by **Roger Deadman,** 40 Firgrove Hill, Farnham, Surrey, England. (Tel: 0252 722641, after 8 pm).

Repairers and associated experts include:

**Fair Spares,**
37 Albion Street,
Rugby,
Staffordshire,
England.
(Tel: 08894 3974)

**Ray Petty,**
31 Highfield Road,
Cove,
Farnborough,
Hants, England.

and (especially for tank repairs and originals)

**John Pearson,**
23 High Street,
Swanscombe,
Gravesend,
Kent, England.

## Books

The ohc models receive much attention in **Norton Singles** by Roy Bacon. Osprey Collector's Library, Osprey Publishing Ltd, 1983.

The 'bible' for Inter owners has long been **Norton Motor Cycles** by Edgar Franks. C. Arthur Pearson Ltd, 1948. Long out-of-print but often available at autojumbles and book sales. **Bruce Main-Smith Retail Ltd.** P.O.Box 20, Leatherhead, Surrey, can supply facsimile copies of factory and other literature on the ohc machines, notably:
**Maintenance Manual and Instruction Book. Models 30/40 up to 1953;** together with a selection of well-illustrated spares lists covering pre-war and 1946-1950 models.

Another BMS publication of value is: **Norton Motor Cycles 1928 to 1955,** covering all roadster models, 348 to 596 cc, with technical data, wiring diagrams, exploded drawings, overhaul information and a rundown on the Norton numbering system, frames and engines, from 1923 to 1963.

An excellent general history of the marque; with some coverage of the International series, is provided by: **Norton Story** by Bob Holliday. Patrick Stephens Limited, Barr Hill, Cambridge, CB3 8EL, England, 1972, and later editions.

Superb action photographs of ohc models, mainly to racing specification, with detailed captions, form a large part of:
**The Unapproachable Norton** by Bob Holliday. Dalton Watson Ltd., 1979. 76, Wardour Street, London W1V 4AN, England

An illustrated history of the Norton motorcycle, in the form of a paperback, is: **Norton** by Dennis Howard. Ballantine Books Inc (USA) 1972. Although copies were originally available in the UK, it has been out-of-print for a considerable time and is not often seen even at autojumbles and book sales.

Authentic photographs of ohc machines, mainly to racing specification, form part of several of the volumes of **The Keig Collection,** in particular Volume 4, published in 1984 by BMS Retail Ltd.

BMS also have in stock **Norton Scene** and **The First Post-Vintage Scene,** containing excellent photographs with detailed captions based on careful model dating, as well as most of the books listed above.

Super Profile

# Super Profile

## PHOTO GALLERY

1. Eight-inch-diameter headlamp carries ammeter and lights switch in customary pre-war style.

2. Hand-adjustable friction-disc shock absorber for the Norton girder fork predates supplementary check springs.

3. Check springs, one each side, attached to upper and lower fork links, damp action of the large main spring of the front fork. They were introduced in the second year of the Internationals, in 1933.

4. Norton footrests in traditional form differ markedly from those of other manufacturers in being complicated, built-up components with a facility for spontaneous disassembly – or, at the least, loosening. They were a characteristic feature of Bracebridge Street production and received short shrift when the firm was taken over by Associated Motor Cycles. (Current prices, noted at a 1984 autojumble, are around £6 each for the 'frame' of a footrest and for the covering rubberwear: £24 in all with, if you are so unfortunate, further expenditure for the hangers!)

# Super Profile

5. Dunlop rubber saddle is smaller than the fabric-covered saddle fitted to less exalted models in the range. Its main advantage, of course, is that it is impervious to water; though Dunlop managed to imply in advertisements that it had other properties to justify a higher-than-normal price. Chrome-plated sleeves over the bolts providing saddle-height adjustment are non-standard.

6. All-iron cylinder and head are part of the standard specification for road-going Inters; light-alloy/bronze variations were available from 1935.

7. Primary-chain case in this form dates from 1934. It is internally flanged in rubber to retain oil.

# Super Profile

8. Scalloped, soldered seams of the 3¾-gallon fuel tank are clearly shown in this shot.

9. André steering damper has friction leaves in a self-contained unit above the steering head.

10. Front wheel takes a 3.00 x 21 in ribbed tyre; eagle-eyed may detect that the cover fitted to the Thomas 1937 Inter is an Avon Speedmaster of much later date.

11. Six-volt 'King of the Road' Lucas battery is rubber-insulated to combat effects of vibration; the up-and-over clips are not normally met with.

# Super Profile

12. A 20in Avon Mk II graces the quickly detachable rear wheel. The rear stand was discontinued in 1938.

13. Front brake has correctly chrome-plated back plate. It measures 7in in diameter. Note speedometer drive.

14. Flexible fuel pipe – usually Petroflex – is standard wear.

15. Inspection cover allows access to the upper run of the primary chain, to assess adjustment.

16. André steering damper is an authentically 'racer' fitment included in the specification of all pre-war Internationals.

31

# Super Profile

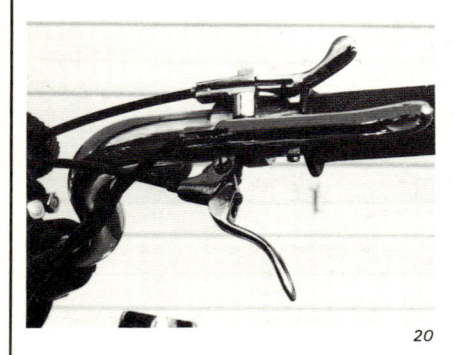

17. "Suitcase" fastening, with lock, for the toolbox is an appealingly idiosyncratic feature of many pre-war Nortons.

18. Riders of pre-war (and post-war, come to that) Inters are able to devote attention to the mph recorder, with no distractions by way of rpm, clock or oil-pressure dials.

19. The narrow, elegantly ended rear mudguard emphasises width of the number plate; the reflector disc, of course, is a non-period addition.

20. Lower pullup lever controls the exhaust valve, enabling it to be lifted from its seat for starting convenience – and, of course, to stop the engine.

21. Silencer is steeply angled; possibly more so than was the case with the machine in original condition. All silencers – other that the Brooklands 'Can' of pre-war fame – inhibit maximum power of the race-developed engine with its generous valve-timing overlap.

# Super Profile

22. The handlebar is mounted in rubber-lined clamps.

23. Here the air-slide control, mounted on a block shared with the front-brake lever, is in the 'closed' – ie, start – position.

33

# Super Profile

24. Wheel-lining, being a time-consuming – hence expensive – operation, is commonly neglected in machine-restoration. Les Thomas, however, has taken no short cuts. The wheels on his International have black centres lined in red.

25. Brake-operating arm of the 1937 model is angled 180 degrees from that on post-war Inters, which have no rear stand.

26. Over-centre spring for the rear stand is precisely angled not to interfere with access to the rear-wheel spindle when the stand is in use. Note the well-made rear-wheel adjusters; compare them with the flimsier devices fitted to the Featherbed model. Lugs and holes in chain stays permit variation in position of foot controls, for competition use.

# Super Profile

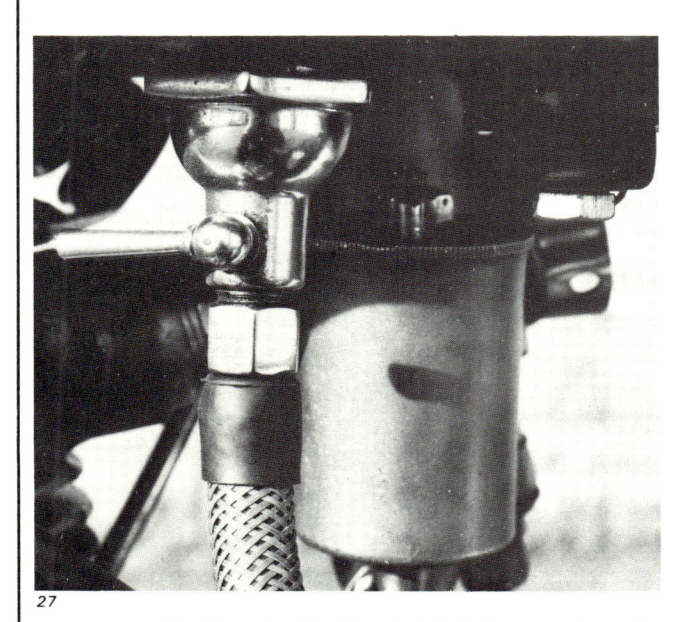

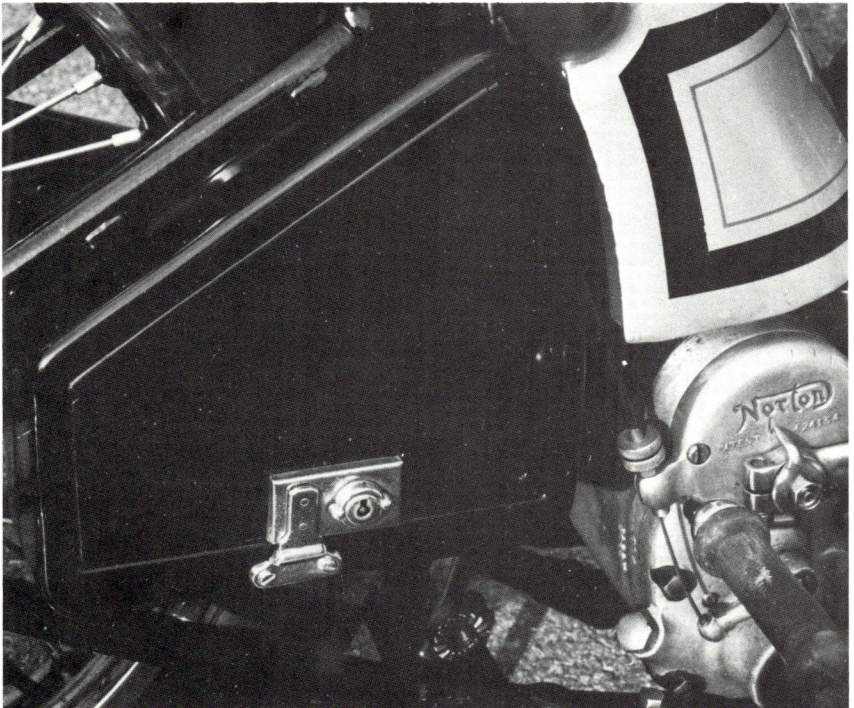

27.

28.

29.

30.

27. Twin fuel taps allow for a reserve supply; float chamber has the traditional 'tickler' for flooding when starting.

28. Breather for the oil tank 'exhausts' into the seat tube.

29. The positive stop box is mounted atop the gearbox; also shown – the clutch cable with knurled adjuster and combined filler/level plug for lubricant.

30. Long through bolts for cylinder and head are standard feature of all Inters – as is oil mist on the head finning ('just' discernible in this photograph), derived from leakage via the rocker arms.

# Super Profile

31. Kneegrips protect tank finish, while interrupting the "line" of the (non-original) striping.

32. Check springs as introduced on early Internationals, and later a standard fitting on all Nortons, were seen also on some other makes, such as Ariel.

33. Hinged filler cap, with screw-down security, was to race specification.

Super Profile

34.

35.

36.

37.

34. Rear lamp was usually built on a push-and-turn principle to permit partial dismantling for easy bulb replacement. Illumination, through both red and clear lenses, is modest.

35. The rubber saddle, usually of Dunlop manufacture, is unaffected by moisture and, hence, was claimed to retain shape, and comfort, longer than the usual leatherette-covered saddle.

36. The full cradle frame, originated in 1927, and used throughout the International's pre-Featherbed period, also became standard wear for the top-of-the-range overhead-valve model, the ES2, in early 30s.

37. The Les Thomas 1937 International has been lovingly restored to near-original condition.

# Super Profile

38. Positive stop box for the heavyweight Norton (once Sturmey Archer) gearbox provides a lengthy movement for the control lever.

39. An outstanding example of 'colour-coding', this Featherbed-frame International of 1956 featured polychromatic-grey finish for frame, forks, tank and headlamp. This model is the property of John Frith of Compton Dundon, Somerset.

# Super Profile

40. First seen in 1950, with a single-cylinder engine installed, the Featherbed frame became more familiar in road-going guise when carrying the Dominator twin-cylinder unit.

41. The famous Roadholder forks are shorter than their pre-Featherbed counterparts, and are provided with two-way hydraulic damping.

42. The pear-shaped silencer was tolerably efficient but no leader in the good-looks department.

43. 'Single-side' front brake with alloy back plate is of 8in diameter. On ohv models in 1956, it was usually incorporated in a full-width hub.

44. Draw-bolt adjustment for the bottom-pivoted gearbox follows long-established Norton practice.

# Super Profile

45. Single-strap tank fixing, with rubber padding, is a feature of Featherbed-era Nortons.

46. The filler cap used on International models was never a mere push-and-turn affair, as featured on some other models in the Norton lineup.

47. Relatively unchanged, internally, from its vertically arranged predecessor, the "horizontal" gearbox used in the Featherbed Inters offered peerless action and long-term reliability.

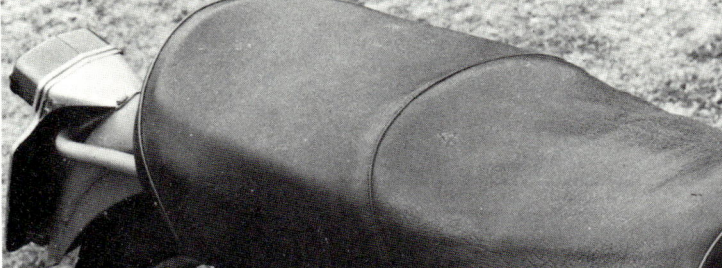

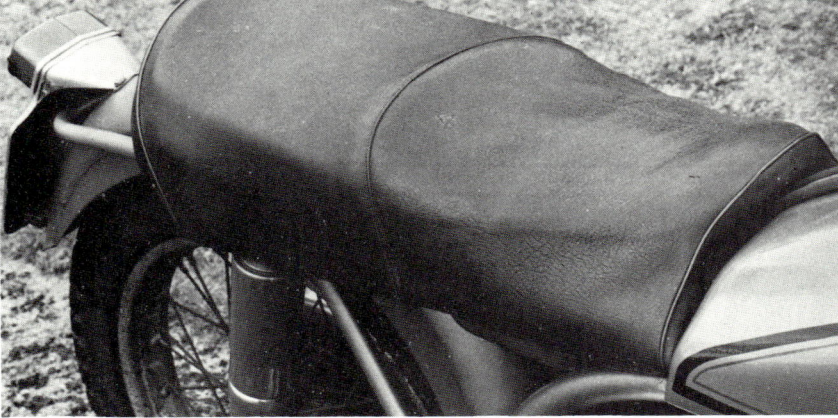

48. Hardly a full-blown nacelle, the fork-top panel groups the few dials and solitary switch neatly and accessibly, and in plain view. The Smiths speedometer is thoughtfully marked at the 30 mph point.

49. The dualseat is wide and rather thinly padded.

50. Where the twins were equipped with less expensive push-pull fuel taps, the International usually retained the more positive, race-style levers.

**Super Profile**

# Super Profile

51. Head-on view emphasises narrowness of the cylinder-crankcase layout, totally obscured here by fork legs.

52. Unavoidably wide, to suit the far-apart top rails of the new frame, the fuel tank holds 3¾ gallons. Its width militates against a first-class riding position – one of the assets of pre-Featherbed models.

53. This round tank badge was fitted from 1955. 'Norton' is in red, the background 'N' motif in silver. The dark quadrants are black, the others silver.

# Super Profile

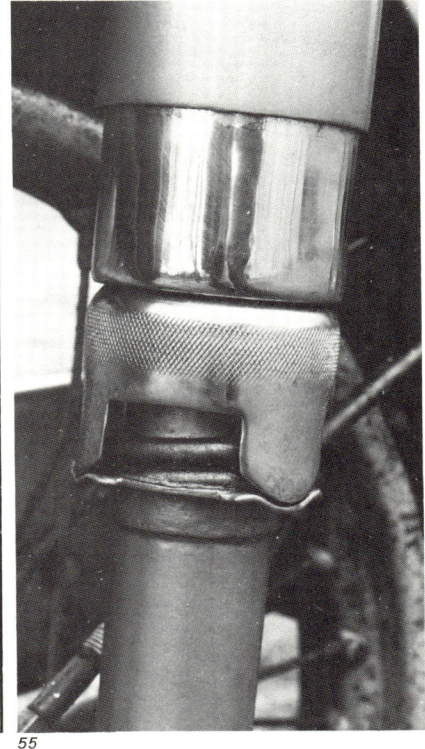

54. The oil tank holds 7 pints and is mounted in rubber.

55. Rear-suspension units on the John Frith-owned model are Woodhead Munroe and offer three position adjustment for spring preload.

56. Speedometer drive is taken from the rear-wheel spindle.

57. Classic proportions of the tall engine remained pleasing throughout the years. The light-alloy cylinder barrel, a standard feature (with the light-alloy head) from the introduction of the Featherbed in 1953, had additional fins, compared with the earlier cast-iron version, and thus a more tapered outline downward from the head.

# Super Profile

58. Chrome-plated bearing surfaces are employed for the fork stanchions.

59. The handlebar carriers are rubber-mounted in the fork-top plate.

**Super Profile**

60. Seat height, springs uncompressed, on a 1956 International is approximately 31in. Weight (dry) is in the region of 375 lb.

61. Rear-chain guard is unusually deep, saving frame work in the area from oil fling.

45

# Super Profile

62. The Lucas Altette horn occupies its usual position, unchanged from pre-war days, and of course gives much the same unemphatic 'warning of approach'.

63. The extra fins at the base of the light-alloy cylinder are clearly shown in this view, and contrast with the unadorned stretch of barrel seen in the all-iron version.

64. Not all Inters were 348 and 490 cc. There was the occasional factory-produced special. This 600 was built in 1948 for Cyril Quantrill, then sports editor of the weekly journal Motor Cycling. He used it through several road-race seasons, at indecently high speeds, while reporting European grands prix. It was attached to a Hughes TT sidecar.

Super Profile

65. Inters suffer, when left unused, from oil drainage into the crankcase. Some owners introduce a tap into the system. Not all are as careful as this owner, who has provided an unmissable memory jog to be acted on prior to starting.

66. The first overhead-camshaft Norton, as designed by the brilliant Walter Moore. This is a 1928 490 cc CS1, with leftside exhaust pipe.

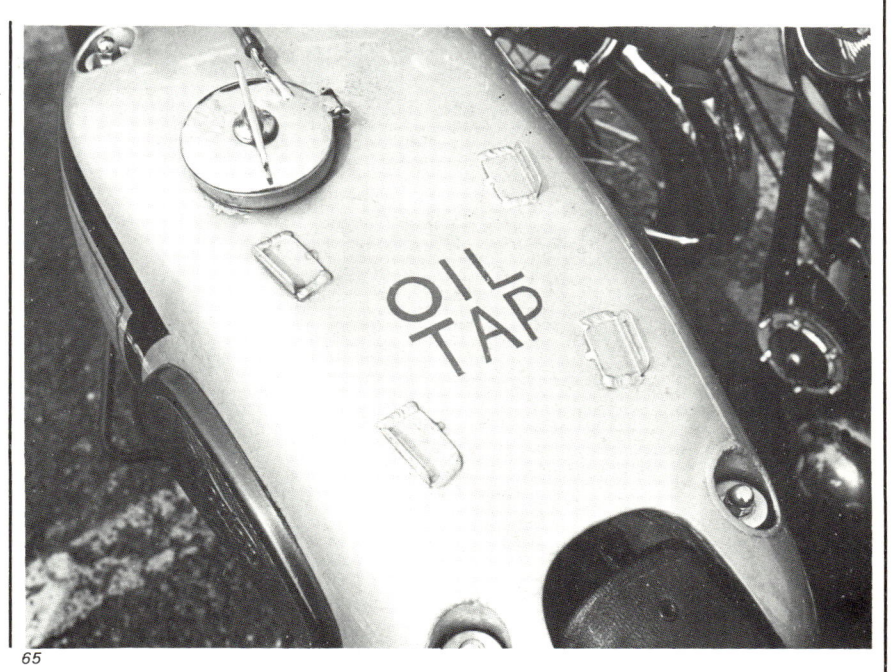

47

# Super Profile

67. The International, suitably modified, was long used for Norton-mounted entries in the British Trophy team in the International Six Days Trial. Here Vic, of the famous Brittain trials-riding family, is seen on his Model 30 in a 1930s ISDT in Wales.

## Super Profile

C1. Superbly balanced proportions of a pre-war International are well illustrated in Les Thomas's 1937 model.

C2. Finish of the tanks is not original. In as-bought trim this Inter probably had chrome-plated tanks with lining in usual Norton colours. Style shown here follows that adopted for the Manx racers, and has come to be accepted for Models 30/40.

49

# Super Profile

C3. Small check springs (one is visible here) supplement action of fork's main spring, providing a damping effect. First fitted to Internationals in 1933, they became a standard feature of all Nortons the following year.

C4. Six-pint oil tank has extended neck to facilitate splash-free filling.

C5. The Norton insignia: a miracle of just-right lettering. Compare this example, on a 1937 tank – a transfer, admittedly – with the fussy surround adopted for the name in the plastic roundel on the Featherbed model illustrated in these pages.

## Super Profile

C6

C7

C6. Kneegrips on pre-war Inters from the mid-30s are of shallow section, in keeping with the enviably narrow tank. Note the scalloping decorating the soldered seams.

C7. Lucas Magdyno is standard equipment on all road-going ohc Nortons.

C8. Tank cutaway was introduced to accommodate the large downdraught Amal TT carburettor.

C8

51

# Super Profile

C9. The manufacturer did not neglect to advertise its name even in areas to which the eye was not usually drawn: here, for example, 'Norton' appears in no fewer than three locations.

C10. Endowed with extra, but not enhancing, areas of polished finish, Len Crane's 1947 International is of interest in having the plunger rear springing which, in original form, was first offered on ohc Nortons in 1938 (when the additional cost amounted to £15).

# Super Profile

*C11. 1948/2 The bolt-through tank was available to special order, with competition in mind. The risk of tank-splitting was supposed to be reduced. Note the loops in the tank top, for attachment of a sponge-rubber pad on which a prone rider could rest his chin.*

*C12. Though differing in detail, colour finish of Featherbed models continued traditional Norton emphasis on silver (grey), black and red.*

C11

C12

53

# Super Profile

C13. Makers differ in their ideas on balance as between front and rear with a centre stand in use; Nortons, with the Featherbed Inter, opted to have the front wheel clear of the ground.

C14. Inter engines date from times when the Allen-head screw was unused; slotted-head screws on this model show evidence of strong wrist work!

C15. Steering damper, with light alloy wing nut, is a far cry from the bulky André unit of pre-war days.

Super Profile

C16

C17

C18

C16. Rear sub-frame of John Frith's model is of small-diameter tubing, brazed to the main frame.

C17. Engine details remain as for the pre-Featherbed models; earlier, however, the light-alloy barrel and head were an option.

C18. The under-dualseat tool tray is visible here.

# Super Profile

C19. The humped shape of the 3¾-gallon fuel tank is clear in this view, together with the greater-than-average width of its rear section.

C20. Plastic tank badge is a 1955 innovation.

56

# ON YOUR BIKE!

Adrian Bradbury

Illustrated by
Eliza Southwood

OXFORD
UNIVERSITY PRESS

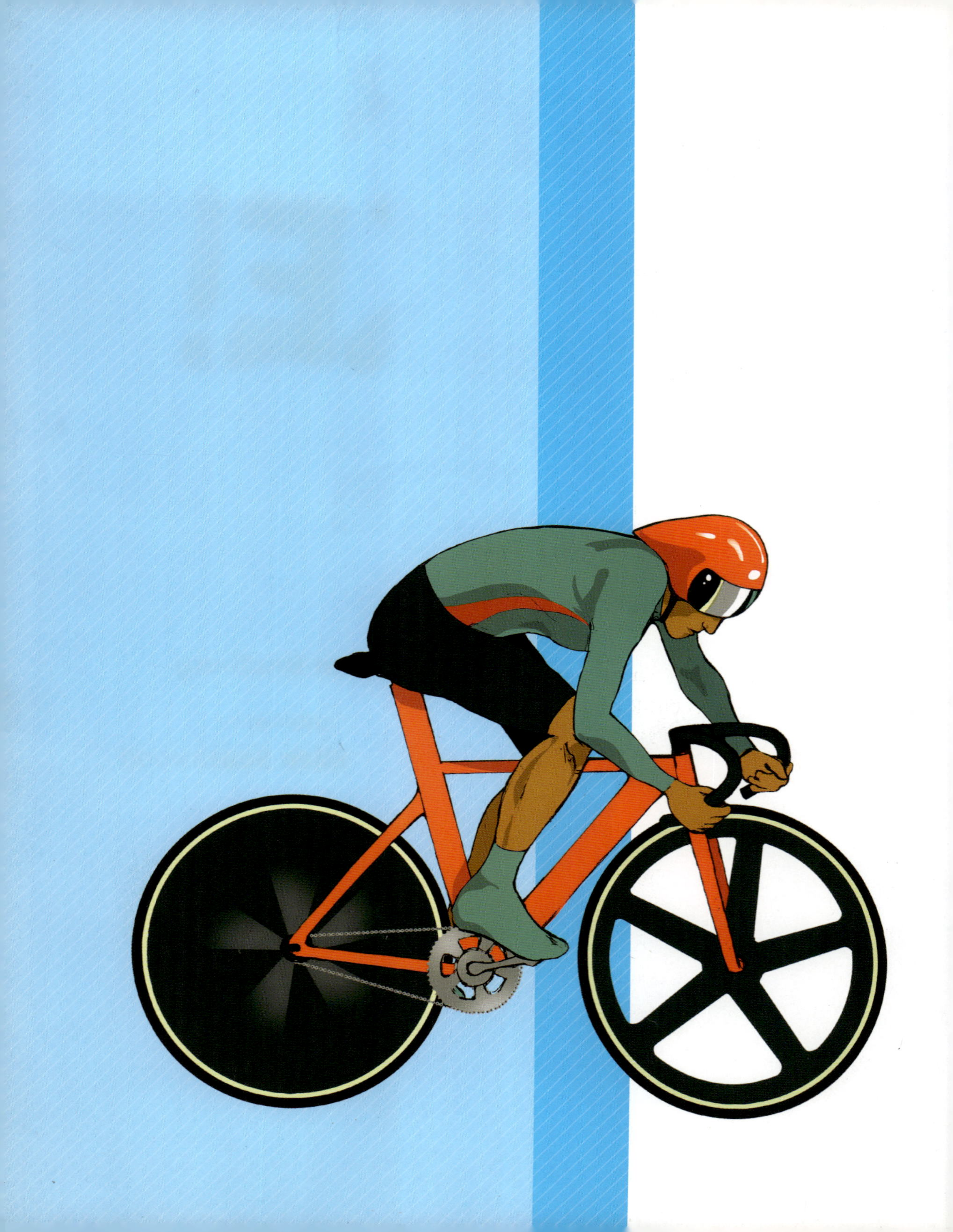

# CONTENTS

| | |
|---|---|
| Introduction | 4 |
| Road Racing | 6 |
|   The bike and kit | 6 |
|   The team | 8 |
|   The races | 12 |
|   The Tour de France | 14 |
|   The tactics | 16 |
|   The life | 20 |
| Track Racing | 24 |
|   The bike and kit | 24 |
|   The events | 26 |
|   Combining track and road | 30 |
|   The life | 32 |
| Off-Road Racing | 34 |
|   BMX racing: The bike and kit | 34 |
|   BMX races | 36 |
|   Cyclo-cross | 38 |
|   Mountain-bike racing | 40 |
|   Trials riding | 41 |
|   The off-road life | 42 |
| Getting Started | 44 |
| Glossary | 46 |
| Index | 47 |

# INTRODUCTION

Go out onto the streets of just about any town or village, anywhere in the world, and you'll see people riding bikes. Some will be cycling to or from work, maybe to save money or help protect the environment. Some will be nipping out to the shops, or just trying to get some exercise after a long day in the office. Some might be parents taking their children for a pleasant ride in the countryside, admiring the birds and flowers as they tootle happily along.

## THIS BOOK IS NOT ABOUT ANY OF THEM!

This book is about professional cyclists and the sport of bicycle *racing*. There's definitely no 'tootling along' for them! Competitive cycling is a serious business. Top athletes, both men and women, devote their lives to riding a bike so that they can go faster and further than anyone else on the planet. They make huge sacrifices to achieve glory on two wheels.

Exciting and challenging, competitive cycling is both an individual and a team sport. There are different categories of racing, depending on where the races take place. The main three are: road racing, track racing and off-road racing.

So, what does it take to be a cycling superstar? It requires **rigorous** training, as well as a combination of strength, fitness, **stamina** and determination. And let's not forget courage – because it can be dangerous!

Keep turning the pages to find out all about professional ('pro') cycling and some of the superstars of the sport. Read about them. Admire them. And then ask yourself the question: Have I got what it takes to be like them?

## DID YOU KNOW?

Bike racing has been a part of every Olympic Games since 1896. The first cycling event at the **Paralympics** was in 1984.

# ROAD RACING

The first two-wheeled bicycle hit the road in 1817 and, knowing people's competitive instincts, the first informal road races probably took place soon after. Bikes have come a long way since the 19th century, but the idea hasn't really changed much: two legs on two wheels, pushing themselves to the limit in their quest to beat the rest.

## THE BIKE AND KIT

The saddle is built for speed and certainly not comfort. You'll just have to get used to it!

The frame is made of very strong but lightweight material – carbon fibre, titanium steel or aluminium.

There are 22 gears, with 11 on each of the two chain rings.

Your shoes clip into the pedals so they can't slip out.

Want to compete at the highest level? You'll need a bike similar to this one, ridden by top road racer Chris Froome. Unfortunately, you'll need deep pockets too, because it comes with a £12 000 price tag!

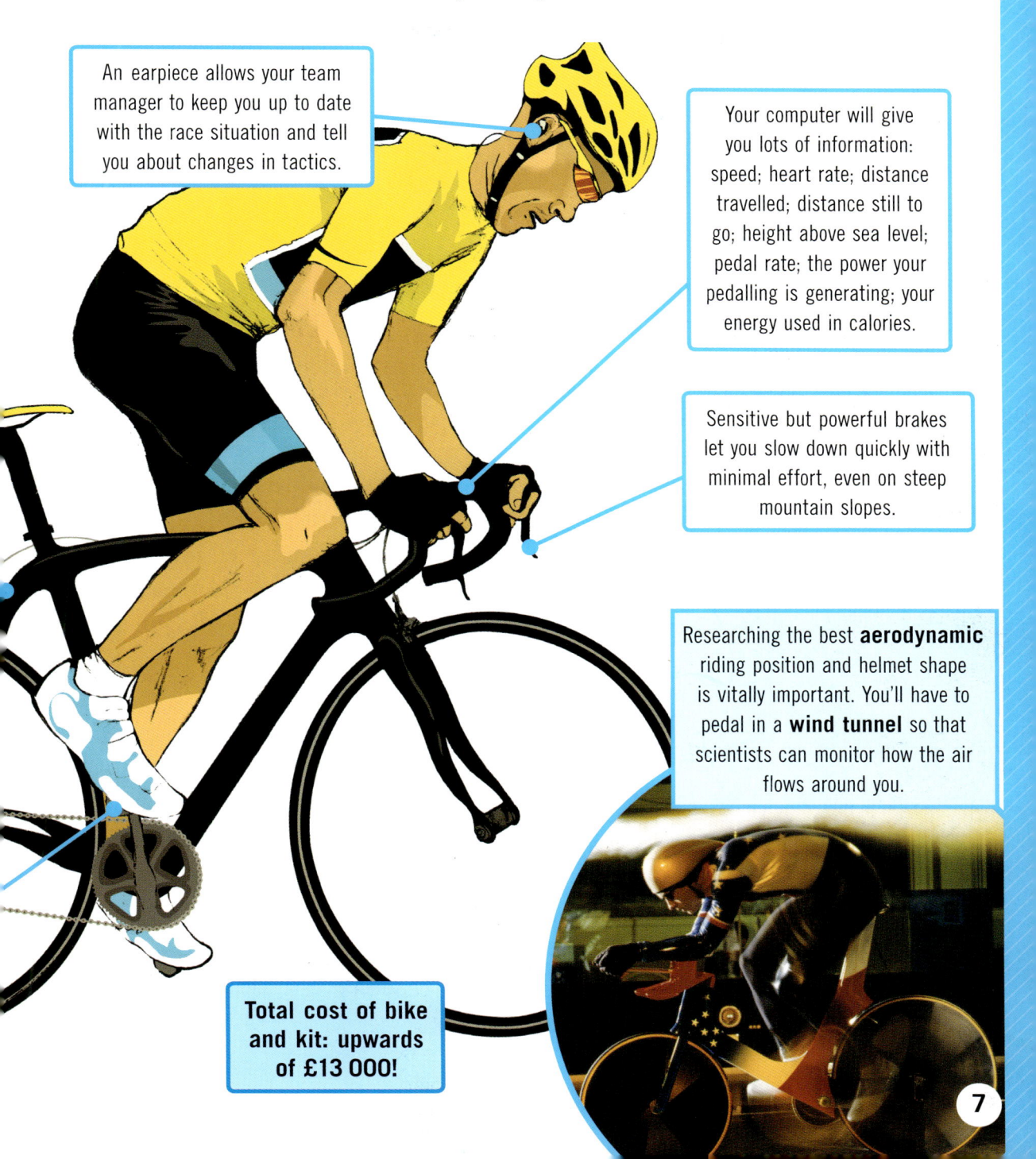

An earpiece allows your team manager to keep you up to date with the race situation and tell you about changes in tactics.

Your computer will give you lots of information: speed; heart rate; distance travelled; distance still to go; height above sea level; pedal rate; the power your pedalling is generating; your energy used in calories.

Sensitive but powerful brakes let you slow down quickly with minimal effort, even on steep mountain slopes.

Researching the best **aerodynamic** riding position and helmet shape is vitally important. You'll have to pedal in a **wind tunnel** so that scientists can monitor how the air flows around you.

**Total cost of bike and kit: upwards of £13 000!**

Once you've made the daring decision to earn your living as a road racer, your first challenge is to find a team. Did you think you could just enter a race and try to win it? Wrong! Road racing is very much a team sport. Without the help of eight team-mates around you, you'd have virtually no chance.

## STARTING AT THE BOTTOM: DOMESTIQUE

You'll almost certainly start your career as a domestique – that's French for 'servant'. (As professional bike racing began in France, many of the terms used are French.) Basically, as a domestique, your job is to do whatever you can to help one of the stars on your team win the race. You do the hardest work for the lowest pay. Your jobs will include:

- Working as a pacemaker. You don't want your star riders wasting any energy, so you, along with the other domestiques, have to take turns setting the pace at the front, while the other riders tuck in behind you.

- Carrying drinks bottles. These will be passed out of the window of one of the team cars. You have to deliver them to the other riders in the team. You might have to carry six at a time!

- Going back to help. If one of the stars has a puncture, or is struggling to keep up, you have to go all the way back and act as pacemaker for them, shepherding them back to the rest of the group.

- Giving up your bike in an emergency! If your star rider gets a puncture and there's no team car handy with a spare, you'll have to give him yours and wait for a replacement yourself. Then you'll have to try to catch up with everyone else.

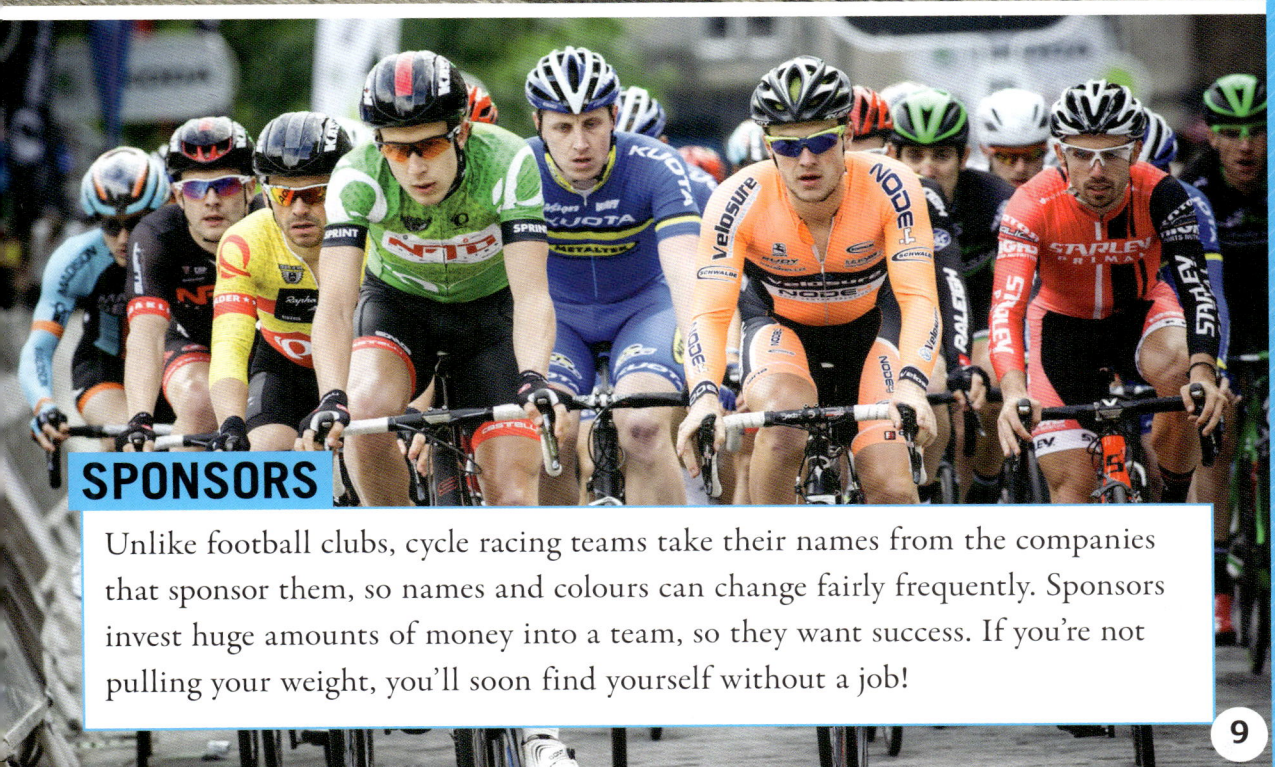

Here a domestique delivers water bottles to his team-mates.

## SPONSORS

Unlike football clubs, cycle racing teams take their names from the companies that sponsor them, so names and colours can change fairly frequently. Sponsors invest huge amounts of money into a team, so they want success. If you're not pulling your weight, you'll soon find yourself without a job!

Still think this is the career for you? Great! If you work your way up to be one of the stars on your team, you'll have to be a specialist. You have two choices:

## 1 SPRINTER

Many races finish on fairly flat roads, and this is where you show your skill. Two or three team-mates will ride in front of you to set the pace, before unleashing you for that final dash to the finishing line and glory! The problem is, all the other teams will be doing the same, so there will be a lot of bikes very close together, all going at almost 80 kilometres per hour. This is definitely NOT a job for the faint-hearted. Crashes are common, and when one bike goes down, it tends to bring down many more.

**THE TEAM**

# 2 CLIMBER

The mountains are your territory. Those sprinters will be left far behind as you power up steep hillsides. Hopefully one or two team-mates will be able to stay with you for a while to help, but in the end it will just be you, in a trial of strength against the other top climbers. You will need incredible willpower to keep pushing yourself when your legs are telling you there's nothing left to give.

## SUPER SKILL!

Top climbers also have to go downhill very fast, which can be extremely dangerous. Mountain roads are narrow, with many hairpin bends. To stay at the front, top riders will often take crazy risks to increase speed and cut corners, even in rain or snow. It is not the time to get a puncture!

## DID YOU KNOW?

The Alpe d'Huez, in France, is one of the most famous climbs in world cycling. Some of the greatest battles in cycling history have been acted out on its 21 hairpin bends over 13 dramatic kilometres. In the 2013 Tour de France, riders had to tackle it twice in one afternoon, with another mountain in between!

## TRICK OF THE TRADE

You may see spectators handing cyclists newspapers at the top of a long climb – these aren't for reading. The cyclists stuff them inside their jerseys to avoid catching a chill on the steep descent, as their sweat dries in the sudden rush of cold air.

As a pro cyclist your team managers will decide which races you ride in. You'll be involved in several different types of race, depending on your talents.

## ONE-DAY CLASSICS

As the name suggests, these are one-off races and the first rider to the finishing line wins. Most of these races involve hills, but are rarely won by pure climbers. They are long, **gruelling** races, held in the spring when the weather is most unpredictable.

Possibly the most **prestigious** one-day classic is the race from Paris to Roubaix, which first took place in 1896. It's known as the Queen of the Classics, but also often referred to as 'The Hell of the North'! Covering up to 290 kilometres in France, the race is famous for its narrow, dusty farm tracks and sections of bumpy cobblestones. The winner will be an **all-rounder** who has the strength to cope with the rain, snow, wind, dust, mud, punctures, broken chains and crashes that this race almost always involves.

THE RACES

12

# STAGE RACES

These generally last for a week, and include one or two mountain stages with some flatter **terrain** to keep the sprinters interested. A sprinter can occasionally win a stage race, as long as there aren't any major mountains involved.

Stage races often make their way around a particular country, taking in all the different landscapes. Some favourites are the Tour of Britain, the Tour of Oman and the Tour Down Under in Australia.

# GRAND TOURS

These are the major prizes in pro cycling: the Giro d'Italia in early summer, followed by the Tour de France and, finally, the Vuelta a España in September. Each one consists of 21 stages over 23 days, with two rest days.

As well as flat and mountain stages, there are also time-trial stages – racing against the clock across a set distance. Special time-trial bikes are used for these stages, with two sets of handlebars and a different riding position. Although the sprinters take the honours during the first week of the tour, as soon as the race reaches the mountains it's the climbers who take over. If several climbers are evenly matched, the race might ultimately be decided by their performance in the time-trials.

As well as the overall first prize, there are prizes for the best sprinter, best young rider and 'King of the Mountains'.

Sir Bradley Wiggins won the Tour de France in 2012, mostly due to his supreme time-trialling ability.

# THE TOUR DE FRANCE

Ever since it was first held in 1903, receiving the Tour de France winner's trophy in Paris has been the dream of every bike racer.

## SIGNIFICANCE OF JERSEY COLOURS

The overall leader of the race wears a yellow jersey. This is because the race was first sponsored by the French newspaper *L'Auto*, which was printed on yellow paper. In the Vuelta a España, the leader wears a red jersey, while in the Giro d'Italia, it's pink!

## EARLY DAYS

In the early days, riders had to race through the night, cheating was common, and – in one particularly brutal year – riders were attacked and beaten up by rival fans as they rode towards a mountain peak!

No help whatsoever was allowed during the race, so riders carried spare inner tubes over their shoulders. If they got a puncture they had to get off and repair it themselves.

## CONTROVERSY

In 1989, the American Greg LeMond overtook his French rival Laurent Fignon on the last stage in Paris, to win the tour by just eight seconds – after 3285 kilometres and over 110 hours of riding! It's an unwritten rule that riders don't challenge the leader on the last day of the tour, but in 1989 the authorities **controversially** made the last stage an individual time-trial, so LeMond was able to race to victory.

## DID YOU KNOW?

To increase interest around Europe, the Tour de France often features stages in other countries. Since 2000, the race has begun in Ireland, England, Belgium, Holland and Luxembourg. It always finishes in Paris.

Before a race starts, the team managers put a great deal of thought into deciding which tactics will help them secure a win. The specialist sprinters or climbers will normally take first place, but sometimes the less glamorous members of the team have their day in the **limelight.**

## GOING FOR A BREAKAWAY WIN

As a domestique, you will spend nearly all of your day as part of the peloton. That's the name given to the main pack of riders. Because many races include 180 or more riders, that's a big pack!

On long, hilly stages, a small group of lower-ranked riders will often break away from the peloton quite early on, speeding off ahead of everyone else and trying to stay in front all the way to the finish.

You might join this group for a chance of glory. Sometimes you may build up a lead of 10 minutes over the peloton. You will feel like a mouse trying to run away from a cat, aware that at any moment it might put on a burst of speed and pounce on you.

*A small breakaway group tries to stay ahead of the chasing peloton.*

THE TACTICS

As one team leads the chase at the front of the peloton, the other racers behind them save energy.

## THE SCIENCE BIT

Riding in a pack, you are protected against air resistance by the riders in front of you. This can save you a huge amount of energy. Scientists have calculated that, by positioning yourself in the middle of the pack, you **expend** only two-thirds of the energy of the riders at the very front.

If you get a puncture, you might try to catch up by riding in the **slipstream** behind a car. Be careful though, because it's not really allowed and you may get fined!

## MONITORING PROGRESS

Your manager will be monitoring your progress from the team car, which drives along between your breakaway group and the chasing peloton behind. The car will have spare bikes on the roof, and a mechanic to jump out and help you if something goes wrong with your bike.

There will also be a medical car with a doctor who can treat you through the window as you ride along holding on to the outside of the car!

Just in front of you there'll be a motorbike with a cameraman perched on the back, filming your every move, while a helicopter hovers overhead to get those dramatic aerial shots.

## THE END'S IN SIGHT

Because there are a lot more riders in the peloton to share the hard work at the front, where the air resistance is strongest, they can make up ground very quickly. Often they will catch the breakaway group just a few hundred heart-breaking metres from the finish, and the sprinters will triumph. Sometimes, however, the peloton doesn't get its timing quite right, and this is what you hope for. Your lungs will be burning, your legs will be screaming with pain, but all the suffering will be worth it if only you can stay ahead of the pack and cross that line first.

THE TACTICS

# WHERE'S THE TOILET?

You'll probably be in the saddle for five or six hours most days, so you may well be thinking: what happens when I need the toilet? Well, usually a group of riders will come to an arrangement where they'll stop, nip into some bushes (or just the side of the road), do what they need to, then get back on their bikes. TV cameras politely look the other way!

## TRICK OF THE TRADE

The 'sticky bottle' tactic: The team car may pull alongside you so that the mechanic can hand you a new drinks bottle. Sometimes this bottle might seem as if it's coated with glue, because it takes a long time for the mechanic to let go of it. All this time you're getting words of advice from the team manager, a free tow from the car and a nice rest! It's not legal, but the race officials usually turn a blind eye, as everyone does it.

As most of the big road races are held in Europe, your working season will be from around March to September. Before that, you'll have one or more training camps. These will be somewhere warm, with mountains – Majorca and the Canary Islands are popular destinations.

## A TYPICAL DAY

Your training days will generally follow a similar pattern to an actual racing day. Races start at different times, but here's an idea of what to expect.

- **7.00 am:** Wake up! You'll be sharing a hotel room with a team-mate. Quick shower, then get your kit on.
- **7.30 am:** Breakfast is a choice of fruit, muesli, porridge, eggs, rice, pasta, bread, energy drinks and coffee. You'll need 4000 extra calories per day to keep your body running.
- **8.00 am:** Team talk to discuss tactics for the day.
- **8.45 am:** Team bus leaves. Another chance to talk tactics. More coffee and snacks on board. Put on sun cream. (Absolutely vital, as you'll spend long hours under the hot sun.)
- **9.30 am:** Off the bus, check your bike and ask mechanics for any last-minute adjustments. Make sure you've got your energy bars and gels. Pin on your race number. Sign in at the start line.
- **10.00 am:** Off you go! Up to 200 kilometres (maybe even more) of cycling ahead.
- **12.00 noon:** Lunch comes in a shoulder bag called a musette, which is held out for you to grab as you speed past a feeding station. It contains little sandwiches or wraps, cakes, more energy bars and gels. Transfer everything to your pockets, then ditch the bag.
- **3–4.00 pm:** Race over! Leaders get whisked off for a compulsory drug test, TV interviews and an awards ceremony. If you're lucky, you'll have enough strength to get off your bike and make your way to the team bus without assistance. More snacks and drinks to **rehydrate**. Massage and treatment for any injuries. Change clothes and relax during the drive to the next hotel. Back at the hotel, there'll be more massages for those aching legs.

THE LIFE

- **6–7.00 pm:** Dinner will include plenty of protein (chicken, beef or fish), carbohydrates (pasta, rice, bread) and vitamins (salads and vegetables). All the food you eat will be prepared and checked under the supervision of the team's own master chef.
- **8.00 pm:** Another team chat to discuss how the race went.
- **10.00 pm:** Off to bed! Tomorrow you have to get up and do the same thing all over again.

## THE DRAWBACKS

Even if you think you can cope with the difficult daily routine, you'll need to consider these other drawbacks to the lifestyle:

- You'll be away from your family and friends for long stretches of time. What if you really miss them?
- You'll have to stick to a strict diet for most of your working life. Can you give up your treats?
- You'll spend much of your time travelling from one hotel to the next. Will you miss your home comforts?
- A serious injury or illness could threaten your earnings, and maybe even end your career early. Could you still pay the bills?
- Your racing career will probably be over when you hit your late 30s. What would you do after that?

### DID YOU KNOW?

If a rider is involved in a crash, they instinctively put their arm out as they fall. This often results in a broken collar bone near the rider's shoulder.

Injuries forced former world champion Chris Boardman to retire when he was only 32. He now works as a TV broadcaster and technical advisor.

# THE REWARDS

- You make a living doing something you love.
- You get to travel the world and ride through some of its most wonderful scenery.
- You have the thrill of competing against some of the world's best athletes, and the glory of winning, either as an individual or as part of a team.
- You'll also be pleased to know that, for all your hard work, you get paid well – but only if you make it into one of the big pro teams. Take a look at this graph to see what you could earn:

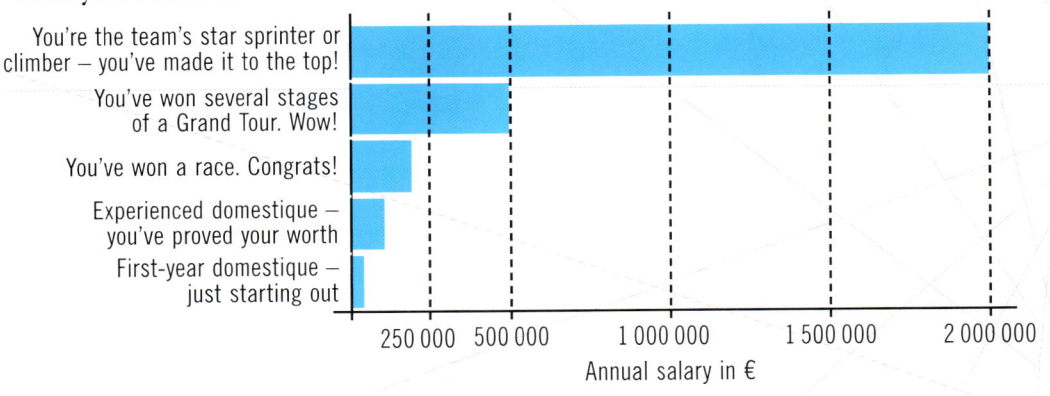

| Category | Annual salary in € |
|---|---|
| You're the team's star sprinter or climber – you've made it to the top! | ~2 000 000 |
| You've won several stages of a Grand Tour. Wow! | ~500 000 |
| You've won a race. Congrats! | ~250 000 |
| Experienced domestique – you've proved your worth | <250 000 |
| First-year domestique – just starting out | minimal |

Any prize money from races is usually shared out between all the members of the team. The big stars can also expect to be swamped with offers from big businesses, who will pay them handsomely to support their products.

Still fancy having a go? Good on you – it looks like you've got what it takes!

Andrew Talansky weeps tears of joy after winning the Critérium du Dauphiné stage race in 2014.

> **You put your life into something and make sacrifices for days like this. Every bad moment, every crash, all the problems make it worthwhile for moments like this.**
>
> Andrew Talansky

# TRACK RACING

Track racing takes place all year round inside a **velodrome**, on a rather odd-looking wooden track. The idea of the sloping sides is that bikes can keep going at full speed around the bends and keep as close as possible to remain at a 90 degree angle to the track. You don't even need to steer around the bends really; the slope just takes you there. Clever!

## THE BIKE AND KIT

The saddle is fitted high so that it pushes your body forward into the best racing position.

The tyres are extremely thin for minimum drag and maximum aerodynamics. Many top riders use tubular tyres — rubber tubes that are inflated until they're hard as iron and then sealed. They are then glued on to the wheels.

The helmet is lightweight but essential: high-speed crashes and falls are one of the hazards of your job!

## GRAEME OBREE

Scottish cyclist Graeme Obree had his heart set on breaking the world one-hour track record – to ride as far as he could in an hour. Graeme decided to build his own bike, 'Old Faithful', and even used bits of a washing machine in the wheels! When he tried to smash the record, Graeme was just one kilometre short. However, as he'd booked the track for 24 hours, Graeme decided to have another go the next day. Afraid that his legs would seize up if he slept, Graeme kept himself awake by drinking so much water that he had to keep going to the toilet.

The next morning, he returned to the track and cycled 51.151 kilometres, breaking the world record by 445 metres!

As a sprinter you'll use normal 'drop' handlebars. Long-distance riders may also have a second set so they can tuck their elbows in to be more aerodynamic.

*Question:* Where are the gears and brakes?
*Answer:* There aren't any! The bike has one gear only, so you have to have explosive power in your legs to get going. You won't need to stop during your race, so there's no need for brakes.

Notice Obree's strange riding position, with his elbows tucked in and his body hunched over the straight handlebars.

# INDIVIDUAL SPRINT RACE

This is a real game of cat-and-mouse, with two racers covering three laps of the 250 metre track. The riders toss a coin. The winner will ask the other rider to lead off in front, while they follow just behind. The first rider will then ride as slowly as they can! Why? They know that if they start off fast, their opponent will just settle in behind in their slipstream, saving energy before shooting past them in the last 100 metres.

The second rider will try to stay high on the track, then swoop down when the sprinting actually starts, which is usually towards the end of the second lap.

Sprints are decided on best out of three races, so both riders have to have a go at leading out.

## SUPER SKILL

Former world champion Victoria Pendleton CBE demonstrates the difficult skill of keeping your balance while riding extremely slowly and looking back over your shoulder to keep an eagle eye on your opponent.

# KEIRIN

This is a sprint for six individual racers. To avoid all the dangers of slow-riding tactics, a comical-looking man in black sets the pace on a little motorbike! The riders follow him as he gradually increases speed to get them up to sprinting pace, then he peels off the track and they go for it!

## PURSUIT

As the name suggests, two riders (or teams) set off at opposite sides of the track and try to catch each other up. Although this rarely happens, the fastest rider or team wins. Pursuit races are usually over four kilometres for men and three kilometres for women.

The riders in each team ride just centimetres apart. They usually change leader every half lap, with the rider at the front swinging up the slope, then down again to rejoin the back of the team.

## TEAM SPRINT

Two three-man teams set off from opposite sides of the track. They ride one behind the other, each using the slipstream of the rider in front.

At the end of the first lap, the front rider drops out, leaving two. After the second lap, the next rider drops out, leaving one rider from each team to battle it out over the last lap. The women's race features just two riders, over two laps.

## MADISON

An odd one, this! Two riders act like a relay team, but only one of them races at a time. The other rider circles slowly around the top section of the track. When they're ready to change over, they have to touch. Usually they will link hands and one will sling the other forwards. Sometimes one will give the other a push from behind. With up to 40 riders on the track, racing for 50 kilometres (200 laps), this event can be mayhem!

### THE HISTORY BIT

Originally, Madison races were held in the Madison Square Garden arena in New York, over six days and nights ... non-stop! A pair of riders might cover over 4000 kilometres during the race.

**THE EVENTS**

# OMNIUM

This is where the all-rounders shine, as the Omnium includes six different races. The winner of each race gets one point, the second two points, and so on. At the end of the competition, the rider with the fewest points is the champion. Possibly the most exciting of the Omnium events is the **elimination** race. All the riders start together, and the one who crosses the line last at the end of each lap is eliminated. The last two riders fight it out over the final lap.

## LAURA TROTT: WORLD CHAMPION AND OLYMPIC GOLD MEDALIST FOR TEAM PURSUIT AND OMNIUM

*Born:* 24 April, 1992, England    *Height*: 1.63m    *Weight:* 52kg

Laura (or 'Trotty') is a great example of someone who overcame health problems to triumph as a sportsperson. She was born one month early, with a collapsed lung. Laura was later diagnosed with asthma, and her doctor encouraged her to take up sport to help with her breathing. When Laura's mum decided to take up cycling to lose weight, Laura and her sister joined in. As a junior rider, Laura was so successful that she wanted to leave school when she was 15 to start cycling full time. Her dad had different ideas though, and made sure she took her GCSEs first. After winning the Junior World Omnium title, she went on to become a star on the professional racing scene. Her sister, Emma, also became a top road racer.

# COMBINING TRACK AND ROAD

Some cyclists compete on both the track and the road, but this is extremely tough. Road racers are generally lighter than track racers, as they have to travel much longer distances. This means a track racer will often have to lose weight to compete successfully on the road, then put the weight back on when they go back to track racing. The two cycling extremes are track sprinters and road climbers:

## SIR CHRIS HOY
### WINNER OF 6 OLYMPIC SPRINT AND KEIRIN GOLD MEDALS

*Height*: 1.85m    *Weight:* 92kg

Sir Chris Hoy's nickname was 'Golden Thighs' – you can probably guess why! His training included two hours in the gym each day, concentrating on building up his legs. The muscle bulk gave him huge explosive power for sprints over short distances.

## NAIRO QUINTANA
### WINNER OF THE 2014 GIRO D'ITALIA

*Height:* 1.67m    *Weight:* 59kg

Nairo came from a poor family in the mountains of Columbia. As a child, his parents couldn't afford the bus fare to and from school every day. Instead, they saved up to buy him a second-hand mountain bike. The fourteen-kilometre trip, twice a day, was ideal preparation for road racing. Nairo's weight is only 65% of Sir Chris Hoy's, ideal for flying up those hills.

## THINKING OF EVERYTHING!

British cycling coach Dave Brailsford had a simple winning strategy: improve every single thing by 1%, no matter how insignificant that thing seemed. The idea was that if you could make everything just a tiny bit better, those improvements would add up to a clear advantage over your competitors. Obviously, Dave looked closely at the bike and kit, but he didn't stop there:

- Riders' diets were examined to try to make them 1% healthier.
- Their training programme was refined to make them 1% fitter.
- The gels used to massage their legs were analysed to find the most effective, making cyclists' muscles 1% more **supple**.
- Research was conducted to identify the ideal pillow for each rider. The riders then took them wherever they went so they could sleep 1% better.
- Even the cyclists' hand-washing technique was improved to make them 1% less likely to pick up an infection!

Now that really is searching for perfection!

World and Olympic champion Joanna Rowsell MBE gives an **insight** into the lifestyle of a professional track cyclist.

## THE LIFE

*What would be a typical training day for you?*
Over the winter track season, each day usually involves two hours on the road, followed by a three hour track session in the afternoon. I have a recovery shake drink after each session. For breakfast I have porridge with honey and fruit, plus an omelette. Lunch and dinner are healthy, balanced meals – something like jacket potato and beans for lunch, and chilli con carne for dinner.

*Do you train alone or with a team?*
I tend to train on my own on the road, but with the team on the track and in the gym. We train together on the track because, in the team pursuit, we need to co-ordinate our moves to get perfect timing. Training together in the gym also helps to build team **morale**.

*How do you organize your day if you have a big race in the evening?*
I ride in the morning to get my legs warmed up, either on the road or on a turbo training bike. I have a mental warm-up routine that I go through on a race day. I sometimes listen to music as I warm up, or just absorb the atmosphere and noise in the velodrome.

*How does track riding compare with road racing?*
I prefer competing on the track, but training on the road. I like the atmosphere of the track and I love the timed events because I enjoy trying to break records as well as win. The track season is during the winter and the road season is from February to September, so I never really get a rest. To take a break (usually two weeks a year) I have to decide which races to miss, because it's not possible to do everything.

*What are the best and worst things about being a professional cyclist?*
The best things are winning races and getting to ride my bike as a job, rather than being stuck in an office. The worst things are travelling a lot, and missing family and friends.

*How tough is it financially for a young rider starting out as a pro?*
It depends on your team. Most will provide a bike and kit. When you are going to races you may well have to cover the cost of travel and accommodation yourself, which is hard. When I train or compete as part of the Great Britain squad, all expenses are covered by them. If I train or compete independently, however, I have to pay my own way.

# OFF-ROAD RACING

If you want a bit more danger in your cycling, why not sample the thrills of off-roading? Test yourself on steep forest paths, muddy tracks and boulder-strewn trails, or get airborne flying over the humps of an indoor track. Better take a deep breath before reading on!

# BMX RACING: THE BIKE & KIT

Notice how low the saddle is! As a BMX racer you'll spend much of your time out of the saddle, so it's not as important as in other types of bike racing.

Only one gear, but you can set it up differently to make it easier or harder to pedal.

BMX bikes have much smaller wheels than a road or track bike. Small wheels are strong and make it easier for the rider to manoeuvre the bike and perform tricks.

BMX racing (that's Bicycle Motocross) took off in 1970s California, as young cyclists tried to copy the stunts of their motorbiking heroes. Soon manufacturers started making specialist bikes, and a new sport was officially born.

The frame is a mixture of carbon fibre and aluminium. Both are lightweight and very strong.

Total cost for the bike: up to £2500.

Handlebars are upright for maximum control.

Wide tyres need to have strong treads in order to grip the dirt track. They also need to act as cushions when you land after travelling over the many humps.

World BMX champion Shanaze Reade in flying BMX action at the 2012 Olympics. Protective gear is a must: helmet, gloves, chest protector, knee and elbow pads. Even with all this, injuries are common. Shanaze's broken bone list includes a knee, a foot, an elbow and a bone at the base of her spine.

# BMX RACES

Although many BMX tracks are outdoors, major international championships are often held on indoor tracks to make sure that bad weather doesn't get in the way of the action.

The track itself must be a dirt surface between 300 and 400 metres long. It's usually four straight sections with humps all the way along them, connected by three sharp bends.

At the start of the race, you'll be one of up to eight riders side-by-side behind a gate at the top of an eight-metre-high ramp. As soon as the gate drops, it's a race to see who can snatch the lead going into that all-important first bend.

Getting the inside position makes it difficult for your opponents to pass you. Being in front makes it much more unlikely that you'll be brought down by another rider who loses control. Crashes are frequent, and when one rider goes down, others usually follow in a domino-effect pile-up!

BMX Champion Liam Phillips on crashes: "It's part of BMX. I wouldn't change it. It's what keeps everyone on the edge of their seat!"

Liam on winning: "I'm not training to be a medal winner but to be an Olympic champion."

Liam on challenges: "I love setting myself big challenges ... It's something that excites me, gets me out of bed every day and makes me work hard."

## DID YOU KNOW?

BMX racers can reach speeds of 56 kilometres per hour, so at the top level, races are over in less than 25 seconds!

37

# CYCLO-CROSS

Cyclo-cross? Think road racing, but off-road and with obstacles thrown in. You'll race for up to an hour around a 2–3 kilometre course, with some parts which are unrideable! These bits might consist of short, steep muddy hills, sandpits, ditches, steps and 40cm-high barriers. Here you have to get off, carry your bike and run. For longer running sections, you put your bike on your shoulder to go faster. Better wear thicker clothing too, as races take place during autumn and winter.

## DID YOU KNOW?

The origins of cyclo-cross may lie in cyclists challenging each other to a race from one village to the next. There were no rules about routes, so they could take short cuts across fields and streams, over fences and hedges or through woods.

At top-level races there will be a 'pit' area at the side of the course, like in Formula One car racing. American cyclo-cross champion Todd Wells explains: "There's usually a lot of mud, ice and sand, and the bikes get heavy, not working great. As you come into the pit, you throw your bike to one of the mechanics. The second mechanic has your other bike. You take three steps then hop onto your new bike. They'll quickly clean your first bike, then three or four minutes later, when you come back, you do it all again."

Cyclo-cross bikes look fairly similar to normal road racing bikes. They need to be strong to cope with the bumpy surfaces, but lightweight too, as they have to be carried. You'll choose your tyres to fit the weather and surfaces that you're racing on, but generally they'll need to be knobbly to get a grip in the mud and dirt.

## SUPER SKILL

Some of the most skilled riders can 'bunny hop' over barriers, which means they stay on their bike and use it to jump over the obstacles. Course managers sometimes try to stop this by putting two or three barriers close together so that riders are forced to get off their bikes.

# MOUNTAIN-BIKE RACING

Mountain-bike racing is a thrilling mix of BMX and cyclo-cross, but without the bike-carrying bit. The cross-country course will typically take you along forest tracks, with steep slopes and huge jumps. You'll cover around 50 kilometres of gruelling racing, so strength and extreme fitness are essential.

If that's not exhausting enough, you may choose to tackle the downhill time-trial course. Here, you're on your own against the clock. Speeds are high, and you'll need nerves of steel to hurtle down a rocky track through the trees before braking at the last moment to get round that sharp bend. It will definitely give you an **adrenalin rush**!

## PRO PROFILE

Marianne Vos was the Dutch Junior Mountain Bike champion three times before switching her attention to road racing and cyclo-cross. After gaining multiple world championships in both those events, Marianne restarted her mountain bike career in 2013 and won her very first World Cup race. Many experts consider her to be the greatest cyclist in history.

## TRIALS RIDING

Balance is the key in trials riding, rather than strength or fitness. To win in this particular mountain-biking race, all you have to do is make your way around an obstacle course inside a time limit, with the lowest number of penalty points. Sounds easy? A glance at some of these challenges should change your mind!

Slow and steady is the secret. One moment's lapse in concentration and you're in trouble! Marshals watch like hawks, and will raise their fingers to give you those penalty points. So make sure you don't:

- touch the ground with your toe (it's called 'dabbing'): first dab means one penalty point, for the second you get two, and so on
- double dab – two dabs at the same time: this lands you with a whopping five point penalty
- touch any obstacle with your hand: five more points
- go over the time limit: sorry, that's five too
- lean any part of your bike against an obstacle: only one point for this one.

Trials bikes take the BMX idea one step further: they often get rid of the saddle altogether! You'll find that standing up on the pedals makes it much easier to keep your balance. Tyres are wide and bouncy, and frames sometimes have holes drilled into them to reduce weight.

# THE OFF-ROAD LIFE

As you'll have gathered, all off-road cycling is going to involve getting dirty, and probably cold and wet too. Unless you're one of the top stars, you're going to spend a lot of time cleaning clothing and equipment. Is it worth it?

You're never likely to make millions as an off-roader. Starting out, you'll have to pay your own way, so if you're not successful, it could cost you a lot of money.

Television and media coverage isn't widespread, so you could easily walk past a group of mountain bike world champions and not recognize any of them. The profile of BMX was raised when it was introduced into the Olympic Games in 2008, but financially, you're still going to trail behind the stars of road racing and track racing

No true off-roader is just in it for the cash, though. It's the thrills, the challenge of competing with not just their competitors but the land and weather too. The hardships are insignificant to them; it's all about the satisfaction of taking part – and winning!

Do you fit the bill?

## NEVER GIVE UP!

In 2006, American BMX rider Kurt Yaeger had his left leg **amputated** at the knee following a motorbike accident. Refusing to give up on the sport he loved, he was back on his bike 18 months later, and is now racing again at the highest level. His bike has a special magnetic pedal to stop his artificial foot from slipping off.

## DID YOU KNOW?

As a top cyclist it's not enough to be physically fit. You'll also have to win two psychological battles: one against your opponents, and one against your own body. Your brain will be sending you a stream of messages: your legs are exhausted – you should stop; you're going too fast – you're in danger of crashing; your rivals look really strong – you might as well give up. Sometimes you may need help to stop listening to these messages. Sports psychologists can train you to ignore all the negativity and doubt, filling your mind with positive thoughts.

**Here's how a few of the world's top cyclists took their first pedal strokes on the road to stardom:**

Shanaze Reade MBE bought her first mountain bike for £1 and started racing when she was 10. As a 17-year-old, she became the British Over-19 BMX champion, beating all the men in that category, and later won gold medals for Great Britain on the track too.

It could all have been different though. Like many top sports men and women, she excelled at several different sports. As a teenager she was interested in the shot put and sprinting before she took up BMX riding.

For Mark Cavendish, as a young mountain-bike racer, the turning point was finding the right bike: "I was always riding a bike, but getting dropped in races. I told my mum it was because all my mates had mountain bikes, so I asked for a mountain bike for my thirteenth birthday and got one. The very next day I went out and beat everyone."

Mark went on to be the most successful Tour de France sprinter in history.

**GETTING STARTED**

44

Swiss rider Fabian Cancellara, known as 'Spartacus', became one of the true hard men of road racing, winning the gruelling Paris–Roubaix classic in 2006, 2008 and 2010, as well as racking up many other famous victories.

When he was younger, Fabian was an expert skier and footballer. Then he found an old bike in the garage and his love of cycling was born.

Track champ Anna Meares was inspired to take up cycling as an 11-year-old, watching fellow Australian Kathy Watt winning gold at the 1994 Commonwealth Games.

It was a two-hour drive for Anna to reach the nearest track so she could train. Sometimes you (and your parents!) need to make big sacrifices to get to the top.

Sir Bradley Wiggins' father was also a professional cyclist, but as a child Bradley preferred football. He fell in love with cycling after watching the Barcelona Olympic Games in 1992. As a 12-year-old he told his teacher: "I'm going to be an Olympic champion, and I'm going to wear the yellow jersey in the Tour de France." And he was right!

**Take your lead from these stars: get out on your bike and enjoy!**

# GLOSSARY

**adrenalin rush:** a feeling of extreme fear or excitement that results in a burst of energy

**aerodynamic:** in a shape that allows air to flow easily around it

**all-rounder:** someone who has talents in several different areas

**amputated:** cut off

**controversially:** done in a way that may cause people to have strong opinions and disagree

**elimination:** a process where some people or things are removed, usually because they are not the best

**expend:** use up

**gruelling:** tiring and difficult

**insight:** a deeper view or understanding

**limelight:** focus of attention

**morale:** feeling of confidence and togetherness in a group

**Paralympics:** short for the Parallel Olympics, for people with disabilities

**prestigious:** famous; important; valued

**rehydrate:** put fluids back into the body

**rigorous:** thorough and very strict

**slipstream:** the space behind a person or vehicle, shielded from air resistance

**stamina:** strength to keep going

**supple:** flexible; able to bend easily

**terrain:** landscape

**time trial:** a race in which each cyclist rides separately, trying to set the fastest time over a set distance

**velodrome:** sports arena specially built for cycling

**wind tunnel:** place where scientists study how air flows around an object

# INDEX

aerodynamic ................................................. 7, 25
brakes .......................................................... 7, 25, 35
Cavendish, Mark ........................................... 9, 44
climber ......................................................... 11, 13, 30
computer ..................................................... 7
costs ............................................................ 7, 25, 33, 35, 42
crash ............................................................ 10, 12, 22, 36-37
diet ............................................................... 20, 21, 32
frame ........................................................... 7, 35, 41
Froome, Chris ............................................. 7, 14
gears ............................................................ 7, 25, 35
handlebars ................................................... 7, 25, 35
Hoy, Sir Chris .............................................. 30
mechanic ..................................................... 18-20, 39
Olympic Games ........................................... 5, 29-30, 35, 42, 46
pay ............................................................... 23, 42
peloton ........................................................ 16-17
protective clothing ...................................... 25, 35
puncture ..................................................... 8, 12, 15, 17
Rowsell, Joanna .......................................... 32-33
slipstream .................................................... 17, 26
sprinter ........................................................ 10, 13, 25, 26-27, 30, 44
team ............................................................ 8, 9, 16, 20
training ........................................................ 20, 32
Trott, Laura ................................................. 29
velodrome ................................................... 24
wheels ......................................................... 7, 25, 35
Wiggins, Sir Bradley .................................... 46
yellow jersey ............................................... 14, 46

# ABOUT THE AUTHOR

After growing up in Manchester, I started my working life as a secondary school PE teacher. Restlessness then set in and I travelled the world, teaching people how to speak English and playing sports whenever I could.

When I returned to the UK, a friend persuaded me to try out primary school teaching. I now teach part-time in Torquay, leaving time to write books, play the piano, drink lots of coffee and stare out of the window at the squirrels.

I've always been a keen cyclist, and find professional cycling one of the most thrilling sports to watch. I hope that after reading this book, you'll be bitten by the cycling bug too!

## Greg Foot, Series Editor

I've loved science ever since the day I took my papier mâché volcano into school. I filled it with far too much baking powder, vinegar and red food colouring, and WHOOSH! I covered the classroom ceiling in red goo. Now I've got the best job in the world: I present TV shows for the BBC, answer kids' science questions on YouTube, and make huge explosions on stage at festivals!

Working on TreeTops inFact has been great fun. There are so many brilliant books, and guess what ... they're all packed full of awesome facts! What's your favourite?